From the
GREAT TRANSFORMATION
to the
GREAT FINANCIALIZATION

From the
GREAT TRANSFORMATION
to the
GREAT FINANCIALIZATION

On Karl Polanyi and Other Essays

KARI POLANYI LEVITT

Fernwood Publishing • Halifax & Winnipeg
Zed Books • London & New York

Editing: Brenda Conroy
Cover design (Fernwood edition): John van der Woude
Cover design (Zed Books edition): www.roguefour.co.uk

Published in Canada by Fernwood Publishing
32 Oceanvista Lane, Black Point, Nova Scotia, B0J 1B0
and 748 Broadway Avenue, Winnipeg, Manitoba, R3G 0X3
www.fernwoodpublishing.ca

Published in the rest of the world by Zed Books Ltd.
7 Cynthia Street, London N1 9JF, UK
and Room 400, 175 Fifth Avenue, New York, NY 10010, USA
www.zedbooks.co.uk

Fernwood Publishing Company Limited gratefully acknowledges the financial support
of the Government of Canada through the Canada Book Fund and the Canada Council
for the Arts, the Nova Scotia Department of Communities, Culture and Heritage,
the Manitoba Department of Culture, Heritage and Tourism under the
Manitoba Book Publishers Marketing Assistance Program and the Province of Manitoba,
through the Book Publishing Tax Credit, for our publishing program.

A catalogue record for this book is available from the British Library
Library of Congress Cataloging in Publication Data available

978 1 78032 649 8 hb (Zed Books)
978 1 78032 648 1 pb (Zed Books)

Library and Archives Canada Cataloguing in Publication

Levitt, Kari
From the great transformation to the great financialization:
On Karl Polanyi and other essays / Kari Polanyi Levitt.

Includes index.
ISBN 978-1-55266-545-9

1. Capitalism. 2. Polanyi, Karl, 1886-1964. I. Title.

HB501.L48 2013   330.12'2   C2012-908251-1

Contents

ACKNOWLEDGEMENTS

My greatest debt is to Henry Veltmeyer, who encouraged me to publish this volume of essays and offered editorial assistance. Of equal importance has been his initiative in the Critical Development Project, a collaboration between Saint Mary's University in Halifax, Nova Scotia, and the Autonomous University of Zacatecas in Mexico. An invitation to lecture at a summer school in Zacatecas in 2009 encouraged me to expand the text to an essay dedicated to the memory of Surendra Patel, reproduced in Chapter 10.

My next debt is to Michael Wiseman, a brilliant young Canadian political scientist and community activist without whose assistance for the past three years I could not have continued to work on the unfinished manuscript of the history of development economics, or on completing the essay "Mercantilist Origins of Capitalism and Its Legacies." I also wish to acknowledge the help received from Marie-Pierre Wallace, Michelle Dupuis and others who have assisted me since the start of my visual disability in the early 2000s.

Finally, I must give thanks to the blessing of good health and the many colleagues and friends whose solidarity and support have enabled me to continue my work in these late years of my life. A very special thanks to Samir Amin for his important contribution on what he calls "the autumn of capitalism" in the Afterword. It is my hope that this volume will encourage younger generations to be fearless in turning the tide of societal alienation and ecological disaster toward the celebration of diversity, creativity and cooperation of peoples and nations.

KARI POLANYI LEVITT — A BRIEF BIOGRAPHY

Kari Polanyi Levitt is Professor Emerita of Economics at McGill University. Born in Vienna and educated in England, the daughter of the celebrated economist Karl Polanyi graduated with a BSc (Econ) in 1947 from the London School of Economics, specializing in statistics. After ten years of engagement in trade union research in Toronto she returned to university and obtained an MA from the University of Toronto in 1959 and an appointment in the Department of Economics at McGill University in 1961. She taught a variety of courses but her special interests were Techniques of Development Planning and Development Economics.

Polanyi Levitt's early research was in the construction of input-output tables of the Atlantic provinces of Canada published by Statistics Canada in 1975. Concurrently she studied the effects of Foreign Direct Investment on host countries, published as *Silent Surrender: The Multinational Corporation in Canada* by Macmillan of Canada 1970 and many times reprinted, and republished in 2002 by McGill-Queen's Press.

Since her first contact with the University of the West Indies in 1961 and as a founding member of McGill's Centre for Developing-Area Studies in 1963, she maintained a continuous relationship with graduate students and faculty of UWI, including collaboration with Alister McIntyre in *Canada-West Indies Economic Relations* (1967) and with Lloyd Best in developing the Plantation Economy paradigm at McGill from 1966 to 1968 published as *Essays on the Theory of Plantation Economy: A Historical and Institutional Approach to Caribbean Economic Development* (UWI Press, Jamaica, 2009).

On the basis of her experience in multisectoral economics, she served as national income advisor for the government of Trinidad and Tobago on the construction of a system of National Accounts (from 1969 to 1973). She undertook a study for the United Nations Economic Commission on Latin America on bargaining with transnational bauxite/aluminium companies (1976); a review of Haiti's National Accounts for the World Bank (1986); and a review of Canada-Caribbean relations for the Canadian Parliamentary Sub Committee on Foreign Affairs (*Hansard*, July 1982).

Polanyi Levitt served as Visiting Professor at the Institute of International Relations at UWI-St Augustine in 1974–75; Visiting Professor at the Department of Economics, UWI-Mona 1977–1979; she taught Theories of Economic Development at the Consortium Graduate School of Social Sciences at UWI-Mona from 1989 to 1995 before her appointment as the first George Beckford Professor of Caribbean Economy (1995–1997), when she compiled *The George Beckford Papers*, published by Canoe Press in 2000. Some of her public lectures and research papers were published as *Reclaiming Development: Independent Thought and Caribbean Community* in Jamaica by Ian Randle in 2005.

Polanyi Levitt is a founding member of the Canadian Association for the Study of International Development (CASID), recipient of the J.K. Galbraith Prize from the Progressive Economics Forum of Canada (2008) and an honorary doctorate from the University of the West Indies (2008). She is Honorary President of the Karl Polanyi Institute of Political Economy, established at Concordia University in 1987. In 1986 she organized a centennial conference in Budapest under the auspices of the Hungarian Academy of Sciences, editing the proceedings as *The Life and Work of Karl Polanyi: A Celebration* (Black Rose Books, 1990). She also co-edited with Kenneth McRobbie, *Karl Polanyi in Vienna* (Black Rose Books, 2000), and manages the literary legacy of Karl Polanyi's work.

In this book the author shares unique insights into the relevance of her father's work in understanding a world in transition from a globalization corrupted by the unlimited accumulation of financial wealth, to the rise of the South and the next great transformation. Polanyi Levitt revisits the Red Vienna of the 1920s, and the debate of Mises and Hayek with Polanyi and others on the feasibility of a participatory socialist economic model, based on associations of workers, consumers, enterprises and municipalities. Polanyi's account of the consequences of the great depression and other essays explain the explosion of interest in his work since the eruption of a crisis more profound and intractable than that of the 1930s.

The second part of the book tracks continuities and change in the trajectory of capitalism from its mercantilist origins in trade and war to the financialization of its heartlands; and the resilience of the non-European world to overcome legacies of colonialism and imperialism and achieve advances in human development on a scale unimaginable when development first came on the agenda in the 1940s. The author's early interest in the work of the pioneers of development economics has assumed new relevance as it becomes clear that only regions which have charted their own course and have not followed the dictates of the Washington Consensus have benefited from liberalized international trade. A final chapter on globalization and development suggests that the protection of territorial sovereignty over natural resources, including land and water, is becoming of ever greater importance.

What makes this book so relevant is that the crisis and death pangs of the neoliberal world are countered by the force of social movements for alternative development. There are many forms that such an alternative could take, but some theoreticians and architects of alternative development are reaching back to the ideas and policy prescriptions of earlier years, particularly to the development decades from the 1940s to the 1970s. It is here where the ideas of Karl Polanyi and Kari Polanyi, Levitt, are so useful in understanding the contours of an alternative development agenda.

— *Henry Veltmeyer, International Development Studies,*
Saint Mary's University.

INTRODUCTION

Four years into the unfolding of the most serious crisis since the 1930s, Karl Polanyi's prediction of the fateful consequences of unleashing the destructive power of unregulated market capitalism on peoples, nations and the natural environment have assumed new urgency and relevance. It was reported that the ghost of Karl Polanyi was haunting the annual conclave of the rich and the powerful at Davos in 2012. In these essays we shed the light of Polanyi's fundamental critique of self-regulating market capitalism on a world in transition from economic dependence of non-European countries on the purchasing power of North American and European consumers. With only a few exceptions, they were written since 1998 and have not been previously published. They should be read against the background of the accelerating accumulation of global finance, which created serious financial crises in Latin America and Asia in the 1990s and eventually engulfed the heartlands of capitalism in a multifaceted political, social and economic crisis that cannot be resolved by Keynesian macro-economic policies alone. Financial and corporate capital has captured governments and has subverted the democratic political process in North America and Europe. Socialism has been devalued by authoritarian Soviet communism, post-modern identity politics and the pervasive influence of neoliberal ideology.

We locate Hayek and Polanyi in the Vienna of the 1920s, and contrast Hayek's ideal of liberty as free enterprise with Polanyi's vision of socialism, which has extraordinary resonance with the contemporary search for bottom-up institutions of democratic self-reliant governance. Another theme in Polanyi's writing is the conflict between capitalism and democracy, treated in the essay on Keynes and Polanyi.

Since the death of my mother, Ilona Duczynska Polanyi, in 1978, I assumed responsibility for the literary legacy of my father. I edited or co-edited two volumes of writings on the life and work of Karl Polanyi[1] and negotiated translations of his works in over fifteen languages. My own work in teaching and research at McGill and the University of the West Indies was in international political economy with special reference to theories of economic development. I am not a specialist in the work of Karl Polanyi, but whether by genetics or shared experience of migrations from Vienna to London and later to North America, I believe I understand what motivated my father in all of his work.

In 1986, a centenary conference organized by the Hungarian Academy of Sciences was combined with the transfer of the earthly remains of my parents from Canada to a cemetery in Budapest. The assembled international participants decided that the neoliberal counter-revolution then gathering increasing influence called for a response in the form of a permanent institution dedicated to the dissemination of the work of Karl Polanyi. In the following year Concordia University accepted a proposal by Marguerite Mendell and myself for the establishment of the Karl Polanyi Institute of Political Economy in Montreal. The institute has hosted a number of international conferences and houses the most comprehensive archive of Polanyi's work, currently being digitalized to make it accessible to scholars the world over.

POLANYI ON CAPITALISM, SOCIALISM AND DEMOCRACY

In the first part of this volume I share with the reader my contributions to Karl Polanyi conferences and similar occasions to reflect on his work. The second part traces continuity and change in the global trajectory of capitalism from its mercantilist origins in commerce and conquest to the threat of financial implosion in October 2008 and shifting power relations in the world economy. It concludes with three essays on the theme of development economics, my subject area of teaching at McGill University and the University of the West Indies. Editorial changes are minimal. Some text has been abridged, while repetitive passages have been eliminated.[2] With the exception of Chapter 2, on Hayek as architect of the neoliberal creed, no attempt has been made to update any of the essays.

In Chapter 1, the book opens with a keynote address to the one-day conference "Karl Polanyi and the Transformation of the Contemporary World System," in Budapest in 2004, which accorded me the honour of Associate Member of the Hungarian Academy of Sciences. It recalls an important article written in 1945 in which Polanyi thought that only the United States believed in universal capitalism and expressed the hope that an international regime of managed trade could enable large regions with different economic and social systems to engage in mutually advantageous economic relations. The suggestion here is that we may again be moving toward a world of major regional blocs as an alternative to a multilateral system dominated by global capital. It concludes with a challenge for a different economic calculus, which values goods and especially services not by market price of supply and demand but by the social value accorded to them by citizens of a genuinely democratic society.

Chapters 2 and 3 situate Polanyi and Friedrich von Hayek in the Vienna of the 1920s—the Red Vienna of my childhood. Polanyi and Hayek arrived in England as émigré intellectuals in the early 1930s. Polanyi's *Great Transformation* and Hayek's *Road to Serfdom* were published in the same year, 1944. The opening sentence of the *Great Transformation* reads: "Nineteenth century civilization has collapsed." Note the present tense of these words written thirty years after the end of the long nineteenth century in 1914. Nowhere was the collapse of that civilization more evident than in Vienna, the glittering capital of the Hapsburg Empire of fifty million people, reduced to the impoverished capital of the six million of the Republic of Austria in 1918. In socialist Red Vienna, Hayek and his mentor, Ludwig von Mises, were the misfits, the remnants of the old order. As recalled by Mises in his memoirs: "To appreciate duly Doctor Hayek's achievements, one must take into account political, economic, and ideological conditions as they prevailed in Europe and especially in Vienna at the time the First World War came to an end" (1976: 183). They were traumatized by the socialist municipal administration that favoured the working classes. They considered socialism of all varieties and economic planning of any kind to be an infringement on personal liberty. They looked back on the liberal utopia of the pre-1914 economic order as an ideal to be recovered and refashioned.

In Chapter 2, we introduce Hayek as the principal figure of the fourth generation of the Austrian School of Economics and follow his career from Vienna to the London School of Economics to his foundation of the Chicago School and the international thought collective of the Mont Pelerin Society. Neoliberal ideology was consciously constructed from European sources but took root in the United States, where it found support among conservative Republicans opposed to New Deal policies. In its most radical form, neoliberalism defines freedom in purely economic terms. Politics is reduced to the rule of law by a strong state dedicated to the preservation of private property and free enterprise.

Chapter 3 introduces the reader to the formative influences on Karl Polanyi in pre-1914 Budapest and Vienna, where Russian revolutionaries of all varieties were welcomed and assisted by family and family friends. We briefly treat the role of Karl Polanyi in the foundation of the Hungarian student movement and the tension between Polanyi's admiration of the courage and idealism of all revolutionaries, including Jesus of Nazareth, and the scientific socialism of doctrinaire Marxism. In Vienna of the 1920s he engaged Mises in the socialist accountancy debates and outlined a model of associational functionalist socialism of democratic decision-making in both the economic and the political sphere.

Chapter 4 is an abridged text of a paper presented to the International Sociological Association in Montreal in 1998. The title, "Back to the Future," refers to the crisis of the 1930s, a subject that returned to academic discourse in the context of the unfolding Asian Crisis of 1997–1998. We summarize Polanyi's account of the crisis, drawing on a lengthy article, "The Mechanisms of the World Economic Crisis," published in the *Oesterreichische Volkswirt* in 1933. The argument is original and important, and differs from explanations of the world economic crisis of 1929–33, which emphasize mistaken policies of punitive German war reparations, the overvalued pound sterling or inexperienced American investors. According to Polanyi, the crisis was the result of the attempt by the victorious Western powers to impose the nineteenth-century liberal economic order—including the Gold Standard—on a continent impoverished by the war, where governments lacked resources to negotiate conflicting claims on the national product by industrial workers, agricultural producers and rentier investors. Before gold convertibility was imposed on weak states of Europe, countries could extinguish domestic debt by inflation. With currency convertibility and capital flight, and no further access to credit, there was no option other than increasing exports at declining prices and incomes to service debt and purchase essential imports. *Plus ca change!* Substitute the Euro for gold convertible currency and the weaker economies of the Eurozone are forced to undertake punishing deflationary contraction under the supervision of the European Central Bank and the International Monetary Fund. Escape from the Eurozone may be the only way to reclaim democratic control over economic livelihoods.

In Chapter 5, the increasing role of global finance in sustaining public and private expenditures in the 1990s invite comparisons with the 1920s and a revisit to the crisis of the 1930s as treated by Keynes and Polanyi. Of special interest in this chapter, and a recurrent theme in Polanyi's writings, is the conflict between economy and democracy, the title of an article written in 1932—a year before the accession of Hitler to office.[3] Where the interest of the captains of industry and the bankers prevailed over Parliaments dominated by socialist majorities, democracy was suspended and fascist regimes were installed. The conflict of capitalism and democracy has returned to contemporary discourse. In a later chapter we note that capitalism was instituted at a time when the majority population had no voice and no vote. Democratic capitalism is as recent as the post-Second World War era. But democracy is in question when corporations can fashion policies in think-tanks and control the media, there is no limit on electoral campaign financing and bond markets can make or break governments.

Chapter 6, on the contemporary relevance of Karl Polanyi's work, was a response to an invitation by the late Anne Chapman,[4] eminent Franco-American ethnographer and former student of my father, to address a workshop of French archaeologists, ethnographers and specialists in Greek antiquity. It is a comprehensive treatment of the principal concepts underlying Polanyi's work. It tracks the regression of democracy under pressure of the neoliberal counter-revolution from the 1970s to the eve of the present crisis.

Chapter 7 is one of the few written in the early days of the rise of neoliberalism. The occasion was a major conference organized by Japan's powerful Ministry of International Trade and Industry at the University of Tokyo in 1982. The objective was to bring Japan into a closer economic relationship with the United States. To this end, a range of high-profile American economists of differing views were invited. It was my good fortune that a Japanese anthropologist, Shinichiro Kurimoto, used the occasion to arrange a modest panel on Karl Polanyi and invited Abe Rotstein of the University of Toronto and myself to participate. The theme of the panel was culture and economics. After the conference, we were able to travel to Kyoto and Nara accompanied by Kurimoto and his graduate student, and I then spent a week in Tokyo. I never learned so much in two weeks, before or since. The embrace of ultra-modern technology by a society more different than any I have experienced attests to the bonds of culture in fashioning the resilience of the Japanese people to overcome adversity, most recently in the devastating earthquake and tsunami.

Chapter 8 is an extract from an address to the twenty-ninth international conference of the Basic Income Earth Network (BIEN) in Sao Paulo in 2010. The principle of basic income as a citizen right is enshrined in the constitution of Brazil, to be implemented as fiscal resources permit. I was asked to respond to the question: would Karl Polanyi have supported a social dividend as a citizen right? This provided an opportunity to add a political rationale to the well-known economic and social arguments in favour of basic income. In the 1950s, my father became increasingly concerned with the trend to conformism in North American society. A basic income, however modest, could assist in sustaining the non-conformity of the independent writer, dissident, artist or activist. The problem of freedom in a modern, technologically dependent society was a constant preoccupation of Karl Polanyi.

THE GLOBAL SOUTH FROM CONQUEST AND EXPLOITATION TO SELF-RELIANT DEVELOPMENT

The second part of the volume, Chapter 9, opens with a partly autobio-graphical presentation to a conference on international trade at the Institute of Development Studies in Sussex, U.K., where I spent some weeks at the invitation of its founder and director, Dudley Seers, in 1976. He had a close association with the West Indies, and the collection of his work published posthumously as *The Political Economy of Nationalism* (1983) reflects the influ-ence of Prebisch and Latin American Structuralism. The chapter explores continuities in structures of dependence of centres and peripheries from the early to the new mercantilism of transnational corporations. These insights derived from my Canadian work on the effects of multinational corporations on host economies (*Silent Surrender*, 1970) and my collaboration with Lloyd Best on structural continuities of the incorporations of Caribbean planta-tion economies into the overseas economies of their respective metropoles. Initiated more than forty years ago, our joint work was published as *Essays in Plantation Economy* in 2009. The text reflects the influence of the Prebisch thesis of deteriorating terms of trade of primary exporting economies of Latin America, the Caribbean and Africa and the demands of developing coun-tries for a fairer new international economic order in the 1970s, definitively rejected by the Western powers. In retrospect, it also reflects the tendency to extend the experience of the above-mentioned regions to the entire Third World, ignoring important differences with Asian economic development.

Chapter 10 is an historical essay dedicated to the memory of Surendra Patel, who foresaw the return of Asia to the world economy long before it became the transformative development of the twenty-first century. If the previous chapter emphasizes continuities, Chapter 10 tracks the changes from the origins of capitalism in the mercantilist era to the rise and decline of Western hegemony. Europe extended its land frontier by conquest and settlement of the Americas and disorganized and retarded Africa by the slave trade, but Asian civilizations, although exploited, were not uprooted in the Age of Imperialism. Europeans did not impose their religion; they did not establish settlements. We trace the imprint of British and later also American institutions and ideologies on Western capitalism in two centuries of their hegemony. We track the Global South through three post-war decades of the taming, followed by three decades of the unleashing, of capital. We conclude that financialization of the real economy, grotesque income inequality and outsourcing by transnational corporations have devastated the social contract in North America and Europe. The principal beneficiary of globalization has been China, whose entry into the world economy has assisted the diversification of production and external markets of other developing countries. We are told that we are experiencing a global crisis, but this is misleading. It is undeniable that that all regions of the world are to some degree affected by the crisis in the epicentres of capitalism, but governments and civil society in regions of the Global South have more autonomy and politics are more effective in popular mobilization for social justice. Superiority of the West in the technology of warfare and the accumulation of financial wealth is a fact, but so is the moral loss of legitimacy of Western hegemony. The paper evolved from a presentation to a Critical Development Studies summer school at the Autonomous University of Zacatecas in 2009 and a Surendra Patel memorial lecture at Saint Mary's University in Halifax in 2010[5] and was completed in 2012. Its broad historical sweep is a response to questions raised by the crisis regarding the future of capitalism.

Chapter 11 is the abridged text of a John Kenneth Galbraith lecture on *The Great Financialization*, written on the occasion of a prize jointly awarded by the Progressive Economic Forum of Canada to Mel Watkins and myself. We track the financialization of the real economy and growing income disparities and revisit *Silent Surrender* and the consequences of commercial and industrial policies governed by criteria of short-term gain. Canada is unique in the Organization of Economic Co-operation and Development in the extraordinary level of foreign ownership of its manufacturing industry, now well over 50 percent. The result is that Canada ranks lowest of OECD countries in research and development and has reverted to dependence on primary—chiefly extractive—exports, including the environmentally destructive tar sands. With the country lagging in the knowledge economy while relying on extractive industries and a strong financial sector, the economic prosperity of the coming generation is unlikely to match that of their parents and grandparents.

In Chapter 12 we note the close correspondence between economic policies and prevailing ideologies. The early pioneers of development economics, including Arthur Lewis and Raul Prebisch, advocated policies of industrialization as a means of escape from export dependence. In the neoliberal counter-revolution, development economics was dismissed together with Keynes in favour of reliance on world prices in the allocation of resources. developing countries were encouraged to engage in outward looking policies of export promotion. We conclude with a critique of economics, which fails to understand that the ultimate source of economic development is in the capacity of societies and governments to liberate the creative energies of the population. This paper, written in 1992, is a rough outline of a larger project on economics and the development discourse, which, at the time of writing, remains unfinished.

Chapter 13 is the response to an invitation by the North South Institute of Canada to review the contribution of theories of economic development to policy, with special reference to the role of development assistance. Development economics addresses three major themes: market and state; trade and development; and growth and equity. Earlier emphasis on the leading role of the state and diversification of economic activity for the domestic market was reversed in the neoliberal era, and national development was reduced to poverty alleviation. We conclude that countries must reclaim policy autonomy over natural and human resources to eliminate gross inequalities of income, assets and opportunities of the majority population. This text was also presented at the conference Globalization and Development, held in Havana in 2006.

Chapter 14 details a program for reclaiming the right to development based on principles of sovereignty, democracy and growth with equity. This implies the reform of the IMF to correspond to changing power relations and the return of the role of the World Bank to the United Nations, as was originally intended. It is a plea for creative thinking and new initiatives to protect the gains of development from devastation by financial hurricanes. The right to development is a citizen right, and the duty to formulate appropriate development policies rests with national governments. At the national level governments are under pressure to respond to the needs of their populations, however reluctantly. At the global level, capital is insulated from the constraints of democratic accountability. Development is an endogenous social project of harnessing human skills and knowledge. To borrow a line from Latin American Structuralism, it is essentially a process from within. It cannot be externally imposed. With reference to the legacy of Arthur Lewis and Raul Prebisch, we reassert the need to reclaim intellectual independence from economic orthodoxies and policies designed by the 10,000 staff of the

World Bank. The chapter is based on my response to an invitation by the then director of UNRISD, Thandika Mkandawire, to a conference on the need to rethink development economics, held in Cape Town in 2001.

A concluding chapter, Globalization and Development: Decline of the West and Rise of the Rest, was written specially for this volume.

NOTES

1. *The Life and Work of Karl Polanyi*, Kari Polanyi Levitt, ed. (1990) and *Karl Polanyi in Vienna: The Contemporary Significance of The Great Transformation*, Kari Polanyi Levitt and Kenneth McRobbie, eds. (2006).
2. Where there was duplication of major passages, we refer the reader to the chapter where the subject is treated.
3. In the interest of avoiding repetition, we have removed similar treatments of "Economy and Democracy" (Polanyi, 1932) from other chapters.
4. Renowned for her work on Mesoamerican civilizations, her final book is entitled *European Encounters with the Yamana People of Cape Horn, Before and After Darwin* (2010).
5. Surendra and Krishna Patel were visiting professors at Saint Mary's University for many years.

PART 1

Polanyi on Capitalism, Socialism and Democracy

1. ON TRANSFORMATIONS
Past, Present and Future?

November is a season for remembering. It is the season of all saints and all souls. A season to take stock of the past and take courage for the struggles of the future. It is a fitting season for this conference, which marks the 60th anniversary of the publication of *The Great Transformation* in 1944. This book has now been translated into fifteen languages, and a new Hungarian edition has been launched, including a translation of the preface by Joseph Stiglitz. The last time we met in this hall was in 1986, when the Hungarian Academy of Sciences hosted an important conference to celebrate the centenary of my father's life and work, and the earthly remains of my parents, Karl Polanyi and Ilona Duczynska, were returned to their final resting place in Hungary. I wish to record a special thanks to the late Joseph Bogner, who presided over the conference from this platform. He was a true friend and we remember him with affection and respect. The platform was also shared by Ilona's ancient Corona Smith typewriter, on which she typed so many of my father's manuscripts and her own memoirs.

October 1986 happened also to be the 30th anniversary of 1956, a historic event that united my parents in a kind of return to Hungary late in their lives. They undertook a project of translating the work of some of their favourite Hungarian poets to English in the only book jointly authored by them, *The Plough and The Pen* (Duczyska and Polanyi 1963). In 1961, three years before his death, my father was invited to Budapest to deliver a series of lectures. Accompanied by Ilona, he was reunited with family members and old friends, some of whom knew him since the Galilee Circle before the First World War. It was his first return to Hungary since he left for Vienna in 1919. This was an important homecoming, a return to Hungary, so central to their lives.

Karl Polanyi's life was, as he noted, "a world life," but its formative years were lived here in Budapest, more precisely in these streets and in this area where we are presently meeting. It was here that he first confronted the philosophical question of freedom in a modern industrial society, a continuing concern throughout his life. On that occasion, I think, he wrote that all he had achieved he owed ultimately to Hungary. I myself have never lived in this country, and I cannot speak your remarkable language, which has given rise to so much original thought in so many areas of science. I was born in Vienna, but as I told Prof. Vizi, I know that my ultimate origins are here. It gives me a special satisfaction to be receiving the honour of becoming a member of your scientific community; it is a sort of return to origins late in my life.

In 1919, my father emigrated to Vienna, where he met my mother; they were married in 1923. There he contributed to an emigré Hungarian publication edited by his friend Oskar Jaszi, and engaged Ludwig Von Mises in a debate on the feasibility of a socialist economy in the pages of the premier German language social science journal.[1] From 1924 to 1933, his position as a senior editor of *Oesterreichische Volkswirt*, the leading financial and economic weekly of Central Europe, enabled him to closely follow European economic and political developments. The first two chapters of *The Great Transformation* are a vivid account of the crises of the interwar years. Many interesting comparisons can be made between the pressures exerted on the weak and fragile succession states of Central Europe in the interwar period and the Structural Adjustment Programs imposed on indebted developing countries in the 1980s and 1990s and indeed up to now.

In 1933, deteriorating political conditions caused Polanyi to leave Vienna for London, but he continued to contribute to the journal until it ceased publication in 1938. In England, he obtained employment as a tutor for the Workers Educational Association (WEA), the adult education extension program of Oxford University. He taught evening classes in provincial towns of Kent and Sussex on international relations and English social and economic history, a subject entirely new to him. There he experienced a profound culture shock. On overnight stays with families in these small provincial towns he discovered the profound cultural impoverishment of the working class in what was then the richest country in Europe, and compared it with the condition of the working class of socialist Red Vienna in impoverished post-1918 Austria, which he much admired. The lecture notes for his WEA classes are the skeleton upon which he later developed *The Great Transformation*.[2]

The principal thesis of this book was that the economic and social upheavals and political tensions resulting from the utopian attempt to restore the nineteenth-century liberal economic order after the First World War were the essential cause of the world economic crisis and of the demise of democracy in most of the states of Continental Europe. With a few exceptions, like France, the Netherlands and Scandinavia, Continental European countries turned inward on national solidarities and adopted fascisms of one kind or another. In a striking passage, he concluded that "in order to comprehend German fascism, we must revert to Ricardian England" (Polanyi 1944 [2001]: 32). It is a profound statement, and one that I think rather shocked English audiences.

I cannot mention German fascism without telling you that I never thought that in my life we would ever again witness fascism in a modern industrial country. In November 2001, at our Mexico Conference I noted that in the U.S. we see a creeping fascism. That was three years ago and I fear we now see a galloping fascism. All of its aspects and manifestations are there. I believe that as social scientists it bears investigation to trace these very unfortunate developments to their historic origins and to the ultimate source of the Anglo-American relationship that has now assumed a military manifestation.

The Great Transformation was first pubished in the United States in 1944,[3] the same year as the publication of Hayek's *Road to Serfdom*. These two intellectuals, both from Vienna, were occupied with the similar problem of freedom in an industrial society, but the diagnoses they made were at polar opposites. By 1945, it was widely believed that the experiences of the interwar years had discredited laissez-faire capitalism and that private enterprise would in the future have to be subordinated to the social objectives of national societies, and indeed this is more or less what happened from 1945 to the mid-1970s. Only the Americans, Polanyi wrote, still believed in universal capitalism, a discredited adventure of the past. In the West, full employment and social security were the first priorities of national policy. In Africa and Asia, the full mobilization of human and natural resources to raise living standards was the principal objective of movements of national liberation. Polanyi (1945: 1–6) envisaged a world of diverse economic and social systems coexisting in managed inter-regional exchange.

In the 1940s and 1950s, some independent-minded economists turned their attention to the problems of economic underdevelopment with important support from the early United Nations. With few exceptions, they came from regions peripheral to the heartlands of industrial capitalism. They came from Scandinavia, Central Europe, including Hungary — Nicolas Kaldor has already been mentioned — India, the West Indies, Argentina, Brazil and Japan. These were the early group of development economists, and many names come to mind. When my father founded the journal *Co-Existence* early in the 1960s as a means of communicating across the Cold War divide, many of these eminent development economists leant their support and joined the editorial board of the journal. We honour their names, and those of you familiar with this field will know that they were indeed eminent: Gunnar Myrdal, Oskar Lange, Jan Tinbergen, P.C. Mahalanobis, Ragnar Frisch, Shigeto Tsuru and the one and only Joan Robinson.

When I first encountered the early literature of development economics in the late 1950s, I hastened to share my enthusiasm with my father. He did not discourage my newfound interest in the subject, but his response was characteristic: "Development, Kari? I don't know what that is."

As we know, he was, at that time, at Columbia University (1947–57) engaged in research on the institutions that governed the organization of economic life in a variety of primitive and archaic societies. He set out to prove the fallacy implicit in the ascription of market mechanisms to pre-capitalist societies. He contrasted the formal apparatus of economics, posited on the behaviour of individual producers and consumers optimizing choices under constraint with the substantive investigation of the role of economic institutions in the organization of economic livelihood. His path-breaking article "Two Meanings of Economics" was greeted with considerable hostility by academic anthropologists. In his search for general principles underlying the organization of the provision of the material necessities of life, he posited reciprocity, redistribution and exchange as patterns of integration. In this optic, the market economy appears as a special case. Polanyi (1944 [2001]: 30) contended that the nineteenth-century market economy was "economic" in the distinctive sense that it chose to base itself on a motive never before raised to the level of justification of action and behaviour in everyday life, namely individual gain.

In an important letter written to a friend of his youth, Beatrice De Waard, he dedicated his work to the "new peoples" of Asia and Africa. He expressed the hope that his ideas would stand vindicated in ten years. He did not live that long, and his ideas took a great deal longer to become vindicated.

As we all know, after the demise of the Bretton Woods monetary order in the early 1970s and various maladies which overcame the capitalist system, including creeping inflation, declining productivity and profits, low or negative real interest rates favouring debtors and a wave of political radicalism in the South, a counter-revolution was unleashed favouring capital. A macroeconomic regime change precipitated the Latin American debt crisis of the 1980s, the Reagan and Thatcher administrations rolled back gains made by labour in the first three post-war decades, and the Bretton Woods Institutions were encouraged to use financial leverage to remove restrictions on trade and capital in developing countries.

Keynes was banished, and development economics was drummed out of the academy. The World Bank took the lead in an intellectual attack on development economics as a sub-discipline of economics devoted to problems of developing countries. The Bank declared that that there was one and only one economics and that economic science could explain the functioning of the economy anytime, anyplace, anywhere, regardless of institutions. Developing countries as diverse as anything you can find from Asia, Africa and Latin America were no different from the leading industrial countries, only poorer. Development economics was demonized as structuralist heresies bordering on socialism.

In the mid-1980s, an influential Swedish trade economist, Assar Lindbeck, was brought to the World Bank as an advisor. He wrote a research memorandum that I will never forget.[4] I could not believe what I was reading. The entire responsibility for the debt crisis was laid upon indebted countries. They were not letting the market work properly, they were not getting prices right. They were imposing wicked subsidies on basic foods and assisting small farmers with loans at concessional rates, a whole list of "erroneous" policies (World Bank 1984). This list of economic sins is very similar to Polanyi's account of charges laid against countries in the context of the stabilization programs of the League of Nations in the 1920s. We now have doctrines of balanced budgets, even enshrined in constitutions, removal of subsidies, freedom of capital transactions and independent central banks with the sole objective of protecting the value of money and the security of investors. By the end of the 1980s Hayek had achieved his declared objective of turning the doctrinal clock back to the 1920s.

Since 1991, which I think may rank as a date as important as 1914, we do not yet know, because that is for future historians to tell us, the neoliberal agenda of deregulation, liberalization and privatization was put into fast-forward mode. In 1994 a word appeared from apparently nowhere: globalization. The word was not found in the two vast volumes of the Oxford Shorter English dictionaries or in the spellchecks of personal computers in 1995. Suddenly it was everywhere; you could hardly read a commentary on economic affairs in magazines or newspapers that did not refer to it. The World Bank in the mid-1990s went as far as to suggest that globalization offered a return to the "golden age of the late nineteenth century," which could bring prosperity to the developing world so long as countries adhered to the market principle. In 1994, the General Agreement on Trade and Tariffs was converted to the World Trade Organization, the North American Free Trade Agreement was signed, and the project to extend it to the entire hemisphere was initiated in Miami.

Liberalization of trade and investment was accompanied by an explosion of short-term global finance far surpassing the requirements of trade. The returns on short-term portfolio investments and the opportunities for capital gains exceeded profits from productive activity. Corporations moved assets from production to finance, and the national accounts of almost all countries showed an extraordinary growth in the contribution of financial services to GDP. In some developing countries this financialization equalled or surpassed the contribution of manufacturing, reflecting the rewards to holders of government debt and other financial assets. This financialization, which accompanied globalization, was a mechanism of transferring real resources from producers and taxpayers to individual or institutional owners of financial assets. Both at the domestic and international levels it has been an engine of inequality and instability. We have seen financial crises more frequent and more severe than those of the 1930s, not in the heartlands of capitalism, but in East Asia, Latin America, Turkey, Brazil, Argentina and Russia. In many developing countries, living standards have plunged not by 2 or 5 percent, but by 30 percent or more.

Whereas capitalism brought great benefits in the form of increases in material production in the nineteenth and twentieth centuries, what we now see is a predatory style of capitalism. In contrast to an earlier era of British hegemony, when the export of capital in the form of long-term bond-financed investments amounted to 6–8 percent of Britain's GNP, the United States is financing its excess public and private consumption by the import of capital from poorer regions of the world, including Japan, China, Taiwan and other surplus countries, amounting to 5 percent of its GDP. While Britain's nineteenth-century overseas investments were principally in railroads, ports and other infrastructure, U.S. foreign investment takes the form of establishment of subsidiaries of transnational corporations. In recent times, these have been more concerned with acquiring existing assets, both private and public, than with the systematic increase in the real productive capacities of countries. This style of capitalism, which privileges finance over production and forced privatization of public assets at fire-sale prices to service debt, resembles the plunder of early mercantile capitalism. A long time ago I described the operations of multinational corporations as a "new mercantilism."

For developing countries this model has been implemented by a complex set of financial negotiations to secure capital account liberalization with conditionalities which impose increasing constraints on the policy space of these countries and put them in a straightjacket, not a golden one but some other form of straightjacket of obligations to external multilateral agencies and financial creditors.

How, we may ask, is imperialist domination of the developing world possible in this day and age? Most Latin American countries and many others in the developing world are now governed by institutions of representative democracy. How is it that neoliberalism has become so entrenched, seemingly regardless of the party elected to power?

The limitations on sovereignty imposed by external obligations to creditors and multilateral institutions alone cannot account for the democratic deficit. A model developed by Osvaldo Sunkel thirty years ago depicts the incorporation of significant strata of industrial, commercial and professional domestic classes into the metropolitan circuits of production, consumption and accumulation. Their aspirations and lifestyles have more in common with those prevailing in the industrialized world than those of their poorer compatriots. In many countries they have benefited from the financing of domestic governments by the issue of domestic debt carrying high rates of interest, and they placed their earnings in foreign banks, safe from financial instability. This is one reason governments elected with wide popular support on progressive platforms find it difficult to deliver the expected results.

We have arrived at a critical moment in history. To gain perspective on possible futures we need to lengthen parameters of inquiry to embrace the history of European hegemony and the evolution of capitalism from its beginnings in mercantilist conquest. The creation of the developing, or underdeveloped world is, historically speaking, a rather recent phenomenon. The continuities over 500 years are best observed from the Caribbean and Sub-Saharan Africa. The establishment of production facilities on capitalist principles was pioneered on the slave plantations of the Caribbean. The legacy of the inferior status of the African diaspora in the Americas has yet to be extinguished. The demographic shock of 300 years of the slave trade disorganized African societies and retarded African economic development and even population growth.

For Polanyi's insights into the historic transformation of agricultural societies to industrial we must turn to the concepts that underlie the narrative of *The Great Transformation*: the *fictitious commodities*, the *disembedded economy* and the *double movement*. While markets have existed since earliest times, it was Polanyi's contention that price-making markets for the fictitious commodities of land, labour and money were an innovation more revolutionary than the mechanical inventions of early industrial capitalism.

The commodification of labour in England is generally dated to the New Poor Law of 1834. But it was preceded by two centuries of systematic dispossession of the peasantry by the enclosure of the commons to create agrarian capitalist enterprises, whether for the rearing of sheep or the cultivation of wheat with wage labour. It is here that we find the source of the cultural impoverishment of the English working class noted by Polanyi.[5] Whether from patrician motives of responsibility or fear of social upheaval, the landed gentry provided a measure of poor relief to large numbers of dispossessed and impoverished people roaming the countryside, until the urban bourgeoisie gained control of Parliament in 1832, and instituted a draconian labour regime.

No such humanitarian considerations applied to African labour transported across the middle passage to work on the slave plantations of the new world from the sixteenth century until abolition in the nineteenth century. If we think of slaves as embodied labour power, bought and sold on a slave market, plantation slavery was a form of agrarian capitalism. The principal capital asset was the stock of slaves, and the sole purpose of the enterprise was the production of a commodity for sale. The Good Hope Plantation, in Jamaica, had 3000 slaves. This was division of labour on a huge scale and at a great level of complexity at a time when Adam Smith was describing the merits of the division of labour in a pin factory employing ten people. The suggestion here is that the technical advantages of the division of labour were pioneered on the plantations of the West Indies. Plantation slavery was a forerunner of capitalist industry.[6]

In the Industrial Revolution, land and labour, people and nature were transposed into factors of production with a market price determined by supply and demand. They were transformed into instruments for achieving the sole objective of increased production of commodities, whether in the form of goods or services. Capital, as a factor of production, has been more problematic in the history of economics and the subject of important controversy, but economists conveniently sweep these aside by the use of a mathematical symbol (k) in algebraic expressions, which may indeed include any number of other so-called factors of production. The economy is presented as an interdependent system of structural and behavioural market relations between transactors imagined as a self-contained and complex mechanism, which can be tweaked and manipulated to explore the functioning and disfunctioning, the equilibria and disequilibria of the economy. This intellectual construct of economics carries a very strong normative message; if economies do not function like this, this is how they ought to function.

The conceptualizations of economic science mirror Polanyi's disembedded economy, which has lifted the economy out of its social and cultural base. The problem, of course, is that this picture of the economy does not conform to reality. The reality is that people work for all sorts of reasons. Some work is remunerated and a lot of work that is done is not remunerated, but economics students are taught that non-remunerated work has no value. The economists' view of nature is equally strange. I remember that in our economics department a test of whether a student could think like an economist was whether that student could understand that natural resources have no value if they are not commercialized or do not have the potential to be so. These are the skills that we teach our students, and this is really very troubling.

Because the disembedding of the economy is in fact socially unsustainable, Polanyi suggested that society protected itself from impersonal market forces in a variety of ways. Polanyi warned, in a frequently cited passage:

> [The self regulating market] could not exist for any length of time without annihilating the human and natural substance of society; it would have physically destroyed man and transformed his surroundings into a wilderness. Inevitably, society took measures to protect itself, but whatever measures it took impaired the self-regulation of the market, disorganized industrial life and thus endangered society in yet another way. (1944 [2001]: 3)

The reference here is to the "double movement" of the explosive spread of the market economy and checks to its expansion by protective labour, civic, social and political movements and the legislative measures enacted by national states.

Polanyi shared Marx's fundamental insight into the historically limited nature of the organization of economic life by the universalization of the market principle, including private ownership of the means of production. Whereas Marx anticipated the eventual breakdown of the capitalist order on account of inherent *economic* contradictions, Polanyi emphasized the contradiction between the requirements of the capitalist market economy for limitless expansion and the human requirement to be sustained by mutually supportive social relations. In Polanyi's account of this existential contradiction the outcome is not determinate. There is no grand design of progress. There are no impersonal historical forces which inevitably move humanity forward.

After the Second World War, a prolonged period of relative economic stability and strong economic growth in Europe and North America encouraged a reading of Polanyi's "double movement" as a kind of self-correcting mechanism. Such illusions were shattered by the impact of globalization in the 1980s and 1990s. Liberalization of capital from national control has accelerated social dislocation and exclusion on a global scale and created polarizing inequalities never before experienced in human history, but there are no international institutions to offset or check the law of accumulation.

We suggest that from the point of view of the developing world, this globalization, neoliberalism, or imperialism, whatever you may want to call it, manifests similarities with earlier penetrations of capitalism into the developing world. From this perspective we may note three waves of capitalist expansion in the 500 years of the modern world system. The initial one, the era of mercantilism from 1500–1800; a second, the creation of the world economy in the nineteenth century, which eventuated in the First World War and the world economic crisis of the 1930s; and the third and present wave, which began with the counter-revolution of capital to roll back the gains made by labour. Each of these has left deep historic traces and legacies on the various regions of the developing world.

North-South relations of dominance and dependence were established in the era of mercantilism. The indigenous civilizations of North and South America were destroyed and their populations decimated. The conquistadors and missionaries came with sword and bible, and the prevailing religion of Europe was effectively implanted in the Americas. The persistence of ethnic cleavage between indigenous peoples and populations of European origin explains the extraordinary inequality of assets, income and opportunity in contemporary Latin America, which far surpass those in any other part of the world. This has contributed to the endemic political and economic instability, which forms the principal obstacle to the achievement of growth with equity.

Asia was at this time, more wealthy than Europe in every way and its manufactures and capacity for material production more sophisticated. Societies were not destroyed or damaged as in the Americas and Africa.

The mutually advantageous relationships between large transnational corporations and their home governments in the current globalization is reminiscent of that of the great trading companies and monarchs of the mercantile era. Mercantilism was about conquest and unequal trade. There was essentially no technical progress.

The second globalization created a world economy. In the nineteenth century industrial capitalism spread from England and Northwest Europe to the rest of the Continent, to North America and at the end of the century also to Japan. There was an enormous increase in productive capacity. Large metropolitan investments in railways, ports and ocean transportation served as infrastructure to an expanding volume of international trade. Surplus labour displaced by industrialization emigrated by the millions to the so-called empty lands of the Americas and other regions.

Peripheral countries were transformed into export economies serving the ever-growing need for foodstuffs and agricultural and mineral raw materials in metropolitan markets. The so-called traditional division of labour between centres exporting manufactures and peripheries exporting primary products was established. A more general legacy of this era is the carving of distinct patterns into the structure of international trade, whereby the stronger metropolitan centres control distribution, finance, communication and access to technology, and the peripheries produce export commodities that now include manufactures. This institutional asymmetry of power disappears from view in the treatment of international trade in economics textbooks, which treats international trade as if it were simply a matter of mutually beneficial exchange between two or more equal partners.

Late industrializers challenged British supremacy, and by the end of the century intensified competition resulted in a prolonged crisis of overproduction. Capital responded by concentration in mergers, trusts and monopolies. Rivalry between national capitalisms extended political colonialism to embrace all of Africa save Ethiopia and vast regions of Asia. Imperialism was accompanied by a discourse of the "civilizing mission" and the "white man's burden." While the economic benefits of new colonial conquests was perhaps marginal in relation to the cost of acquiring and defending them, the damage to the social fabric and natural environment was far reaching and long lasting. This was the "golden age" which advocates of neoliberal globalization hold up as a model to be replicated on a now larger global scale.

It all came crashing down in the imperialist war of 1914–18, followed by a world economic crisis in 1929–33. In Latin American history, 1929 marks the end of a century of export-dependent economic development. Imperialism was discredited, and peripheral countries set their hopes on industrialization as a means to escape export dependence. By the beginning of mass decolonization in 1945, it was believed that territorial colonialism was a thing of the past.

Prior to the accession of the George W. Bush administration to office in 2000, globalization was manifested principally by the exercise of economic and financial power. I suggest what this really adds up to is a project to impose Anglo-American institutions and an Anglo-American style of capitalism on the world. Since 2000 the U.S. has adopted an explicit policy of the unilateral exercise of military power, including the implementation of a doctrine of "space superiority." Colonial wars seem to have returned. The United States has undertaken to exercise hegemony by the establishment of military outposts on a global scale. I believe that the project of American empire is bound to fail. So far they have been unable to digest the occupation of the relatively small country of Iraq. It may last a little longer than Hitler's promise of 1,000 years of peace in Europe, but I don't think it is a viable proposition, though it can bring terrible damage to the world.

By the end of the 1990s, it had become evident that neoliberal policies had failed to produce economic growth with stability and had greatly widened disparities of income in Latin America, where there is now a critical reassessment under resurgence of popular pressures to deliver the benefits of economic development to the masses. In Sub-Saharan Africa, where the World Bank implemented hundreds of Structural Adjustment Programs, living standards have fallen, wars have ravaged the continent and HIV/AIDS has decimated the population. Unlike Latin America, where neoliberalism had captured the imagination of a generation of economists, Africans charged with implementing these programs did so under duress of the fiscal burden of debt service. They never believed in this neo-colonial management of their affairs by the staffs of the Bretton Woods Institutions (BWIs). There is a growing consensus that African development requires a totally different approach, respectful of indigenous institutions and values and based on the appropriate allocation of the great resources of the continent for the economic and social requirements of their diverse communities.

With some exceptions, the BWIs exercized minimal influence over national economic policy in East, South East and South Asia. While participation in international trade and investment has played an important role in the economic success of the region — China is emerging as the world's second largest economy and Americans are currently obsessed with the outsourcing of services to India — the wellspring of the extraordinary economic growth in East Asia is firmly domestic. In one way or another, the state has provided economic and social infrastructure in education and research, and assisted industry to climb up the value chain by strategic incentives and control over access to credit and foreign exchange. They have replicated the success of European late industrializers in a mere twenty or thirty years. In this connection, the work of the early development economists is being revisited.

There is reason to expect the emergence of a powerful East Asian regional formation, including China, Japan, Taiwan and Korea, associated with the ASEAN group of countries. India, with a population approaching one billion, a strong industrial base and high levels of tertiary education and a middle class approximating 300 million with significant purchasing power, is negotiating long-standing problems with Pakistan and also China. This is the background against which we assess the prospects of the U.S.-led drive to restructure the world in the image of its own institutions, because that is what the globalization agenda is all about. Initiatives toward regionalism in the South are also evident in Latin America, the Caribbean and Africa. The love affair of elites in the European transition countries with the United States is fading. Some countries have joined the European Union and others aspire to do so.

Because of the present imbalance of power in the world, any form of world government, however attractive it may appear, would be an instrument for the maintenance of the status quo. From the point of view of the developing world, an objective for the foreseeable future could be the formation of large regions of economic integration with political institutions of governance appropriate to geographic and historical realities. Only China and India or perhaps the entire South Asian region have the size, diversity and historical and political coherence to stand alone as viable regions. Such a reconfiguration of the international system implies a reform of the international financial order to replace the dollar as the hegemonic reserve currency. Keynes's plan for a special-purpose money for clearing international balances deserves re-examination.

Such an imagined future constitutes a significant retreat from the universal capitalism of globalization. Regionalism could embrace diversity of its constituent parts as indeed is the case in the European Union. Economic, social and indeed political institutions of the various regions would be quite different. Such arrangements would permit the re-allocation of resources on a regional scale to meet the requirements of domestic consumption. Trade would perform its proper function of benefits of mutual exchange. The resources devoted to trade would no longer displace or constrain domestic development. It is a variant of Polanyi's model of an international economy. His historical investigation of the place of the economy in society and his deconstruction of the roles of money, markets and trade points to a variety of economic institutions which indeed can coexist as they do in a modern mixed economy, and markets will always have an important role to play. All of this is possible if regional economies are to some degree closed to allow the allocation of domestic resources to be sheltered from prices prevailing in the stronger economies. The set of prices appropriate to one region may be different from the set of prices appropriate to the resource allocation of another.

The richest 25 percent of the world's population consumes 80 percent of the world's limited natural resources. If there is to be any way of closing these enormous gaps, the regions of China, Asia, Latin America and Africa will have to be able to provide their populations with the basic amenities of modern life. They will have to have access to the natural resources required to do so. This implies an absolute decline in the use of these resources in the capitalist heartlands. It is difficult to conceive how the capitalist organization of the economy, based on ever-growing consumer demand, can adjust to what amounts to a radical change of lifestyles. Unfortunately, it is more likely that military power will be used to appropriate scarce resources.

We conclude that the contradictions between the requirements of the capitalist economy for unlimited expansion and the requirements of people to live in mutually supportive relations cannot be resolved without a civilizational change to transform institutions governing economic life. This is a long-term process, but in the history of humanity the past two centuries of industrial capitalism are a moment. As Heilbronner (1992: 103) reminds us, none of the great economists, not Smith nor Marx nor Schumpeter nor Keynes, projected a long untroubled future for capitalism. Nor did Karl Polanyi. Many non-profit initiatives of civil society are examples of social solidarity based on cooperation, not competition, on association, not individual gain. Important as they are, however, they cannot substitute for democratic control of the state, which remains essential to the organization of economic livelihood in a modern society in the North as in the South.

The transformation of the capitalist order requires a new calculus of the value of work, the value of human needs and the value of nature; basic human needs of security, affection, respect and protection have no place in formal economics. Economic decisions have to be made. But the value system must be one that accords with the realities of real people living in real societies and a very real dependence on the natural environment and its very real limitations. Economics has to return to some very basic questions of use value and exchange value. We have to take into account the real value of human effort and work, and that is very different from its market value. We have to protect nature and our social and cultural heritage. People do not like to be valued and respected only for the income they can earn and to be totally disrespected if they are not able to earn income for whatever reason. The reconciliation of criteria of technical efficiency with distributive justice and democratic process was the problem which Karl Polanyi attempted to solve in the debate with Ludwig Von Mises, mentor of Friedrich Hayek, on the feasibility of an associational democratic socialist economy. He did not solve the problem, but the legacy of his research into institutions of non-market exchange, the use of single purpose moneys or reciprocal and redistributive arrangements of various kinds may expand the boundaries of the possible. This is the challenge that Karl Polanyi has presented to us and to future generations.

NOTES

This chapter was the keynote address, entitled "The Transformation of the World System: Some Insights from the Work of Karl Polanyi," to the conference "Karl Polanyi and the Transformation of the Contemporary World System," Budapest, Hungary, November 5–6, 2004.

1. See, for example, Karl Polanyi, "Sozialistische Rechnungslegung" in *Archiv fur Sozialwissenshaft und Sozialpolitik*, Bd. 49, 2, pp. 377–420 and Ludwig V. Mises, "Neue Beitrage Zum Problem der Sozialistischen Wirtschaftsrechnung" in *Archiv fur Sozialwissenshaft und Sozialpolitik*, Bd. 51, 2, p. 410. See Chapter 3 for greater

    detail on the Polanyi–Von Mises debate.

2.   They are held in the archive of the Karl Polanyi Institute of Concordia University, Montreal, Canada.

3.   An English edition, published by Victor Gollancz Ltd., followed in 1945 with the title *Origins of Our Time*.

4.   For further details, see Chapter 12.

5.   A reminder of the agrarian origins of English capitalism is furnished by Ricardo's concept of diminishing returns at the margin of cultivable land. The economics of the firm derived from the economics of the farm.

6.   The slave trade and the slave plantations were enormously profitable and accounted for one-quarter of England's imports in the eighteenth century.

2. HAYEK FROM VIENNA TO CHICAGO
Architect of the Neoliberal Creed

Karl Polanyi's *The Great Transformation* was first published in the United States in 1944, and Friedrich von Hayek's *Road to Serfdom* was published in England in the same year. Both authors were concerned with freedom in a modern complex society, but their conclusions were diametrically opposed. Hayek considered socialism and economic planning of any variety a threat to personal liberty. Freedom, he argued, must be grounded in an economy of property rights and free competitive markets for labour and capital, guaranteed by the rule of law and secure from political intervention. Polanyi was a socialist who believed that the economy must be subordinate to social priorities determined by political processes of democratic governance. While he rejected Soviet central planning as excessively bureaucratic and authoritarian, for Polanyi it was not the Soviet experiment but the rise of fascism that constituted a civilizational challenge to the values of the West. Whereas Hayek looked back on the bourgeois economic order of the nineteenth century as a liberal utopia, Polanyi ascribed the collapse of that civilization to the subjugation of the economic livelihood of individuals and nations to the dictates of impersonal market forces. We recall his conclusion that, "to comprehend German fascism, we must revert to Ricardian England" (Polanyi 1944 [2001]: 32).

Both Hayek and Polanyi arrived in England from Vienna in the early 1930s. Hayek was working in the offices of the Austrian Chamber of Commerce, where he had established a modest institute for the study of the business cycle, when he was projected from relative obscurity into the prestigious Tooke Chair of Economic Science and Statistics at the London School of Economics by Lionel Robbins in 1931. The intention of this appointment was to counter the influence of Keynes and his unorthodox policies of monetary expansion, feared as dangerously inflationary by the financial interests of the City. Polanyi was, at that time, tracking the world economic crisis as it spread from the collapse of the Vienna Creditanstalt westward to France, Britain and eventually the United States in his weekly column in the *Oesterreichische Volkswirt*. As the shadow of fascism crept over Central Europe,

Polanyi was asked to resign his position on the editorial board and his salary was terminated. He left for England in 1933. Polanyi and Hayek did not know each other personally. They lived in different worlds in the Vienna of the 1920s. While Hayek looked back on the liberalism of the Belle Époque of pre-war Imperial Vienna, Polanyi admired the Red Vienna of the 1920s as a remarkable achievement and model of municipal socialism.

In this chapter and the next, we locate Hayek and Polanyi in the Vienna of the 1920s, where socialist majorities had dominated politics since the foundation of the Republic of Austria in 1918. A special target of Hayek's polemics in the 1920s was the regime of rent control and public housing, which effectively eliminated private high-rental residential construction (Hayek 1929). Working-class families were now privileged in access to low-rental, bright, spacious, modern apartments with parks, kindergartens and other communal facilities. These programs, together with a sweeping educational reform based on Alfred Adler's theories of psychology, plus the large-scale participation of the working people of Vienna in a remarkable variety of cultural, recreational and educational activities organized by the socialist municipal administration, made Red Vienna a world-class showpiece of avant-garde urban lifestyle.

The elite of the intellectuals of Vienna were socialist sympathizers. In Vienna alone 350,000 people belonged to social democratic organizations, while socialist trade unions comprised 700,000 workers. "Never before or since," wrote Ernst Fischer,[1] "has a Social Democratic Party been so power-ful, so intelligent or so attractive as was the Austrian party of the mid-1920s" (1959: 143). According to another contemporary,

> [the] piecemeal reforms were to be the first building blocks of a future socialist society…. The ultimate justification of socialism derived from our expectation that it would usher in a new man, a new morality…. The essence of being a socialist is the holding of certain ethical positions about justice and about duties to our fellow man. (Zeisel 1985: 123, 131)[2]

Hayek came from a good patrician family. He served as an officer in the Great War, obtained a doctorate in law and political science from the University of Vienna in 1922 and spent a year in New York (1923–24) before returning to join Ludwig von Mises' Privatseminar. In the setting of intellectual Vienna of the 1920s, Hayek, his patron Mises and their associates were the misfits — the remnants of old Imperial Vienna's privileged urban elites, whose security had been shattered, whose savings had been decimated by wartime and post-war inflation and whose taxes were financing the pioneering housing programs of Red Vienna. In their parlours and favourite coffee houses they fed their fears of the dictatorship of the proletariat.

Mises and Hayek were frightened by the 1926 Linz Program of the Social Democratic Party, which resolved to defend Austria's democratic constitution — by armed struggle if necessary — against threats by the conservative Christian Social Party to crush the working class and its organizations. The heirs of the liberal tradition of the 1860s made common cause with the rising forces of clerical fascism in their fear of the working classes. The suspension of Parliament in 1933 was followed by the violent destruction of the working-class movement in February 1934, leaving the country defenceless against Hitler's occupation in 1938.

THE DEMISE OF AUSTRIAN LIBERALISM

Hayek was born in Vienna at the turn of the century (1899) as the brief era of the liberal constitutional order established in the 1860s — which privileged the rising class of bankers, manufacturers and merchants and found its social support base among middle-class urban Germans and German-speaking Jews — was being challenged by anti-capitalist populist movements of the Right and the Left.

During the last quarter of the nineteenth century, the program the liberals had devised against the upper classes occasioned an explosion of the lower. The liberals succeeded in releasing the energies of the masses, but against themselves, rather than against their ancient foes. The Catholics, routed from the school and the courthouse as the handmaiden of aristocratic oppression, returned as the ideology of the peasant and the artisan, for whom liberalism meant capitalism and capitalism meant Jew. Laissez-faire, dressed to free the economy from the fetters of the past, called forth the Marxist revolutionaries of the future (Schorske 1981: 117).[3]

The appeal of the conservative Christian Social Party was founded on the sense of betrayal of the "little man," the petty producers and small artisans, who felt menaced by liberal capitalism. The targets of the party were the "free thinking, highly educated and often Jewish capitalists and their somewhat strong belief in Manchester Liberalism, materialism and positivism" (Kitchen 1980: 36).

Here it is important to understand the high-profile role played by German-speaking (largely assimilated) Jews in the economic life of Imperial Austria. This was true particularly of those areas that subsequently became the Republic of Austria. Commercial and professional opportunities abounded because of the almost complete absence of a native bourgeoisie. This was not true of Bohemia or Moravia, where German capitalists played the key role. As the centre of the Hapsburg Empire, Vienna attracted a large Jewish immigration.[4] A very considerable number of the rich bankers and industrialists of Vienna and the Alpine provinces were Jews — possibly the majority. Jews were also prominent in the liberal professions. In the minds of the Austrian people, the terms "Jew" and "capitalist" tended to merge (Borkenau 1938: 92–117; Craver 1986: 22–3).

Whereas the populism of the Christian Socials was anti-capitalist and anti-Semitic, the social democratic challenge to the liberal capitalist order was squarely based on the class interests of the workers, who had largely been excluded from its economic benefits and had no political voice in Parliament. The Austrian Social Democratic Party was founded by Victor Adler in 1889 at the Hainfeld Congress, which united moderate and radical groupings into one party. Its political base was principally among the urban working class. Its ideological foundation was based on Marx and Lassalle. The movement believed in progress, industrialization and the historical inevitability of socialism.

In 1907 the working class won universal, equal and direct suffrage in the Imperial Austrian Parliament following a massive demonstration organized by the Social Democratic Party in Vienna. Mises describes the event in his memoirs: "Vienna was completely paralyzed, and 250,000 workers marched on the Ringstrasse past Parliament in military fashion in rows of eight, under the leadership of Party officials." Mises complained that the "Social Democrats had extorted this right by force," they "attempted to intimidate and bring Parliament to heel through terror," because, as he explained, "the Austrian constitution had expressly forbidden public outdoor meetings in front of Parliament" (1978: 89). It is clear that Mises found this manifestation of the will of the masses to achieve the right to vote quite terrifying. In the first election with universal suffrage, the Social Democrats won 83 of 516 seats in the Imperial Austrian Parliament. To add one more dimension to the complexities of the politics of Imperial Austria, we must explain that the Hapsburg administration perceived the cosmopolitan Socialists as less dangerous to their continued rule than the strident nationalist assertions of the Czechs and Slovenes. It was possible to meet the socialist demands for the vote and for social-reform measures, whereas the nationalist aspirations of the non-German regions could not be accommodated within the structure of the Hapsburg regime.

In commenting on the demise of nineteenth-century Austrian "liberal culture" in the years of Vienna's *fin de siecle*, Schorske acknowledges the continuity of that tradition in the philosophy of the social democrats: "Of all the filial revolts aspiring to replace the [liberal] fathers, none bore the paternal features more pronouncedly than the Social Democrats. Their rhetoric was rationalist, their secularism militant, their faith in education virtually unlimited" (1981: 119). The politics of post-First World War Austria were taking shape in the contest between the Catholic Conservatives and Socialists: Black versus Red.

THE BIRTH OF THE FIRST AUSTRIAN REPUBLIC

To fully comprehend the virulent individualism and antisocialism of Mises and Hayek, we have to consider the cataclysmic circumstances surrounding the birth of the First Austrian Republic (1918) from the ruins of Imperial Austria-Hungary. The knowledge of the impending end of an era of security, stability and the enjoyment of high culture had permeated the atmosphere of Vienna in the decade preceding the outbreak of the Great War: a sense of impending end of the world (*Weltuntergang*), of "things falling apart." Ernst Fischer described it as follows:

> As a rule, things tended to come to Austria later than elsewhere; not so the premonition of impending catastrophe, the heightening of sensibility, the loss of reality. Something was coming to an end — not only the monarchy, not only the century, but a whole world "fawned upon by decay," as Georg Trakl has it in one of his poems. Those who were most sensitive to all this because so ambiguously poised between civilization and anti-Semitism, between privilege and ignominious rejection were the intellectual Jews, along with the old patrician families, a stratum of cultivated bureaucrats and the elite of the Social Democratic Workers Party. They were Vienna at its most interested and interesting. (1959: 76)

Post-war Vienna, its numbers swollen by pension-hungry officials from all over the former Austro-Hungarian Empire, was joined with three neighbour- ing and four Alpine provinces to create the "new" Austria, a rump of six- million German-speaking leftovers after the secession of Czechoslovakia and Yugoslavia and large territories ceded to Poland and Romania. The oversized former metropolis of a multinational empire of fifty million was regarded with horror by the Alpine provinces as "Red" and "Jew-ridden." The new republic was generally believed to be non-viable (*nicht lebensfahig*). Socialists had traditionally looked to union with Germany, an option vetoed by the Allied powers; the more conservative-minded dreamed of a Danubian federation of the former Imperial territories. Meanwhile the country became increas- ingly dependent on external assistance from the victorious Entente powers.

The long-awaited collapse of the Hapsburg order of things preceded the establishment of the First Republic in November 1918. In October 1916, Fritz Adler, son of Victor Adler and passionate opponent of the war, became an instant hero when he assassinated the Prime Minister of Austria. He was lionized by the population of Vienna, profoundly disillusioned with the war and angry at those who profited by it while death stalked the battlefronts. The 1917 Russian October Revolution put socialism on the agenda in Central Europe — and aroused the deepest fears of the ruling classes. The Austrian Social Democratic Party had by then abandoned its ambiguous position concerning the war and in January 1918 organized a number of general strikes. The Imperial authorities were no longer able to supply the soldiers at the front and industrial workers in the cities with food and clothing. The Socialists had organized Austria's soldiers and industrial workers into soldiers' and workers' councils, which soon became the only functioning administration in the land able to deal with increasingly severe shortages of food and heating fuel. Revolution was on the agenda throughout 1918 (Reventlow 1969; Hautmann 1971). Victor Adler died on the eve of the proclamation of the First Austrian Republic in November 1918, and Karl Renner was named the first Chancellor of the provisional government. The sister republic of Hungary was established in October 1918, with Count Karolyi as its first president. The Hapsburg-era was finished. In March 1919, Bela Kun displaced the Karolyi regime. The short-lived Hungarian Soviet Republic was defeated in August 1919 by a combination of forces, including military intervention by neighbouring states. In Austria the leadership of the powerful 350,000-member Social Democratic Party successfully prevented ultra-Left forces from pushing the situation toward the establishment of a Hungarian-type revolutionary regime.

The Socialists emerged from the elections of 1919 as the strongest single party, with 48 percent of the votes, and entered in a coalition with the Christian Social conservatives, who controlled the four Alpine provinces. Otto Bauer became foreign minister and first head of the Socialization Commission. Joseph Schumpeter briefly served as Minister of Finance, from March to October 1919.

In the spring of 1919, Bauer introduced his socialization program calling for the gradual public administration of large coal, iron and steel plants and the eventual control of all sectors of the economy (Rabinbach 1983: 24). This was not a program of expropriation, but rather one of restricted gradual socialization. It had, at its inception, the full support of Schumpeter, who warned of the need to exclude from this program those industries that depended heavily on the availability of foreign exchange.

As part of the reconstruction program, Schumpeter proposed a capital levy, in his words, an "enormous incursion into the private rights of the propertied classes…. We have to do it." This capital levy would be directed exclusively towards the repayment of the war debt. Additionally, he proposed the creation of an independent central bank, stabilization of the currency, indirect taxation to equalize the burden and an industrial strategy to attract domestic and foreign capital (Marz: 1984: 323).

Schumpeter quarrelled with Bauer, who disagreed with the need for foreign loans, while his intransigence on the capital levy alienated the conservative Christian Socials, who withdrew their support for the program. Schumpeter resigned, and in 1924 he left Austria for Bonn, and thence for Harvard in 1932. According to Marz, "for one side he was too radical and for the other too pragmatic, too self-willed" (1986: 330). The socialization issue gave rise to a rich literature in which a number of Austria's leading economists participated, including Schumpeter, Lederer and Neurath — and also Karl Polanyi. Bauer (1919) advocated a form of guild socialism, while Mises (1920, 1922) contributed a blistering attack on the feasibility of any form of socialist economy.

While the debate concerning the feasibility of a socialist economy waxed hot, the population of Vienna was literally freezing and hungry. The new Austria, torn from its traditional sources of supplies of food and raw materials, was in chaos. The Czechs refused to ship coal. The hyperinflation was not terminated until mid-1922. Unemployment stood at 300,000 in the early 1920s. Austria was surviving by virtue of allied food aid and charitable activities of foreign nongovernmental organizations. National output did not recover pre-1914 levels until 1928–29. The coalition broke down, and the socialization programs were effectively suspended after Ignaz Seipel became Chancellor in May 1922. He stabilized the currency, one new schilling equalled 10,000 kronen, with the assistance of a League of Nations program not dissimilar to the conditionalities of IMF adjustment programs. Thousands of public servants were fired, remaining subsidies were removed, new taxes imposed, and the proposal for capital taxation suspended. A League of Nations supervisor was installed to oversee the implementation of the stabilization program, which "corresponded to the train of thought dominant in contemporary academic economics. An economy weakened by the disease of inflation, this theory pronounced, can be restored to health only by severe fiscal and monetary discipline" (Marz 1986: 499).

This was the context in which Mises expounded his views, which were, as Fritz Machlup recalls, unpopular with the majority of people considered as the intelligentsia:

> Mises fought interventionism while almost everybody was in favour of some government action against the "evil" consequences of laissez-faire. Mises fought inflationism while a large majority of people was convinced that only a courageous expansion of money, credit and governmental budgets could secure prosperity, full employment and economic growth. Mises fought socialism in all its forms, while most intellectuals had written off capitalism as a decaying system to be replaced either peacefully or by revolution, by socialism or communism. Mises fought coercive egalitarianism while every "high-minded" citizen thought that social justice required redistribution of wealth and/or income. Mises fought government-supported trade unionism, while progressive professors of political science represented increasing power of labor unions as an essential ingredient of democracy. Hayek became the most forceful exponent and defender of the economic and political views of Mises. (Machlup 1981: 10–11)[5]

The Austrian School of Economics

To understand Hayek's place as a fourth generation star of the Austrian School of Economics, it is important to appreciate that neither its founder, Carl Menger, nor Menger's two (rival) successors — Eugen von Böhm-Bawerk (1851–1914) and Friedrich von Wieser (1851–1926) — were radical antisocialists. Böhm-Bawerk was a true liberal and his Privatseminar in the decade before 1914 was enriched by important controversy with Marxist thought regarding the nature of capital. Participants included Joseph Schumpeter and Ludwig von Mises, as well as socialist figures such as Otto Bauer, Karl Renner, Rudolf Hilferding and Otto Neurath (Marz 1986). Austro-Marxist approaches to macro-economic policies were conditioned by the intellectual formation of those of its leading lights who were trained in economics in the best years of the Austrian School before 1914.

Bohm-Bowerk's contemporary, Friedrich von Wieser, was the holder of the chair in economics at the University of Vienna during nearly two decisive decades. He was no laissez-faire liberal. His socioeconomic credo was summarized as follows:

> Building on a strong Catholic and conservative foundation he was an interventionist liberal … with quite an admixture of racist sentiment who still found it possible to admire Marx. Above all, he was an admirer of the state as guided by the supreme wisdom of his own bureaucratic class. (Streissler 1986)

The anti-interventionist and antisocialist current in the Austrian School, which so appealed to Lionel Robbins in the 1920s, was the singular contribution of Ludwig von Mises (1881–1973) and was ultimately carried into the Anglo-American world by his protégé, Hayek. Here it must be noted that Mises's extreme anti-interventionism was not shared by all the members of his seminar. In an excellent summary of the principal tenets of the Austrian School, Fritz Machlup (1981), a contemporary of Hayek and one-time member of Mises' Privatseminar, pointed out that "consumer sovereignty" and "political individualism" were additions by the Mises branch of Austrian economics.

Mises' Privatseminar

Although Vienna remained one of the best three places to study economics during the 1920s and early 1930s (the others being Stockholm and Cambridge, England), the centre of research activity shifted from the University of Vienna to the Privatseminar and research institute. Mises, who commanded respect as the most able of the third generation of the great Austrian School, did not have a chair at the university; nor did Schumpeter. He earned his living by working in an administrative capacity as Secretary of the Vienna Chamber of Commerce. His Privatseminar, which met twice a month in his office, from its foundation in 1922 to 1934, when he departed for Geneva, was nevertheless considered by Oskar Morgenstern as "far more important in the 1930s than anything that went on in the University" (Craver 1986: 14). According to Hayek, this was already so in the 1920s. Clearly, Mises was the central figure in the Viennese economics community. Many of the regular participants of the seminar subsequently achieved international recognition, including Fritz Machlup, Gottfried von Haberler, Oskar Morgenstern, Gerhard Tintner, and Paul Rosenstein-Rodan. The seminar was not confined to economists and included also sociologists, historians, mathematicians, philosophers, and a number of men from the banking and business community. An invaluable source of recollections of the Mises seminar has been provided by one of its regular participants, Martha Steffie Braun (Browne 1981: 1986).

Many of the participants also belonged to another "circle," founded by Hayek and J. Herbert Furth in 1921, which they called the Geistkreis, where a wider and more philosophical range of topics was discussed: music, literature, history, political philosophy, relativity theory and more. Hayek's circle excluded women, whose participation was confined to serving tea and cookies (Browne 1981: 1). Throughout the 1920s there was a close relation between the Mises group in Vienna and the U.S.-based Rockefeller Foundation, which enabled Austrian economists of the Mises-Hayek circle to visit the United States and brought foreign economists to Vienna. Among the economists who visited Vienna were Howard Ellis, Albert G. Hart, Ragnar Nurkse, Alfred Stonier, Hugh Gaitskell and John van Sickle, an American whose connections with the Rockefeller Foundation were particularly useful to regular members of the group (Craver 1986: 15).

Despite his contempt for empirical research, Mises let himself be persuaded by Hayek to set up an institute for business-cycle research on the model of the U.S. institutes, which Hayek had visited in 1924. It was located on the premises of the Chamber of Commerce and initially financed by contributions from the business community.

In January 1927, Hayek was installed as director of the newly formed Institut fur Konjuktursforschung. It was a shoestring affair with a staff of only two clerks, until the Rockefeller Foundation provided major funding. Hayek brought in Oskar Morgenstern (who succeeded him as director after his departure for London) and enabled another economist friend, Gottfried Haberler, to obtain temporary employment (Craver 1986: 19). After the departure of Hayek in 1931 and Mises in 1934, Morgenstern emerged as the central figure in the Vienna economics community. The work of the institute became more scientific, mathematical and econometric with the participation of trained mathematicians such as Abraham Wald and Gerhart Tintner. Subsequently, Morgenstern collaborated with the brilliant Hungarian mathematician, John von Neumann, in the foundation of game theory.

HAYEK AT THE LONDON SCHOOL OF ECONOMICS

As noted earlier, Hayek was invited to the LSE by Lionel Robbins, a friend and admirer of Ludwig von Mises and one of the few English economists acquainted with the German language and the Vienna School of Economics of the 1920s. John Hicks recalled that Hayek created quite a stir among the group of young economists whom Robbins had gathered around him when he became professor and head of department in 1929. This group, Hicks wrote,

> [shared] a common viewpoint, or even, one might say, a common faith. Some of us, especially Hayek, have in later years maintained that faith; others such as Kaldor, Abba Lerner, George Shackle and myself have departed from it, to a greater or lesser extent…. The faith in question was a belief in the free market or "price-mechanism" — that a competitive system free of all interferences by government … would easily find an equilibrium. (Hicks 1981: 2)

The appointment of Hayek was part of a deliberate effort by Robbins to shore up the ideological stronghold of economic liberalism at the LSE after a brief period during which the economics department had been headed by Hugh Dalton (1926–27), who later served as a Labour Party Chancellor of the Exchequer, and Allyn Young. Appointments of conservative economists included Frederic Benham and Arnold Plant.

The influence of the Austrian School on the teaching of economics in the English-speaking world was transmitted not through Hayek, but rather through Robbins, whose 1932 *An Essay on the Nature and Significance of Economic Science* has served as the classic definition of its subject matter as "the theory of allocation of scarce means among alternative uses" (Kirzner 1986: 140–47). This formal definition thereafter displaced Marshall's more substantive but less elegant one. As Joan Robinson observed in her Richard T. Ely lecture, "the date of publication was unlucky. By the time the book came out there were three million workers unemployed in Britain and the statistical measure of GNP in the USA had recently fallen to half its former level." The book appeared, she commented with characteristic acidity, "when means for any ends at all had rarely been less scarce" (1972: 1).

In 1931, the Labour Party of Ramsay Macdonald had joined the Conservatives in a National Government engaged in slashing public expenditures and cutting the wages of Britain's working class in defence of the pound sterling and the interests of the City. The prevailing view of the community of academic economists was that the massive unemployment was due to excessively high real wages.

At this time, the group of young Cambridge economists associated with J.M. Keynes were developing highly unorthodox theories which challenged these wisdoms, and they were, no doubt, regarded by the rentier interest of the

City as threatening to financial stability and the edifice of the Empire. Hayek was brought to London as a counter-attraction to Keynes (Robinson 1972: 2). His theories were by no means easy to understand but were undoubtedly comforting insofar as his antisocialism was matched only by his aversion to monetary expansion as an instrument of policy. The traumatic experience of the post-war inflations certainly contributed to Hayek's reluctance to rely on monetary expansion.[6] We recall that the Board of Governors of the LSE had a close relationship with the City.

Hayek's trade-cycle theory,[7] which he taught in undergraduate classes throughout his years at the LSE, rejected underconsumption or deficiency of demand as an explanatory mechanism. Injections of credit during recessions would, according to his theory, only make matters worse by creating an artificial boom, followed by a worse slump. The theory was one of intertemporal discoordination insofar as changes in the availability of credit and interest rates affect the relative prices of future goods against present ones and thus affect the resource allocation between more and less roundabout production: Hayek explained that injections of credit were likely to exacerbate the discoordination and delay the adjustment between the production of producer goods and consumer goods (Garrison and Kirzner 1987).

Joan Robinson has given us a graphic account of Hayek's 1931 visit to Cambridge, where he covered a blackboard with his famous triangles. It appeared that he was arguing that the slump was caused by excessive consumption, which reduces the stock of capital goods. What looks like an oversupply of capital and a lack of demand for consumer goods is in reality too high a demand for consumer goods and an insufficient supply of capital (Rosner 1988). R.F. Kahn, who was at that time working on his explanation of how the multiplier equates savings with investment, asked Hayek the following question: "Is it your view that if I went out tomorrow and bought a new overcoat that would increase unemployment?" Hayek responded: "Yes, but (pointing to his triangles on the board) it would take a very long mathematical argument to explain why."

THE ROAD TO CHICAGO

Of all of Mises' younger friends and colleagues none was more faithful than Hayek in his dedication to combating socialism. The Vienna debate "Economic Calculation in a Socialist Commonwealth" (1920) took place in a world in which there had never yet existed, and there did not at that time exist, a functioning socialist economy. The situation was somewhat different when the debate concerning a centrally planned economy was taken up again in Britain in the 1930s, after the publication of Oskar Lange's and Frederick Taylor's famous articles that showed that shadow prices could be used by planning authorities, an approach already pioneered by Enrico Barone as early as

1909, which had not previously come to the attention of Mises. As Michael Polanyi — physicist, philosopher, brother of Karl and founding member of the Mont Pelerin Society — who shared Hayek's fears of central planning, pointed out: "If planning is impossible to the point of absurdity, what are the so-called planned economies doing? And how can central planning, if it is utterly incapable of achievement, be a danger to individual liberty as it is widely disowned to be?" (from "The Logic of Liberty," 1951, quoted in Cristi 1986).

At the peak of the great debates on post-Second World War reconstruction in Britain that laid the foundations of the welfare state, Hayek published a polemical tract against all varieties of economic and social planning. *The Road to Serfdom* (1944) attracted little attention in England but considerably more in the United States, where it was serialized in the *Reader's Digest* and interpreted as an attack on the New Deal.

Initially wishing to be based in Europe post-war, Hayek chose to emigrate to the United States. But neither the Law School, the Business School, nor the Economics Department at the University of Chicago were prepared to make Hayek an offer because *The Road to Serfdom* was not considered a scholarly work meriting an academic appointment. Eventually the president of the university arranged a Volker-funded position on the Committee of Social Thought in 1950, and Hayek thus became the doyen of what would become known as the Chicago School.

In tracing out Hayek's contributions to the formation of neoliberal thought and the transition towards a neoliberal world order, *The Road from Mont Pelerin* (Mirowski and Plehwe 2009)[8] details the important part played by a mid-Western businessman, Harold Luhnow, a conservative opponent of the New Deal who converted the philanthropic Volker Fund into a proto-think-tank dedicated to combating the perceived threat of social legislation to liberty. In 1945, Luhnow arranged to meet with Hayek, who was then on a book tour promoting *The Road to Serfdom*. Luhnow proposed to provide funding for a version of the book that would speak more directly and accessibly to an American audience. Hayek consulted Henry Simons of the University of Chicago Law School, and, on the basis of their long-time intellectual friendship, a more ambitious project emerged. The close relationship between Hayek, Simons and University of Chicago president, Robert Hutchins, facilitated the establishment in 1946 of the Free Market Study (FMS), underwritten by Luhnow and headed by Aaron Director, a close associate of Hayek and brother-in-law of Milton Friedman. Members of the FMS included Theodore Schultz, Milton Friedman and Frank Knight from the Economics Department, Edward Levi and Wilbur Katz from the Law School, and representatives from the Volker Fund. The FMS had a twofold mission: to produce an American version of *The Road to Serfdom* and to reformulate traditional liberal doctrine and legislation to the changing industrial landscape. The FMS was followed by the (also Volker-funded) Antitrust Project (1953–1957), which concluded that, in contrast to classical liberal doctrine on monopoly, competition is a sufficient condition to contain corporate market power. There was, according to this revisionist doctrine, no danger to individual liberty from monopolies or oligopolies. Only the trade unions constituted a violation of liberty because they denied the worker the right to negotiate individually with the employer.

The Volker Fund eventually got their American "corporate neoliberal" version of *The Road to Serfdom* in the form of Milton Friedman's *Capitalism and Freedom*, which has never been out of print since its first publication in 1962. What is interesting here are the differences between the neoliberalism of this flagship publication of the Chicago School and traditional liberalism. Contrary to the minimalist governments of classical liberalism, neoliberalism requires a strong state to enforce private property and promote free enterprise, extending the sphere of operations of the private sector to public enterprise and public services. The application of economic calculus to sociology, as in human capital theories, is associated with Gary Becker of the University of Chicago, a Nobel laureate in economics. Neoliberalism also projects the theories and assumptions of economics to the political sphere. James Buchanan, Nobel laureate in economics and co-author of public choice theory, studied under Frank Knight at the University of Chicago. The concept of the marketplace of ideas or the vote as an extension of consumer choice defines the public good out of existence. The democratic process is devalued once politicians and public officials are assumed to be acting in their self-interest. If politics succumbs to economics and economics is ruled by money, we arrive at plutocracy. In the extreme case, the suppression of civic liberties to enforce the rule of law by an authoritarian state is best described as fascism, as in the case of the well-documented support of Pinochet by Hayek and Friedman.

THE MONT PELERIN SOCIETY

If the launch of the Chicago School was one leg of the neoliberal enterprise, the establishment of the Mont Pelerin Society (MPS) was the other on the long road to the implementation of neoliberal policies in the last quarter of the twentieth century. Or, if you prefer an anatomical analogy, the authors of *The Road from Mont Pelerin* suggest that the Chicago School and the Mont Pelerin Society were joined at the hip.

At a time when economic planning and socialism were in the ascendancy and laissez-faire liberalism was in deep intellectual retreat, Hayek invited a select number of like-minded persons from academia and business to a private meeting in a mountain village in Mont Pelerin, Switzerland. An inner circle consisting of Hayek, Mises, Michael Polanyi, Raymond Aron, Louis Baudin, Wilhelm Röpke and Alexander Rüstow had attended a previous meeting in France in 1938 at the Colloque Walter Lippman. Almost half of the forty or so participants at Mont Pelerin came from the United States, including Hayek's fellow Austrians Mises, Machlup and Haberler, and representatives of the Volker Fund, which, together with the Foundation for Economic Education, financed the U.S.-based contingent. The predecessor of Credit Suisse covered all local costs.

The objective of the MPS was to arrive at a neoliberal position regarding a variety of important issues, such as antitrust policies, collective bargaining and foreign aid to underdeveloped countries. The project was innovative and ambitious, transdisciplinary and cosmopolitan. It sought to construct what has been variously described as a neoliberal thought collective, an invisible international college and a comprehensive transnational discourse community. There was no manifesto, and the time horizon was long — possibly several decades, even several generations.

The roots of neoliberalism were in Europe, where the economic crises of the twenties and thirties had profoundly discredited classical laissez-faire liberalism, but it was in the United States that it found more fertile soil. The intellectual centres of neoliberal thought in Europe were at the LSE in England, Freiberg University in Germany, and the Institut Universitaire des Hautes Études Internationales in Geneva. The Institut, founded and directed by William Rappard, employed Mises and Röpke and hosted most of the early MPS meetings. European neoliberals understood that a return to free market principles would have to be socially grounded in a corporate state with collective bargaining. American MPS members were largely hostile to trade unions. Originally there was diversity of opinion within the MPS, but as the project evolved, the libertarian variant of Hayek and Mises largely prevailed. The leading architect of the construction of the neoliberal ideology was Hayek, and from the beginning, corporate funders, principally American, British and Swiss, were essential to gaining influence in universities and the political arena.

Hayek understood that the production by academics of articles and textbooks could not reach the public without the intermediation of "secondhand dealers in ideas" (Hayek 1949). This somewhat contemptuous reference by Hayek was to the intellectuals and journalists associated with specially created institutions for the diffusion and popularization of neoliberal thought. The Foundation for Economic Education, which employed Mises and the journalist Henry Hazlitt, who wrote for *Newsweek*, was established in 1946. This novel technique of creating public opinion became the template for all subsequent neoliberal think-tanks. It was followed by a British version, the Institute of Economic Affairs, founded by Antony Fisher in 1955. The Centro de Estudios Economico-Sociales, established in Guatemala City in 1959 by Manuel Ayau, was the first such institute in Latin America.[9] In the 1970s the Heritage Foundation was created by future MPS president Ed Feulner.

CONCLUSION

The measure of the success of Mont Pelerin, and the arrival of neoliberalism as a legitimate economic and political ideology, was the award of the Nobel Prize to Hayek in 1974 in recognition of his contribution to economics. The award, however, was shared with an eminent intellectual adversary, Gunnar Myrdal, the architect of Sweden's social welfare system.

By the 1980s, the membership of the MPS had grown to over a thousand, but the real importance of the society was the nurturing of neoliberal ideas in the 1950s and 1960s, at a time when New Deal policies and issues of civil rights dominated American politics. It is a mistake to see neoliberalism exclusively in terms of the neoclassical economics associated with the Chicago School or the policies that served Reagan, Thatcher and the Washington Consensus. Ultimately, it is the ideological appeal of individual liberty and distrust of government which has had the most profound consequences in undermining social institutions of solidarity and social cohesion, which are the prerequisites of effective democratic government.

NOTES

This chapter is based in part on a paper prepared for a conference on Hayek at the Université de Montréal on January 29, 1988, and in part on materials included in "The Origins of Market Fetishism," which was published by *Monthly Review*, 41, in June 1989.

1. Ernst Fischer was a journalist, writer and leading figure in the Communist Party of Austria.

2. Hans Zeisel, with Paul Lazarsfeld, pioneered survey techniques in sociological research in Vienna and later in the United States. He was a close family friend and authored the entry of Karl Polanyi in the *Encyclopaedia of the Social Sciences*.

3. Schorske's study of the politics and culture of Vienna is a classic — a superb interpretive essay on the ambiance of pre-1914 Vienna.

4. In 1860, the number of Jews in Vienna numbered about 6,000. By 1918, numbers approached 200,000 — after Warsaw and Budapest, the largest urban concentration of Jews in Europe.

5. Frtiz Machlup studied economics at the University of Vienna under the informal tutelage of Mises, and left for the United States in 1933 where he held various academic positions at Buffalo, Johns Hopkins, and Princeton.

6. My grandmother told me that in the hyperinflation of 1922 people stopped counting the value of money; they weighed bundles of paper money on scales against kilograms of bread.

7. The theory is elaborated in *Prices and Production* (1931)

8. Our account of the role of Hayek in the Chicago School and the Mont Pelerin Society has been informed by the excellent and informative contributors to *The Road from Mont Pelerin* (Mirowski and Plehwe 2009). The publication is meticulous in its use of documentary evidence and draws selectively from a large body of studies, particularly Bernhard Walpen's *Die offenen Feinde und ihre Gesellschaft: Eine*

hegemonietheoretische Studie zur Mont Pelerin Society (2004) and Ronald M. Hartwell's *A History of the Mont Pelerin Society* (1995).

9. From his position in Geneva and later the Foundation for Economic Education in New York, Mises maintained contact with like-minded economists in Latin America. In 1941, he received an invitation by Luis Montes de Oca, the outgoing head of the Mexican Central Bank, to shore up opposition to the radical reforms of the Cardenas administration. He remained for another year as a visiting professor at the National University (UNAM), where he advocated for the privatization of the national railway system. The issue of development and underdevelopment was first placed on the neoliberal agenda by Mises in 1951, and four of the eight meetings of the MPS in the 1950s were devoted to this discussion.

3. THE ROOTS OF POLANYI'S SOCIALIST VISION

Karl Polanyi was, as noted earlier, all his life, a socialist. Many have given the best years of their lives to political and social movements motivated by a socialist vision of a free, cooperative, democratic and just society based on the social ownership and control of the economic resources of the nation. My father shared such a vision. I know that I am not alone in wondering what he would have to say about the developments of the last few years — about the prospects for humanity and for socialism. Those of us who were privileged to have known him expect that he would have said something unexpected, something that would cut across the conventional terms of the discourse. In this brief intervention, I can do no more than bear testimony to what I know, to share with you some memories and bring to your attention themes and threads which linked his quasi-religious commitment to freedom of thought and individual responsibility for our actions with a decentralized, "bottom-up" vision of a cooperative socialism.

Polanyi's socialism was rooted in early family influences, the "free-think-ing" anti-clericalism of the Hungarian student movement (Galilei Circle) and the intellectual milieu of Red Vienna of the 1920s. His socialism was neither that of traditional European social democracy, nor that of centralized com-munist planning. It was more akin to the third stream of the European socialist tradition — the populist, syndicalist, quasi-anarchist and corporativist one. Among his heroes were all the Russian revolutionaries of the late nineteenth and early twentieth centuries. Other important influences included Robert Owen and English guild socialism; the democratic functional socialism of Otto Bauer; Max Adler's insistence on the socialist mission of the working class to raise the cultural level of society above the commercial ethic of the bourgeoisie; and last but not least, a re-reading of *Capital*, which brought to the fore Marx's alienation critique of capitalism. In terms of economic analysis, he favoured the Vienna School over the more mechanistic labour theory of value because it introduced volition in the form of choices by consumers and producers. The choices in his functionalist model of a socialist economy were not however those of maximizing/minimizing atomistic individuals buffeted by "impersonal" market forces, but negotiated choices of associational collectivities operating within the complexity of a democratic civil society. Polanyi's socialism has been located on the margins of Austro-Marxism.[1]

As we move into the final years of the twentieth century, the wreckage of socialism is all around us. The communist regimes of East Europe have imploded and collapsed. They have compromised socialism in all its forms, Marxist and non-Marxist, reformed communism and social democracy. The deluge of disenchantment is undeniable. But yesterday's triumphal victory of free enterprise capitalism — the "end of history" — already sounds hollow, a superficial, shortsighted and ignorant response to revolutionary changes in economic and political relations on a world scale. The excesses of the Reagan-Thatcher era of neoliberal deregulation, ideologically driven privatization and abandonment of governmental responsibility for full employment and social justice are tearing apart the social fabric of Western capitalist societies. In the countries of the former Soviet Union and East Europe whole populations are being subjected to risky economic experiments which have projected millions of people into abject poverty and economic insecurity. The poisoned seeds of a resurgent Great-Russian nationalism are being sown by American economic advisors, including academics from prestigious U.S. universities. Meanwhile, scores of developing countries are now in trusteeship to international financial institutions and appear to have no alternative to compliance with the extreme liberalization conditionalities of the IMF and the World Bank. These agencies have used powerful financial leverage to strip indebted countries of the policy instruments essential for the protection of the economic security of the majority of their populations. They have bulldozed "level playing fields" to expose domestic markets to competition from unrestricted imports and foreign investment. Far-reaching changes in the regime governing international trade and investment threaten to strip these countries of the remaining vestiges of national sovereignty. Since the mid-1980s, global net international transfers of official financial resources have reversed direction, and now move from South to North.

The shadow of the future is looming over us with frightening momentum. The certainties of yesterday are dissolving with every passing day. Signposts are collapsing. Established nation-states are fragmenting. We are being tossed about in a turmoil of conflicting currents, manifested both in the realities of the world we live in and the conceptualizations which have formed the basis of our understanding of that reality. Progress, development, socialism, political Right and Left are among the terms whose meaning is not as clear as it once seemed to be. The passing of an era is more clearly evident than the shape of the present, not to speak of the future. This is manifested in the proliferation of "posts" as in "post-industrial," "post-modern," "post-communist" and the deconstruction of concepts that have served the social sciences since they emerged from the Enlightenment.

Even our small, privileged and peaceful corner of the world in Canada is not unaffected by the forces of change. Who would have believed even a few years ago that Canada as we know it might not exist for much longer? But the revolutionary nature of the period we are living through goes far beyond the changes in global politics, which are now making it impossible for cartographers to prepare atlases that will not be out of date before they are printed.

My father died in 1964, as the thick ice of the Cold War was beginning to crack, giving way to what appeared to be the possibility of reform and renewal of socialism in East Europe, and of peaceful coexistence. He greeted the Hungarian revolution of 1956 as a movement of socialist reform and renewal, led by a cultural avant-garde of intellectuals and poets. In 1961, he initiated the journal *Co-Existence* as a vehicle for dialogue across the Cold War divide. Karl lay dying in the Toronto Western Hospital when the page proofs of the first issue of *Co-Existence* arrived from Scotland. The second issue carried an obituary, which I wrote at the insistence of my mother. I tried to put on record my father's social and personal philosophy, as far as possible in his own words, drawn from fragments of published and unpublished writings and letters. I cannot do better than reproduce once again the following passages from "Karl Polanyi and *Co-Existence*" (Levitt 1964):

> His life spans the period of modern socialism and through his intellectual heritage reaches beyond the 77 years that ended on April 24 1964. All his life a socialist, he was never associated with any political party. Nor did he participate in any political movement.

This is not quite true because as a young man in Budapest he was associated with Oskar Jaszi in the foundation of the bourgeois Radical Party. It is, however, true of the rest of his life from emigration to Vienna in 1919 to his death in Toronto.

> Never doctrinaire, he many times cut across the main trends of debate within the socialist movements of Europe. Although not a Marxist, he was much less a social democrat. Although a humanist, he was eminently a realist. Although aware of the reality of society, and the constraints that this reality places upon the actions, values and ideas of all of us who inescapably live in society, his life was guided by an inner necessity to exercise freedom of action and thought and never to give in to determinism and fatalism. Hence the quotation from Hegel he many times cited.

The following lines from Hegel may not be as Hegel wrote them. They are however exactly as my father scribbled them on index cards as his own obituary:

Brich mit dem Frieden in Dir
Brich mit dem Werte der Welt,
Besseres nickt, als die Zeit
Aber auf's Beste sie sein.

(In rough translation: Break with the peace within you / Break with the values of the world (around you) / You cannot be better than the times (you live in) / But (strive) to be of the best.)

Karl Polanyi was born in 1886, three years after the death of Karl Marx and the birth of John Maynard Keynes. During his early years spent in *fin de siecle* Vienna and Budapest, mass-based social democratic parties gave voice to the aspirations of the rapidly growing new industrial working classes of Germany, Austria-Hungary and East Europe. Socialism spelled a new dawn, a secular religion promising the extension of democracy to the economic and social spheres. According to orthodox Marxism, as embodied in the 1891 Ehrfurt program of the German Social Democratic Party, the transition from capitalism to socialism was historically inevitable — guaranteed by the "scientific" laws of historical materialism. In Czarist Russia, which was far behind Central Europe in terms of economic development, where the industrial working class was small and weak and the great majority of the population was still rural — including millions of landless or hopelessly indebted peasants — popular struggles against the repressive Czarist regime were more direct and elemental.

The spirit of the Russian revolutionaries of the late nineteenth and early twentieth centuries came into the lives of the Polanyi children and their cousin Ervin Szabo through the close family friendship of the Polanyis with the Klatchkos. Karl's mother, Cecile Wohl, had been sent from Vilna to Vienna by her father when she was seventeen, accompanied by another young girl, Nyunia, daughter of the Mayor of Simferopol. Nyunia married Samuel Klatchko, a Narodnik revolutionary who at the age of fourteen had run away from his rabbinical home in Vilna and later founded a Utopian community in the United States (named after N.V. Tchaikovski). When this venture failed, he settled in Vienna, where he became the non-party envoy of all the illegal parties and movements then existing in Czarist Russia. Klatchko met many of the great early Russian revolutionaries — Plekhanov and Axelrod included — and Leon Trotsky was a daily visitor to his bookshop on the Karlplatz in Vienna until his death in 1911.

In Klatchko, the cousins Ervin Szabo and Karl Polanyi found a friend and mentor, their first great teacher. The Klatchkos and the Polanyis spent many summer vacations together on the Semmering in Austria. Shortly before his death, my father jotted down some reflections on the life of Klatchko and noted that "he was the kindliest man I ever met." The Klatchko home in

Vienna was an underground post serving assorted Russian revolutionaries, and the Polanyi apartment offered shelter to these nameless heroes of resistance to Czarist oppression. I recall my father's accounts of men arriving cold and hungry, feet wrapped in newspapers, to stay for a while before moving on to their next revolutionary assignment. They made a deep impression on my father. Indeed, he held all revolutionaries in high respect — including, as he once said, the foremost of them all, Jesus of Nazareth. Culturally, he was a Russophile and an Anglophile — as was his father, whom he held in respect bordering on adoration. In a letter of 1963 addressed to me on the anniversary of the death of his father he wrote: "My father's pure unadulterated idealism of the Western brand (unspoiled by the Hungarian standards of the nineteenth century) infiltrated my upbringing and it was this *melange* of Russian and Anglo-Saxon atmosphere that reached the Galilei students by way of my person."

The reference is to his role as co-founder and first president of the Hungarian student movement in 1908. According to him, the inspiration was the Russian student movement, embracing thousands of secondary school (gymnasium) students as well as those attending universities. The Galilei Circle signalled a philosophic and scientific renaissance, a challenge to the backward character of the university — from which Karl was expelled in 1909, thus having to finish his studies in the provincial university of Cluj (in modern-day Romania) — and to the pervasive morass of clericalism, corruption, opportunism, privilege and bureaucracy. It was a call to progressive free thinkers to liberate the individual spirit by a cultural revolution based on the rejection of superstition and metaphysics, and the introduction of modern science, art and sociology. Although the Galilei student movement was not explicitly socialist, one of the old-timers recalled that "knowledge of socialism, Marxism, historical materialism, was always the object of our educational activities" (Levitt and Mendell 1987: 18).

The latter were impressive by any standard. According to Polanyi, the 2,000 members delivered more than 2,000 tutorial lectures in the first year alone. Over the years the Galileists, as they were called, taught tens of thousands of illiterate workers and peasants to read and write (Polanyi 1960). The Galilei movement was to be free in spirit, keep clear of party politics and dedicate itself to raising the level of social consciousness by learning and teaching, appealing to the many thousands of students living in poverty. Polanyi's social philosophy can best be described as idealist, populist and voluntarist. He admired the work of his anarchist cousin Ervin Szabo, the guild socialism of G.D.H. Cole and the Utopian Socialism of Robert Owen. He rejected the crude determinism of orthodox Marxism, which served as the official ideology of the Social Democratic Party. For him the impersonal forces of history were no substitute for conscious, principled and courageous action: "Courage and integrity," he wrote, "are not questions of political programme or policy. They are matters of temperament and moral character of the individual."

In the First World War Karl Polanyi served as a cavalry officer in the Austro-Hungarian army. He was at that time in his early thirties. In an article published many years later, he tells us that his vocation was revealed to him during the war, in the Russian winter, on the cold steppes of Galicia, when he was physically ill, deeply depressed and haunted by a semi-religious sense of responsibility for the fate of humanity. His was not the role of the revolutionary, or the statesman, but the often lonely role of the teacher and scholar. The task: to discover and reveal the origin of the cataclysm which caused millions to suffer and perish in prisons and in the infernos of wars (Polanyi 1918, 1954). Schumpeter observed that an individual's basic ideas are fully formed by the age of thirty. But another three decades were to pass before the appearance of his most important single work, whose English edition bore the significant title *The Origins of Our Time* — now better known by its American title, *The Great Transformation.*

Following the defeat of the Hungarian revolution of 1919, my father emigrated to Vienna where he met my mother, Ilona Duczynska. Ilona has been well described as a sovereign revolutionary — a romantic, heroic and beautiful young woman with a distinguished record of revolutionary activity, including imprisonment on charges of treason and sedition for distributing anti-war propaganda in the munitions factories and army barracks of Budapest. Ilona was the darling of the Hungarian communist emigration in Vienna; however, it was no communist, but Karl Polanyi, who captured her heart. As he wrote in a letter commemorating the anniversary of his father's death, "[he] adored my mother who belonged culturally to the Russian world, and I myself was in love with the thought of the Russian girl ideal. (Actually our Viennese Russian friends grew up as our own family to me.) And so Ilona, who was Polish and a revolutionary, 'filled the bill,' I suppose. Our luck!"

MARX, BAKUNIN AND THE MOSCOW TRIALS OF 1922

The reflective mode and chosen abstinence from involvement in political activity coexisted within my father's psyche with a passionate engagement on the side of revolutionaries — men and women who proved the courage of their convictions by direct action. In a long-forgotten article entitled "The Intellectual-Historical Background of the Moscow Trials," Polanyi (1922) penned a prophetic commentary on the tragedy of a political trial in which the Bolsheviks depicted social revolutionary groups as common counter-revolutionaries and agents of the bourgeoisie. The social revolutionaries had programmatic differences with the Bolsheviks concerning land reform (the agrarian question), the communes and the reactivation of the local Soviets, which had been all but disbanded.

The groups under attack in 1922 had fought side by side with the Bolshevik and the Menshevik factions of the Russian Social Democratic Party against Czarist reaction and had participated in the October Revolution. They were, my father explained, the inheritors of the traditions of the Social Revolutionary Party, founded late in the nineteenth century by Shytlovsky and Rappaport. Although weaker in numbers than the social democrats, they were "characterized by a many sided flexibility in forms of direct action — the ignition spark of revolutionary energy, rather than its storage battery. They had pioneered an ideological opposition to social democracy on Russian revolutionary soil."

The differences pertained less to program than to tactics, methods and the ethics of revolutionary praxis. In this article, Polanyi raised fundamental questions of socialist revolutionary ethics — "basic differences which, from the beginning of the working-class movement, have existed between two conceptions of revolutionary behaviour, two irreconcilable and contradictory orientations which not infrequently compete for the soul of one and the same individual."

The Social Democratic Party was, without question, the vehicle of the Marxist working-class movement which, in accordance with the objective conditions obtaining in Russia, was based on economic issues, concentrated on organizational strengths and led mass political struggles. The political orientation of the social revolutionaries, by contrast, was based on subjective factors of personal initiative and revolutionary *elan*, on Bakuninist direct action by the peasantry and by the radical intelligentsia. Their methods were conspiratorial — the preparation and execution of direct action and of guerrilla warfare. But this distinction manifested itself more in matters of revolutionary conduct, tactics and methods, and in the ethical ambiance of the movement, rather than in programmatic differences of the two parties. The Social Revolutionary Party was not an anarchist party, but a socialist one. Its ideology was definitely not that of Bakunin, but followed the teachings of Marx.

"The Moscow Trials [of 1922] are but the most recent chapter of the fratricidal struggle whose hidden seeds were sown in the early days of the modern working-class movement." Polanyi's argument reaches back to the historic injustice done by Marx and the leaders of the First International to Bakunin, the Russian nihilist and pupil of Proudhon.

> From the beginning of the 1860s onward, every significant grouping of Russian revolutionaries was under the influence of Bakunin. His boundless and passionate hatred of authoritarianism, his love of freedom, the shining integrity of his personality, created in Russia an eternal revolutionary tradition of unforgettable fame: the commitment of a Vera Zasulich, of a Sofya Perovskaya.

Polanyi continues:

> Bakunin was exactly Marx's age. Twice condemned to death by reaction, several times incarcerated and physically chained to the prison walls, Bakunin served thirteen years of hard labour in the mines of Siberia. Rebellion, assassination and revolution followed his footsteps throughout Europe. He founded the first clandestine international revolutionary organization in Italy. He called it the League of Social Revolutionaries.

Some years later Marx founded the First International. In 1868 Bakunin and his organization joined the International, whose foundations he had, in fact, built. But between the flaming love of freedom and the deterministic revolutionary spirit of Marx, there stretched an unbridgeable rift. Bakunin disapproved of Marx's position with respect to the peasantry and also to such remnants of Hegel's philosophy as remained part of Marx's thinking at the time, and influenced Marx in an *etatist* (statist) direction. Bakunin detested nothing more than authoritarianism and bureaucracy, centralization and nationalization: "I want society and collective or social property to be organized from the bottom up by way of free association, and not from the top down by means of any authority whatsoever" (Bakunin, quoted in Polanyi 1922: 396).

Polanyi describes how Bakunin was slandered by the leaders of the International, accused of being a Czarist agent and a common thief who had appropriated party funds. None of these charges was sustainable. Nevertheless, Bakunin was expelled from the International in 1872, which by that point, for all intents and purposes, had ceased to exist, and soon thereafter was formally disbanded: "The Second International came to grief forty years later on account of the same problem of revolutionary ethics." Polanyi concluded:

> Although Marx was correct in almost all of his contentions in the conflict [with Proudhon and Bakunin], virtually no unprejudiced Marxist will today deny that the methods which were used in that struggle against Bakunin resulted in a moral degeneration of the entire working-class movement with fateful subsequent consequences. In our view Marx had a deeper and more fruitful understanding of the revolutionary mission of the proletariat. But just as fifty years ago the judicial murder of Bakunin impoverished the working-class movement of the entire world by sapping its revolutionary morality and energies, so one fears that the obnoxious methods of the bloody Moscow replay may deplete the Russian revolution of its ideals and force *whose absence will, some day, cost the Russian working people very dearly.* (my emphasis)

SELF-RELIANT, BOTTOM-UP PARTICIPATORY SOCIALISM

While Karl and Ilona followed the historic events of the early years of the Russian revolution with the closest interest — as manifested by their collection of heavily annotated pamphlet literature of the era, which survived our several migrations and is safely in my possession awaiting further research — Karl immersed himself in the study of the Vienna School of Economics. Among the books he read were the classic works of Menger, Böhm-Bawerk, Wieser, Schumpeter, Mises and Hayek, as well as British and American marginalists and the early writings of Keynes. As already mentioned, he also reread Marx's *Capital.* Some of the books he studied at this time, many of them annotated, are now deposited with the Polanyi Institute in our archives in Montreal. In the 1920s Polanyi conducted a mini "private seminar" from the family apartment in the Vorgartenstrasse — documented in remarkable detail in an unpublished manuscript by one of his students, the late Felix Schaffer, who emigrated to New Zealand, where he became a professor of economics at Wellington University. Polanyi lost no time in challenging Ludwig von Mises, the doyen of Austrian economics, to a debate on the feasibility of a socialist economy in the pages of the *Archiv fur Sozialwissenshaft und Sozialpolitik.*[2]

The feasibility of any kind of socialist economy was a hotly contested subject of debate among students of economics. Mises had pronounced it to be impossible, with all the authority of his status as the principal intellectual successor to Böhm-Bawerk. As expected, there was a reply by Mises, further contributions by Weil, Marshak and a further response by Polanyi. This is not the place to go into details of the arguments of Polanyi's lengthy — and in places obscure — article of 1922, which has been summarized, analyzed and critiqued by several scholars, although an English-language version still awaits a translator looking for a formidable challenge.[3]

In brief, Polanyi's attempt to construct a positive theory of socialist economy, where the abolition of private property and class antagonism between owners and workers would open the way for the exercise of social responsibility by all citizens, was rooted in his aversion both to market economy and to the administered centralized command economy. He considered both of these to be forms of "unfreedom." His model was essentially one of cooperative associations of producers, consumers and communities (municipalities etc.) jointly determining the allocation and distribution of resources in a process of negotiation whereby economic efficiency criteria would be consciously moderated by social policy as determined by the members of these associations. This was not a market-less economy, nor an economy without money. Nor was it the "capitalism without capitalists" of the Lange-Taylor-Dickenson variety, developed in the English-language literature on socialist planning of the 1930s.

To appreciate the "socialization debates" of post-1918 Vienna, we must bear in mind the strength and sophistication of contemporary working-class organization and the great appeal of the Austrian Social Democratic Party. In an article published in 1925 in *Der Kampf* — the official party organ, founded by Karl Renner and Otto Bauer in 1908 — Karl Polanyi presented the case for a model of functional (associational) socialism in terms of the praxis of really existing working-class and popular organizations, as illustrated in the following passages (emphasis as in Polanyi's original 1925 text):

> Socialist theory cannot impose a "scientific socialist" model on a historical vacuum, but rather must seek to point present realities in a socialist direction. The treatment of this problem by socialist theory is meaningful and justifiable only to the degree to which its results prove to be fruitful in the *praxis* of the working-class movement.
>
> *The most obvious deficiency of the approach of the centrally planned economy relates to its failure to encompass the concrete reality of the working-class movement and the historical mission it embodies.* The presently existing capacity of the trade unions, industrial associations, co-operatives and municipalities to contribute to a socialist economy is entirely overlooked by the theoreticians of the administered economy. All these formations are, as we will show, *organs of the "inner overview" of the economy,* with great significance for socialist development. The evolution of this "transparency" can be illustrated with respect to the political party, the trade unions, co-operatives, industrial associations and socialist municipalities.

Polanyi rejected the administered economy model as flawed by a productionist "crude naturalism whereby the economy is conceived merely in terms of tangible objects, machines, raw materials, etc." He conceived the economy as a social-natural process whose principal elements are: 1) human needs; 2) human work and effort *(Arbeitsleid);* and 3) means of production. Of these three aspects of the macro-economy,

> the administered economic approach concerns itself exclusively with physical and material things, i.e., means of production, inclusive of labour power. We must pose the question whether this approach is at all concerned with the other two aspects of the economy: human needs, and human effort? Means of production are visible, tangible aspects of the external world that can be counted and measured. *The needs and efforts of another human being would be comprehensible to us only if we could imagine ourselves in the situation of another person, feel and live his needs, his pain and effort, enter into his inner self.* (emphasis in original)

Such an approach to the "inner overview" is basically quite different from the "external overview" relating to material objects and things. For the command economist, Polanyi wrote, "economics narrows down to the area of production: needs and efforts slip into the background. As regards *needs,* these are simply assumed to be known. Whether it is at all possible, within a planned administered economy, to achieve the "inner overview" depends on the *means and modalities* available."

Polanyi notes that one of the tools available to the planner is statistics. "Inner and qualitative phenomena however escape statistics: *Statistics are thus the classical means of the external view of the economy.*"[4] Polanyi stresses the role of (really existing) economic, political and cooperative organizations and associations as a modality informing planners of the needs ("inner overviews") of citizens in their manifold roles as consumers, workers, agricultural producers, etc.

"Of far greater significance [than statistics] is a second means available to the planner: i.e., *organization,*" Polanyi continues by stating that organizations not only generate information passed from "lower levels" to "higher levels" and thus contribute to policy formulation, they must mediate conflicts and contradictions within their membership in order to function effectively:

> The conflicting interests and objectives of members have to be recognized, assessed and negotiated into balance. … The trade union is more than an organ regulating the external phenomenon of the price of labour power as a means of production. It is also an instrument, a means of "inner transparency." Whereas the capitalist order can address itself only to the determination of the price of labour power in the labour market, we have here a fundamentally different modality of addressing the problem of the inner, subjective assessment of organized workers concerning *Arbeitsleid* — admittedly still within the limitations of the capitalist wage determination.

Polanyi notes that the same is true of industrial associations, democratically organized consumer cooperative movements, or socialist town councils. "All of these organizations share the characteristic that they each contribute to the ability to comprehend one or other of the basic elements of the economy as a whole."

These organizations of the working class have a second, very important characteristic. They are not artificially created by fiat to some preconceived administrative model, but are the outcome of independently created organizations of the working class. This development from the "bottom up" from the "inside outward" constitutes their capacity of democratic surveillance *(Ubersichtsleitung).* The principle underlying these organizations is a different one from that which underlies the administered economy model.

> It is neither that of power, or coercion, or authority, nor the abstract principle of legal or constitutional rights. Rather it is in the broad-

est sense of the word, the principle of comradely cooperation, the principle of relations among equals, or genuine self-organization.

Our principal conclusion is that self-reliant organization (Selbstorganisierung) is an instrument for the achievement of "inner transparency" *(Innere Ubersicht)* over the specific aspect of daily life that has given rise to the establishment of the organization.

Whoever has joined with others to form a consumer cooperative to meet the need for consumer goods, has contributed to an organ of inner democratic surveillance over the intensity and direction of the needs of its members. Whoever has joined with others for the defence of an occupation or profession to form a trade union, has contributed to the creation of an organ of inner democratic surveillance over the intensity and direction of the various views of its members concerning working conditions and *Arbeitsleid.*

When workers belonging to different occupations or sectors within an industry combine to create an industrial association, they have created an organ of inner democratic surveillance over the various branches and departments that constitute the industry as a whole.

Whenever residents of a locality have joined with others for the satisfaction of their collective needs within the framework of a socialist municipal community, they have created an organ of inner democratic surveillance over the intensity and direction of their collective needs as residents of a neighbourhood or city.

These insights concerning the contributions of trade unions, industry associations, cooperatives, socialist municipalities and socialist parties to the achievement of an overview of economic life, are by no means irrelevant to the ultimate aims and objectives of the working-class movement. The functional democracy, defined by Otto Bauer as "the constant cooperation of comrades in the service of the interests of the whole and the effective performance of each individual within his particular occupation and function," is possible only if each individual is conscious of his particular function. Bauer is absolutely correct in his insistence that the educational work to be done is *the* problem of socialist organization.

REREADING *THE GREAT TRANSFORMATION*

I believe that my father conceived his vocation to be that of an educator, in the broadest sense of the word. More exactly, a socialist educator, with a vocation to lift our consciousness above bourgeois conditioning, which has invested commodity market relations with the aura of social-scientific truth. All of his subsequent scholarly work can be seen in this light. It is a tribute to the moral force of his spirit that his work has retained a freshness and a relevance which continues to speak to us across the decades which have passed since it was written. Recent years have witnessed a renewal of interest in his work, which is ever more frequently cited. A re-reading of *The Great Transformation* comes across as an urgent appeal to associate in solidarity to protect communities, peoples and nations against the atomization of society and the cannibalization of the cultural and natural resources of the planet, by the rapacious forces of global capital markets.

Karl Polanyi's vision of a free, cooperative, democratic and just society based on social ownership and control of economic resources lives on because it is not grounded in technological or economic determinism. It was nourished by the indomitable human spirit that he so admired in Bakunin, Zasulich and the other early Russian revolutionaries — and all other rebels who confronted authoritarian power, including Jesus of Nazareth. His Christianity — at no time practised within the institution of any church — was grounded in the communion of humans. Freedom, so central to his concerns throughout his life, was grounded within "the reality of society." But the reality of society, and the constraints which this reality places upon the actions, values and ideas of all of us who inescapably live within society, do not release us from the responsibility to exercise freedom of action and thought and never to give in to determinism and fatalism. Hence the quotation from Hegel, which he many times cited, "The creative necessity of man to assert his will to conquer the world of the spirit, and so to acquire fullness of life," was for him the guiding dialectic of action, indeed of life.

The liberal illusion that society is shaped only by men's wishes and will is a hoax: "This liberal illusion was the result of a market view of society which equated economic with contractual relationships and contractual relationships with freedom." Laissez-faire philosophy, he wrote, has split up

> man's vital unity into "real" man, bent on material values, and his "ideal" better self. It is paralysing our social imagination by more or less unconsciously fostering the prejudice of "economic determinism." Today we are faced with the vital task of restoring the fullness of life to the person, even though this may mean a technologically less efficient society.

Central to his critique of economic determinism, whether of the liberal or the Marxist variety, was the concept of the embeddedness of the economy in social institutions. This concept "permits the transcending of an industrial civilization through a deliberate subordination of the economy to the ends of the human community."

The demise of "really existing socialism" has put new wind into the sails of market-driven policies on a world scale. It is no exaggeration to say that the post-communist restructuring of the international economic order is ruthlessly subordinating the human community to market forces seeking short-term financial gain on a global scale. In a letter written a few days before his death, my father recorded his last words on socialism: "The heart of the feudal nation was privilege; the heart of the bourgeois nation was property; the heart of the socialist nation is the people, where collective existence is the enjoyment of a community of culture. I myself have never lived in such a society."[5] It is unlikely that any of us living today will have the experience of living in a truly socialist society. Moreover, the "really existing" socialism of East Europe was fatefully flawed by authoritarian political structures, as noted by Polanyi seventy years ago in the prophetic passages cited in this paper. What can be stated with certainty, however, is that the attempt to impose on the rest of the world a radical Anglo-American vision of the autonomy of market forces, backed by sanctions to subordinate nations, peoples and communities to the rights of property, is a Utopian project which threatens to unleash uncontrollable reactionary political forces. It is incompatible with democratic governance, cultural diversity and pluralism, and ultimately the protection of the biosphere that sustains life on Earth.

Polanyi's ideas are finding ever-widening expression. In a significant contribution to the *Guardian* newspaper, a leading British daily, Will Hutton wrote:

> If it were only a battle of ideas, the situation would be less serious but it is the veto on politics placed by the global capital markets. Its judgements about governments' credit-worthiness and sustainability of policy are the ultimate arbiter — and much more important than the opinion of national electorates. (Hutton 1994)

The threat to democracy could not be stated more clearly. Credit ratings affect government policy more immediately and more effectively than opinion polls or the results of elections. The same columnist went on to note:

> The world has been here before. Karl Polanyi's seminal book of fifty years ago, *The Great Transformation,* traced the rise of the great twentieth century political extremisms, fascism and communism, from the ashes of the free market experiment of the nineteenth century…. Free trade led to social misery which the minimalist nineteenth century state could not check … and the supremacy of commercial values over those of trust and cooperation undermined the very bonds upon which the market depended…. Is it too fanciful to see the process repeated 100 years later?

It is becoming ever clearer that the subordination of the economy to the ends of the human community must be moved to the top of all other agendas, for the sake of survival on this planet. This requires a reassessment and a rethinking of the current development discourse, including the present emphasis on ever more liberalized trade, deregulation, specialization, economic integration, globalization and further material growth in the rich industrialized countries of the West. Here Polanyi's insistence on reciprocity and redistribution as complementary to the market in a socially cohesive and ecologically sustainable modern economy is of major significance. If we cannot set limits on the reach of the market, economic forces will destroy the capacity of society to resist disintegration and the capacity of the biosphere to renew itself. Public ownership and social and economic planning must be rescued from their current status as heresies. The vision of socialism as a co-operative, democratic and just economic order based on the social ownership and control of natural and man-made resources, united by the enjoyment of a community of culture, embodies the best of the legacy of the European enlightenment.

NOTES

This chapter is based on a paper entitled "Karl Polanyi as Socialist," delivered at the Fourth International Karl Polanyi Conference, Montreal, Canada, 1992.

1. Polanyi's "Neue Erwagungen zu unserer Theorie und Praxis," published in the Austrian socialist revue *Der Kampf* in 1925, was reprinted under the rubric "On the periphery of Austro-Marxist Theory," in *Austro-Marxistische Poitionen*, edited by G. Mozetic (1983). Other authors similarly situated by Mozetic were Paul Lazarsfeld, Alexander Gerschenkron, Ernst Fischer, Kathe Leichter and Rudolf Hilferding.

2. See, for example, Karl Polanyi, "Sozialistische Rechnungslegung" in *Archiv fur Sozialwissenshaft und Sozialpolitik*, Bd. 49, 2, pp. 377–420 and Ludwig, V. Mises, "Neue Beitrage Zum Problem der Sozialistischen Wirtschaftsrechnung" in *Archiv fur Sozialwissenshaft und Sozialpolitik*, Bd. 51, 2, p. 410.

3. See, for example, Peter Rosner, "Karl Polanyi on Socialist Accounting" and Marguerite Mendell, "Karl Polanyi and Feasible Socialism" in Levitt 1990.

4. "Statistics are not, however, a magic solution because they can inform us only about measurable, i.e., external, realities such as the quantity of people, wealth, acres, consumption of commodities. Moreover, they are useful only in their ex post and not their ex ante aspect" (Polanyi 1925).

5. From a letter written to Rudolph Schlesinger, editor of the journal *Co-Existence*, founded by Karl Polanyi in 1964.

4. BACK TO THE FUTURE
The World Economic Crisis of the 1930s

In recent years, Karl Polanyi's *The Great Transformation* has been cited with increasing frequency. Written seventy years ago, the book was well received when it was first published in the United States in 1944, and resulted in Polanyi's visiting appointment at Columbia University. In England, where it was published a year later under the title *The Origins of Our Time*, it had little impact. Although many who have read *The Great Transformation* report that it made a lasting impression, and it became a minor classic, reprinted and translated into many languages and rated one of the greatest hundred books of the twentieth century,[1] it is only recently that Karl Polanyi has emerged as an important thinker whose work is routinely referred to in the contemporary literature of international political economy, economic sociology and ecology — even by the occasional economist.

The explanation is not difficult to find. *The Great Transformation* is a powerful critique of the liberal "utopia" of the universalization of the market principle, popularly known as "globalization." "Our thesis," he wrote on the opening page, "is that the idea of a self-adjusting market implies a stark utopia. Such an institution could not exist for any length of time without annihilating the human and natural substance of society; it would have physically destroyed man and transformed his surroundings into a wilderness" (Polanyi 1944 [2001]: 3). Fifty years ago this language might have seemed excessive.

The book, subtitled "The Political and Economic Origins of our Times" was about the "great transformation" which followed the breakdown of the liberal international economic order in the crash of 1929–33. In this chapter we review Polanyi's commentaries on the world economic crisis as it unfolded and attempt to draw insights about the global financial crises of the 1990s from his methodological approach. His location in Vienna as a journalist and political analyst of a leading financial and economic weekly placed him at the centre of the political and economic upheavals of post-First World War Continental Europe[2] culminating in the fateful collapse of the Kreditanstalt

— a major bank in Vienna founded by the Rothschilds — with consequences spreading westward to England and the United States.

In the 1920s, large American short-term credits enabled Germany to service unsustainable reparation payments to France and Britain, and the latter two to repay war debts to the United States. After the pound returned to gold convertibility at pre-war (now-overvalued) parity, it was underwritten by American credits. In 1931 the "golden thread," which had deficit countries on a very short leash, snapped. According to Polanyi, this is when the long nineteenth century finally came to an end.

The second chapter of *The Great Transformation* — "Conservative Twenties, Revolutionary Thirties" — summarized the revolutionary transformation of the early 1930s:

> Its landmarks were the abandonment of the gold standard by Great Britain; the Five Year Plans in Russia; the launching of the New Deal; the National Socialist Revolution in Germany; the Collapse of the League [of Nations] in favour of autarkist empires. While at the end of the Great War nineteenth century ideals were paramount, and their influence dominated the following decade, by 1940 every vestige of the international system had disappeared and apart from a few enclaves, the nations were living in an entirely new setting. (23).

The experience of the thirties was cataclysmic. Contrast, for example, Keynes's elegy to the pre-1914 world with his later views on the prospective post-1945 world. In *Economic Consequences of the Peace* (1919), Keynes describes idyllic life in pre-First World War England, where "internationalization was nearly complete in practice," as a "paradise" in which "the inhabitant of London could order by telephone, sipping his morning tea in bed, the products of the whole earth ... by the same means venture his wealth in the natural resources and new enterprises of any quarter of the world, and share without exertion, or even trouble, in their prospective fruits" (1971c: 129). By 1944 Keynes concluded that unregulated capital movements had proved too dangerous between the wars and that the post-war order must include permanent capital controls, both inward and outward.

ECONOMIC LIBERALISM AS A MODEL FOR THE TWENTY-FIRST CENTURY?

The Bretton Woods order, constructed by Anglo-American negotiators toward the end of the Second World War, encouraged the liberalization of trade while permitting member countries to maintain national control over capital movements. Fixed exchange rates were restored, but medium-term finance was made available to enable member countries to traverse temporary balance-of-payments crises without pushing them into deflation and recession. This international regime of embedded liberalism was complemented by a domestic compromise of capital and labour brokered by the state — the so-called Keynesian consensus. In the post-colonial nations, the absence of an effective domestic bourgeoisie placed responsibility for national economic development on an active developmental state.

The rise of the neoliberal counter-revolution following the economic and political turmoil of the 1970s is too well known to require elaboration. Suffice it to say that the golden age of the nineteenth-century liberal order was refurbished and presented as an inevitable trend toward a globalized world of winners and losers: a world of intensified economic competition requiring the subordination of all aspects of social and cultural life to economic success, by individuals and by nations.[3] The power of the media has created the impression that this is a technologically driven trend beyond the control of national or international governmental intervention. To survive in this globalized world, countries must subordinate domestic concerns to competition in external markets.

Neoliberal policy prescriptions include disinflationary monetary policies, deficit reduction, the partial dismantling of the welfare state, flexible labour markets and independent central banks. Third World countries have been subjected to Structural Adjustment Programs, including large devaluations, on the theory that a change in the external value of the currency could switch production from domestic to export markets, like the flow of traffic can be diverted by a road sign. The privatization of public enterprise, initiated by Thatcher in Britain, was added to the arsenal of IMF/World Bank structural adjustment measures in the late 1980s. Countries were judged by their success in implementing market-oriented reforms with little regard for the social consequences. The patient was considered to be improving so long as the medication was administered as prescribed. The means became ends. Economics became ideology. Accelerated liberalization of cross-border capital flows was urged on developing countries as a way to attract capital and sustain economic growth. In the 1990s, Mexico and South Korea were rewarded for financial liberalization by inclusion in the OECD, the club of the rich and successful. The price of admission proved to be very costly to both these countries. The liberalization of the capital account triggered the Mexican peso crisis of 1995 and the Asian Crisis of 1997.

Private capital was enthroned as the engine of growth, and owners of financial assets have been favoured over debtors and borrowers by restrictive monetary polices and high real interest rates. These policies put recessive strains on the productive sectors and downward pressure on real wages while generating large gains for the holders of paper claims to a share of the national product. Finance began to act as a mechanism for transferring income from wage earners to the holders of financial assets, manifested in incontestable evidence of growing income disparities, most strikingly in the Anglo-American world. This "market-friendly" model of winners and losers is not only inequitable in the distribution of the gains from growth, it is financially, politically, socially and ecologically unstable — and ultimately unsustainable. Underlying instabilities have been overlaid by a veneer of prosperity for the influential and opinion-making educated professional and commercial classes, both in developed and in developing countries. They have been the principal beneficiaries of the high earnings and capital gains of a vast structure of financial paper claims.

THE GLOBALIZATION OF FINANCIAL CRISIS

A major financial hurricane on the scale of the 1930s is in the making, gathering speed and power from the hypertrophic mass of short-term global finance circling the globe in search of gain and shelter from risk, bouncing from country to country. The surge of short-term capital flows encouraged by financial liberalization and supported by the G7, the International Monetary Fund (IMF) and the World Bank, has brought the world to the brink of a major financial crisis. Policy advice about what to do points in diametrically opposed directions: the IMF — and the U.S. Treasury which now dictates policy to the Fund — is pressing for the acceleration of financial liberalization and their encoding in new Articles of Agreement on capital account liberalization. More cautious voices are recommending measures to contain global capital movements, whether by a variant of the Tobin tax or by international agreement to legitimize national capital controls. This is only the beginning of a major re-thinking of doctrines and policies which have, until recently, enjoyed a virtual monopoly in national and international governmental circles.

From the mid-1990s, the accumulation of financial savings in commercial banks and pension and managed mutual funds seeking high returns and capital gains constituted the supply side of the surge of capital into the fast growing economies of East Asia. Under pressure from the Western powers, domestic financial liberalization opened these economies to large inflows of mostly short term-credits; the borrowers were private banks and non-bank corporations. High growth rates, low inflation and small public-sector deficits sucked in large capital flows in excess of the needs of economies with very high rates of savings. In 1997 the Bank of International Settlement issued a warning to commercial banks that they were overextended in high-risk emerging (mainly Asian) markets; the warning was ignored.

The ink was hardly dry on a report by the IMF praising the high-growth performance of Thailand when a real-estate bubble and bank failures there brought the IMF steaming into the region with a large bailout package and a set of restrictive policy measures, which aggravated a balance-of-payments crisis that should have been dealt with quietly by negotiation with private creditors and private debtors. Contagion spread to neighbouring countries. Bank closures and high interest rates bankrupted viable businesses while failing to restore confidence in currencies. By the autumn of 1997 and the spring of 1998 the Asian Crisis had devastated economies that had sustained high rates of economic growth for decades. Domestic factors, which had been used to explain their previous successes, were now blamed for the crisis.

The collapse of the high-growth economies of East Asia has impacted Japan, where a mountain of non-performing bank loans and several years of economic stagnation have plummeted the value of the yen. There are fears that the worst recession in fifty years in the world's second largest economy could trigger a full-scale global recession. Japanese savers, distrustful of banks following high profile scandals, are either keeping their cash at home or investing it in safe havens in the United States. Further deterioration in the region is checked by the cooperation of communist China with the United States in resisting pressures to devalue the yuan — expected to set off another round of debilitating devaluations and bankruptcies in the stricken economies of Asia.

The political consequences of the economic hurricane that has lashed the Asian region have begun to unfold. Massive street demonstrations removed leaders in Thailand, Korea and Indonesia, and a Japanese prime minister was voted out of office. The shift in popular rhetoric is toward the people. It is widely believed that the Western orthodox financial medication has made the crisis worse — a view shared by many Western economists. A more extreme view is that the Asian economies have been deliberately destroyed and pushed back to colonialism by Western capitalists and governments. Challenges to economic globalization are growing. Although exports have increased in volume, competition for markets in America and Europe have plummeted prices and shaved profit margins. It is increasingly difficult to see how these economies can export themselves out of the recession. Unemployment is growing, not only in the former Tiger economies but also in China. A rising tide of anti-Western sentiment is reported as threatening trade liberalization agreements and creating a fortress mentality.

Meanwhile back in Washington, the International Monetary Fund is running out of money. The $35 billion committed to Thailand (4) Korea (21) and Indonesia (10) from IMF resources depleted the Fund to a degree that endangers its ability to extend substantial loans to the next casualty of the global financial crisis. Although the top brass of the International Monetary Fund made reassuring statements that the threat of default by Russia at the end of May 1998 was no cause for panic, panic is the only word to describe the fears that reign in the corridors of power in Washington. Fears of the political consequences of the failure by Yeltsin to protect the rouble from a devastating meltdown caused Republicans to join Democrats in lifting Senate obstruction to a replenishment of IMF resources. Popular discontent in a great country with a vast arsenal of nuclear weapons was sufficiently menacing to put American domestic politics and well-founded criticisms of the IMF on hold — for a week or two! At time of writing, the $4.8 billion in credits released to Russia have not halted the flight of capital.

Financial, economic and political instability in Russia is not the only smouldering bush fire. Last week it was revealed that Pakistan is on the brink of default. The IMF was blocked from releasing funds by a U.S. embargo on assistance to countries that test nuclear weapons. Again, panic struck. Within days, U.S. policy reversed itself and sent a message to the IMF that Pakistan was to be exempted from the embargo. India however, less dependent on foreign capital and consequently less dangerously indebted, was not exempted. A smouldering financial crisis in South Africa — a country long on the watch list of the IMF — hit the pages of the newspapers. By July, the Rand had lost 25 percent of its value since its currency was first attacked late in May; there are dangers of further speculative attacks, as capital flees the country. A major crisis in South Africa could carry the whole of Southern Africa into recession. In Iran, where student demonstrations support the president who is locked in conflict with ultra-conservative religious forces, economic and financial stability is now threatened by falling oil prices. Even strong currencies of countries like Australia and Canada have felt the impact of the Asian Crisis as capital seeks safe haven in the United States. Commodity exports to Asia are in decline, and currency trading sharks are active in troubled waters.

In Australia, international speculators reduced the value of the currency to its lowest level in twelve years, despite large interventions by the Central Bank. The danger of further attacks on the currency persist. It is believed that the ultimate target of the currency speculators is China's yuan. A deputy governor of the Reserve Bank of Australia ascribed the Asian Crisis to excessively large — and volatile — inflows of short-term capital. He criticized IMF policies of imposing high interest rates and obliquely suggested that, in the absence of regulation of international capital flows, fragile emerging economies must protect themselves against the virus of short-term lending, particularly by — and to — banks. An electoral backlash by the victims of a decade of radical liberalization is veering policy toward rebuilding productive industries and slowing the pace of trade liberalization.

In its annual report published in June 1998, the Bank of International Settlements (BIS) warned that the growing institutionalization of financial markets could undermine financial stability. Institutional investors of North America, Europe and Japan (investment companies, insurance companies, pension funds and money managers) hold an estimated $21 trillion — more than the combined GNP of the eighteen countries concerned. A marginal portfolio adjustment by the investor can be a major event for the recipient. Institutional investors were not blamed for the Asian Crisis, but the BIS considered that the increasing importance of professional investors and their methods of doing business offers scope for herd-like behaviour and potential damage. The commercial banks, who were by far the most important lenders (of short-term funds) in emerging markets of Asia and continued to increase their exposure well into the autumn of 1997, appear to have been primarily responsible for the fatal mismatch for borrowers when the crisis struck.[4]

Where will the next crisis hit? We don't know, but one can safely assume that there will be more acute crises, until somewhere a large developing or transition country is pushed over the brink of default — which could trigger a cascade of other defaults. It was by declaring unilateral moratoria on debt repayment that Latin American and other debtor countries averted economic collapse in the 1930s. The global financial crisis we have described suggests that a large overhang of inflated financial claims will either crash or will be reduced by a combination of debt forgiveness, stock market adjustments and negotiated write-downs.

For a number of years the electorate of Western Europe have endorsed — or at least tolerated — the restrictive fiscal policies of their governments. But the social fallout of policies geared to external competition at the expense of domestic living standards is blowing up political storms. The election of social democratic governments in almost all the countries of Western Europe — even though their policies are not very different from the governments they replaced — is not without significance.

Democracy is kicking in to administer a countervailing revision of policies which privilege greed over equity and security. The ideological hegemony of neoliberalism is loosening its grip. In the language of Polanyi, society is moving to protect itself from the lash of market forces. Democracy is striking back at economics. For a discussion of the conflict between capitalism and democracy treated in Polanyi's essay "Economy and Democracy" (1932), see Chapter 5 of this volume.

LESSONS OF THE WORLD ECONOMIC CRISIS OF 1931–1933

The gripping rhetoric that pervades *The Great Transformation* originated from Polanyi's Central European experience. Central and Eastern Europe were far more profoundly affected by the First World War than the victorious Western powers of England and France, where the gloss faded from the pre-1914 Belle Époque, but bourgeois life continued much as before — as described by Keynes in the passage already quoted. The coupon-clipping rentiers of the English leisure classes continued to invest abroad, as if not very much had changed. City interests returned the pound to its golden pedestal at pre-war valuation, in defiance of Britain's slippage as the premier exporting country of the world and the unsustainable burden of reparations imposed on the defeated central powers.

In a remarkable study written in 1933, "The Mechanisms of the World Economic Crisis," Polanyi traced the origins of the 1931–1933 crisis back to the social and economic costs of the Great War. Production in Central and Eastern Europe as well as Russia did not recover to 1913 levels until late 1928. The scale of human and societal destruction was of such magnitude that the social fabric could not sustain the forces of adjustment to a post-war equilibrium. In his view it was "one single economic crisis" that had only been postponed as the burden of adjustment shifted from one region to another.

In this paper Polanyi provided an exemplary political economy analysis of conflicting class interests in the post-war adjustment to diminished levels of real resources. There were three major social claimants: the *bondholders* (rentiers), who had financed the war and without whose confidence in currencies and credit capitalist economies could not be reconstructed; the *workers*, who had carried the moral and political burden of the war and were promised a reward of more rights and more bread; and the *peasantry*, who appeared to be the only bulwark against the threat of Bolshevism on the continent.

In the victorious countries, strong currencies favoured the interests of rentiers. The democratization of public life in England increased the number of eligible voters from eight million pre-war to twenty-eight million. When the war finished, there were no excuses for failure to deliver on the promises of "homes worthy of heroes." Nobody in Britain believed in the necessity to restrict living standards after the war. When the realities of the diminished economic capacity of England began to dawn, the entire burden of adjustment to defend — and increase — the value of rentier incomes was placed on the working classes.

In the defeated countries, the rentier classes were devastated by inflation. The workers likewise were not protected from the fallout of the crisis, but they had priority. Installed in the seat of political power, the worker (and ex-soldier), who had borne the greatest burden of the war, demanded the promised rights and the promised bread. The third party to the trilogy was the peasantry, whose general *Weltanschauung* (worldview) allied it with the forces of conservatism. A viable social framework demanded the protection of rentier interests by the defence of currencies, protection of worker incomes by the stabilization of real wages and protection of farm incomes by the stabilization of commodity prices. In the war-impoverished, capital-depleted economies of Continental Europe, the satisfaction of all these demands was impossible. But when the viability of society comes into conflict with what is economically impossible, economic possibilities are stretched one way or another. The way they were stretched was by interventions, including politically negotiated foreign credits. Although the eventual collapse was inevitable, it could be — and was — delayed by sacrificial interventions.[5]

> The mother of all interventions was the war itself. All the interventions of the post-war era were costly attempts to protect society against the shock of the brutal destruction of economic and social equilibrium. They were not the *cause* of the crisis. The effect of inter-

> ventions — sometimes misconceived and shortsighted in implementa-
> tion — was to postpone the solution to the crisis. But they created new
> disequilibria, which exacerbated the consequences of the original
> major intervention of the war. (Polanyi 1933, emphasis in original)

Excess demand of the three major categories of income earners could be met from only three sources:

- by domestic redistribution in favour of privileged classes. Where workers and peasants were favoured, the burden fell on the middle classes and on industrial capital by property taxes and the unfairest of all taxes — liquidation of savings by inflation. Real incomes of agricultural producers were maintained by protective tariffs — at the expense of urban consumers.
- by consumption of capital; domestic capital was eaten away by inflation and the sale of assets to foreigners.
- by external borrowing and increased indebtedness, on a vast scale.

Countries financed their deficits by perpetual external borrowing. Weaker national economies sought assistance from stronger ones. Years of apparent stability, a run of strong growth and a deceptive appearance of equilibrium were punctuated by new economic and financial difficulties, until suddenly, at the height of the American boom, the elastic band snapped. The interdependent deficit economies went into an irreversible slide, and the whole stabilization structure collapsed.

The geographic displacement and consequent postponement of the crisis was facilitated by credit mechanisms of unique capacity and flexibility.

> While the world economy was destroyed by the war; resurrected after the war; and slid into uninterrupted decline at the end of 1928, the system of credits has not ceased to develop since the financial innovations introduced during the war. An amazing mobility and magnitude of international credit was accompanied by intermittent constriction and malfunctioning of the real economy.

The source of this system of credits was the cooperation of the victorious powers in mobilizing credit to finance the war: "Never in the history of modern capitalism had credit been so politicised." A close relationship developed between the commercial banks and note-issuing authorities (central banks) in London, New York and Paris.

> The source of this ultra-modern pipeline for the distribution of credit to the whole of Europe, which brought gold to water the parched plains of central Europe, was the unfathomable wealth of America. The enormous profits which America made in the war were searching

for investments. The reconstruction of Europe appeared as an excellent business, which could also revive American exports. Unequalled in wealth — and inexperienced — the investors who now appeared on the scene requested only that this credit mechanism should be fuelled by their resources. If we now find it incredible that the world could have been so mistaken about the true balance sheet of the war, the explanation lies in part with the financial claims which were considered good. The sum total of allied war debts was estimated at $25 billion dollars.

It was believed that claims on Russian war and pre-war debtors estimated at 35 billion gold francs were good. In 1925, after Britain and Germany had returned to the Gold Standard, there was talk of a 16 billion gold mark reparations issue as if it were a normal business deal.

> The value of all these claims have now been written down. What is remarkable is that prior to the write down, owners of these papers thought they were rich.... The credit mechanism endowed by contemporaries with virtual mythical powers, were the principal actors in the ten-year postponement of the crisis.

THE COURSE OF THE CRISIS

Polanyi traced the geographical course of the crisis — from East to West. The actors were the *defeated states*,[6] the *victorious states* (England, France, Belgium and Italy) and, in a class by itself, there was the super-victor: America.

1918–1924

The process starts in the East with the reconstruction of the defeated states — with assistance from the victors and America.[7] The high point was the restoration of the Gold Standard in Germany, financed by Dawes Plan loans, almost half of American provenance. The reinstatement of the Gold Standard stripped the defeated states of the secret reserves of inflationary finance. Their structural deficits were increasingly covered by foreign loans; the burden of these debts was thus transferred to the victorious states, whose currencies were at that time far from secure.

1925–1928

In addition to the deficits of the defeated states, the victorious states had their own problems. From the time of the re-establishment of the Gold Standard, the defence of the currency assumed top priority. By central bank cooperation, England shifted the burden of maintaining the external value of the pound to the United States (by U.S. short-term credits). "From this time on, the secret purpose of American credit policy was not so much assistance to Europe, as support for England." The high point was the negotiations between the Bank of England governor, Norman, and the Federal Reserve governor, Strong, in May 1927. In August of that year, the United States adopted a "cheap credit policy," which lasted till February 1928, and prepared the way for the Wall Street crash of October 1929. The American crypto-inflation signified effective support for the European currencies that had returned to the Gold Standard — by the availability of cheap credit.

1929–1933

The deficits of the European defeated and victorious states were effectively shifted to America and covered by the steady growth of U.S. credits over the previous ten years. America financed the Dawes Plan and re-negotiated British and French war debts and the servicing of its own loans — in addition to putting wasted efforts into supporting English stabilization, bad German investments and the accumulation of East European private-sector deficits in financial institutions in Vienna. Vienna's Kreditanstalt crashed on May 12, 1931, the Reichsmark declined, the English pound devalued. On April 19, 1933, the dollar was floated. "The constriction of the world economy and the chaotic instability of currencies resemble conditions prevailing in the immediate aftermath of the war."

Critics who ascribed the economic crisis to policy errors such as the text-book example of the return of the pound at pre-war parity, or the Central European belief that the English bank rate was too low to sustain the value of the pound, were taken to task. Alternative policies, Polanyi maintained, "were only alternative paths to the same undesirable outcome." English exports became uncompetitive when France and Belgium devalued their currencies by 80 percent. England chose to privilege its rentier class, whereas France and Belgium devalued the (foreign) assets of their rentiers. Had England gone that route, there would have been a reduction in the export of capital considered essential to the maintenance of British exports. Had England raised the bank rate, which in any event never fell below 4.5 percent — far above historically prevailing rates — this would have aggravated the acute economic crisis in England. The fact that English rentier incomes were protected (by overvalued exchange rates) assured the continued flow of British long-term investments to Continental Europe — assisted by the flow of cheap money from New York to London.[8]

From the start, the elastic band which bound the ever more fragile equilibria of the deficit economies were the American credits. "But the transmission belt which carried the deficits of even the strongest European economies to the credit ledgers of American financial institutions was the re-established gold standard." European national economies were forced to adjust their weakened economic capacities by adherence to the rigid rules of the Gold Standard. Their increased indebtedness to American creditors occurred

silently, but no less effectively than negotiated loans. Whereas the stabiliza-
tions in Central Europe were sustained by cheap credit available on London
money markets, the restoration of the pound sterling at pre-war parity was
sustained by nothing less than the American silent inflation of 1926–1929.

From August 1927 to February 1928 the discount rate of the New York
Federal Reserve Bank was a mere 3.5 percent. The result was an enhanced
economic boom in the United States and Europe as a flow of American
credits supported European currencies. Foreign investments to Germany in
1927/28 topped $2 billion. In July 1928 the New York rate was raised to 5
percent to check a speculative bubble on the stock market. The supply of
long-term capital to Europe dried up. In the first half of 1929 the value of
European bonds floated in New York was a mere $101 million, compared
with $449 million in the first half of 1928.

Up until 1925, American protectionist and credit policies sustained living
standards in the United States and Europe by accepting gold for payment
of imports and by the extension of credits. After the restoration of the Gold
Standard in Europe, the debtor states could withstand the pressure on their
currencies only because inflationary cheap money policies in the United States
were instrumental in an enormous increase in foreign lending to Europe. When
American inflationist policies were reversed, financial pressure on debtor states
triggered the world crisis. Neither gold nor new money was available to finance
payments deficits.[9] Debtor states now had no alternative to the increase in
the export of goods. Europe and overseas raw material exporting countries
since 1928/29 have flooded markets with exports at virtually any price. The
trend of universally falling world prices manifested in 1929 was the prelude
to the world crisis. Then came the credit crisis of 1931, the decline in world
trade in 1932 and the collapse of currencies in 1933. The geographic displacement and postponement of the economic deficits had run their course.
If inflation succeeded in saving the social fabric, it could not save humanity
from a prolonged and painful process of adjustment.

Polanyi cited Professor J.B. Condliffe (1933: 277), principal author of the
Economic Yearbook of the League of Nations for 1932/3, in support of his analysis:

> The real difficulties did not manifest themselves as long as the cur-
> rencies of most of the debtor states were independent of each other,
> exchange rates were flexible, and inter-governmental debts unregu-
> lated. But as currencies returned to the gold standard, exchange rates
> were fixed, and debt payments were officially negotiated, tensions in
> the newly reconstructed international financial mechanism increased.
> For a few years, from 1925 to 1929 debt service was effected without
> radical adjustment of national economies by means of large flows of
> capital to the debtor states, principally from the United States. From
> 1928 and continuing in 1929, capital flows diminished. As pressures

on debtor states increased, prices declined and credits dried up, the difficulties of international adjustment precipitated the collapse of the whole structure of international payments.

THE SIGNIFICANCE AND RELEVANCE OF POLANYI'S INTERPRETATION OF THE CRISIS

In many ways, Polanyi's summary of the world economic crisis of the 1930s accords with received conventional wisdom. What then is interesting about this article — aside from the fact that it was written in 1933, without benefit of hindsight? How does it differ from the second chapter of the *The Great Transformation*? What can we learn about our present — and our future — from Polanyi's account of the past?

The first thing to note is the role played by the First World War in Polanyi's account of the economic crisis of 1929–33: "the conjunctural crisis of 1929–33 [was] only the most dramatic phase in a general crisis which had its origins in the War." Conventionally, the war of 1914–18 marks the close of the "long nineteenth century." For Polanyi the historical break — the great transformation — set in with abruptness, in the early thirties. The world economic crisis of 1929–33 was the last and final chapter of the nineteenth century.

Next we note the role of the United States as the "super victor" of the First World War and the close relationship between central bankers and commercial bankers in New York, London and Paris. Although the source of the American funds that underpinned the complex structure of credit extended to European states was private, these credits were politically negotiated transfers of resources. "It is the curse of politically motivated interventions," Polanyi wrote, "that eventual adjustments entail new and more painful interventions."

On the domestic front, we note the emphasis on the political priority of assuring "the viability of society" — what now is called the preservation of social capital or concern for the social fabric in stressful transformations of the economic order or severe insufficiency of economic resources to meet expectations of improvement in living conditions.

This raised issues of domestic income and asset distribution. Here we note Polanyi's attention to the political impact of economic mechanisms. For example, the rentier classes in England were privileged by an overvalued exchange rate, whereas the Russian, German, Austrian and Hungarian middle classes were pauperized by hyperinflation. In this context, he observed that it is mistaken to consider only those policies that are intended to benefit the workers or the peasants as "interventionist."

> The convenient implication here is that … protection of the currency, no matter how artificial or draconian, is not considered interventionist; the distributional effect on rentier income is not explicitly taken into account. An approach to economic stabilization which depends

exclusively on the sanctity of contract is of little value as a practical tool of economic and financial policy.

Polanyi's approach to the analysis of the world crisis of the 1930s invites the following questions concerning the unfolding financial and economic global crisis of the 1990s.

One
Did the Cold War victory of the Western powers over the former Soviet Union result in the destruction of an international political order which: 1) provided a framework for four decades of strong economic growth in the mixed economies of the developed and most of the developing world; 2) respected the authority of the United Nations and the sovereign rights of member states; and 3) checked the United States — now the only world superpower — from attempts to impose its economic system and ideology on the rest of the world? After its defeat in 1914–18, Germany rose to unleash a second terrible war in Europe, in which Russia defeated Hitler's armies and lost twenty million people. What are the possible political consequences of the humiliation of a great power — with an arsenal of nuclear weapons — whose population has been subjected to a form of mafia capitalism which has enriched perhaps a million and impoverished most of the rest of the people?[10]

Two
The Asian Crisis of 1997/8 has been greeted as proof of the superiority of the Anglo-American model of "free enterprise" over the failed "crony capitalism" of the Asian "tigers" whose achievements of decades of strong growth with relative income equality and high educational attainment were, until recently, described as "miraculous." Having trashed Russia, is it now the intention of the United States to use economic and financial leverage to destroy the cohesion of Asian societies to restructure forms of capitalism that they consider not sufficiently "open" or deregulated? Is there a hidden agenda — to block a regional economic formation under Asian control?

During the Cold War, the United States encouraged — and assisted — East Asian countries to engage in successful "developmentalist" policies of state intervention, under authoritarian rule. Would the United States have permitted the fourth largest country in the world (Indonesia) to fall into a black hole of chaos and poverty if there were still a credible threat of "communism"? What anti-Western backlash may be expected from Asian countries, which, until recently, were proud of their economic achievements due to their hard work and sacrificial high rates of domestic savings?

Three
Turning from international politics to international finance, have the lessons of the dismal inter-war years been forgotten? The Bretton Woods system was

constructed to prevent countries with balance-of-payments shortfalls from being forced into recession and unemployment. But the IMF interventions in East Asia did exactly the opposite — banks were closed, viable companies were forced into bankruptcy, and high interest rates were imposed to protect the value of local currency denominated assets of foreign creditors.

These policies were not only wrong and damaging — they were also ineffective. A balance-of-payments crisis in a small country triggered a global crisis of confidence and massive capital flight, following interventions by the International Monetary Fund. The IMF is not only short of financial resources, it is short of intellectual resources. Its economic analysis and policies have been challenged by a number of eminent economists, most importantly by Joseph Stiglitz, Chief Economist and Senior Vice President of the World Bank, former chair of the President's Council of Economic Advisors and a highly respected academic expert on financial markets. The question here is: who is calling the shots at the IMF? And in whose interest? And how much longer can the world afford to balance on the brink of a precipice before falling into the vortex of a generalized economic crisis?

Four

Back to the globalization of financial crisis. No less an authority than Alan Greenspan (1998) warned that "global financial markets, engendered by rapid proliferation of cross border financial flows and products, have developed a capability of transmitting mistakes throughout the financial system in ways that were unknown a generation ago." He suggested that, "the Asian economies could not provide adequate profitable opportunities at reasonable risk in the 1990s to absorb the surge of capital inflows ... which reflected ... the diversification of Western equity markets' huge capital gains to a sector of the world which was perceived as offering above average returns." Greenspan considered:

> Cross border interbank funding as potentially the Achilles' heel of the international financial system. Creditor banks expect claims on banks, especially banks in emerging economies, to be protected by a safety net and, consequently consider them to be essentially sovereign claims. Unless those expectations are substantially altered — as when banks actually incur significant losses — governments can be faced with the choice either of validating these expectations or of risking serious disruption to payments systems and to financial markets in general.

The threat to the stability of the world economy is real, grave and imminent. British Prime Minister Tony Blair stated that Japan's faltering economy is the gravest threat to the world economy in twenty years. George

Soros, financier and master currency speculator, expressed fears that "Japan is suffering from conditions reminiscent of the thirties," that "we're on the edge ... on the brink of a slow down as the crisis intensifies in Asia" (Soros 1998a). He criticized the IMF for imposing conditions on borrowing countries but not on the international banks that lent to them. He predicted that "the current bull run on stock markets will be followed by a massive crash: if inexperienced investors are all seized by panic and quit the market together, there will be a crash" (Soros 1998b). Scorned by academic economists, Soros has demonstrated his understanding of the instability of financial markets in the real world of successful currency speculation.

Five
Polanyi saw the rigid rules of the international Gold Standard as the crucial transmission mechanism which sustained international capital and postponed adjustments to underlying disequilibria — until the whole structure of credit collapsed under stress of the social and political forces in Europe. Today, we have a system of flexible exchange rates. From the strictly technical aspect of exchange rate policy, this is the polar opposite of fixed exchange rates. Indeed, we now look back on the exchange rate stability of the pre-1971 Bretton Woods order as a lost "golden age." How then can we say that there are similarities between the 1930s and the 1990s?

The globalization policies of deregulation, privatization and liberalization of trade and finance have placed deflationary pressures on the real economies of the major industrial countries. High interest rates and the fiscal and monetary discipline which liberalized financial markets have imposed on policy-makers — who see international financial market "credibility" to be the foremost policy goal — have slowed economic growth, reduced the purchasing power of wage earners and intensified global competition. Investment in real capital has been channelled to export markets, where excess capacity in internationally traded commodities, including manufactures, is putting downward pressure on world prices — and profits.

Unlike the 1930s, when countries engaged in devaluations to gain trade advantage, countries are now forced into (unwanted) devaluations by capital flight and speculation against weak currencies. If weak countries attempt to defend their currencies, their central banks are soon stripped of reserves; the countries then fall into the clutches of international creditors whose interests are protected by international financial institutions on the principle of the "the sanctity of contract." Laissez-faire, as Polanyi suggested, is instituted, maintained and policed by rules and regulations imposed by states. An elaborate structure of international political and economic arrangements has created a "liberal" economic order which favour creditors over debtors, finance over production, the rich over the poor. There are no winner countries in this thoroughly disordered system. The winners are the banks and more generally the holders of paper claims to assets that far exceed the capacities of the real economies to honour them. The losers are the great majority of working people of all countries.

As in the thirties, the crisis is moving from East to West. But the scale is immensely greater. The East is no longer East Europe — it is Asia with its population of two billion. The "world" is no longer Europe and its overseas extensions in North and South America. The scale of the impending crisis is truly global. But official responses have not measured up to the challenge. There are many voices of reason, good sense and good advice. In this paper, I have brought you the voice of Karl Polanyi — across distance and time — in the hope that his warnings of the perils of unleashing gain as the principle governing the livelihood of peoples and nations, may contribute to solutions.

NOTES

This chapter is based on a paper entitled "Back to the Future: Insights from Karl Polanyi's analysis of the world economic crisis of the 1930s," presented at the International Sociological Association XIV Congress of Sociology, Montreal, 1998.

1. *Time Magazine*, 17 March 1977.
2. For a complete discussion, see *Karl Polanyi in Vienna*, Polanyi-Levitt and McRobbie 1998.
3. In the *World Development Report 1995*, the World Bank invited developing countries to return to the "golden age" of earlier globalization of 1850–1900. "Globalisation is unavoidable … whether a new golden age arrives for all depends mostly on the responses of individual countries" (53–4).
4. The largest set of creditor banks in Asia were European, followed by Japanese and North American.
5. While noting that reparations and war debts contributed to economic pressures, Polanyi was explicit in placing primary emphasis on policies that sought to stabilize the domestic incomes of rentiers, workers and peasants.
6. Russia, Austria, Hungary, Bulgaria and the succession states carved from the eastern war regions like Rumania, Yugoslavia, Czechoslovakia, Poland and Greece. Last but not least, there was Germany.
7. The Austrian (1923) and Hungarian (1924) currencies were stabilized with help from the League of Nations; at the same time, Greece, Bulgaria, Finland and Estonia were structurally adjusted (*saniert*). Rumania, Poland, Czechoslovakia and Yugoslavia received French credits; even Russia was a candidate for economic assistance.
8. Flotation of foreign bonds in London amounted to $651 million in 1927; reduced to $525 million in 1928 and a mere $228 million in 1929.
9. In mid-1929, the United States and France accounted for 59 percent of the world's monetary gold.
10. When Anatoly Chubais, then Deputy Prime Minister of Russia, went to Washington to beg the IMF for emergency assistance to prevent imminent default on debt service and to protect the rouble from devaluation, he had to sit outside the door of the conference chamber for five hours while the request was being considered.

5. KEYNES AND POLANYI
The 1920s and the 1990s

In the fractured decade of the 1970s, a counter-revolution in economics restored the neoclassical doctrines prevailing before the Great Depression. By the mid-1980s, the economics profession had furnished the political directorates of the West and the Bretton Woods Institutions with theoretical justifications for policies of monetarism, liberalization, deregulation, privatization, balanced budgets and independent central banks. Capital was poised to roll back gains made by labour in the Western industrial world and developmental policies in the Third World. The 1990s witnessed devastating financial and economic crises of increasing frequency and severity in Latin America, East Asia, Russia, Brazil, Turkey and most dramatically, Argentina. By 1998, two decades of these policies had brought the world to the brink of the first global deflationary downturn since the 1930s. Developing countries were forced into painful devaluations by capital flight and speculation against weak currencies.

As in the inter-war period, when stability of employment and democratic governance were sacrificed to the stability of currencies, economic livelihoods are now subordinated to the macro-economic prescriptions of the Washington Consensus. Complex provisions of multilateral agencies are designed to protect the special interests of creditors and investors from popular political pressures. Global finance is undermining the foundations of the productive economy. Now, as then, there are no effective international institutions for the negotiation of political conflict and financial disorder.

Relentless pressure to open economies to trade and capital flows is eroding the coherence of national economies. Workers and agricultural producers are exposed to competition on a world scale, driving down real wages and commodity prices to benefit a relatively small number of large transnational corporations, which control access to technology and markets. Rich countries like Canada can no longer afford the universal right to free education and health care available at a time when GNP per capita was half of what it is today. Why? We are told it is because we must sacrifice social security to remain competitive. Governments engage in competition to lower taxes to

71

attract and maintain investors. Competitiveness has become enthroned as the operating principle of public policy.

As the world economy lurches from crisis to crisis, and savings are drawn into speculative financial markets, average growth rates in the industrial heartlands of capitalism are at a historical low.[1] For a decade, Japan was mired in a Keynesian liquidity trap, where interest rates close to zero failed to stimulate consumption or investment. A prolonged boom fuelled by the wealth effect of a rising stock market in the United States was followed by the liquidation of billions of dollars of asset values. We are living Keynes's nightmare of a "casino economy" of speculators and rentier capitalists and Polanyi's false utopia of the self-regulating market. This neoliberal economic order favours creditors over debtors, finance over production, and the rich over the poor. A growing underclass of marginalized persons is excluded from formal circuits of employment, production and consumption. Hundreds of millions of poor people in poor countries are simply redundant to the requirements of the global capitalist economy. The system is chronically inequitable and endemically unstable. Ultimately, it is politically unsustainable.

Keynes is making a return from intellectual banishment by mainstream economics. Distinguished economists have joined scholars of other disciplines in drawing attention to the importance of Polanyi's insistence that economic policy must be subordinated to broader social objectives. His warning of the perils of subordinating social, cultural and environmental needs to the dictates of the market speak to us as though they were written today.

The end of the Cold War promised a peace dividend and a bright future for capitalism. However the political, economic and financial environment required for the expansion of international business is problematic. What in fact we are witnessing is a realignment of the political landscape on a global scale, including neocolonial military adventures reminiscent of the imperial rivalry of the late nineteenth century. Historic fault lines are opening. States are fracturing under pressure of resurgent nationalisms. Inequalities are rising almost everywhere. Equity, social justice and democracy are subordinated to the requirements of a predatory style of capitalism, a kind of primitive accumulation more interested in seizing and controlling existing assets, both private and public, than in real productive investment. Politicians and politics are devalued. There is a pervasive sense of apprehension. The environment is threatened by irreversible degradation. Life in the industrial heartlands is characterized by deep insecurity and uncertainty. An industrial revolution in China, explosive growth in India and a demographic crisis of the costs of an aging population suggest a shift of growth points to Asia. A new generation of political leaders in Latin America and similar rumblings in Africa are challenging the claims of the G8 to set the development agenda.

In 1991 the U.S. emerged as the unrivalled military superpower, and the dollar continues to serve as the principal world reserve currency. However, one may ask how long can the U.S. can maintain its position as top metropole given the contradiction between the requirements of business for a peaceful, orderly, internationally regulated world and destabilizing domestic and international consequences of the American project of global military domination?

For Keynes, "the great problem of the age is to free modern industrialism from the fetters of financial capitalism" (Dillard 1948: 102). Polanyi thought that only the U.S. believed in universal capitalism; he envisaged a world of managed trade between regional blocks with diverse economic and social institutions. The circumstances are different and historical analogies always hazardous, but we believe that Keynes's and Polanyi's accounts of the events of the inter-war years can shed light on our current disordered world. To fashion political institutions that permit policy space for the non-European world to allocate their natural and human resources to the attainment of a modern standard of material welfare, while protecting the environment from further damage, it is essential to assert democratic political control over disintegrating forces of unconstrained economic growth. The insights of Keynes and Polanyi can assist us in restoring and rescuing public spaces from Keynes's "economic juggernaut."

THE POWER OF IDEAS

European intellectuals of the generation of Keynes (b.1883) and Polanyi (b.1886) were conditioned to assume responsibility for the welfare of society. Whether as public intellectuals (Keynes) or socially engaged scholars (Polanyi), *they believed in the power of ideas to affect the course of world events.*

Although they came from different backgrounds, Keynes and Polanyi shared a generational experience for which the First World War was a traumatic event that closed an era. For Polanyi, an almost personal sense of the responsibility of his generation for the Great War and all its consequences motivated his search for *The Origins of Our Times* — the original title of *The Great Transformation.* Keynes and Polanyi complement each other; Keynes was a brilliant economist and committed public servant, a product of the best traditions of English liberalism; Polanyi was an economic and social historian whose intellectual formation — and physical location — were Central European and his orientation was socialist.

More than any other great economist, Keynes was motivated by the desire to influence policy. Keynes believed that "capitalism, wisely managed can be made more efficient for attaining economic ends than any other system yet in sight" (1971a: 294). What he found profoundly objectionable was "the fostering, encouragement and protection of the money making motives of individuals" (293). His utopia was a society of abundance, leisure, beauty, grace and variety, where "love of money" is regarded as a mental disease (329). Polanyi shared the aversion to love of money. However, his critique of "market society" reached beyond that of Keynes. Polanyi questioned the very existence of "economic motives" as fundamental human attributes. For him, industrial capitalism was unique in human history in elevating gain to the fundamental principle of economic organization. Like Marx before him, Polanyi found the "the origins of our times" in the birthplace of the Industrial Revolution.

> For the origins of the cataclysm, we must turn to the rise and fall of the market economy. In order to comprehend German fascism, we must revert to Ricardian England. Market economy, free trade and the gold standard were English inventions. These institutions broke down in the nineteen twenties everywhere — in Germany, Italy and Austria the event was merely more political and more dramatic. But whatever the . . . final episodes, the factors that wrecked that civiliza-tion should be studied in the birthplace of the Industrial Revolution, England. (Polanyi 1944 [2001]: 30)

Polanyi warned that "the self adjusting market could not exist for any length of time without annihilating the human and natural substance of society" (3).

The 1920s was the last gasp of the long nineteenth century, which ter-minated in the world economic crisis of 1929–33. Both Keynes and Polanyi ascribed a principal role to the international monetary order as the transmis-sion mechanism that placed politically unsustainable pressures on countries forced to adjust to the dictates of financial markets in the interests of rentier bondholders. Keynes's analysis was drawn from the experience of England, where the Gold Standard assured the value of large overseas investments in fixed income instruments and the burden of adjustment fell on the working class. Polanyi's analysis described the impact of adjustment on Germany and the weak and peripheral succession states of Central and Eastern Europe, as countries attempted to defend the value of their currencies by sacrificing democracy to "sound finance" and linked this to the rise of fascism.

The 1990s witnessed an attempt to accelerate policies initiated in the early 1980s, designed to recreate the "golden age" of 1870–1914, promoted and marketed as "globalization." The neoliberal project is the creation of an all-embracing "free" global market for goods, services and capital — but not labour. In the industrialized world, countervailing social and political pressures (Polanyi's double movement) have subordinated to some degree the freedom of capital to the public good. When this system is transposed to a world scale, no such mechanisms exist and we have a kind of global apartheid. Labour is confined within national boundaries, but capital is mobile. Weak states are stripped of fiscal and administrative resources to negotiate conflicting interests.

The mechanisms by which this predatory style of capitalism is capsizing viable economies and impoverishing the human and environmental resources of the developing world are financial. They are encoded in rules governing international finance and investment and enforced by creditor interests acting through multilateral organizations, including the Bretton Woods institutions and the World Trade Organization. The effect is to reproduce — incompletely, less automatically and with complex political negotiations — the mechanisms of the Gold Standard.

A CENTRAL EUROPEAN VIEW OF THE WORLD ECONOMIC CRISIS, 1918–33

For Central and Eastern Europe, the First World War was a political earthquake that trashed Imperial Germany, splintered the Austro–Hungarian Empire into a set of weak and fragile succession states and witnessed a historic socialist revolution in Tsarist Russia. The Soviet Union inherited Tsarist conquests in Central Asia and the Far East. The remnants of the Ottoman Empire were occupied by Britain and France, with fateful consequences for the entire region of the Middle East and North Africa, consequences that can still be seen in the headlines of today.

In Vienna, a world had ended. The glittering capital of a multinational empire of fifty million became the capital of the rump Republic of Austria — a country of six million, too small and too poor to be considered a viable state. The first government of the Republic was formed by the Social Democratic Party, and the first finance minister was Joseph Schumpeter (who soon departed for Germany). Chaos and inflation reigned. The provinces were rural and Catholic; Vienna was cosmopolitan and socialist. Educational reforms and model public housing projects of the socialist administration of "Red" Vienna of the 1920s made a deep impression on Polanyi — a triumph of social and political forces over unfavourable economic circumstances.

From 1924, his position as senior editor of *Oesterreichische Volkswirt*, the leading financial and economic weekly of Central Europe, placed him in the eye of the storm of economic and political upheavals in Continental Europe. From this post he followed the unravelling of attempts by the Western powers to restore the pre-1914 economic order and its eventual break down in 1931, when a financial crisis in Vienna spread westward to England and ultimately to the entire world economy. In 1933, when the deteriorating political climate did not permit the journal to keep a prominent socialist on their editorial staff, he left for England but continued to write for the journal.

To underline my emphasis on the significance of Polanyi's Central European perspective, we note that a major feature article, "The Mechanisms of the World Economic Crisis," written in 1933, starts with the words: "From a Central European perspective." The thesis of the article was as follows:

> The entire post-war period, including eight years of miraculous prosperity in the United States, sustained economic growth in several other countries (Canada, Argentina etc.) and the multifaceted

technical, economic, currency and trade policy adventures of this whole dismal historical epoch, right down to the crash of 1929 and the world depression of 1933, *is one single economic crisis which manifests itself in different forms as it traverses and transforms the world.*

The economic crisis of the first post war years was not resolved — just postponed. *"Equilibrium in one location was achieved by shifting the burden of adjustment, deliberately or otherwise, to other economic regions and sectors....* When the unavoidable day of reckoning arrived, it not only re-ignited old smouldering fires, but the entire crisis assumed depths and dimensions which made all previous experiences pale by comparison.

Polanyi located the origins of the world economic crisis in the scale of the human and societal destruction of the war: "The social fabric," he wrote, "could not sustain the forces of adjustment to a post-[First World War] equilibrium." According to pre-war growth rates, industrial production in Europe should have approximately doubled between 1913 and 1933. Instead it increased by only 60 percent. In 1933, it fell below 1914 levels. The political-sociological shock of the war implied that it would take many years to achieve equilibrium. However, the social framework could not be sustained unless political leaders could satisfy the expectations — and prevent the disappointments of — three major social claimants: bondholders, workers and peasants. "In the victorious countries, bondholder interests had priority. Their financial sacrifices had won the war; their faith in the stability of currencies and credit was the basis of the post war reconstruction of society." In the defeated countries the resources were insufficient to meet the claims of all three groups. Lacking reserves, they became increasingly indebted. With the re-establishment of the Gold Standard by the victorious powers, inflation and devaluation were impermissible and defeated countries had no other choice but to attempt to export themselves out of debt in conditions of declining prices.

Polanyi traced the geographical course of the crisis from the weaker peripheral countries of the East to the stronger economies of Western Europe and eventually the United States. The availability of cheap money in the United States from 1926 to mid-1928 flooded Europe with credits. When in July 1928 the New York Federal Reserve rate was raised from 3.5 to 5 percent to check a speculative stock market bubble, the supply of capital to Europe dried up. Loans were recalled. The pound sterling abandoned gold convertibility. Ten thousand American banks went bankrupt. The trend of universally falling world prices in the late 1920s was the prelude to the world crisis. Then came the credit crisis of 1931, the decline in world trade in 1932 and the collapse of currencies in 1933.

POLITICAL DESTABILIZATION BY CURRENCY CRISIS

In *The Great Transformation,* Polanyi described the stabilization programs implemented through the League of Nations in Geneva to restore currencies in Central and Eastern Europe:

> According to Geneva social organization had to be wholly subordinated to the restoration of the currency. Deflation was the primary need. Domestic institutions had to adjust as best they might. The deflationists" ideal came to be "free economy under a strong government" but while strong government meant what it said — namely emergency powers and suspension of public liberties — "free economy" meant in practice the opposite of what it said — namely government adjusted prices and wages. While the inflationary governments condemned by Geneva subordinated the stability of the currency to stability of employment and incomes, the deflationary governments put in power by Geneva used no fewer interventions in order to sub- ordinate the stability of incomes and employment to the stability of the currency. (Polanyi 1944 [2001]: 233)

"To liberal economists the gold standard was a purely economic institution: they refused even to consider it as a social mechanism" (20). Confidence in the credit worthiness of foreign borrowers rested on a system of fixed exchange rates and guaranteed convertibility. The value of outstanding liabilities greatly exceeded the capacity of the borrowing countries to service these debts, and eventually the whole structure of credits unravelled and collapsed. Polanyi commented: "Never in the history of modern capitalism has credit been so politicized" (Polanyi 1933). Comparisons with the politically motivated and politically negotiated rescue packages and Structural Adjustment Programs of the IMF in the 1980s and 1990s are too obvious to merit further comment.

Polanyi documented the universal faith in the capacity of the Gold Standard to deliver stability and normalcy, which must be understood against the background of the devastating inflations that ravaged national currencies in Central and Eastern Europe after the First World War. Middle-class savings were wiped out. Horrendous fortunes were made by speculators. "Currency has become the pivot of national politics" (Polanyi 1944 [2001]: 24), countries "literally starved themselves to reach the golden shores" (27).

> Vienna became the Mecca of liberal economists because of a brilliantly successful operation performed on Austria's Krona, which the patient unfortunately did not survive. In Bulgaria, Greece, Finland, Latvia, Lithuania, Estonia, Poland and Romania, the restoration of the currency provided counter-revolution with a claim to power. In

Belgium, France and England the Left was thrown out of office in the name of sound monetary standards. (25)

"There was hardly an internal crisis in Europe that did not reach its climax over an issue of external economy. Students of politics now grouped countries not according to continents but according to the degree of their adherence to a sound currency" (23). "Invariably the danger was to the currency, and with equal regularity the responsibility was fixed on inflated wages and unbalanced budgets" (229).

Eventually it all collapsed, ushering in the "great transformation." Germany, under National Socialism, re-inflated the economy by large public expenditures on war preparations and social programs. Labour was repressed and profitability restored to capital. Russia adopted five-year plans. Smaller countries of Europe abandoned the Gold Standard and partially closed their economies as international trade and investment collapsed. In the U.S., the New Deal measures instituted by President Roosevelt directly challenged entrenched financial interests by massive public expenditure on the employment of the unemployed in a variety of innovative programs.

ECONOMY AND DEMOCRACY

In a remarkable article, "Economy and Democracy," published in the *Oesterreichische Volkswirt* in December 1932, on the eve of the accession of Hitler to power, Polanyi described the impasse of Continental European politics in the inter-war years with the freshness of the contemporary observer. In the victorious Western countries, where rentier interests were favoured, Polanyi observed that Left-wing governments went down on the currency question: "In the defeated countries, it was democracy which went down to defeat under the combined pressures of the trauma of the war, the economic crisis … and the degeneration of party politics which diminished the authority of democracy." He added:

> In the name of economy and democracy the right and the left are feuding. The left is grounded in democracy, the right in the economy. The resultant disjuncture between economy and democracy is stretching the tensions of a catastrophic polarity. The world of political democracy gives rise to forces that intervene in the economy, disturb and constrain the economic process. In response, the economy mounts a general attack on democracy as the embodiment of irresponsible and unrealistic hostility to the world of business.

Labour entrenched itself in Parliament, where its numbers gave it weight. Capitalists built industry into a fortress from which to lord the country (Polanyi 1944 [2001]: 244). Polanyi's account of the indictment of the economy against democracy (and often against politicians) included responsibility for inflation, subsidization, protectionism, trade unionism, monetary management, costly and senseless support for individual enterprises, public assistance and rehabilitation of specific industrial sectors, excessively high wages and social expenditures. This reads like a list of macro-economic policy errors and "price distortions" ascribed by the IMF to "populist" governments which lack sufficient "political will" to implement structural reforms. *Plus ca change*! This indictment, as well as the "unrelenting decline in prices, production and consumption, and the mounting misery of mass unemployment were laid at the door of democracy.... Politics, political parties and Parliaments lost credibility. Democracy fell into disrepute. Broad strata of the masses, both right and left, turned against democracy" (Polanyi 1932).

> In many countries, where parliamentarism and democracy were recently established, as in Germany, Italy, Poland and most of Eastern Europe, economic interests deserted democracy and civil rights. In the post-war period the working classes manifested greater intellectual and moral resistance to dictatorships than did the bourgeoisie.

Polanyi reminds us that militant liberals — from Maucaulay to Mises, from Spencer to Sumner — expressed their conviction that popular democracy was a danger to capitalism (Polanyi 144 [2001]: 226). This suggests that current initiatives to bind nations and societies to supranational rules beyond reach of popular democratic political forces are an illustration of Polanyi's contention that democracy is incompatible with the "self regulating market" (now global). The term is perhaps misleading because, as he explained, laissez-faire is not a natural state of affairs, but rather an economic order which cannot function without institutions that safeguard the primacy of markets over all contesting priorities. More specifically, the capital market, because a liberal economy requires "absolute confidence in the continuity of titles to property" (242). This indeed was the central issue in the contest over the proposed Multilateral Agreement on Investment and the new regime for investment proposed under the auspices of the WTO and the Free Trade Agreement of the Americas. The globalization agenda *explicitly* seeks to subordinate popular democratic politics to the security of investor rights and property claims, now extended to trade in "services" and "trade related intellectual property."

THE GREAT TRANSFORMATION

As mentioned earlier in this volume, Polanyi located the ultimate cause of the rise of European Fascism in the inter-war years in the utopian attempt to subordinate society to the rule of the market. The birthplace of this revolutionary doctrine was nineteenth-century England. Like Marx, Polanyi recognized commodification of human and natural resources as a revolutionary innovation that released productive forces and created the untold wealth of the industrial civilization of the nineteenth century.

While Marx believed that capitalism would ultimately fail because of inherent economic contradictions, Polanyi's emphasis was on the social and ecological consequences of the commodification of people and nature. He posited that the growth and expansion of markets would inevitably encounter social contradictions and engender social and political measures and movements to defend society against the disintegrating forces of the market. This he called the "double movement." It is important to understand that this was not a self-correcting mechanism to moderate the excesses of capitalism but an existential contradiction between the requirements of a capitalist market economy for unlimited expansion and the requirements of people to live in mutually supportive relations in society. We note that the much quoted text at the bottom of the first page of *The Great Transformation* concerning the utopianism of the idea of the self-regulating market and its disastrous consequences is followed by: "Inevitably, society took measures to protect itself, but whatever measures it took impaired the self-regulating market, disorganized industrial life, and thus endangered society in yet another way."

It was Polanyi's contention that the market-system ("economy") is necessarily in perpetual conflict with popular forces in society ("democracy") and, in its purest form, cannot tolerate democratic intervention. In its purest form, it is fascism.

> The fascist solution to the impasse reached by liberal capitalism can be described as a reform of the market economy achieved at the price of the extirpation of all democratic institutions, both in the industrial and the political realms. The economic system which was in peril of disruption would thus be revitalized, while the people themselves were subjected to a re-education ... comprising the tenets of a political religion that denied the idea of the brotherhood of man in all its forms, achieved through an act of mass conversion, enforced against recalcitrants by scientific methods of torture. (245)

Is this not a fitting description of Pinochet's Chile, widely acclaimed as an economic success?

KEYNES AND THE DEFLATIONARY CLASS BIAS OF THE GOLD STANDARD

Keynes described the class war between rentier capital and the industrial working class of Britain in the 1920s — then the richest country in the world. The source of wealth of the rentier British leisure class — whose idyllic prewar lifestyle Keynes described in a much-quoted passage[2] — was their large holdings of foreign portfolio investments in bonds and equity. The financial anchor which protected the value of these assets was the stability of the

British currency, which had maintained a fixed and unchanging parity in terms of gold since 1818. Prior to 1914, Britain's formal and informal colonies of conquest and settlement, together with investments in the U.S. and Europe, yielded back flows of rentier income of as much as 10 percent of GDP. Between 1870 and 1914, British capital exports averaged 5 percent of GNP. This far surpasses rates of net foreign investment flows from any source country today. The entrenched social class structure of Britain was sustained and re-enforced by an export-oriented economy in which the contribution of wages to purchasing power in domestic markets was of little significance to the investing community. Wages were considered purely as costs, a view shared by the economics profession of the day.

After the First World War, the restoration of the pound at pre-war parity with gold became the priority objective of the Bank of England, acting on behalf of the interests of bondholders and the City of London as premier financial centre of the world. Although large back flows of interest, profit and other service exports were sufficient to cover about one-third of Britain's commodity import bill, export earnings were no longer running at levels that could sustain the volume of new purchases of Canadian and Latin American bonds, which British investors wanted to make to maintain and increase their rentier incomes. The (overvalued) pound was under pressure, and the Bank of England borrowed short on the New York money market to shore up unsustainable levels of long-term capital outflows. Either British investors would have to reduce foreign investment or the money wages of coal miners would have to be cut to regain the competitiveness of Britain's most important single export.

Keynes understood that what appeared to be a technical matter of a "moderate gap" between sterling at $4.40 and its pre-war parity of $4.86 was really a class conflict between workers and rentiers interested in protecting the value of their overseas investments by means of high interest rates (Keynes 1971a: 223). This had a twofold effect of attracting money from New York and imparting a deflationary bias to the domestic economy, resulting in levels of unemployment of 10 percent and more. The Bank of England and the Treasury decreed that exports be increased to sustain the value of the pound. Mine owners were encouraged to demand wage cuts and miners were told to "export or die." Economists lent their weight to these policies and maintained that British prosperity and reduction in unemployment depended on a reduction in money wages.

Keynes charged that these policies resulted in persistent unemployment and underutilized capacity in Britain's domestic industries. Wages in the export sector should not be forced down to accommodate the export of capital by rentiers. Investment should be directed to the home market by an easy credit policy. Keynes warned Mr Churchill, then Chancellor of the Exchequer:

> It will not be politically safe to admit that you are deliberately inten-
> sifying unemployment in order to reduce wages.…
>
> On grounds of social justice no case can be made out for reduc-
> ing the wages of the miners. They are the victims of the "economic
> juggernaut." They represent in the flesh the "fundamental adjust-
> ment" engineered by the Treasury and the Bank of England to
> satisfy the impatience of the city fathers to bridge the moderate gap
> between \$4.40 and \$4.86. (215, 223)

Automatic monetary adjustment by the rules of the Gold Standard favoured the propertied classes at the expense of the labouring classes: "The
gold standard with its dependence on pure automatic adjustment … is an
essential emblem for those who sit in the top tier of the machine" (224).

When miners refused to take wage cuts, they were locked out. The trade
unions called a general strike (1926), which frightened the capitalist class sufficiently that demands for further wage cuts were moderated. In defence of
the value of the pound, budgets were trimmed, adding an additional million
to the ranks of the unemployed. Well before the American stock market crash,
unemployment in Britain was close to three million and remained at that level
until the Second World War. The overvalued pound was defended by interest
rates too high in relation to expected returns in the domestic economy. The
result was an excess of savings over investment and an "underemployment
equilibrium." The only way the Bank of England could set a rate of interest
sufficiently low to allow a level of investment equal to what the community
wanted to save, while maintaining the value of the pound, was to subject
the economy to a crushing deflation. "This can only attain its end," Keynes
charged, "by intensifying unemployment without limit until the workers are
ready to accept the necessary reduction of wages under pressure of hard
fact" (229). By contrast, investors gained by deflation: lower prices benefited
the receivers of interest at the expense of the rest of the community. This
consequence of deflation, Keynes commented, "is deeply embedded in our
system of money contract" (229).

THE KEYNESIAN REVOLUTION IN ECONOMICS

In the 1920s, the academic establishment did not consider unemployment to
be a subject meriting their attention. They followed the master; Marshall had
devoted only two pages of his *Principles* to the subject. Professor Pigou, who
inherited Marshall's chair in economics, published *The Theory of Unemployment*
in 1933, in the depths of the depression. In this work, he concluded that
unemployment, beyond that which is frictional, was due to trade union collective bargaining and government interference in labour markets by minimum
wage legislation. Between 1932 and 1935, only three papers on the subject of
unemployment appeared in the *Economic Journal.* One of these was Professor

Cannan's Presidential Address to the Royal Economics Society, in which he concluded that "general unemployment appears when (workers) are asking too much ... [the world] should learn to submit to declines in money income without squealing" (Cannan 1997: 38). Lionel Robbins, who succeeded Professor Cannan's chair at London University, denied there had been any breakdown of the capitalist system: "It is not capitalism, it is interventionism and monetary uncertainty which are responsible for the persistence of the slump" (Routh 1989: 269). Readers may recognize the influence of the ideas of Friedrich von Hayek, who was brought from Vienna to the London School of Economics by Professor Robbins to combat the theories of Keynes and his Cambridge associates, believed to be dangerously inflationary by the City.

Keynes knew that policy advice, no matter how brilliantly argued, could be brushed aside so long as orthodox economic doctrines went unchallenged; to change the way the world thought about economic problems, he would have to invent a new paradigm. In the early 1930s, Keynes and a group of young academic colleagues set about the task of constructing an analytical model, which could show that a free market economy can reach equilibrium with underutilized capacity of capital and labour. The institutional stylized facts embodied in the model were inferred from observation of the realities of capitalist economies of the time. Underlying the model is pervasive uncertainty. Hence, the formulation of the trilogy of the consumption function, the demand for money and the marginal efficiency of capital, in terms of psychological propensities, attitudes and expectations. In the useful language introduced by the Scandinavians, all three of these variables are *"ex ante"* or "intended." None of them can be modelled exactly because all three embody uncertainty, which, unlike risk, is not subject to treatment by the calculus of probability.

Keynesian economics has been attacked for its lack of foundation in microeconomic utility theory. The charge is valid. Keynes departed from an individual to a group-centred conception of behaviour (the consumption function; the demand for money). Unlike the subjective concept of "utility," Keynes's analytical categories are subject to measurement and estimation — ex post. It was his genius to have invented intellectual constructs that captured important economic realities and provided a guide to policy-makers which has endured as a useful economic paradigm for the management of a modern mixed economy.[3]

Initially Keynes won more acceptance in the U.S., where a young genera- tion of New Deal economists embraced his teachings before they penetrated the more conservative British academic establishment. In England he gained the confidence of the Treasury as a practising technocrat and by his active participation in the management of British Second World War finance, de- tailed in *How to Pay for the War* (Keynes 1971a: 367). He was charged with the responsibility of negotiating the Bretton Woods Agreements with the United States on behalf of the government of the U.K.

THE END OF LAISSEZ-FAIRE: CURRENCY AND CREDIT CONTROLS

By 1944, Keynes had abandoned his earlier belief in laissez-faire. "Experience between the wars," he wrote, "clearly demonstrated the mischief of unregulated capital movements" (1944) and "it is widely held that control of capital movements, both inward and outward, should be a permanent feature of the post war system" (Keynes 1971b: 129). In *The End of Laissez-faire*, Keynes proposed the deliberate control of currency and credit by a central institution and social mechanisms of "coordinated intelligent judgement" to determine how much a community as a whole should save, how much savings should go abroad in the form of foreign investments and whether the capital market distributes savings into the most nationally productive channels (Keynes 1971a: 293). If these proposals sound radical today, it is only because the neoliberal counter-revolution has turned the clock back to the 1920s. Keynes challenged received economic doctrine of his day — and would surely contest the same (recycled) doctrines today. He rejected socialism as a feasible or desirable alternative to capitalism, but he also rejected laissez-faire as a realistic view of the existing capitalism of his day, or as a point of departure for the formulation of policy.

Keynes concluded that the post-Second World War international economic order must provide participating countries with policy space to maintain full employment. He advocated permanent capital controls. Keynes proposed an International Clearing Union with special purpose money akin to Special Drawing Rights (SDRs) whereby central banks would clear outstanding credit and debit balances. In order to prevent the kind of disequilibrium that currently prevails in the international economy, surplus countries would be penalized. The International Clearing Union — a kind of world central bank — was to be financed by the creation of a fund many times exceeding the resources of the International Monetary Fund, established at the Bretton Woods Conference. This fund was to be backed by real resources of commodities, including gold. Keynes's design of the Bretton Woods system would have assured countries access to medium-term finance to bridge temporary balance-of-payments shortfalls, without pressures to deflate by recessionary demand compression, as required by the rules of the Gold Standard. In the negotiations between Britain and the U.S., which eventuated in the establishment of the IMF, Keynes was at a severe disadvantage *vis-à-vis* his American counterpart because Britain was massively indebted to the U.S. and the latter was determined to dismantle the British preferential system and the sterling bloc. Although the U.S. dollar was the unrivalled top currency in the post-war international financial order, dollar convertibility to gold and national exchange controls of other major currencies provided an international monetary discipline which lasted until massive loss of gold reserves caused the United States to suspend gold convertibility in 1971. Since currencies were officially floated in 1973, the United States has been able to settle overseas commitments by dollar denominated credits. The outcome of dollar hegemony has been the thoroughly disordered international financial system which the original Keynes plan sought to prevent.

SOME INCOMPLETE NOTES ON A LARGER RESEARCH AGENDA

As the twentieth century recedes, watershed events emerge from the noise. The First World War, followed by the world economic crisis of 1931–33 definitively terminated the nineteenth-century liberal economic order. The attempt by the victorious powers to reconstruct it in the 1920s failed because none of the permissive conditions that had sustained economic liberalism in the long nineteenth century survived the political earthquakes that followed the war. Britain's long role as top metropole ended when the pound sterling was unlinked from gold in 1931. Within twenty years, its vast colonial empire in Asia and Africa was rolled back. A similar fate awaited the Dutch, the French and other European powers.

Following Keynes's advice to "study the past, in light of the present, for the purpose of the future" we compare Keynes's and Polanyi's analyses of the 1920s with the 1990s. Of course, the world has changed in many important respects. If there are similarities, there are also great differences. Future historians may consider the victory of the Western powers in the Cold War as a watershed event as important as 1914. It terminated the post-Second World War economic and political order.

For convenience we frame my comparison with a generalization of the four institutions which Polanyi identified as supporting the nineteenth-century economic order, now claimed as an earlier globalization: a hundred years peace in Europe sustained by the balance of power between rivalling major powers served the peace interest of international *haute finance;* the British pound sterling with unchanging gold value from 1818 and the City of London as premier financial centre of the world sustained the international Gold Standard, which secured the value of international investment; the self-regulating market and free trade were the ideal national economic institutions of the era; Polanyi's fourth institution was the constitutional state, which transferred political power from the *ancien régime* to the bourgeoisie — with franchise limited to the propertied classes, the state became the agent for the institutionalization of laissez-faire and the disembedding of the economy from society. Polanyi's discussion of the role of the state was largely confined to the national sphere. Naval and military supremacy and direct and indirect political colonialism assured the security of rentier incomes in overseas investments.

The Geopolitical Order

Shortly before the defeat of the axis powers in the Second World War, the foundations of the post-war political order were laid by Roosevelt, Churchill and Stalin at Yalta. The veto accorded to the five permanent members of the Security Council of the United Nations secured the territorial division of Europe between the Western powers and the Soviet Union, sustained by the mutually assured destructive capacity of the two nuclear superpowers. The contest between communist and capitalist powers was played out in major military conflicts in Korea and Indochina and scores of smaller wars in Africa, Latin America and Central Asia. Nuclear weapons, however, were never used again after Hiroshima and Nagasaki.

A closer examination of the geopolitical landscape emerging from the collapse of the Soviet Union reveals profound and multidimensional political instability. The landmarks of the Cold War have vanished. The ultimate consequences of the humiliation and impoverishment of Russia — intended or unintended — are as yet unknown. Historic fault lines associated with great power rivalry for control over the Balkans and the former regions of the Ottoman Empire have reopened. The collapse of the Soviet Empire has contributed to resurgent nationalisms and solidarities based on ethnic and religious identities.

The proximate origin of the Jihadist fundamentalism that has attacked the U.S., its allies and the regimes it supports in the Middle East is to be found in the arming and training of thousands of Islamic fighters in the Cold War cause of resisting Soviet occupation of Afghanistan. The inability of the E.U. to settle the first military engagement on the European Continent since the end of the Second World War, in the former Yugoslavia, followed by fundamental disagreement between Britain and other European countries that supported the war in Iraq, and France, Germany and others that did not, revealed the absence of consensus regarding a common policy on European security.

The fiscal burden of the reunification of Germany seriously compromised the principal engine of European growth. Pressures to roll back gains made by labour and the introduction of economic reforms to sustain external competitiveness have met with popular opposition, a manifestation of Polanyi's double movement. An ideological divide led by Britain is opening a rift in the Keynesian compromise that sustained the success of the European project for forty years.

Unlike the early post-war years, when American economic and financial power was unrivalled, the capitalist world economy now rests on a multipolar base, with Europe, Japan and the emerging economic powers of China, India and the tiger economies of Asia greatly exceeding the U.S. in productive capacity. Although the military expenditures of the U.S. now exceed the combined expenditures of the next ten powers, their declared aim of achieving global military dominance is dangerously unrealistic; they have been unable to secure the occupation of two relatively small countries, Afghanistan and Iraq.

The unilateralist position of the George W. Bush administration constituted a break with previous U.S. administrations, democratic or republican. It is difficult to conceive how these policies can serve the interests of American security or indeed of American capitalism.

There is little evidence that international political institutions now have the capacity to negotiate realistic political solutions, which take into account the legitimate interests of peoples and states. All the multilateral institutions are now in crisis, including the Security Council and other institutions of the United Nations. The globalization project requires a peaceful and stable international political order. In the circumstances described above, the continued liberalization of international economic relations is problematic. So perhaps also is the future of U.S. hegemony.

The International Financial Order

The essence of the Gold Standard was its automaticity in bringing external payments of nations into balance and its class bias protecting the value of property incomes and assets from depreciation by inflation. As Polanyi noted, a social mechanism protected rentier incomes while shifting the risk inherent in a capitalist market economy onto the productive classes of workers, peasants and entrepreneurs. At the international level, as Keynes explained, the burden of adjustment to disequilibria, whether caused by business cycles, deteriorating terms of trade or other economic shocks, fell exclusively on debtor countries. How, we may ask, could this inequitable system survive for so long? How could the pound sterling maintain a fixed gold value for a hundred years? How could the rentier leisure classes of Britain sustain their comfortable lifestyle while engaging in ever increasing overseas investments amounting to 6–7 percent of GNP by 1914? In brief, because the domestic franchise was limited to propertied classes, while debt service on portfolio investment was guaranteed by colonial and quasi-colonial governments.

The international financial institutions negotiated by Britain and the U.S. at Bretton Woods replaced the Gold Standard by a modified version of the Keynes plan, created to facilitate adjustment of member national economies to temporary balance-of-payments disequilibria. Conditionalities were minimal. Capital controls, enshrined in article VI of the constitution of the IMF, were the norm and central banks had exclusive rights to trade in currencies. The U.S. emerged from the Second World War as the hegemonic capitalist power and the major source of international finance and investment. Currencies were pegged to the dollar, which was convertible to gold until 1971. Gently rising prices favoured growth of the real economy. Historically unprecedented rates of economic growth in developed and developing countries were sustained for thirty years. World trade grew faster than world output but national finance served its economic role of channelling savings into investment in the expansion of real productive capacity.

When the dollar was freed of the discipline of gold convertibility, an explosion of international liquidity fuelled inflationary pressures. Floating exchange rates and the progressive unleashing of capital from national control favoured labour in the industrial world and sovereign borrowers in the developing world, as real interest rates were low, sometimes negative. To restore profitability of capital a disinflationary shock in the form of hardline monetarism was administered in 1979/80. This crashed the economies of indebted Latin American and other middle-income developing countries. Economies were restructured to reduce domestic absorption and increase export earnings to service unpayable mountains of debt.

For the next two decades, the interests of investors were sustained by enormously complex arrangements devised by multilateral financial institutions employing many thousands of highly paid professional staff to negotiate Structural Adjustment Programs and supervise the design of national budgets in scores of developing countries. Less efficiently and less completely, the effect has been to replicate the discipline of the Gold Standard, with no automaticity and a great deal of planning. We are reminded of Polanyi's much quoted dictum that "laissez-faire" was "indeed planned."

In the 1990s, finance, not trade, has determined exchange rates.[4] While devaluations were initially forced on developing countries to shift internal resources from non-tradable to export sectors and balance external payments, in the 1990s exposure of pension and mutual funds to exchange rate loss in emerging markets encouraged fixed exchange rates. To defend currencies from speculative attack, ensure convertibility and prevent precipitous devaluations, central banks have been obliged to hold large reserves. In the absence of exchange controls, capital flight inevitably results in depletion of reserves and impoverishment of debtor countries. From the Mexican crisis of 1994 to the Asian crisis of 1997, the magnitude of IMF-negotiated bailout packages to rescue foreign investors became ever larger.

By 1998, there were serious fears of a possible global financial meltdown. The whole dismal experience, including ever-increasing bailouts revealed the absence of an effective international financial institution capable of dealing with such an eventuality. Senior Fund officials, who argued the case for the IMF as a "lender of last resort" for the international monetary system, were ridiculed by Treasury officials. Only the U.S., they were told, has the power to create internationally acceptable reserve currency, and such replenishments require authorization of Congress.

From this point forward, the disequilibrium in the international financial order has greatly increased. Abandoning all pretence of fiscal discipline, a surplus of $200 billion in 1999 was turned into rapidly increasing annual deficits exceeding 5 percent of GDP in 2003. Approximately 45 percent of U.S. Treasury bonds of the huge federal fiscal deficit was financed by foreign capital. The world's strongest economy has become the world's largest debtor.

Excess private and public consumption, including military expenditures, are financed by the transfer of real resources from capital-exporting surplus countries and debt-burdened deficit countries. In effect, China and the rest of the world are financing the capacity of U.S. consumers to purchase their exports by depositing reserves in low-yielding U.S. government securities. This whole unstable structure now rests on the continued confidence in the value of the U.S. dollar and its continuing role as the world's leading reserve currency. In these conditions, how long can confidence in the U.S. dollar hold up? A question posed with increasing frequency. The outcome of dollar hegemony has been the thoroughly disordered international financial system, which the original Keynes plan sought to prevent.

The Self-Regulating Market on a Global Scale

In Polanyi's schema, the self-regulating market was a national economic institution moderated by social counter movements. Financial capital and populations moved freely across national borders. Production facilities were generally domestically owned. The large export of portfolio capital financed private and public infrastructure. The value of interest and profits was secured by government guarantees and the rules of the Gold Standard and financed one-third of Britain's commodity import bill before 1914. Millions of peasants displaced by agrarian capitalism migrated to "empty continents" and assured the supply of food and agricultural raw materials by extending the land resource available to the metropole.

By contrast, the U.S. pioneered the modern corporation and the culture of consumerism within its vast domestic market, subsequently extended to foreign countries by the establishment of production facilities abroad. After the Second World War, Foreign Direct Investment (FDI) became the principal form of private long-term capital, accompanied by official development assistance for economic infrastructure. Whereas U.S. FDI made important contributions of capital, technology and market access in the first three post-war decades, in the 1980s and especially in the 1990s, FDI increasingly assumed the form of mergers and acquisitions of private and public assets. The foreign sales of subsidiaries and affiliates of U.S. corporations have long exceeded U.S. exports of goods and services. Transnational corporations have become increasingly powerful and influential in the formulation of public policy. They financed the think-tanks and universities that, as mentioned earlier in this text, furnished the political directorates of the OECD with the neoliberal policy agenda of globalization.

The globalization project is nothing less than the attempted recreation of the nineteenth-century liberal economic order on a global scale. To assure the "self-regulating" nature of the system required more than a golden straightjacket. It required new international political and economic institutions to protect the property rights of investors from the exercise of sovereignty by national governments. According to the World Bank: "One effect of globalization is to expand the options available to private individuals and firms while reducing those of policymakers" (1995b: 5).

The failure of socialism and the collapse of the Soviet Union encouraged the illusion that globalization was, whether desirable or not, unavoidable. In 1994, the General Agreement on Tariffs and Trade (GATT) was transformed into the WTO. Its mandate was not confined to the arbitration of trade disputes but included provisions intended to bind countries to agreement on so-called trade related issues such as intellectual property rights. In the same year, the U.S. proposed the establishment of a Free Trade Area of the Americas, which went far beyond free trade issues to secure investor rights. The FTAA was intended to extend the NAFTA of 1994 to embrace the entire continent.

In 1995, the OECD-initiated Multilateral Agreement on Investment to guarantee national status to foreign investors, was aborted in the face of popular opposition mobilized by NGOs. Also in 1995, the Mexican economy collapsed. In 1997, the East Asian Crisis threatened to derail the globalization agenda. In 1999, mass protests at the Seattle meetings of the WTO stalled progress and reverberated around the world. At Cancun in 2003, the Global South blocked progress on the contentious "Singapore issues." By 2005, all that remained of the FTAA was a Free Trade Agreement with the small countries of Central America. It has been the greatest fear of the international financial community and the large transnational corporations that social and political costs of crises will cause countries to abandon "globalization." Hence, the exclamation of relief by Stanley Fischer, Deputy Director of the IMF, commenting on the Asian Crisis of 1997, that globalization had survived its first crisis (1999).

Since the 1980s and 1990s, a predatory form of Anglo-American "shareholder" capitalism has uprooted socially "embedded" mixed economies. The social, cultural and natural environment has increasingly been invaded, degraded and subordinated to criteria of private profitability. Objectives of full employment and social security in the industrial world have been replaced by the overriding objective of competitiveness in external markets. National institutions and standards that have protected vulnerable sectors and provided comprehensive systems of social security are being sacrificed. In the developing world, policies of national economic planning and national industrial development, which enabled East Asian and some other countries to build a strong industrial base for domestic and export markets have become problematic due to commitments to bilateral and multilateral institutions, including the World Trade Organization.

Late twentieth-century globalization has created a world more uniform in economic institutions — but immensely more inequitable.[5] Capital is globally mobile — while immigration of labour to rich countries is highly restricted. Poor people in poor countries are not required as producers or consumers.

They are "excess population," a source of potential political instability and a threat to the security of foreign investments. A distinguished Canadian of an older generation has no inhibitions in expressing his fear that global corporate power is tending toward fascism. I quote from "Remembering" by Eric Kierans and Alter Stewart, past president of the Montreal Stock Exchange, minister in Quebec provincial and Canadian federal governments, McGill university professor and erstwhile colleague:

> We are not born to live in a corporate world, yet that is the world we are moving toward. We have created a society in which so much of the world's riches are accumulated in so few hands — a curve that grows steeper every year — that we are headed for fascism or chaos. Either the few will control the many by force of arms — the example of old South Africa springs to mind — or the mob will rule. When people have nothing to lose as more and more of them are plunged into poverty for the enrichment of others they must either subside or rebel; and there is an end to community, responsibility and society. (Kierans and Stewart 2001: 253)

Capitalism and Democracy

Perhaps the most current legacy of Polanyi pertains to the conflict between economy and democracy. The nineteenth century constitutional state was the instrument used by the bourgeoisie to institute a laissez-faire capitalist market economy in England, unencumbered by popular franchise or trade unions (Eichengreen 1996: 195). As representative government was extended to the adult population, the state became an arena of contest between economy and democracy, between the requirements of the capitalist economic order and the social and political demands of citizens.

After the Second World War, full employment and social security tipped the balance of political power toward labour. In the 1980s, capital regained control over public policy. Since that time, deregulation of trade and capital markets has subordinated living standards of citizens to the property rights of investors.

When measures affecting the livelihood of people are locked into supra-national agreements, enforced by punishing penalties, there is effectively no democracy. In Hirschman's unforgettable words, "exit trumps voice." Property rights of holders of paper claims (investors) prevail over Parliaments, where they exist. Constitutions are regularly suspended or re-written by creditor-driven stabilization programs. Multilateral institutions have become instruments for the imposition of economic imperialism.

In the schema of Rodrik's "political trilemma," in the absence of world government, deep economic integration is incompatible with democratic governance (1999: 1). Democracy, whether at a local, sub-regional or national level, operates in public social space. Although there are global social movements, the nation state remains the principal political arena of democratic contestation.

UNIVERSAL CAPITALISM OR REGIONAL PLANNING?

In an article of the same title published in 1945, Polanyi expressed confidence that the post-war order would subordinate economics to social objectives. Only the United States, Polanyi wrote, believed in "universal capitalism" (1945). In the 1940s, it was widely held that capitalism was discredited by the disasters of the 1930s, "within the nations we are witnessing a development under which the economic system ceases to lay down the law to society, and the primacy of society over that system is secured" (Polanyi 1944 [2001]: 259). He envisaged a regionalized world of coexistence of different economic and social systems linked by negotiated and managed trade.

Polanyi was wrong in his prediction that universal capitalism was a dead doctrine, but his vision of the coexistence of regional economies with different and diverse economic institutions linked by flows of trade, knowledge and people has new relevance for the world today. Serious crises in excessively open and export dependent economies are likely to redirect attention to domestic markets, not on a national but on a larger regional scale. China and India are perhaps the only countries that have the cultural and historic coherence and population size to undertake economic development based on production for the satisfaction of the basic needs of people. This is not an argument for autarky but for the exercise of sovereignty over economic and social policy. In Latin America, a new generation of populist political leaders is responding to a profound disillusion with neoliberal policies. Similar currents are stirring in Africa. The common struggle against entrenchment of property rights in the WTO has forged political and economic links between major regions of the Global South. Given the severe imbalance of power between the developed and the developing world, it is difficult to imagine that a multilateral financial and economic order would not be biased to favour the rich and the mighty. Regional formations would have to furnish themselves with financial institutions to complement the management of external trade and investment.

In this context, the original Keynes plan for a world clearing union, endowed with special purpose money, which could coordinate economic transactions in a multipolar world of regional economies with widely different economic and political institutions, merits re-examination. Keynes was a liberal; Polanyi was a socialist. However, Polanyi's definition of socialism as "the tendency inherent in an industrial civilization to transcend the self-regulating market by consciously subordinating it to a democratic society" is broad enough to embrace political liberalism, social democracy and a variety of associational forms of democratic socialism (Polanyi 1944 [2001]: 242).

NOTES

1. For the period 1986–1995, average growth of GDP in the major advanced economies was 2.7percent and 2.6 percent for 1996–2005. Corresponding rates for Newly Industrialized Asian economies are 8.1percent and 4.3 percent (IMF website).
2. Keynes described life in pre-1914 England, where "internationalization was nearly complete in practice," as an "El Dorado" in which "the inhabitant of London could order by telephone, while sipping his tea in bed, the products of the whole earth, by the same means venture his wealth in the natural resources and new enterprises of any quarter of the world, and share, without exertion, or even trouble, in their prospective fruits" (Keynes 1971a: 11).
3. In 1935, he wrote to George Bernard Shaw: "I believe myself to be writing a book which will largely revolutionize — not I suppose at once, but in the course of the next ten years — the way the world thinks about economic problems" (Skidelsky 1992: 520).
4. The value of total derivatives trading ($5.7 trillion a day) combined with daily turnover in the foreign exchange market ($1.9 trillion) gives us a figure of $7.6 trillion/day for 2003, a figure larger than the annual value of global merchandise exports for the same year (Bank for International Settlements, April 2004). "In the late nineteenth century, there was less than one cent's worth of mergers and acquisitions for every one dollar of 'real' investment. Fast forward another hundred years, and for every one dollar of 'real' investment there were over two dollars put into mergers. In other words, over the entire period, mergers have grown roughly 300 times faster than 'real' investment" (Nitzan and Bichler 2004: 38).
5. From 1960 to 1970 the increase of the ratio of the highest 20 percent to the lowest 20 percent of holders of income was minimal (30:1 in 1960 to 32:1 in 1970), by 1980 the ratio had increased to 45:1, by 1989, 59:1, and by 1997 it had risen to 74:1 (UNDP 1999).

6. LEADING CONCEPTS IN THE WORK OF KARL POLANYI AND THEIR CONTEMPORARY RELEVANCE

When my father was teaching a course on general economic history at Columbia University in the 1950s, he was engaged in research on economic life in primitive and archaic societies. At the time I could not understand his preoccupation with the trade of the Trobriand islanders or interpretations of Babylonian scripts. It all seemed to me so far removed from the problems of our times. Only years later did I appreciate that his research in economic anthropology was motivated by the determination to prove that nineteenth-century market economy was unique. Recall his oft-repeated statement: "Never before in human history has the principle of gain been elevated to the organizing principle of economic life" (Polanyi 1947 [1968]: 43). His extensive research into non-market exchange in primitive and archaic societies challenged the preconceptions of anthropologists and historians who imposed on pre-capitalist societies concepts of scarcity and price-making markets derived from the claims of economics to universal validity.

To rid the study of economics of what he once called "our obsolete market mentality," he posited three general patterns of integration of economic activity: reciprocity, redistribution and exchange. These patterns were universal in the sense that they could be found in all systems of the organization of economic life, including contemporary market economy. Polanyi's approach was comparative. There was in his work no suggestion of progress or any implication that modern societies are more advanced or more developed than those of the past. I think this is why he questioned the concept of development.

His rejection of development did not reflect indifference to the emerging nations of post-colonial Asia and Africa. On the contrary, it was his hope that his warning of the destructive effects of subordinating society to the requirements of the market economy could save humanity from disasters more profound than anything experienced to date. In a letter to a friend of his youth, Beatrice De Waard, in 1958, six years before his death, he wrote:

> My life was a world life — I lived the life of the world. But the

world stopped living for several decades, and then in a few years it advanced a century! So I am only now coming into my own, having somewhere lost 30 years on the way — waiting for Godot — until the world caught up again, caught up to me. In retrospect, it is all quite strange, the martyrdom of isolation was only apparent — ultimately, I was only waiting for myself. Now the scales are weighed against us — against you, against me — because in ten years, I would stand vindicated in my own lifetime. My work is for Asia and Africa, for the new peoples. The West should bring them spiritual and intellectual assistance; instead the west is destroying the tradition of the nineteenth century and is even demolishing its Victorian ideals.... My ideas at last are drawing opposition and that is a good sign, I would dearly love to live to fight for them, but man is a mortal being.[1]

Fifty years had to pass before the originality of Karl Polanyi would emerge from relative obscurity to be embraced in so many quarters as a definitive critique of the fateful effects of the subordination of society to economic market criteria. Not until the Asian Crisis of 1997 and disasters of instant market capitalism in Russia would his work be cited in thousands of speeches, papers, articles and policy statements.

Many authors have provided excellent expositions of the principal thesis of *The Great Transformation* (1944) and its relevance to contemporary globalization. But none might give him more satisfaction, given his wish to engage the intellectual adversary, than to be identified as the most effective critic of the neoliberal project for the twenty-first century by a senior fellow at the Cato Institute, a leading Right-wing think-tank.

> He has emerged in recent years as a kind of patron saint of globalisation's critics. George Soros notes his intellectual debt in his acknowledgments at the beginning of *The Crisis of Global Capitalism*. Dani Rodrik, of Harvard University and author of *Has Globalisation Gone Too Far?* refers to him frequently. John Gray, a professor at the London School of Economics who wrote *False Dawn: The Delusions of Global Capitalism*, titled his first chapter "From the Great Transformation to the Global Free Market." These arguments are an almost perfect inversion of the truth. The tragedies of the 20th century stemmed, not from an over-reliance on markets, but from a pervasive loss of faith in them. (Lindsey 2001)

Without doubt, Polanyi's critique of the nineteenth-century market economy and its fateful consequences resonate most strongly with critics of globalization. *The Great Transformation* is the best known of Polanyi's works, now translated into some twenty languages. The basic insights germinated during formative years in Hungary and journalistic experience in Vienna. Ten years of teaching and research at Columbia University, from 1947 to 1957, provided the opportunity to extend his historical research on economic livelihood back to archaic and primitive societies. There was a constant theme in his world of thought. It was his insistence that there are no impersonal forces, which absolve us from personal responsibility for the fate of fellow human beings. Ideas matter, when people cease to believe in the legitimacy of the powerful, their power is in decline.

A WORLD LIFE

Polanyi's life was indeed a "world life" marked by three emigrations. He was born in 1886, in Vienna, but the family moved to Budapest shortly thereafter, and his formative years were Hungarian. He grew up in a comfortable upper-middle-class family. His father was a civil engineer and a successful railway contractor until a prolonged season of bad weather ruined the business and the family descended into genteel poverty. His mother, daughter of a rabbinical scholar from Vilna, then in Russia, was known for her role in hosting gatherings of Budapest's literary, artistic and intellectual elite. The Polanyi children received a superb home education, including instruction in Latin and Greek, English, French and German. Karl graduated from the University of Budapest in 1912 with a doctorate of law, the only university qualification he ever had. He was prominent in Hungarian intellectual life as the founding president of the Galilee Circle, a student movement, which undertook educational activities on a remarkable scale of 2000 classes per year. The ideology was one of Western Enlightenment, opposed to obscurantism, clericalism and the moribund political order of the Hungarian monarchy.[2]

He was twenty-eight in 1914 when he enlisted in the Austro-Hungarian army as a cavalry officer and served on the Russian front. He was hospitalized and in 1919 he emigrated to Vienna, where he was soon followed by a large exodus of Hungarians fleeing the White Terror.[3] Among them was Ilona Duczynska; they were married in 1923. The Russian Revolution of 1917 was fighting for its existence in a prolonged civil war. Polanyi joined the wide-ranging debate on how a socialist economy could be constructed. It was in this context that he studied the works of the leading exponents of the Austrian School of Economics. For many years he struggled to construct a socialist economic model, which would combine economic criteria of technical efficiency with social and cultural requirements and democratic decision-making. Eventually, he abandoned this exercise and found in history and anthropology a more effective means of developing insights regarding the place of the economy in society. He remained to the end of his life a socialist.

From 1924 until he left for England in 1933, Polanyi was a senior member of the editorial staff of *Oesterreichische Volkswirt*, specializing in international affairs. Kari joined him in 1934. Ilona remained to engage in the struggles of the illegal opposition to Austrian fascism until 1936, when she also came to England (Duczynska 1978).

In his initial years in England he was associated with a small group of intellectuals and religious leaders who called themselves the Christian Left. He contributed an essay titled "The Essence of Fascism" and co-edited *Christianity and the Social Revolution* (1935). Among other contributors was Joseph P. Needham.[4] To this group he brought a continental perspective and introduced them to Karl Marx's *The Economic and Philosophic Manuscripts of 1844*.[5] In 1937, recommendations by R.H. Tawney and G.D.H. Cole assisted him in obtaining employment as a tutor with the Workers' Education Association, teaching courses on international relations and English social and economic history in small provincial towns. At this time he contributed articles on current affairs to various Left and liberal publications. Although *The Great Transformation* was written at Bennington College, Vermont, from 1940 to 1943, it was in England that he found the origins of the disasters that befell Europe from 1914 to 1945.

From 1947 to his retirement in 1953, Polanyi taught a course in general economic history as a visiting professor at Columbia University, and from 1953 to 1957, he co-directed an interdisciplinary research project with Conrad Arensberg on economic aspects of institutional growth. The results of this research were published as *Trade and Market in Early Empire, Economies in History and Theory* (1957). Several of his graduate students contributed to the volume, among others, Anne Chapman, who invited me to this conference. *Dahomey and the Slave Trade*, with an introduction by Paul Bohannan, was published posthumously with the assistance of Abraham Rotstein in 1966. A former student, George Dalton, produced the useful collection of essays by Karl Polanyi, *Primitive, Archaic and Modern Economies* (1968), and Harry Pearson edited a posthumous volume of Polanyi's writings, *The Livelihood of Man* (1977).

In 1950, the Polanyis made their home in Canada, in Pickering, Ontario, because Ilona was barred from entering the United States on the grounds of former communist activities in Hungary (1917 to 1920) and in Austria (1934 to 1936). Both my parents died in Canada and now rest in a cemetery in Budapest.

The most frequently cited biographical source on the life of Karl Polanyi is a chapter in Peter F. Drucker's memoirs called "The Polanyis" (1978: 123–40).[6] In this highly entertaining exercise in imagined recollections of his friend Karl and other members of the family, almost none of the facts are correct; indeed some are manifestly absurd. Drucker was perceptive in noting that the Polanyis sought "a new society that would be free and yet not "bourgeois" or "liberal"; prosperous and yet not dominated by economics; communal and yet not a Marxist collectivism." But he could not have been more wrong in dismissing Karl Polanyi as a "minor figure" whose "failure

… signifies the futility of the quest for … the perfect — or at least the good — society," or his research on economic organization of past civilizations as a retreat "into academic busyness" (138).

POLANYI ON THE GREAT TRANSFORMATION

Polanyi's thesis was that the economic and social upheavals and political tensions resulting from the utopian attempt to restore the nineteenth-century liberal economic order, including the Gold Standard, after the First World War were the essential cause of the world economic crisis and of the demise of democracy in most of the states of Continental Europe in the 1930s. Like Keynes, he understood that the Gold Standard was a social mechanism designed to restructure the domestic economies of debtor countries in the interest of rentier financiers. His account of the vulnerability of the small and weak peripheral states of Central and East Europe to a pull on the "golden thread" reads like a preview of IMF stabilization programs. In the succession states of Central Europe international creditors instituted regimes of external supervision under the auspices of the League of Nations operating from Geneva. The League of Nations employed no more than a few hundred people. Today, the IMF and World Bank employ many thousands of highly paid professionals and consultants to institute a long list of macro and micro economic measures designed to impose balanced budgets and "free markets" on indebted developing countries. *Plus ca change.*

In describing the role of international finance in restoring Rightist regimes in Europe, Polanyi noted:

> In Belgium, France, and England the left was thrown out of office in the name of sound monetary standards. An almost unbroken sequence of currency crises linked indigent Balkans with the affluent United States through the elastic band of the international credit system which transmitted the strains of the imperfectly restored currencies first from Eastern to Western Europe, and then from Western Europe to the United States. (Polanyi 1944 [2001]: 23–4)

Europe leaped from crisis to crisis until an unsustainable pyramid of debt collapsed in 1931. National fascisms, Soviet five-year planning and the New Deal were protective reactions to save societies from economic and social collapse.

FICTITIOUS COMMODITIES

Contrary to a commonly held belief, there was nothing natural or inevitable about the nineteenth-century market system. As Polanyi demonstrated, laissez-faire liberalism was designed by the early English political economists and instituted by the power of the state. In a frequently quoted passage, Polanyi concluded that "laissez-faire was planned" while the protective reaction against the discipline of the market was "spontaneous" (Polanyi 1944 [2001]: 147). The extension of price-making markets to embrace the fictitious commodities of land, labour and money was an innovation more revolutionary than the mechanical inventions of early industrial capitalism. Land, labour and money are "fictitious" commodities because unlike true commodities they are not produced for sale. Natural resources including land are God-given; people do not have children to provide workers for the labour market; and money is a social convention. While commodity money has been used as currency, modern money is essentially a bookkeeping entry validated by the sanctity of contract and codified in law. Historically, money was the first to be liberated from regulation prohibiting usury, for centuries deemed sinful by Christian doctrine.

The divorce of agricultural producers from their means of subsistence by the privatization (enclosure) of communal lands created a new underclass of vagabonds and paupers. The threat to social stability was countered by measures of poor relief and wage subsidy. The critical step in the creation of an industrial proletariat in nineteenth-century England was the abolition of poor relief by the draconian New Poor Law of 1834, which gave legal sanction to the degradation of wage labour. It was instituted by the reform Parliament of 1832, which subordinated the landed oligarchy to the urban and industrial bourgeoisie. The majority of the population had no voice and no vote. Trade unions were outlawed.

The result was the unleashing of productive forces and the accumulation of capital. But wages failed to rise above subsistence until the second half of the nineteenth century. The classical economists were concerned with capital accumulation, economic growth and the distribution of incomes from production. They largely ignored the dispossession, displacement and human degradation by the destruction of social relations in which economic livelihood, social status, pride in craft and cultural expression had previously been embedded.

Polanyi insisted that the creation of a self-regulating market by the commodification of land, labour and money required nothing less than the subordination of society to the requirements of the market economy. His central thesis was that the nineteenth-century liberal economic order was "economic" in a different sense from that in which all societies have been limited by the material conditions of existence. It was "economic" in the distinctive sense that it chose to base itself on a motive never before raised to the level of justification of action and behaviour in everyday life, namely individual gain (Polanyi 1944 [2001]: 30). Prior to the rise of industrial capitalism, markets were never more than accessories of economic life. In that regard, the generalized market economy of modern capitalism stands as an exception. As "improvement" (read "efficiency") conquered "habitat" (read "security") and labour, land, money and the essentials of life became commodified, the economy acquired an existence of its own driven by "economic" laws of its own, whether conceived in neoclassical or Marxist terms.

THE DOUBLE MOVEMENT

Regarding the creation of the self-regulating market, Polanyi warned, in a frequently cited passage:

> Such an institution could not exist for any length of time without annihilating the human and natural substance of society; it would have physically destroyed man and transformed his surroundings into a wilderness. Inevitably, society took measures to protect itself, but whatever measures it took impaired the self-regulation of the market, disorganized industrial life and thus endangered society in yet another way. (Polanyi 1944 [2001]: 3)

The reference here is to the "double movement" of the explosive spread of market economy and checks to its expansion by protective civic, social and national movements. Polanyi interpreted legislation regarding public health, factory conditions, social insurance, public utilities, municipal services and trade union rights in Victorian England as countervailing measures to check the societal effects of the unfettered expansion of capital. He noted that on the Continent, governments of widely different political complexions enacted similar measures, including protection of industries and agriculture threatened by ruinous competition. These measures were instituted by state interventions at the national level. Following the First World War, social conflicts arising from draconian financial requirements to conform to the rules of the Gold Standard could not be mediated by the democratic process and resulted in the rise of authoritarian and fascist regimes in most of Continental Europe. It must be understood that Polanyi's "double movement" is not a self-correcting mechanism to moderate excesses of market fundamentalism but an existential contradiction between the requirements of a capitalist market economy for unlimited expansion and the requirements of people to live in mutually supportive relations in society.

When the world emerged from the Second World War to construct the international institutions which framed the post-war era, it was generally accepted that the market economy would have to serve national objectives of full employment and social security. Polanyi foresaw a world of regional blocs of diverse social economic systems. The tide, it appeared, had turned against the unrestricted domination of the economy by capital. Social control was restored over the economy. This was the "great transformation" that closed the book on the economic liberalism of the English classical political economists. The Bretton Woods international financial order permitted policy space for industrial countries to pursue full employment and social security financed by redistributive fiscal arrangements. Developing countries were able to engage in import substituting industrialization and long-term economic planning.

As Polanyi reminds us, however, the measures taken by society to protect itself could impair the functioning of the market and set in motion a counter-attack by capital to free itself from social constraints. This indeed is what has been happening since the crisis of the 1970s, when declining productivity and profits, low or negative real interest rates favouring debtors and a wave of political radicalism in the South unleashed a neoliberal counter-revolution.

The liberalization of trade and capital in the last quarter of the twentieth century has once again freed capital from regulation — now on a global scale. The dictates of financial capital are again governing markets. Combined with the predominance of transnational corporations, the democratic political process in national societies is undermined and corrupted. Provisions of the World Trade Organization regarding investment, competition, government procurement and intellectual property are specifically designed to bind states to supranational agreements to protect investors from legislation at the national level. Inequality has escalated to unprecedented levels but there are no international institutions to moderate the polarizing effects of the liberalization of capital. Fiscal resources that sustained the welfare state in the industrialized countries are eroding. Indebted developing countries are in the grip of conditionalities which do not permit them to follow strategies of economic development that proved successful in the past.

A prolonged period of relative economic stability and strong economic growth in Europe and North America encouraged a reading of Polanyi's "double movement" as a kind of self-correcting mechanism. Such illusions were shattered in the 1990s. The surge of portfolio capital seeking high returns and capital gains in emerging markets of Asia and Latin America precipitated a series of severe financial and economic crises — most dramatically in the high growth economies of East Asia. The lessons of *The Great Transformation* were recovered and Polanyi emerged from relative obscurity to feature in academic discourse and journalistic comment.

THE DISEMBEDDED ECONOMY

Instability, insecurity and serious financial crises associated with globalization have led scholars and policy-makers, including the World Bank, to embrace institutional reform and good governance. The "embedded economy" has gained currency in policy discourse, and in this connection Polanyi is frequently cited. The assumption here is that corruption is uniquely attributable to politicians and that countries would benefit from the introduction of Western political institutions and practices, and that empowerment of civil society could substitute for the traditional role of the state. In reality, the rolling back of the state has *dis*-empowered civil society. The reduction of public provisions of health and education has impoverished people, and agglomerations of private economic power, including mercenaries, have undermined public authority and the rule of law. The result has been to diminish the capacity of societies to determine the allocation of their own resources. As never before, the economic livelihood of people is beyond national control instanced by financial crises triggered by footloose capital, the relocation of production facilities to cheaper sources of labour and the destruction of domestic food production by liberalized imports. In this regard, globalization has *dis*-embedded economic life on an international scale.

The concept of the disembedded economy is central to Polanyi's contention that the nineteenth-century liberal economic order — the template of contemporary globalization — was economic in a different sense from the provision of economic livelihoods in all previous societies. In describing the economy as a distinct and separate sphere of human activity, Polanyi wrote:

> The disembedded economy ... stood apart from the rest of society.... In a market economy the production and distribution of material goods in principle is carried on through a self-regulating economic system of price-making markets. It is governed by laws of its own, the so-called laws of supply and demand, and motivated by fear of hunger and hope of gain.[7]

Social relations of extended family, community and all other ties of traditional society are displaced by special economic institutions such as private property and the economic motive of individual gain. Because the disembedding of the economy was socially unsustainable, Polanyi suggested that society protected itself from impersonal market forces in a variety of ways.

Fred Block dismisses the disembedded economy and contends that Polanyi's real discovery was the "always embedded economy." He maintains there was a shift from Polanyi's earlier Marxist influence to a later revision of his views and only time did not permit him to revise the manuscript of *The Great Transformation* to resolve this contradiction: "Polanyi glimpsed, but was not able to name or elaborate the idea of the always embedded market economy."[8] By discarding the disembedded economy, Block moved Polanyi into the mainstream of socioeconomic discourse. The effect is to obscure the radical implications of the existential contradiction between a market economy and a viable society. There is a suggestion here that Polanyi was influenced by Marxism in the turbulent inter-war years and there was an ideological shift during the writing of the book in the United Sates from 1940 to 1943. Such an interpretation misses the point. It fails to understand what Polanyi accepted and what he rejected in Marx.

Polanyi shared Marx's fundamental insight into the historically limited nature of the organization of economic life by the universalization of the market principle. His account of the societal consequences of the commodification of money, land, labour and indeed the essentials of life recall the alienation theme in the writings of Marx. What he rejected was the Ricardian labour theory of value and the economism of historical materialism. Whereas Marx anticipated the eventual breakdown of the capitalist order on account of inherent *economic* contradictions, Polanyi emphasized the contradiction between the requirements of the market economy for limitless expansion and the social requirements of people to live in mutually supportive social relations. In Polanyi's account of this existential contradiction the outcome is not determinate. There is no grand design of progress. There are no impersonal historical forces which inevitably move humanity forward.

As we enter the twenty-first century, we witness societal disintegration manifested in displaced populations, pandemics, ethnic and religious conflicts, and irreversible damage to the natural environment that sustains life on Earth. Our world is arguably more turbulent and dangerous than Polanyi's. The impulse of social protection of societies threatened by the concentration of economic, financial and increasingly military power may be mobilized by appeals to solidarities as diverse as class, race, ethnicity, caste, religious belief and nationalisms. The rhetoric of populist politics may lean to the Left or the Right. Where the conflict between the "economic" and the "social" cannot be resolved there is chaos. It is not by coincidence that Polanyi's warning of the fateful consequences of liberating capitalist market relations from social control has such resonance today.

RECIPROCITY, REDISTRIBUTION AND EXCHANGE

We first encounter reciprocity and redistribution in Chapter 4 of *The Great Transformation*, drawn from Polanyi's early readings of the anthropological writings of Malinowski and Thurnwald. To introduce a measure of order into the endless variations of the organization of economic life, Polanyi posited three forms of integration: reciprocity, redistribution and exchange. To be effective as integrative mechanisms, reciprocity requires movements between designated symmetrical groupings as in kinship relations; redistribution of goods in and out of a centre requires centricity and is generally accompanied by hierarchy; and exchange requires a system of price-making markets. These patterns of integration do not derive from the summation of individual acts but are conditional on the existence of specific institutions. They do not represent stages of development; no sequence in time is implied. However "economic systems" may be classified according to the dominant form of integration, corresponding to the manner in which labour and land are instituted in society to produce the material requirements of life. Thus, in communal societies kinship relations of reciprocity predominate in the allocation of land and labour:

> In the floodwater empires, land was largely distributed and sometimes redistributed by palace or temple, and so to some degree was labour, at least in its dependent form. The rise of the market to a ruling force in the economy can be traced by noting the extent to which land and food were mobilized through exchange, and labour was turned into a commodity free to be purchased in the market. (Polanyi 1957: 255)

We note Polanyi's consistent reference to people and nature, labour and land, toil and soil as the ultimate economic resources of every society, and the institutional modalities regarding land are no less significant than those regarding labour.

In the history of economic thought, "man" and nature as the original sources of wealth is a forgotten contribution of the Austrian School of Economics. The emphasis on labour as the ultimate source of value derives from English political economy, elaborated by Ricardo and appropriated by Marx. Natural resources acquire value only when labour is applied to their extraction or use. In neoclassical economics, they have value only if they are scarce; hence, the well-known paradox, that air and water have no value because they have no exchange value, and diamonds are valuable because they are scarce. The unsustainable impact of the commodification of natural resources has attracted environmental economists to Polanyi's critique of market economy and market society.[9]

Polanyi rejected Marxist historical "stages" of slavery, feudalism and capitalism based on the predominant labour regime as historically untenable. Polanyi's three patterns of integration have an interesting correspondence with Samir Amin's three modes of production: the primitive communal, tributary and capitalist. It must be noted that elements of all three patterns of integration are found in every society. Reciprocity relations of kinship persist in varying degrees to modern times, redistributive institutions may be found in communal societies and play a crucial role in all variants of national capitalism, and markets, as Polanyi noted, are not a new phenomenon.

POLANYI'S HISTORICAL AND THEORETICAL CONTRIBUTION

The Economy as an Instituted Process is perhaps the most comprehensive account of Polanyi's attempt to construct a general theory of the organization of economic livelihood. In this approach, based on a substantive definition of economics as man's relation to land in providing the essentials of life, the market as the principal integrative mechanism is a special case (Polanyi 1957). His unpackaging of the triad of trade, market and money from the baggage of assumptions drawn from the modern market economy and formalized in mainstream economics opened a large and promising area of research of economic institutions in archaic and primitive societies.

Because the self-regulating market is, as Polanyi illustrated, an unattainable ideal fraught with social and ecological disaster, social institutions constrain and regulate the market, and public goods are provided by the state, whose fiscal operations also finance more or less comprehensive redistributive measures. Reciprocity exists beyond relations of kinship in social obligations of all kinds. International trade is not exclusively commercial and may be motivated by political arrangements of mutual advantage. It is generally subject to international agreement. National currencies are a form of special purpose money particularly where there is exchange control. Informal arrangements of local special purpose money may facilitate exchange within a community. Barter is a form of non-market exchange, and non-market elements are present in a variety of cooperative associational or non-profit activities. When the formal economy breaks down or otherwise fails to clear markets, non-market exchange plays a crucial role in survival strategies of individuals, communities and enterprises.

Globalization presents a challenge of how to reconcile participation in international trade with the requirement of societies to be anchored in social and cultural institutions. When the state is unable to mediate conflict, support individual and community creativity, provide economic and social infrastructure and ensure that the gains of economic growth are shared by all, the benefits of growth will be captured by upper-income earners. Market forces of polarization will disembed the economy from traditional social relations and people will seek solidarities of community, ethnicity, religious belief or other solidarities of the excluded. Polanyi's rejection of economic motives of individual gain as fundamental to human nature and his research into a diversity of patterns of economic organization suggest that economic livelihoods can be instituted in a great variety of ways. This, however, is incompatible with the universalization of the market principle. It implies a civilizational transformation in accord with the fundamental need of people to be sustained by social relations of mutual respect.

NOTES

This chapter is based on a paper prepared for a conference on the anthropological contribution of Karl Polanyi, Nanterre, Paris, June 10–12, 2004. An earlier version was published in French as "Les principaux concepts dans le travail de Karl Polanyi et leur pertinence actuelle," *Autour de Polanyi, Vocabulaires, théories et modalités des échanges*, Ph. Clancier, F. Joannès, P. Rouillard, A. Tenu (eds.) (Paris: Colloques de la Maison René-Ginouvès 2005).

1. Letter written in 1958, cited in Levitt and Mendell (1987: 7–39).
2. For a useful collection of papers on the Polanyi family and Karl's contribution to Hungarian intellectual life presented at the centenary conference in Budapest

1986, see Levitt 1990. For historical documentation, including memoirs on the life of the Polanyi's in Vienna in the 1920s, see McRobbie and Polanyi-Levitt (2000: 255–328).

3.   The White Terror refers to the repressive regime of Admiral Horthy that succeeded the short-lived communist revolution and intervention by Czech and Romanian armies in 1919.

4.   Joseph Needham, Christian Socialist and eminent scholar, best known for the volumes *Science and Civilisation in China* (1954).

5.   This was first published in Germany in 1931 and smuggled out of the country to Switzerland when the Nazis came to power.

6.   Drucker came from Vienna to the United States, where he became a leading authority on the modern corporation.

7.   In a seminal article entitled "Aristotle Discovers the Economy," in *Trade and Market in the Early Empires* (Polanyi, with C.M. Arensberg and H.W. Pearson 1957, p. 68), Polanyi returned to a central theme of *The Great Transformation*.

8.   Fred Block (2001): "Only time did not permit him to rewrite the earlier part. We can make systematic use of Polanyi's insight in the GT once we have 'unpacked' the text and shown the tensions between Polanyi's original Marxist architecture for the book and the new ideas he developed as he was writing them."

9.   See, for example, Herman Daly.

7. CULTURE AND ECONOMY

With all due respect to my fellow economists who yesterday surveyed the frontiers of economics it is painfully clear that economics is not capable of guiding us safely into the next century. Albert Einstein, whose genius hastened the unlocking of the secrets of nuclear power, was tormented by the doubt that "the creations of our mind shall be a blessing and not a curse to (hu)mankind" (1931: 6). He died, we are told, with a doubt whether it might have been better had he not enabled us to create the means for our physical destruction. "The Chinese sages," he is said to have told Leo Szilard, "were right: it is best to do nothing."[1] He was a deeply moral man and thus he warned us that "concern for man and his fate must always form the chief interest of all technical endeavours." This, I suggest, is most particularly true for the so-called social sciences.

I can do no more than sketch out an incomplete agenda of topics in the social sciences that must — to use Karl Polanyi's words — be "subjected to total reconsideration." Incidentally, as regards Karl Polanyi's life work, I would like to put it on the record that throughout his life, my father was concerned with the existential condition of humanity — "the problem of freedom in a machine age and the regeneration of the creative traditions of the cultural West." His extensive researches into the organization of the substantive economy of primitive and archaic societies — with the aid of his now well-known paradigm of reciprocity, redistribution and exchange as forms of integration — were a gigantic detour in aid of proving that the nineteenth-century market economy, better known as free-enterprise capitalism, was a "fateful error," a historic aberration that threatens the future of humankind with destruction because it alienates individuals from each other and from nature. His intention was not to provide academic economic anthropologists with an intellectual toy to explore "distant" and esoteric cultures. It was rather to suggest that never in human history, or human experience, has the economy been disembedded from society in the manner in which that was done in the English Industrial Revolution, which opened the Pandora's Box of exponential economic growth accompanied by exponential social dislocation.

The insights so richly and vigorously presented in his seminal work, *The

Great Transformation (1944 [2001]), were derived from the breakdown of the world capitalist system in the 1930s; the end of the era of hegemonic Britain and the pound sterling; and the abandonment of the Gold Standard as enforcer of the rules of the game. These insights were gained from Polanyi's Central European perspective of smaller and weaker countries tied to the credit strings of the City of London and the Bourse of Paris. Western financiers could demand budget cuts, wipe out social programs and dismiss public servants much like indebted Third World countries today are subjected to IMF and World Bank tutelage.

Polanyi conceived of nation states as sharing a "collective community of culture." He concluded that they were forced to defend their social fabric by refusing to submit to the dictates of the "self-regulating, all-embracing cash-nexus." We are now another forty years down the road and capitalism got a new lease on life after the Second World War with a new hegemonic power to cast the umbrella of its military might over the world. The relations of humiliating dependence have extended to the far corners of what is loosely called the Third World, which was not considered to be part of the world economy or even world polity as recently as 1944/45, when the post-war economic and political order was established. The era of U.S. hegemony however will be much briefer.

The closing of societies in response to the social devastation of the Depression took many forms. One was European fascism, in corporative catholic varieties (Italy, Austria, Spain, Portugal, Poland, etc.) and in a more virulent German national socialism. The social democratic protective response was blueprinted in the Beveridge Report, with its principle of the right of people to be free of destitution whether by involuntary unemployment, sickness or old age.

We are now at the end of the era of U.S. hegemonic power within the trilateral economic multipolarity of North America-Europe-Japan. The Bretton Woods system has broken down. Small nations and Third World countries are now able to exercise economic and political power, as instanced by OPEC, or the Iranian revolution. The international economy is in chaos. We live in a world of two superpowers whose potential capacity for destruction far outreaches their legitimacy either in terms of economic performance, or in terms of respect for liberty and freedom, or more generally in terms of creative human achievement. We live on the brink of nuclear destruction. If we are saved from that fate, how can we ensure that "the creation of our minds shall be a blessing and not a curse for mankind?" Our notions of "economic man" are due for a total reconsideration, according to Karl Polanyi.

I refer to economics, with its simplistic and deeply erroneous assumption concerning human nature and "man" in society. Let me indicate briefly an agenda of three fallacies so we can attempt to repair the damage. Not that it will be easy given the power which can be, and has been mobilized to subject and "open up" human societies to the dictates and dominance of capital over labour, of money over man.

Fallacy No. 1: "Economic Man"

The concept of a maximizing and minimizing individual motivated by the desire to get the most for the least effort by a calculus of "utility" and "disutility" is an absurdity, but we have been socialized by dominant Western European institutions and ideologies to behave as if this were indeed the nature of human beings. Putting it simply, greed and laziness have been enthroned as basic human motivations (called "real" because they are "material"), whereas the human need for love, companionship, community, respect, creativity, a sense of purpose to the meaning of life and harmony with nature are considered secondary (or "ideal" because they are not believed to be essential to man as producer and consumer). Such a warping of human behaviour is a consequence — and a necessity — of the universalization of commodity relations. Here the basic texts are the opening chapters of Marx's Capital, in which he so powerfully explains that behind the exchange of commodities lie social relations. From here Karl Polanyi derives his concept that capitalism has created the "fictitious" commodities of labour power, land and money. But children are not conceived and nurtured because parents are creating the "supply side of a labour market." The Creator has not endowed us with fertile land, water or useful minerals in order that these become commodities to be bought, sold or owned as private property. As for money and its price (interest), this is a social construct for the benefit of society, and all societies prior to ours considered it sinful and illegal to permit usurous interest by those with power to extract it. Today that power lies with governments, to a considerable degree, and currently the government of President Reagan is using the price of money to transfer real resources from other countries to the U.S., from the poor and the weak to the rich and the strong.

The truth is that man is a social being, not an animal, not input-output machines, like a cow or a pig or a slave. That must be the beginning of our reconstruction of the place of economy in society. The reality of society, as Karl Polanyi was so insistent upon, means more than the triviality that we live in society and cannot escape it. It means that within each of us is the need for the protection of a communal and social support system that accords us self-respect and dignity, and thus personal freedom.

Fallacy No. 2: Economic Determinism

This is a philosophy shared by technocratic capitalism and by technocratic Marxism. It is the ideology of technocracy, which would have us believe that modern industrialism must universally and everywhere assume the particular characteristics which it acquired in its European and American manifestations. The laws of exchange which govern the capitalist economy are made out to be the general laws of society. Socialism as we know it in its Soviet form suffers from the same ethnocentric arrogance. So, writes Polanyi, economic determinism is as unacceptable from socialist as from capitalist ideologues, and the central question of man in society is "how to organize human life in a machine society."

Here lies the significance of his twenty years of research into economic anthropology from which he concluded that nothing "is more obvious to the student of anthropology than the variety of institutions found to be compatible with practically identical instruments of production." It follows that economics must be dethroned as the queen of the social sciences. We must seek to reverse the trend to over specialization, to reintegrate the study of man in society, to understand the relationship between the manner in which man's livelihoods are secured, and the manner in which men in society organize the polity within the larger reality of the cultural matrix of each and every society. We must recognize that we are blessed in the diversity of our cultures, that we need the familiarity of our particular cultural milieu and that it is humanly intolerable to be forced to live under alien cultural values.

To me the paradise of the Garden of Eden, of biblical mythology, is not an original state of bliss but is the remarkable fortune of humankind on planet Earth to be blessed with abundant variety in nature and culture. The dangers of eating of the fruits of the tree of knowledge are the fears expressed by Albert Einstein that we can, with knowledge untempered by morality, destroy the richness of human existence. Our science fiction points to the hell on Earth that could await us in a world in which technocracy would triumph over humanity.

Fallacy No. 3: Economic Freedom Equals Personal Freedom
To descend from the philosophical to the more immediately mundane, I would like to close by identifying a more obvious fallacy — the idea that economic liberalism and free enterprise are the way to expand personal freedom. This idea, which many of us believed was well and truly discredited, has re-emerged as the philosophy of the new Right and informs official policy of the government of the United States. The roots of the idea go back to the era of the emergence of Europe from feudalism and the cry that a people should have the right to the fruits of their labour, that the peasants, not the landlords, should own the products of the sweat of their brows. This was the original case for the rights of property over the rights of privilege of feudal tyrants. The extension of the principle of the rights of property to gigantic impersonal accumulators of capital — to transnational corporations and transnational banks — is bizarre and totally unacceptable. Thus, the destabilization and political overthrow of regimes which limit the power of capital to dictate the rules of the game — as in the imposition of economic "liberalism" by ferocious political repression as in Chile, masterminded by

the Chicago School of Friedman — is so gross that it has offended wide strata of U.S. liberal opinion.

The current U.S. initiatives to open-up Third World societies to the unrestricted rules of the game designed to safeguard capital — and particularly foreign capital — will be met, must be met, by measures to insulate and close national societies. If pressed too hard, the results will be disastrous to the future of the now wealthy and industrialized societies and will unleash a reaction of popular protest and civil war of the so-called South against the so-called North that will take many forms, not excluding the revival of fundamentalist and irrational religious forces.

Thus the international economic and political order must proceed with due respect to the sovereignty of nations, which are the political manifestations of modern cultural communities. In an effort to outline the basis of a viable and humane order of things, Polanyi identified what he called four vistas of a humanist socialism:

1. pluralist democracy, i.e., freedom within society,
2. national independence, i.e., freedom from imperialist domination,
3. industrial culture, i.e., acceptance of modern technology as a fact, and
4. a socialist international order, i.e., the coexistence of different cultures and respect for national sovereignty.

In this perspective, the nation remains the fundamental cultural as well as political unit of society. In a letter written late in life, Polanyi argued:

> Few words in political sociology are so perverted as nation, national or nationalistic. After the feudal nation, came the bourgeois nation, which is now being superseded by the socialist nation. The essential connotation is always about the communion of humans. The heart of the feudal nation was privilege; the heart of the bourgeois nation was property; the heart of the socialist nation is the people, where collective existence is the enjoyment of a community of culture. I myself have never lived in such a society.[2]

But socialism, as Polanyi conceived it, must be redefined as beyond mere property terms, as a quality of life where the economy is embedded in non-economic social relations. Material needs and their satisfaction — the technology of production — are merely accessories to a tissue of society, a web of social relations which inhere in lives under humane conditions.

We should not, cannot afford to be afraid of restoring morality to the social sciences. As Einstein, the greatest natural scientist of our era, warned us, concern for humanity and its fate must always form the chief interest for all technical endeavours. For this we may not get rewards within the narrow confines of our academic institutions, but we can enjoy the satisfaction of having contributed a little trickle to a human stream that is asserting the will of life to conquer destruction and death.

NOTES

This chapter is based on a presentation to the panel, "Culture and Economic Systems," at the 1982 International Conference on Economics and Management, Tokyo, July 14–15, 1982.

1. As related by Leo Szilard to Karl Polanyi in conversation. Szilard was a close friend of the Polanyi family.

2. Letter to Rudolph Schlesinger, prospective editor of the journal *Co-Existence*, founded by Karl Polanyi in 1964.

8. SOCIAL DIVIDEND AS A CITIZEN RIGHT

When I first met the remarkable Senator Eduardo Suplicy of Sao Paulo in Montreal, he asked me whether my father would have supported a basic income as a citizen right and invited me to this conference to respond. When the question was first put to me I had no answer. He never addressed the subject and, perhaps, he had never heard of it. This sent me back to re-reading many of my father's writings. To break into the question of basic income, I think it useful to attempt a brief summary of the social philosophy of Karl Polanyi.

We have heard a number of references to Amartya Sen's work and his definition of development as freedom to exercise choice by the enhancement of the capabilities of individuals. It is difficult to disagree with personal development as the aim of social development. But Sen's approach derives from classical liberalism in the best sense of the word, whereas my father's social philosophy was grounded in what he called the reality of society. By this he meant that humans are by nature social animals and, as such, we do not and cannot live outside society. Any notion of individual freedom has thus to be conceived of in terms of our relationship to society. My father was a socialist, but he insisted on the importance of maintaining personal freedom and personal liberty in society, as is clear from the last chapter of *The Great Transformation*, "Freedom in a Complex Society."

Karl Polanyi was a passionate man. He strongly believed that intellectuals have a social responsibility. In early articles and speeches in Hungary, he took upon himself and his generation, *Our Generation,* as he called it, the moral responsibility for the ravages of the Great War. For him, freedom was inseparable from responsibility. I believe his critique of market society was grounded in an aversion to the commercialization of daily life and, more generally, the impersonalization of social relations. In his view, any form of socialism would have to ensure the responsibility of people for their communities, their societies and their democracies. For these reasons, he distrusted the idea of a centrally planned economy, with its inherent concentration of political power.

In England, my father was a lecturer for the Workers' Educational Association, the adult education extension of Oxford University. The subjects he was required to treat were contemporary international relations, and English social and economic history. Like Marx before him, he found the origins of industrial capitalism in England — specifically in the thirty years from 1815 to 1845, when the legislative and supportive infrastructure for markets in labour and land were instituted. The free market for money was of course older, dating to the abolition of laws prohibiting usury — considered as sinful by Christian doctrine. Together, the markets for labour, land and money had the effect of disembedding the economy from society. The economy assumed a life of its own and society was reconfigured to serve the requirements of the economy. This was a very strange and historically unprecedented state of affairs, which however released enormous energy of economic growth.

My father's intellectual ancestry, I suggest, runs from Karl Marx to Max Weber to Ferdinand Tönnies and to two economic anthropologists: Turnwald of Germany and Malinowski of Vienna. I mention this in connection with basic income because not at any time in human history, recorded or unrecorded, do we find that individuals or individual families were permitted to fall into destitution or suffer starvation, other than when the community as a whole fell on hard times. In primitive societies, failing harvests could bring severe shortage of food, but individual families could never be without the basic necessities of life while the rest of the community was provided for. The idea that fear of hunger and love of gain were the motivating drivers of economic life is historically very recent — as recent as the early nineteenth century. For these reasons alone, without taking the story any further, I can say that a share in the social product as a citizen right would have won Karl Polanyi's support, both as a means of decommodifying access to economic livelihood and on grounds of moral justice.

I suggest there are three distinct reasons why my father would have supported the basic income principle: one is economic, one is social and, not least important, one is political. The economic arguments are well known and have many times been repeated. You do not need to be a Keynesian to understand that people in need receiving a basic income will spend it on consumption goods, thus creating market opportunities for producers. Furthermore, the accelerating rate of technological innovation requires ever less labour input to industrial activity, from mining and manufacturing to transportation and commerce. And this is true on a global scale. In these conditions, it is no longer reasonable to consider earnings from wage employment to be the only — or even the principal — entitlement to the social product. In light of the increasingly precarious nature of the labour market, a basic income provides a platform from which people can organize economic activities with some relief from the debilitating stress of making ends meet.

The social argument is one of justice. Where there is a perception of social injustice, there will be problems of social cohesion. In these conditions, the state will be ineffective in negotiating conflicting claims on the social product. Such a society lacks the capacity to advance in terms of economic development. It is now recognized that societies that are more egalitarian and that are less riddled by inequities and injustices, have been more successful in achieving economic growth and development. Speaking as an economist, I believe that mobilization for effective economic development ultimately rests on the degree of social cohesion and the perception of social justice, releasing the energies generated by the hope and belief of the people that their sacrifices and efforts will result in a fair and equitable share of the social product.

The third reason why my father would support a basic income relates to his concern about freedom in a technologically advanced society, as expressed in the last chapter of *The Great Transformation*. In the 1950s, while teaching at Columbia and commuting between New York and Canada, he became increasingly preoccupied with the trend towards uniformity, conformity and what he called "averagism," manifested in reluctance to dissent from prevailing opinions. This was the United States in the 1950s, and he suggested that a highly advanced technological society had within it the seeds of totalitarianism. I remind you that he wrote this before the role of the media had become so evident, before the total corporate control of the media had become so powerful and certainly before what we witnessed in the United States after September 11, 2001, when the cost of dissent from official views became prohibitive.

My father believed that the protection of liberty required the institutionalization of non-conformity. He saw this as a virtue of English classical liberalism. But these liberties were available only to the privileged upper classes benefiting from the rentier incomes of the late nineteenth and early twentieth centuries. Incidentally most of this came from Britain's colonial possessions and extensive overseas investments. This was the era of the Belle Époque in England and France, in Vienna and more generally in Western Europe. It produced great cultural achievements, but it was confined to limited sectors of the population. My father was familiar with classical Greek literature and particularly admired Aristotle, whom he credited with the discovery of the economy as a distinct sphere of social life. But Greek democracy was dependent on the work of slaves. In bourgeois society, of which my father's family were beneficiaries, cultural expression was effectively limited to a privileged elite.

Polanyi believed that creativity was a basic human attribute and need; the capacity to exercise creativity must embrace all of its people. In his view a popular culture was the collective wisdom, knowledge, tradition and common sense of ordinary people. This had nothing to do with pop culture, rather that different societies would create different democracies rooted in the collective pool of their unique popular culture. This is developed in an unpublished essay, "Jean-Jacques Rousseau: Is Freedom Possible?"[1] This fascinating essay treats the classical issues of liberty and equality in the era of the Enlightenment. He finds in the writings of Rousseau support for his contention that the ultimate foundation of government must rest on the reservoir of wisdom, knowledge, tradition and common sense of the people that is the popular culture. This is the context in which he would have supported basic income as a citizen right for the political and cultural objectives of non-conformity and dissent. A guaranteed subsistence income could enable musicians, artists and writers to express the dreams of their society, political activists to challenge prevailing doctrines and ideologies and people who aspire to advance economically to gather the resources required to do so.

Finally, I must say that I was happy to hear from our Brazilian colleagues that economic and social development is back on the agenda. The country's achievement in increasing industrial capacity while reducing poverty by massive expenditure on social and physical infrastructure is impressive. It shows that it is indeed possible to combine strong economic growth with equitable social policy. But the ultimate wealth of a society cannot be counted in money. Adam Smith was quite right about that: the wealth of a nation is the skill and effort of its people. Development is a creative social process and its central nervous system; the matrix which nourishes it is located in the cultural sphere. Development is ultimately not a matter of money or physical capital, or foreign exchange, but of the capacity of a society to tap the root of popular creativity, to free up and empower people to exercise their intelligence and collective wisdom.

NOTES

This chapter is based on a paper delivered at the 13th Basic Income Earth Network Congress at a roundtable entitled "Basic Income as a Public Policy to Enhance Democracy and Global Justice," Sao Paulo, Brazil, 30 June 30–July 2, 2010.

1. There is a version of this article written in 1937 and a similar but slightly different undated version believed to have been written some time in the 1950s.

PART 2

The Global South from Conquest and Exploitation to Self-Reliant Development

9. STRUCTURAL CONTINUITY AND ECONOMIC DEPENDENCE IN THE CAPITALIST WORLD SYSTEM

This essay contains no facts, no statistics, no algebra and a minimum of references. It makes no claims to originality. It is not concerned with trade theory, nor even with the theory of development. What is here attempted is a sketch of a framework within which the mechanisms of the unequal economic relations between so-called developed and so-called developing countries are revealed. Or more precisely, the mechanisms by which the former colonial territories of the metropolitan powers have been and continue to be incorporated into the expanding world capitalist system. The purpose of such a framework is to guide developing countries toward economic decolonization, liberation and self-reliance, and away from a pattern of integration which grants the controlling centres — and the multinational corporations headquartered there — a cumulative advantage of power and wealth. While the centralizing and polarizing forces within the world system derive from the dynamics of capitalist economic relations, enforcement or defiance of the "rules of the game" within which the complicated nexus of economic transactions are instituted is ultimately a matter of political power. It is therefore self-evident that no theories which confine themselves to the economic dimension, whether of the classical, neoclassical, neo-Ricardian or Marxian variety, can provide even the crudest explanation of the persistence of the unequal relationship between rich countries and poor. Nor can economics alone explain how a very narrow strata of elites in developing countries can maintain themselves in power in the face of the increasing poverty, dispossession, alienation and apparent human redundancy of the peoples of many Third World countries.

The search to find the roots of the present condition of underdevelopment in the legacy of the past was the starting point of all the serious work from scholars and working economists in Latin America and other peripheral regions. Nevertheless, we must create from the detail of historical experience, abstractions sufficiently institutional to be realistic and sufficiently general to be relevant to the great variety of situations found in the countries peripheral to the growing points of the world economy. Thus, the study of economic history is absolutely necessary to, but is not a substitute for, the constructions of models of the political economy of the world capitalist system, however inadequate this or other efforts may be.

The relationships described here have been observed by many others, some of whose work is accessible and well known. Without disrespect or lack of appreciation for the scholarship and insights contained in the very large and exponentially increasing body of literature relating to the subjects of monopoly capitalism, imperialism, dependency, unequal exchange, unequal development, the transnational corporation and much more, I feel it necessary to identify the roots from which my perceptions originate.

I have learnt most from the school of everyday life because knowledge experienced and understood is transferable. Furthermore, as the late Joseph Schumpeter observed, significant ideas begin with an intuitive perception; the rest is in a sense rationalization. The perception of exploitation, in the case under discussion here — exploitation of people in the Third World for the benefit and advantage of people in the rich countries of Europe and North America — is the knowledge of the school of everyday life, the universities of the blocs and *quartiers populaires* which surround the growing cities of every developing country. There you can hear, if you wish to listen, more profound insights into the ultimate impossibility of organizing the basic livelihood of people on the principle of the unlimited greed of the rich and the powerful than you are likely to find in academe. Moreover, to those here to whom the absence of facts, figures or formulae may imply that this paper is a theoretical speculation drawn up in an ivory, concrete, steel or glass tower I wish only to say that I have spent the last twelve years of my life in compiling statistics, specifically systems of input-output and other intersectoral national accounts both in Statistics-Canada and in the Ministry of Planning and the Central Statistical Office of Trinidad and Tobago. Tedious and sometimes soul destroying as such work may be, it yields a very rich insight into the relationship between industrial organization, domestic and external economic and financial structures, and the ramifications of the operations of transnational corporations, including all aspects of inter-affiliate sales. Perhaps more important, the mathematics and routines of compiling and analysing matrix form data sets, imprints a perspective of the general interdependency of structures on the mind, as a habit of thought.

CAPITALISM AND DEVELOPMENT

There are three main roots to the sketch that is outlined in this paper. I believe it helpful to explain them as an alternative to the more conventional but less indicative procedure of citing a full set of references. The first is the influence of the ideas of my father, Karl Polanyi, the power of whose insight I did not grow to appreciate until the early 1960s. His world of thought in turn derived from the writings of Marx and the experience of the events of his own lifetime. What Polanyi shared with Marx was not Marxist economic determinism nor the class struggle but rather the insight that capitalism - as the ultimate alienation of people from nature and society — is not a viable system.

It is neither possible nor necessary to trace the circuitous route whereby I eventually came to gain an appreciation of the work of Karl Polanyi, save to record the fact that through circumstances largely fortuitous and beyond our control we shared important formative experiences of everyday life. We came as refugees from fascism from the socialist Vienna of the 1920s and early 1930s to England, the birthland of the capitalist world and the shrine of civil liberties. Here the monuments to William Blake's Dark Satanic Mills were all around in the form of the brick, soot and grime of the East End of London, the bleak urban sprawls of South London, the even worse scars of Manchester and Liverpool and the coal valleys of Wales — along with two or three million unemployed workers, including young women from Wales and Ireland who came to prostitute themselves in domestic service in London. We were received with charity and efforts were made to reassure one that foreigners, even those speaking with accents and of dubious complexion, were more or less acceptable to English society, provided a total adaptation to native cultural values, class structures and prejudices could be made. Young as I was, I came too late. After the war we independently found ourselves in North America — in Toronto to be exact — near the frontier of the uncontrolled and rampant individualism and visually offensive commercialization that characterizes the heartland of capitalism of the post-Second World War era. It is also relevant to record that I was throughout and beyond my formative years a fairly orthodox Marxist — although well trained in the paradigms of classical, neoclassical and Keynesian economics — and later became a student of development economics. My father rejected all of that, and for years we had an amicable running argument. I now recall that in the later 1950s he told me that he did not understand what was meant by development, nor was he interested: the problem, he said, was how to institute a continuous supply of the material requirements of life given our knowledge of industrial technology, without the "disembedding" of the economy from society, which, according to him, was the prime characteristic of what he chose to call the self-regulating market economy, but which we more generally know as capitalism. It took me a long time to appreciate the essential truth of this statement. The other thing he told me at about the same time was that Chapter 1, Verse 1 of the conventional wisdoms of development economics, i.e., W.W. Rostow's *Stages of Economic Growth,* was a noxious book. This was long before Rostow's activities as the guru of U.S. counter-insurgency tactics in Latin America became known to anybody outside the conspiratorial group itself. Although this book and its author are now in disrepute, the basic approach continues to permeate development economics and policies.

THE CARIBBEAN PERSPECTIVE

Next in importance in my understanding of the structures of power in the world system is my association for the past fifteen years with West Indian economists and the New World Group, founded by Lloyd Best.[1] This group had no ideology save for the common perception of the need to discard alien metropolitan models and to find the solutions to the problems of the Caribbean from internal resources — beginning with intellectual ones. It was an ideology of decolonization and self-reliance, without reference to capitalism, socialism or black nationalism. It is not surprising that the approach leads to the diagnosis of the problem as one of neocolonial dependency or that it shared some of the features of Cepalist Structuralism. Nor is it surprising that the group disintegrated in the early 1970s under the stress of unresolved conflicting ideologies, specifically the relative emphasis to be placed on class, race and nation as the key to decolonization in the Caribbean.

Whatever the similarities with the analyses and debates among Latin American economists and intellectuals, the Caribbean has a unique experience. It is the region of the original and, in a sense, the ultimate act of capitalist alienation: the establishment of total institutions in the form of slave plantations, where alienated labour power was the principal physical capital asset of the planters and merchants, who organized this first form of Foreign Direct Investment in the Third World. The venture was magnificently successful. It consisted of the uprooting, transplanting and re-socializing of African labour so as to produce a staple for export to Europe which, when sold, would yield profits to European merchants and planters worthy of the wildest dreams of the great merchants of the maritime cities of the Mediterranean and Atlantic seaboard (Best and Levitt 1968, 1976).

The continuity of structures of economic and social power from the days of slavery to the present is a fact of daily life, whether expressed in the sophisticated language of the academics or slogans painted on walls. In either case the message is the same: four hundred years of exploitation. It may be true that the structural continuity of the system from the past of the merchant companies to the modern transnational corporation is a particularly Caribbean perception — although I doubt it — but then the philosophers say you can see the universe in a grain of sand. From a study which commenced with the explicit aim of understanding the structure and mechanisms of a Caribbean plantation economy, the conclusion emerges that the general institutional framework within which metropolitan dominance and peripheral dependence are interlinked is the single most important determinant of the distribution of gains from production and trade — not only between metropole and periphery, but also amongst classes within peripheral society. Insofar as this general institutional framework is an international one, the relevance of its structural continuities is in no way restricted to the Caribbean nor ultimately to the incorporated countries of the Third World. Thus, we now hear about the "Latinamericanization" of the United States, the alienation of the affluent and the redundancy of the hard-hat wearing, pork-chop eating, blue-collar worker of North America.

THE CANADIAN CONNECTION

The third input which is relevant here relates to my involvement in the Canadian "foreign ownership" debate initiated by Walter Gordon, who was eased out of his position as minister of finance in Lester B. Pearson's government essentially because of his nationalist views with respect to the excessive influence of United States business and government on Canadian policy. It soon became apparent that the issue was not one of the costs and benefits of foreign capital but rather the totality of the effects on the host country of the penetration of its economy by subsidiaries of U.S.-based multinational corporations.

In developing the case against permitting these companies uncontrolled access to Canadian raw materials and markets, I discussed in the book *Silent Surrender* the phenomenon of the transnational corporation in light of what economic theory had to offer by way of explanations, and I also indicated the principal economic and political issue raised for a dependent host country — even where that country is not underdeveloped in the usual sense of the term (Levitt 1970). Because this book was written in language deliberately purged of academic jargon and perhaps because the case in review was that of Canada, which might not appear to have any lesson of relevance to Third World countries, the book was largely ignored as a contribution to development literature. However, in the study of the effects of Foreign Direct Investment on the host country, the Canadian case — as distinct from Canadian governmental policy or lack thereof — remains important.

Not the least aspect of the "Canadian connection" relates to the incomplete life work of Stephen Hymer, starting with his important and unpublished PhD thesis of 1960. The number of academic economists who were prepared to challenge the mainstream of the profession in Canada on the question of foreign ownership in the mid-1960s was very small. Essentially it consisted of Mel Watkins, Abe Rotstein, Steve Hymer and myself. The first three were invited by Mr. Gordon to form the core of a task force which produced *Foreign Ownership and the Structure of Canadian Industry* (Government of Canada 1968). The Watkins Report, as it was known, was subsequently disowned by the Canadian government as too nationalistic and by Watkins himself on the grounds that it did not go beyond the cost-benefit approach in its search for basic alternatives to a dependent capitalist economy dominated by foreign corporations. Incidentally, a later study commissioned by the government of Canada, published in 1972, elaborated on both the argument and the documentation of the Watkins Report and *Silent Surrender*. If its recommendations are trivial compared with the excellent material contained in that report, the fault is clearly not that of the anonymous public servants who wrote it (Government of Canada 1972).

It is no coincidence that the most incisive and effective efforts to place the multinational corporation within the framework of the world economy and to explain the coincidence of its hierarchical structure with that of the world capitalist economy was the work of a Canadian. Although Hymer lived and worked in the United States, he associated himself with Canadian nationalist sentiment *vis-à-vis* the economic domination by U.S.-based corporations, as witness by his crucial contribution to the Watkins Report. Here I can do no better than quote Watkins, who records that,

> on the issue of industrial structure Hymer wins the prize for relevancy. By shifting the topic from the sterile world of the theory of international economics to the less tidy but more interesting institutional world of industrial organization, Professor Hymer puts his finger on a fact much neglected by economists prior to 1960, namely that most foreign direct investment was accounted for by a small number of firms operating in industries that the economist calls oligopolistic.[2]

Stephen Hymer was born and raised in Montreal and was a graduate of McGill University, but I did not meet him until 1967. From that time until his death in 1974 we exchanged ideas in infrequent but long and stimulating discussions. It was Hymer who directed me to the literature on industrial organization, particularly to A.D. Chandler's work on the modern corporation and to Jane Jacob's work on cities, and from whom I learned to study the world of corporations by reading what they write about themselves and for themselves. The last conversation we had lasted twelve hours through the night of January 1, 1973, and ranged from Marxism to astrology, from the Yankee merchants of Boston to the new patterns of the international division of labour. The loss of Stephen Hymer was more than the loss of a friend and a colleague, it was the loss of an exceptionally original and powerful mind — a man who, with several dozen important articles and statements behind him, had only just arrived at the beginning of his intellectual potential (Levitt 1982).[3] It is a comment on the provincialism of Canada that Hymer's work is less known in the country of his birth and citizenship than in the United States, Europe or the Third World. Indeed, it was this provincialism that he gave as his principal reason for remaining in the United States, despite efforts by Mel Watkins and others to try to persuade him to return to Canada. On this particular matter Stephen had the last word, in typical fashion even from the grave, in the form of a brief obituary in the Canadian national newspaper, the *Globe and Mail*, under the headline "Watkins Economist Dies at 38." That God in his wisdom cut short this life has, I think, strengthened the resolve of many of us who knew Stephen Hymer and seek only to produce work which appears to be relevant to our human condition, to the best of our limited abilities.

Hymer left us with some of the most graphic descriptions of the hierarchical structures of the transnational corporation, with its top-level decision-making headquarters located in a few major capitals — New York, London, Tokyo, Frankfurt, Paris and Moscow — forming an inner ring between roughly the fortieth and fiftieth parallels. From these radial points of strategic planning instructions flow out and information flows in from a whole hierarchy of functional centres of direction, those of the lowest order, relating to the details of production, being the most dispersed and in the hands of nationals of the country of location. I do not know of any more vivid description of the structure of the predominant economic enterprise of contemporary capitalism:

> The new international economy will be characterized by a division of labour based on nationality.... Day-to-day management in each country is left to the nationals of that country who, being intimately familiar with local conditions and practices, are able to deal with local problems and local government. These nationals remain rooted in one spot, while above them is a layer of people who move around from country to country, as bees among flowers, transmitting information from one subsidiary to another and from the lower levels to the general office at the apex of the corporate structure. In the nature of things, these people for the most part will be citizens of North Atlantic countries (and will be drawn from a small culturally homogenous group within the advanced world), since they will need to have the confidence of their superiors and be able to move easily in the higher management circles. Latin Americans, Asians and Africans will at best be able to aspire to a management position in the intermediate coordinating centres at the continental level. Very few will be able to get much higher than this, for the closer one gets to the top, the more important is "a common cultural heritage." The majority will be little more than middlemen helping to organize their countries' labour for sale abroad. (Hymer 1973)

It is a strange coincidence that, by way of his admiration for the writings of Marshall McLuhan, Hymer's vision links with the central theme of Canada's only original economist — or more exactly economic historian — the late Harold Innis. Revered in name but in typical fashion largely ignored by Canadian economists, Innis made the crucial connection between empire and communication. The latter was more than the title of one of his later books and the evident inspiration of his disciple, Marshall McLuhan. It was the unifying theme of his monumental life work, from his PhD thesis on the Canadian Pacific Railway to his subsequent interpretation of Canadian economic history in terms of the structural legacy of successive export staples in his best-known work, *The Fur Trade in Canada* (1930), to his later books on communication in the wider sense of the evolution of the transmission of information from oral, to print, to electronic media.[4]

In his work Innis traced the manner in which the commercial relations between periphery and metropole have shaped the economy, the society and the structure of government of the northern part of North America, now Canada. He analyzed the relationship between the staple (predominant commodity) and the pattern of economic development in terms of the symbiosis between what he termed the "centre" and the "margin" of Western civilization two decades before the relationship was formulated as one of "great industrial centres" and "peripheries" by Prebisch in the 1940s. Furthermore a generous and careful reading of Innis reveals his perception of the key connection between merchants and monopolies on the one hand, and the use of the state apparatus of the peripheral country on the other, to reinforce the power of the former by means of manipulation of the latter:

> The economic history of Canada has been dominated by the discrepancy between the centre and the margin of western civilization... agriculture, industry, transportation, trade, finance and governmental activities tend to become subordinate to the production of the staple for a more highly specialized manufacturing community. These general tendencies may be strengthened by governmental policy as in mercantile systems. (Innis 1930: 385)

Innis was a populist, a foe of monopolies and of the state because he perceived the latter as an instrument reinforcing the former. In the context of the 1930s he was an antisocialist because he, like many others to this day, equated socialism with statism. Neither Social Democrats nor Marxists regarded Innis as being of importance. He was moreover an institutionalist so traditional economists, whether classical, neoclassical, Marxist or Keynesian, dismissed him. But important ideas do not die. They have a way of persisting. It is now commonplace to observe that information is power and that the ultimate strength of the transnational corporation lies in its centralized system of communication. It has been said, for example, that "what distinguishes the modern multinational enterprise from large international corporations of earlier centuries is its global management strategy made possible by the technology of communication" (Nye 1974).

Yes and no, because one can argue with equal force that control over long distance communication with attendant control over channels of distribution is precisely the element of structural continuity from the old chartered companies to the transnational enterprises of today. Indeed, this is my argument in this essay and has been my argument all along. It is the reason I continue to maintain that it is useful to see the present configuration of the world capitalist system as a new mercantilism of economic and political power with structural continuity back to the era of chartered companies and the armies and navies of the competing metropolitan states of the Atlantic seaboard of Europe.

This does not deny that the complementary perspective of growth and change, of capital accumulation and the extending international division of labour, is equally valid. It is however a more familiar one — at least to economists — and has the limitation of removing from view the structures of power by which the processes of accumulation are instituted and maintained. In its classical and Marxist versions, it is excessively mechanistic, as witnessed by the common assumption of most proponents of both these schools that a surplus over the needs of subsistence is in some way a natural or inevitable phenomenon rather than one that is instituted by power relation. It is, as I suggested at the beginning of this paper, an advantage of studying the world capitalist system from its periphery that the experience of daily life so clearly demonstrates that there is nothing natural or inevitable either about surplus or about accumulation and that there is no solution to underdevelopment by any variety of economistic approaches.

It is clearly impossible within the limits of this essay to do more than sketch out the basic argument, which can be summarized in the form of two themes:

1. the mechanisms of the subordination of peripheral regions and countries to metropolitan capital; and
2. the accumulation of capital as the progressive disembedding of successive layers of social life by the ever wider and deeper reach of commercialization.

It is strange how economists have a blind spot. They can readily see that the rich will be strong, but they seldom see the reverse relationship: that the strong become rich and stay rich because they are strong. The ultimate enforcement of the "rules of the game" remains the military, political and economic power of what Joan Robinson once called the Top Nation, or perhaps we should say the Top Nations. When the power wanes and threats cease to be so operative, the rules of the game can change quite quickly.

With the United Nations Declaration on the Establishment of a New International Economic Order (United Nations General Assembly 1974), the Third World countries challenged the legitimacy of the general institutional framework within which foreign trade and foreign investment proceeds. They declared that economic decolonization must follow political decolonization:

> The greatest and most significant achievement during the last decades

has been the independence from colonial and alien domination of a large number of peoples and nations which has enabled them to become members of the community of free peoples…. However, the remaining vestiges of alien and colonial domination, foreign occupation, racial discrimination, apartheid and neo-colonialism in all its forms continue to be among the greatest obstacles to the full emancipation and progress of the developing countries and all the peoples involved…. It has proved impossible to achieve an even and balanced development of the international economic order. The gap between the developed and developing countries continues to widen in a system which was established at a time when most of the developing countries did not even exist as independent states and which perpetuates inequality.

I know it is fashionable to be cynical about this Declaration, but I maintain that no set of institutions, however powerful, can survive for long without legitimation. Historians tell us that the present severe income differentials between Europe and the rest of the world are of rather recent origin — possibly less than 150 years! Adam Smith referred to India and China as great civilized nations which produced the finest silks and cottons known to Westerners — not as backward underdeveloped countries.

The severely inequitable distribution of power and wealth in the world today plainly cannot last even to the end of this century, short of the imposition of a centralized world-wide regime of repression of the kind prophesied by George Orwell for 1984. This is one of the possibilities. The other is that the world system will continue to undergo transformation either with the semi-voluntary agreement of the rich countries or by the unilateral use of every lever of power, including armed conflict, by governments and liberation movements in countries comprising the 75 percent of the world's people who receive 25 percent of its income, probably starting in Southern Africa. I am not naive. The Third World is not a bloc, any more than their governments represent the interests of all classes and all citizens. Far from it. But it is important to understand that the era of the hegemonic dominance of the most recent Top Metropole, the United States of America, is drawing to a close. We have to go back to the days before British world supremacy to find a multicentred world economy, when we find war between rival metropoles the rule rather than the exception. War between great powers in contemporary technological conditions is evidently self-destructive to all, "winners" and "losers" alike. Thus, we do not know whether the Orwellian nightmare can become a reality or not.

We abstract from the diversity, the complexity and the remarkable changes which have characterized European commercial and capitalist expansion into the areas and regions of the world now called underdeveloped in order to focus on the remarkable structural continuity of the general framework within which economic relations between metropolitan and peripheral countries have been instituted since the first merchant-pirate-venturers set forth in search of trade, conquest and plunder at the end of the fifteenth century. These are essentially the imperialist structures whose legitimacy and inevitability is now being challenged. The challenge is ultimately directed at the Euro-centred world capitalist system, and I am using European in its wider sense to include, together with Europe, the major countries of European settlement, i.e., the United States, the white dominions of the former British Empire (Canada, Australia, etc.), the southern cone of South America and the dominant European fragments in regions of conquest such as Southern Africa and Palestine. It is implicit in this argument that capitalism is an integrative mechanism for the disembedding of economic activity from all other aspects of society and that it is essentially a European innovation. Indeed, it appears to have a special affinity to the Protestant regions of Europe, as Max Weber and R.H. Tawney long ago suggested. From its inception, it has been structured to generate a surplus in a fashion that assured that the control over the process of accumulation is concentrated in the mercantile-financial sectors located in the metropolitan centres of the system. The purpose of identifying the elements of structural continuity in the evolution of this world economic system is not to suggest that they are immutable. To the contrary, the purpose is to lay bare the narrow and hierarchal structure of the lines of communication of economic power, as contrasted with the geographical diffusion of production and consumption implicit in the accelerating international division of labour.

Here, then, are five mechanisms, or five rules of the game, that govern the unequal relations between metropolitan and peripheral countries. This schema derives from my work with Lloyd Best on Caribbean plantation economy (Best and Levitt 2009: 47–48).

1. Division of the world into spheres of influence of the major metropolitan powers (Inter-Caetera)[5]
Every peripheral country or region normally finds itself within the dominant sphere of influence of one of the major metropolitan powers. This remains true long after the dissolution of formal political colonialism. The metropolitan powers, which rivalled each other in trade and war and expanded their empires overseas, were and to a large degree remain the maritime nations of the North Atlantic: Portugal, Spain, the Netherlands, Belgium, France, Britain, later Germany and the Yankees of the Eastern Seaboard of the United States, later again Japan and the United States of America (Russia and Austria-Hungary built inland empires, the latter long ago disintegrated; the former today constitutes the Soviet Union, its Eastern European Bloc and spheres of influence in bordering countries, including India). Of all these

metropolitan powers, Britain was the only one that remained undisputed Top Nation for a century (1815–1914), and London remains a leader among the principal financial centres of the capitalist world economy. The era of United States hegemony was briefer, significantly less extensive in relation to the size of the world economy of the post-Second World War period and very much less stable.

As the system becomes more integrated, societies in metropolitan countries become more similar (homogenized), trade and investment between them increases, and the costs to all centre countries of war between them become prohibitively high, best illustrated by the U.S.-Soviet detente, accompanied by significant new links of trade and transnational corporate relationships. Peripheral lines of communication however, tend to remain exclusive with respect to the metropolitan sphere of influence within which a country finds itself by virtue either of past colonial conquest or shifting patterns or spheres of influence of major powers. Lateral ties between peripheral countries remain weak even where their respective metropoles are integrated into trading blocs or common markets. Transnational enterprises maintain a close relationship with the governments of their home countries, or to be more exact, penetrate key sectors of the state bureaucracy, particularly those which administer foreign economic policy. This is most clearly observable with respect to the relationship between U.S.-based transnational corporations and the government of the United States. Patterns of Foreign Direct Investment to this day reflect colonial spheres of influence. According to data of vintage late 1960s, two-thirds of Belgian and French affiliates in developing countries were located in Africa, principally French-speaking Africa. The more balanced distribution of British investments in developing countries followed the greater spread of its former Empire: 30 percent in Asia, 30 percent in Africa; 26 percent in the Western Hemisphere and 13 percent in the Middle East. The geographical concentration of United States influences was reflected in the fact that 70 percent of U.S. direct investment in developing countries was located in Latin America and the Caribbean, the rest being distributed equally in Asia, Africa and the Middle East. Metropolitan intervention in defence of their economic and strategic interests, not excluding those of their national corporate citizens, is a daily fact of life — most noticeable in the U.S. sphere of influence. The organizational and technological instruments have advanced past gunboat diplomacy, but who in any corner of the Western Hemisphere could honestly say that manipulation, interference and intervention by the United States is not a constraint to be taken into account by governments and oppositions alike.

2. International division of labour between centre and peripheral countries (the Muscovado Bias)[6]

Peripheral countries typically specialize in terminal activities: the production and extraction of agricultural and mineral raw materials and their simple processing on the one hand, and the domestic distribution or assembly of metropolitan goods (screwdriver assembly) on the other. This is obviously valid for the simple export-import economies. It largely continues to be valid for import-substituting industrialization that produces metropolitan-type goods with metropolitan technology, capital equipment and intermediate components, whether wholly controlled (direct investment) by foreign companies or in joint ventures with the local private or the local state sector. The peripheral economies remain fragmented (truncated, disarticulated) — their waves of growth and stagnation largely remain dependent on erratic changes in demand and supply conditions for their exports of agricultural and mineral raw materials and on changes in prices of imports. Thus, the so-called commodity and terms-of-trade problems remain acute. Current trends to locate cheap labour export manufactures or highly polluting primary processing activity outside the geographical boundaries of the metropolitan centre countries has not basically altered the pattern of industrialization in peripheral countries.

The major motive for investments or joint ventures of foreign companies in Third World countries remains access to raw materials. Direct investment in import substituting manufacturing in developing countries remains concentrated in a few large ones — Argentina, Brazil, Mexico, India and Spain accounting for 60 percent in 1967. Most of this remains terminal activity, i.e., either the processing of primary materials or assembly type activity with a high import content of capital equipment, parts, components and technology services.

As for "export platform" cheap labour manufacturing by transnational enterprises in Taiwan, Hong Kong, borderland Mexico, the Philippines and Singapore, this represents the ultimate in fragmentation and might be termed "technological truncation." The point is best illustrated by an example drawn from a study commissioned by the OECD which cites the following "typical export oriented project":

> The main motivation of the company was to reduce the production costs of certain labour-intensive components. The parent company was a large multinational enterprise handling sophisticated electronic products, which it exported to 22 countries, including six LDCs. The investment was approximately $350,000. The function of the LDC factory was to assemble sub-components, which were shipped in by air from the parent company, and to ship them back as finished components. The market for the output was entirely under the investor's control and the only technology transferred was in the form of production methods. The profitability to the investor of a feeder plant such as this has to be measured on the basis of production cost savings to the enterprise as a whole.... On this basis the project had a pay back period, after tax, of only eight months. It was the company's

> view that an investment recovery must be rapid and the scope of the operations limited in order to permit rapid redeployment should the environment or company requirements shift. (Reuber et al. 1973)

It should be noted that the technology transferred is restricted to the assembly of sub-components provided by the metropolitan-based parent firm into components whose market is entirely under parent company control.

3. Monopoly control by metropolitan countries and companies over lines of communication to peripheries (Navigation Laws)[7]

A constant feature of the world economic system since its mercantile inception in the sixteenth century has been metropolitan control over channels of distribution and lines of communication between centre and periphery. This control reinforces the hierarchical and centralizing pattern of the international division of economic activity between metropole and periphery. Negatively, there is an absence of lateral lines of distribution and communication between peripheral countries. Metropolitan control over access to credit, markets and information — including technological know-how — is reinforced by metropolitan control over shipping, airlines, telecommunications and electronic data processing systems. The organizational structure of the transnational corporation coincides with the metropolitan location of control over communications in the widest sense of the term.

The exports of peripheral countries cannot reach metropolitan markets without the intermediation of metropolitan-based agents, distributors or companies; likewise these same monopolistic mercantile elements control the procurement of finished intermediate and capital goods imports into peripheral countries.

The metropolitan control over access to information and technology, and even over the educational accreditation of professional and bureaucratic personnel of peripheral countries, likewise reinforces patterns of integration and control. The same hierarchical patterns of control obtain within multinational corporations as between head office functions and production operations located in peripheral countries. Thus, monopolistic control of overseas production and trade has been a constant feature of the world capitalist system, as has the close relationship between the enterprises engaged in economic exchange with peripheral areas and the metropolitan state. Viewed from a peripheral perspective, monopoly capital is not a recent phenomenon dating from the late nineteenth century any more than primitive accumulation is only an historical phenomenon predating the emergence of industrial capitalism.

The flexibility and mobility accruing to the controlling centres, from which the companies have allocated and re-allocated the productive resources of the expanding world economy to their advantage for the past four hundred years, is a basic structural constant of the system.

4. International monetary system (Metropolitan Exchange Standard)[8]
The fact that the system requires a metropolitan exchange standard whereby local currencies are convertible to metropolitan currency and profits are predictable and remittable is well understood and requires little elaboration. Initially, money in peripheral countries consisted of metropolitan coins and various sorts of accounts receivable by merchant houses in the form of bills. Later there was the Gold Standard and the pound sterling exchange standard. After the Second World War there was, for a while, the dollar standard. The point here is that peripheral countries must be placed into a position where the only "real" money is foreign, or "hard," money and the only commodities which really have a price are those which are internationally traded. This ensures the perpetual primacy of the foreign trade sector over competing domestic claims on resources of land, labour and skills. This mechanism ensures the net transfer of real resources from developing to developed countries through trade. The lower the protective barriers of the developed countries, the more effectively does this mechanism work. Thus, transnationals are generally advocates of free trade, both in raw and partially processed raw materials and in manufactures. The present disorders in the international monetary system plainly threaten the stability of peripheral incorporation into the world economy. The effect of the breakdown of the system in the 1930s was a significant — if involuntary — shift towards self-reliance, particularly in some of the Latin American countries. The re-enactment of a breakdown of the international system of money and payments is likely to produce self-protective disengagement from the world capitalist system on a more extensive scale.

5. Preferential concessions within sphere-of-influence blocs (Imperial Preference)[9]
It follows from the division of the world into metropolitan spheres of influence that concessions with respect to market access and related credits and aid are normally made within the area of spheres of influence. Thus, we have the old Commonwealth preferential system, the European Community preferential system, including the Lomé Convention of preferential access to the European market by former African, Caribbean and Pacific colonies, and the Inter-American system in the Western Hemisphere. Multilateralism suits the relationship of metropolitan countries with each other, but does not suit their interests in peripheral countries where preferential systems are a kind of neocolonial remnant and, incidentally, act as a convenient device for heading off the lateral combination of commodity producers, thus reinforcing ties between local oligarchies and their traditional metropolitan business partners and political allies.

CAPITAL ACCUMULATION AND POLARIZATION

Accumulation of capital proceeds by the disembedding of successive layers of social life by the ever wider and deeper reach of commercialization. The process of capital accumulation is both disruptive and inequitable in nature. It is not the exception but the rule that the rich get richer while many of the poor become poorer. Within a nation state there are economic and political processes that result in a measure of redistribution between the rich and the poor — between capital and labour, if you wish. Between rich and poor nations there are no such processes. According to international trade theorists, movements of capital and goods equalize factor incomes. Whatever the merits or demerits of this theory, there is no evidence that this happens with respect to trade with Third World countries for reasons implicit in the previous section of this essay. Plainly, between countries there are no fiscal or other effective measures of redistribution except unilaterally asserted changes in political bargaining power. Furthermore, the classical, neo-Keynesian and Marxian models of capital accumulation and growth were essentially conceived in terms of a closed economy, with a foreign trade sector tagged on as an afterthought.

The perspective which accords to the structuralist view of this paper is one which sees capital accumulation as a progressive disembedding of social relations as an increasing number of activities generally called economic are commercialized, i.e., made the objects of market relations at prices or exchange values determined by supply and demand. This process is continuous, and the sequence does not so much constitute stages as layers of further and further penetration of the social fabric by exchange or market relations. The word market as used here implies neither the existence of competitive markets nor the absence of manipulated or administered prices. Indeed both monopolistic and monopsonistic relations are a normal means of forcing people into ever more profound situations of dependence and alienation.

This process is not inconsistent with income growth. Indeed, the world system as a whole has a very strong growth dynamic, although growth is normally polarized. It is hardly necessary to point out that the progressive alienation or disembedding described here is instituted by the use of state power, legitimated by the growth of private goods and services it engenders, and legalized by the rights of private property, sometimes extended by the state to corporations as legal persons.

Briefly then, there is a sequence whereby the merchant who originally trades in long distance goods emerges as the controlling pinnacle of the hierarchy, which Hymer described so graphically. In a sense, everything eventually becomes capital, and the accumulation of capital becomes the only objective of the system. Goods, money, labour, land, information (technology) and raw political power become commodities. To be more exact, goods apart, they are what Polanyi called "fictitious" commodities, i.e., aspects of human existence that are treated as if they were created to be bought and sold. The point is important because plainly neither land nor labour power are commodities in the sense of things *produced* for sale, but the essence of the capitalist relationship is that they are treated as if they were commodities for sale. The same holds for money and technology, not to mention political influence, as reflected in the statement that "everybody has their price."

In sequence, the process starts with commodities, i.e., goods produced to be traded. Next comes money. It is hardly necessary to recall that it took centuries to break the resistance of European society to the sin of usury — the sin of letting the market determine the price of money. Next was the long process of divorcing agricultural producers from their means of subsistence to create markets for land and labour power. In this entire process of primitive accumulation, which, as Marx explained, is essentially that of divorcing the producer from the means of production — which are also the producer's means of independent survival — the merchant, or if you prefer, those who control access to money or financial capital, have been second in importance only to the state itself. Referring to the role of the merchant in the putting-out system, Marx relates how previously independent craftsmen, "who wove and spun as a secondary rural occupation," were separated from their means of subsistence and brought under the merchants' control:

> The capitalist has prepared neither the raw material, nor the instrument, nor the means of subsistence for the weaver and the spinner. All that he has done is to restrict them, little by little, to one kind of work in which they become dependent on selling, on the *buyer*, the *merchant*, and ultimately produce only *for* and *through* him. (Marx 1973: 510, emphasis in original)

The controlling relationship of the capitalist-merchant as here described is essentially not different from that of the metropolitan controlled companies in their relations with peripheral economies. In fact, it is a graphic description of the process whereby specialization is forced upon an economy of primary producers for, little by little, it becomes dependent on the unequal relationship with the metropolitan trading partner for the import of goods and services which previously were not essential to survival. Indeed the move to relocate manufacturing or assembly of components to cheap wage countries can be seen as an international putting-out system.

Neocolonial or peripheral capitalist development requires institutions that separate the independent producer from the means of livelihood. It requires the uprooting of communities and the alienation of land. The population must be forced into participation in the international economy on penalty of starvation. This is achieved by a combination of measures well known to colonial administrators — the alienation of land, imposition of taxes payable in cash, whether as head tax or as levies imposed on basic necessities, by labour laws and a set of similar devices. Previously existing economic, social and even cultural institutions must be destroyed. People must be uprooted and driven into the labour market, where they may or may not find work. They must be made to beg for employment — and they do. They must be made to beg for the privilege of selling their produce at virtually any price — and often they do. They must be made to sell their soul for cash income. And so from time to time there are rebellions, riots and revolutions. The economy is thus eventually "disembedded" from society. In an extraordinary letter written in 1920 by a United Fruit manager to a company lawyer, we read the following graphic description of this process in Honduras: "We must produce a disembowelment of the incipient economy of this country in order to increase and help our aims. We have to prolong its tragic tormented and revolutionary life. The wind must only blow in our sails, the water must only wet our keel" (Barnet and Muller 1973: 87).

The process never stops. After money, labour and land (including natural resources) comes know-how, technology and information. Socially generated by complex processes of intergenerational transfer of knowledge, technology is becoming the private property of corporations. Technological dependence is complementing financial dependence as a principal lever for the exercise of monopoly power in relations between metropolitan and peripheral countries.

The above is no more than a sketch of the continuity of the process of capital accumulation, the continuity of the elements of power and monopoly which have always characterized it, and is offered as an antidote to the Eurocentric notion that monopoly capitalism or imperialism date from the end of the nineteenth century.

CONCLUSION

In summary (and to conclude) what is implied here is:

1. The essence of capitalism is the primacy of capital over all other social relations. It is the subordination of people and nature to the requirements of accumulation.
2. Capital is neither machines and equipment, nor money. It is the power to divorce people and whole societies from *direct access to the means of subsistence* and to force individuals and, in the case of peripheral countries, whole nations into an exchange of the fruits of their labour and the riches of their lands for access to metropolitan goods that are made to become necessities of life.
3. Peripheral producers are subordinate to metropolitan capital. Where the locus of production is peripheral, the locus of control is usually metropolitan. Thus, for example, plantation slavery, plantation wage labour and peasant cash crop production for export are to be seen as different

means of instituting regimes whereby producers are forced to yield, cede or sell their labour, or the fruits of their labour, on exploitative terms to metropolitan buyers. Differences in the labour regime are subordinate.

4. An extreme state of dependence of a peripheral economy corresponds to an extreme state of disarticulation or truncation of its productive structure — in other words, participation in the world economy on terms of extreme and fragmented specialization. Specialization in primary exports is the traditional and familiar form (cheap labour component assembly or other variants) of the new international "putting-out" system.

5. Monopolistic and monopsonistic market structures for the peripheral purchaser of imports and producer of exports *are* the normal not the exceptional condition. Deteriorating terms of trade for primary producers are to be explained by structures of economic and political power. The producer is in a vice with respect to the monopsonistic position of the metropolitan buyer, distributor or processor. Where these transactions are internalized within an integrated corporation, the share of the peripheral producers in the final selling value is low. The price paid for imports is normally higher than metropolitan consumers pay for the same goods. Where imports come in the form of intermediate goods for local processing or assembly, the monopoly position of the supplier is enhanced because local employment is now contingent on imported inputs.

6. Industrialization by invitation, as it has appropriately been labelled in the Caribbean, creates a new middle class composed of the salaried employees of foreign companies and senior level government officials, as well as self-employed professionals and local business owners. This new strata, together with the older landed and commercial elites, form a social group whose average incomes are very much higher than those of the urban worker, not to mention the rural producer and the unemployed. Socially and otherwise they are integrated into the international system in terms of consumption patterns and lifestyles.

The conclusions which follow point in the direction of strategies of collective self-reliance in order to decrease vulnerability and increase the bargaining power of Third World countries. They point in the direction of the need to re-allocate resources of peripheral countries to meet directly the material and social requirements of their people, even at the cost of partial temporary disruption of economic transactions. In other words, there must be deliberate efforts to dismantle the structures of dependency imposed on these economies by their past and continuing incorporation into an international economic system that has inherent tendencies to pile up wealth in its rich metropolitan centres and to create conditions of poverty and destitution in its peripheries.

NOTES

This chapter is based on a paper originally prepared as a "semi-paper" for a conference entitled "New Approaches to Trade," Institute of Development Studies, University of Sussex, September 8–12, 1975.

1. For a collection of works by many of these West Indian economists, see George L. Beckford (ed.) *Caribbean Economy, Dependence and Backwardness*, Institute of Social and Economic Research, University of the West Indies, Kingston, Jamaica, 1975. It also contains a useful select bibliography.

2. From the Preface by Mel Watkins in Kari Levitt (1970).

3. A posthumous publication of Hymer's essays was published as *The Multinational Corporation: A Radical Approach: Papers by Stephen Herbert Hymer*, edited by R.B. Cohen et al. (1979).

4. Note that Innis's use of the term "staple" is interchangeable with "commodity" today.

5. "Inter-Caetera" refers to a fifteenth-century papal bull dividing the world between Spain and Portugal.

6. The "Muscovado bias" refers to the export of raw sugar for refinement in the metropole.

7. "Nagivation Laws" refers to the exclusive control of communication between a metropoles and their respective colonies.

8. "Metropolitan Exchange Standard" refers to the fact that the periphery can only transact in metropolitan currency so the only "real" money is metropolitan money.

9. "Imperial Preference" refers to special privileges accorded to colonies by their respective metropoles.

10. FROM MERCANTILISM TO NEOLIBERALISM AND THE FINANCIAL CRISIS OF 2008

In this essay dedicated to the memory of Surendra Patel, we complement his work on technological transformation with a brief history of the origins and geographic spread of industrial capitalism and the ascendance and un-ravelling of Western hegemony. The financial crisis of 2008 has thrown into relief the contrast between the rapacious accumulation of wealth by large agglomerations of corporate economic power in the Global North and the dynamic national energy of the youthful populations of regions of the Global South. As the growing points of the world economy are shifting from North and West to South and East, Asia is reclaiming its historical importance. We attempt, in the words of Keynes, to "study the present in the light of the past for the purposes of the future" (Johnson and Moggridge 1972: 173–4).

THE INDOMITABLE OPTIMISM OF SURENDRA PATEL

I had the good fortune of meeting Surendra Patel a long time ago, in the early 1970s at the United Nations Conference on Trade and Development (UNCTAD) in Geneva, where he was working on technology transfer. We next met in Halifax, Nova Scotia, in 1975, at the International Development Research Centre-supported conference "The New International Economic Order," chaired by Gerry Helleiner. Surendra gave the keynote address, and I was invited to comment as a discussant. Krishna was present, and by that time we had formed a friendship that continued during the many years when Surendra and Krishna Patel were distinguished visiting professors at Saint Mary's University in Halifax.

The principal subject of Surendra Patel's lifelong research was techno-logical transformation and development in the Global South, in the service of the United Nations, where he was director of the Technology Division of UNCTAD prior to his retirement in 1989. Patel was a model development economist who combined a detailed command of data with a profound com-mitment to radical change. It was his good fortune to receive his early training as a student in the United States under Nobel-laureate Simon Kuznets, an outstanding pioneer of development economics. I like to think that he learned a great deal from Kuznets of how intelligent conclusions can be reached from long-term projections of growth rates and an understanding of the power of compound interest. Surendra joined the early United Nations in New York as the first Indian employed in the production of the World Economic Survey, under the direction of Michael Kalecki, considered by some to have been the most important macro- and development economist of his generation. Using Marxian categories of the department of producer goods and the department of consumer goods, Kalecki arrived at conclusions with similarities to those of Keynes's *General Theory of Employment, Interest and Money* (1936) concerning instability and long-term unemployment within a capitalist system. Many European Continental economists were as familiar with Marxian as with Anglo-Saxon economics. This was also true in Japan and, more generally, in Asia. The 1950s was the era of McCarthy. Kalecki was forced to leave the United Nations and return to Poland; Patel was permitted to remain, but his movements were restricted to the immediate vicinity of the United Nations in New York.

In 1964 UNCTAD was established under the direction of Raul Prebisch, and Patel was personally invited by Prebisch to join the staff. In a seminal paper, *The World Economy in Transition 1850–2060*, published in a festschrift honouring Marxist economist Maurice Dobb (Feinstein 1967), Patel established that prior to the Industrial Revolution there was no discernable increase in GDP per capita and that the Industrial Revolution itself did not bear fruit in terms of increased living standards until the middle of the nineteenth century. As industrialization was undertaken by an increasing number of countries, late-comers were able to benefit from "the accumulated treasure house of world technology" and "could short-circuit the jump from one stage of technical development to another by a massive adaptation of the existing knowledge" (Patel 2007: 9). Patel established that as countries entered the world economy to the benchmark year of 1960, average annual per capita growth rates progressively increased, in the following manner:

> 1.2 to 1.4 per cent in England and France; 1.6 to 1.8 per cent for Germany, Denmark, Switzerland, the U.S. and Canada; 2.1 to 2.8 per cent for Norway, Sweden and Japan; 4 per cent or higher, depending upon the estimator, for the Soviet Union. And as high as 6 per cent and above during the last 15 years for a number of countries. (Patel 2007: 8)

From this analysis, Patel concluded that "the growth rate of output has progressively tended to rise over the last century, and this trend can be expected to continue" (15). On the basis of these trends and a leap of faith, he anticipated that "the world [was] set for an incredible economic explosion in the century to come" (21). Where most development economists could see only failure (growth without development; growth without employment) and it was fashionable in the West to dismiss development as yesterday's agenda, Patel insisted upon the recognition of the simply spectacular record of the Global South since 1945.

Writing some twenty-five years later in a UNU/WIDER publication (Patel 1995), Patel's earlier optimism was validated. He documented the achievements of the Global South in sustaining average annual growth of over 5 percent over a period of forty years, from 1950 to 1990, by a population ten times larger than that of the developed world. Significant economic transformation included increasing urbanization and a declining share of agriculture in GDP; increasing industrialization and share of manufacturing in exports; an increase in the rates of savings and investment; and an unprecedented expansion of capital formation, including health and education, both public and private. While the development gap in terms of GDP per capita was large and continued to increase, the social gap was significantly reduced: life expectancy increased from around thirty-five to sixty or seventy years; infant mortality rates declined from about 250 to 70 per thousand; literacy rates rose to 50 percent in Africa and 80 percent in Latin America; and while there were ten times more students enrolled in higher education in the North than in the South at the start of the post-war era, forty years later the numbers were approximately equal. These achievements were described by eminent development economist Paul Streeten as a "spectacular, unprecedented and unexpected success" (quoted in Patel 1995: 220).

In *Development Distance Between Nations*, written with Krishna and Mahesh in 1995, Surendra expressed his belief that "a significant narrowing of the distances between the levels of living in the North and South will not take hopeless centuries. The task needs only 50 to 70 years, or simply the life cycle of a person just born" (Patel, Patel and Patel 1995: vii). In an article entitled *East Asia's Explosive Development*, he noted that East Asia had "in one giant leap covered its social distance from the West" and that "the emergence of this rival centre on the world stage [had] fundamentally altered the old balance of world economic power" (2007: 180).

We conclude this brief tribute to our colleague and friend Surendra Patel by sharing his words of advice to planners, strategists and theorists of the South:

> Quite clearly, the expansion of intra-country trade has been the most important stimulus to the development of East Asian countries. Equally clearly, the new economic centre of East Asia will also play an important developmental role by serving as a large potential market for the exports of other developing countries. East Asia "has achieved a critical mass in sustaining a chain reaction of mutual

prosperity" (Ball 1993: 29). In the process, the old pioneers of the Industrial Revolution will have yielded to the newly industrialized East Asia. The four-century eclipse of Asia by the West will have ended, and a new stage in world economic history will have begun. (Patel 2007: 182–83)

When Surendra was working in the early United Nations in New York in the 1950s, nobody imagined that China could in the next sixty years become the growing point of the world economy and the world's leading exporter of manufactures. The 550 million people of China were at that time among the poorest people on Earth, with per capita GDP substantially below traditional subsistence levels, contributing a mere 5 percent to world production; India's GDP per capita had barely increased since the mid-eighteenth century.[1] Patel's optimistic evaluation of the achievement of the Global South, which he greeted as a "miraculous" achievement of catch-up growth by the majority of the people of the world, was a result of his long historical vision of the technological revolution as just a brief moment in the evolution of human civilization.

Eurocentrism has greatly exaggerated the economic development of Europe compared with that of Asia prior to the advent of industrial capitalism. As recently as 1820, China's economy was larger than that of Western Europe; production in Asia was nearly twice that of all of Europe including Russia. Adam Smith, writing in 1776, considered China to be the most stable and advanced — although not the most dynamic — civilization of his time.

In 1700 there was no substantial difference in the income and wealth of Eurasian civilizations; living standards were approximately equal in China, India and most of Europe, although by that time considerably higher in Western Europe. While in Mogul India and Qing China manufacturing was more extensive and the quality superior to Europe, it was not in these older civilizations but in the unlikely small nation-states of northwestern Europe that technology was first harnessed to achieve an explosive increase in production. Whereas the surplus of pre-capitalist civilizations was invested in palaces, temples and churches, and canals, irrigation and other public works, industrial civilization resulted from the investment of the economic surplus in the enhancement of the productive forces of industry and agriculture.

To realize the profitability inherent in the increase in the productivity of labour associated with the early Industrial Revolution, commerce and conquest were reconfigured from the acquisition of spices and fine textiles from distant lands, to the acquisition of markets for the industrial exports of the metropoles. As a small island with limited land resources, England could not have sustained the productivity-enhancing innovations of the early Industrial Revolution without access to colonial markets and imported raw materials and cereal grains to feed its rapidly growing industrial proletariat. Industry and empire were an inseparable continuum from mercantilism to free trade imperialism and colonialism.

Although Patel's account of technological transformation suggests that the industrialization of Europe did not impact the rest of the world until the mid-nineteenth century (1850–70), it was in the three centuries of mercantilism (1500–1800) that the explosion of European conquest and commerce determined the contours of what we now call the Global South. It was in this period that the emerging states of the Atlantic seaboard of Europe began their ascent to world dominance and industrial capitalism was incubated in England.

For two centuries, approximately 1780 to 1980, Western capitalism achieved a historic fifty-fold increase in world output and seven-fold increase in world population. But the progressive financialization, liberalization and commoditization of Western economies since 1980 — led by the United States and Great Britain — is reminiscent of the mercantilist origins of capitalism in commerce and dispossession. The innovation of techniques of proprietary control over technology and markets has become more profitable than innovation in production through the concentration of financial wealth, the creation of rents by corporate capital, the dispossession of land, the plunder of natural resources and even the establishment of plantations — now for biomass to be used as fuel.

MERCANTILIST ROOTS OF CAPITALISM: CONTINUITIES AND LEGACIES

Capitalism was born in historically specific circumstances; in the competition of emerging maritime nation-states of the Atlantic rim of Europe in an alliance of the merchant class and the national sovereign for commerce and conquest, trade and war, wealth and territory. It was not by superiority in production, but by superiority in commerce and conquest that primitive accumulation transferred resources from the non-European world to European metropoles. The explosive dynamic between the small nation-states of the Atlantic seaboard has been attributed to the fierce competition between them; constant conflict for control and protection of sea-lanes east and west encouraged the progressive improvement of shipbuilding, skills of navigation and maritime warfare. At that time, shipbuilding was a strategic industry supported by the state, analogous to the aerospace industry of today, and control of the sea-lanes was as important then as control of airspace is today.

The principal economic institution of mercantilism was the joint-stock chartered company. The companies were granted monopolies by the sovereign to operate in specially designated areas, engage in trade, set-up ports and forts, raise armies and dispense justice. They comprised a complex operation of shareholders who ventured their capital, merchants who advanced the supplies and sold the commodities in domestic and third markets, mariners who undertook the risks of the voyages, and behind them the artisans who built the ships and fashioned the trade goods. Their activities, commonly described as trade, are better understood as commercial enterprise in which the costs of assembling and outfitting the sea voyage along with attendant risks were large in relation to the value of European trade goods exchanged for exotic commodities in Asia or slaves on the coasts of Africa.

Underlying structures of economic dominance and dependence established in the era of mercantilism continue to characterize relations of trade and investment between the North and South. From the old mercantilism of the chartered companies to the new mercantilism of the transnational corporations, control over channels of distribution and communication remain the principal means of exercising economic power. By their control over access to markets — and later also technology — they are in a position to capture the major share of the surplus generated by producers, indeed some of the largest transnational corporations of our times do not engage directly in production. Formal economics erases the institutional structures of power that underlie international economic transactions.

Unlike the chartered companies of the old mercantilism that operated at the will and with the benediction of the sovereign, the transnational corporations of a new mercantilism have penetrated the corridors of power in the West and effectively control the political process. Governments are hostage to the judgement of capital markets. The failure of U.S. and British governments to limit the power of financial capital in the wake of the 2008 crisis has demonstrated the degree to which the democratic process has been undermined.

The Creation of the Global South

The legacies of European commercial expansion to Asia are very different from Europe's territorial expansion across the Atlantic. Europe had long traded with the East by intermediation of Arab and other Asian traders to access the exotic products of the more advanced civilizations of Asia. With the capture of the ports of the Levant by the Ottomans and the ultimate fall of Constantinople in 1453, the action moved from the Mediterranean to the Atlantic seaboard. Portuguese and Dutch mariners, soon followed by the English, captured strategic locations from the Cape to Ceylon, Goa, the Malacca Strait and Formosa, among others, to access trading opportunities in the Indian Ocean and the China Seas, and in 1492 Columbus set out to find a westward route to China. In the following year the Pope divided the entire world between the two great Catholic powers — the East to Portugal, the West to Spain. When the Portuguese reached Japan, Japanese authorities, upon hearing of European ravaging of American civilizations, closed their ports to all European traders until the nineteenth century, a decision which may account for the success of Japan in economic and imperial expansion from the late nineteenth century.

The Dutch East India Company was established in 1602 with a capital ten times greater than that of the English East India Company (established in 1600) and a charter granting monopoly of all trade east of the Cape of Good Hope, including the Indian Ocean, the China Seas and the Pacific as far as the Straits of Magellan at the southern tip of South America. Without the huge profits generated from its monopoly of the Indonesian spice trade, Amsterdam could not have established the first permanent stock exchange. But the population of the Netherlands was too small to provide the personnel necessary to engage in successful naval warfare with the French or English in the Atlantic, or to establish permanent settlement colonies or plantations in the New World; declining economic power was accompanied by financialization and, in the seventeenth century, Amsterdam became the principal financial centre of Europe.

The English East India Company engaged in the initially less profitable trade of high quality cotton piece goods. From the mid-eighteenth century, the Company occupied regions of India, including Bengal, the industrial centre of Indian cotton textile production, and effectively assumed government from the disintegrating Mogul Empire, extracting increasing tribute from peasants and imposing punishing conditions on suppliers of fine cotton exports. The leading industry of the English Industrial Revolution was cotton textiles, and the powerful Lancashire industrialists obtained prohibitive tariffs against Indian cotton imports while cheap English textiles entered India duty free. In 1857, the British brutally suppressed a rebellion by the Indian Army and imposed crown colony government; this is known as the Great Indian Mutiny in Britain and the First War of Independence in India. The English East India Company enjoyed great social prestige and its college employed Thomas Malthus. As senior employees of the East India Company, James Mill and John Stuart Mill had intimate knowledge of the impoverishment of the Indian handloom weavers by the imposition of British cotton products and the Company's role in the Chinese Opium Wars, which contributed to mass addiction and the humiliating incapacity of the government to deal with civil war, famine and semi-colonization.

The accumulation of capital from trade with Asia was substantial but modest compared with the benefits that accrued to Europe from its westward expansion, which effectively embraced all of the Americas to extend its land frontier by the establishment of colonies of conquest, exploitation and settlement. The conquest of the Aztec and Inca Empires and the large shipments of gold and silver to Europe in the sixteenth century monetized feudal obligations and accelerated the accumulation of capital. It also assisted in compensating for Europe's relative poverty in trade goods; the fine imbalance of trade with the East for spices from Indonesia and silks and other manufactures from China was covered by shipments of silver. The destruction of Amerindian civilizations and the decline of their populations by exploitation and disease resulted in the marginalization of the indigenous peoples together with their cultures and languages. Christianity was imposed. The official language of every state of the Americas is one or another European language.

Throughout the colonial period, the economic and social elites of Latin America maintained close commercial and cultural ties with European metropoles. Political independence was not accompanied by a reform in land ownership, which remained highly concentrated. The philosophy of the Enlightenment did not penetrate into the social fabric — the institutions of representative government were largely controlled by rival factions contesting for power over the state. Land owners profited from the export of temperate and tropical foodstuffs and, later, also mineral commodities to Europe and North America. The virtual exclusion of indigenous peoples and the inferior status of populations of African descent have endowed Latin America with deep ethnic and class cleavages and inequalities of income, wealth and opportunities exceeding anything found in other regions of the Global South. There is a deficit of national cohesion. In many countries, elites effectively do not pay taxes. The state is in perpetual fiscal shortfall. The frequency of political and economic crises and the temptation of populist governments to deal with distributional conflict by printing money are ultimately due to the unresolved legacies of the origins of Latin American society.

Colonies of Exploitation

Colonies of exploitation were established by investment in land and the import of a supply of slave labour for the sole purpose of producing a valuable commodity for profitable sale in the Metropole and third markets. The sugar plantations established in Northeast Brazil, the Caribbean and the littoral of South and Central America were essentially a capitalist operation, where the purchase of enslaved labourers was the principal investment of the planter. Indeed the price of the enslaved person was determined by supply and demand, and the estimated labour power embodied in the man or woman according to height, weight and age. Sugar was Britain's single largest import in the eighteenth century, and the exports of the tiny island of Grenada were eight times more valuable than the exports of Canada. In the English-speaking Caribbean, the planters were generally the younger sons of the landed classes of England because property passed to the first-born son. Plantations were encumbered to relatives or mortgaged to merchants in the metropole. The profitability of the plantations sustained the profitability of the slave trade, which also secured Britain's naval and military superiority. In the continental countries of Brazil and the southern United States, where land was not scarce and the labour regime was less harsh, the populations of slaves increased by natural reproduction and populations of European origin shared spaces with descendents of Africans. Both in Brazil and in the United States, the legacy of slavery remains to be extinguished in terms of the social and economic status of African-descended populations.

The scale of the slave trade is illustrated by the fact that prior to the nineteenth century the number of Africans transported across the Atlantic significantly exceeded European population movements to the Americas. The ultimate cost of the slave trade to Africa was larger than the lives consumed on the mines and plantations of the new world. The knowledge that there was a market for gold and captives at the coast depressed trans-Saharan trade and encouraged local chiefs and rulers to engage in wars to sell captives to merchants in exchange for trade goods. The introduction of guns exacerbated conflict. It has been estimated that the number of Africans who perished in these wars was greater than the ten to fifteen million Africans shipped across the Atlantic as slaves. The demographic shock of the loss of so many millions of men and women in the prime years of their working lives was reflected in the stagnation of population growth on a vast continent of only 75 million people in 1820.

Colonies of Settlement

When England emerged victorious over France in 1815, after more than a century of rivalry and war in the Americas, Asia and finally Europe, the land stolen from the indigenous populations of North America was set to become the major power of the English-speaking world. Many of the early settlers were escaping religious persecution and sought to establish a new society free from the oppressive class structures of Europe. Their right to the lands they cleared and cultivated were grounded in the doctrines of John Locke, whereby the labour applied to common lands legitimated property titles. The defence of settlements from attack by indigenous peoples displaced from the territories that provided their traditional livelihoods explains the extraordinary provision of the right to bear arms in the U.S. constitution. The constant state of warfare inherent in the westward expansion, later expressed as the Manifest Destiny of the United States, is a formative element of its national psyche. Early political and financial institutions were highly decentralized and there was a general distrust of the power of government. The founding fathers constructed the U.S. Constitution of checks and balances of the legislative, judiciary and executive to safeguard individual liberty from the concentration of power in the office of the president.

Early American industrial development was based on balanced growth of farmers and artisans exchanging their products in a free market, which was protected from external competition by high tariffs from the establishment of the republic until the Second World War. This strategy favouring develop-ment of the expanding domestic market, considered by Adam Smith to be the "Natural Path," was articulated by Alexander Hamilton, first secretary of the treasury (1789–95) in his *Report on the Subject of Manufactures* (1791). Hamilton believed the primary object of nations is to supply themselves with subsistence from their own soil; manufacturing nations should, as far as possible, use domestic raw materials, and import substitution for manufactures should be encouraged and assisted where the external terms of trade are unfair and the trading partners want to "[sell] everything and [buy] nothing" (Hamilton 1791 [2007]: 24). The sparsely populated ever-expanding open frontier encouraged the introduction of labour-saving devices on farms and households and business opportunities for industrial-scale manufacturing; thus the combine harvester, the tractor, the general purpose pick-up truck. The iconic example of the labour-saving household device was the sewing machine, initially powered by foot or by hand and marketed directly to housewives in distant lands on hire-purchase instalment plans by the Singer Company. Geography favoured the development of rail and road transport, and, ultimately, the U.S. pioneered assembly-line mass production of the automobile, facilitating suburbanization and the acquisition of a range of consumer durables. Indeed development driven by consumption created the culture of consumerism, the soft power of twentieth-century American capitalism.

The impact of five hundred years of European conquest and colonialism has been very different in the diverse regions of the Global South. Although plantation slavery was not abolished until the 1860s, the American Revolution set the United States on a course of self-sustaining economic development while Latin America and the Caribbean, and also Africa, were destined to become export-dependent peripheries supplying agricultural and mineral raw material to the industrial centres of Europe and the United States. They became dependent on metropolitan markets as drivers of economic growth. Dominated by European and later also American political, commercial and cultural influences, indigenous national enterprise was stunted or explicitly suppressed.

By way of difference, although exploited, the societies of Asia were not destroyed in the era of mercantilism. They were not uprooted. Village life continued much as before — tribute had always been paid to one or another ruler. The Europeans did not impose their religion and they did not establish settlement colonies. It was not until the Industrial Revolution, and the search for new markets and investments, that the nations of Western Europe extended colonial control over Africa and most of Asia in the late nineteenth century. Free trade imperialism and colonialism impoverished India, humiliated and devastated China, and exploited labour in the mines and plantations of Southeast Asia. But resistance to the subjection of Asian civilizations to European colonialism was organized by a variety of national political movements. Struggles for independence contributed to national identity, but most importantly, the older civilizations of Asia escaped the worst consequences of European colonialism — a loss of self-esteem; in various ways with important differences they have chartered their own paths to economic development.

East and South Asia were much poorer than Latin America, the

Caribbean, the Middle East and even Africa in the 1950s.[2] Latin American and Caribbean economic growth was strong until the onset of the debt crises of the 1980s, but the predominance of traditional oligarchies in primary export activities, together with dependence on multinational corporations both in extractive and import substituting industries, critically inhibited the development of export manufacturing. By contrast, in the former Japanese colonies of Korea and Taiwan, the concerted determination of governments and national enterprise enabled these countries to compete in external markets in state-of-the-art transportation equipment and electronics. Political and economic elites rejected policies of short-term comparative advantage based on cheap labour in favour of nurturing ever-increasing value-added industries.

ENGLAND AS PIONEER OF INDUSTRIAL CAPITALISM

In the seventeenth century, Britain challenged and defeated Dutch naval power and commercial hegemony; in the eighteenth century, Britain contested world hegemony with France and, as noted, assured an English-speaking future for North America. The seamless transition from British to American hegemony in the course of the transformational crises from 1914 to 1945, and their continuing special relationship, testifies to historical commonalities and a shared ideological foundation of individual liberty and free enterprise grounded in the institution of private property. Two centuries of British and subsequently American hegemony in the capitalist world order have endowed the English-speaking world with an imperial mission to bring order to an unruly world, by force if necessary. We trace this common heritage to the birth of industrial capitalism in England.

The conditions prevailing in England were unique. The English Revolution of the seventeenth century had stripped the monarchy of effective power, but it was not a bourgeois revolution in the continental sense of the proclamation of universal citizen rights. Under British constitutional government, sovereignty was exercised by a Parliament controlled by a hereditary oligarchy of landed and commercial elites. This governing class was socialized to rule on the playing fields of select private so-called "public" schools and in the halls of Oxbridge. In the nineteenth century, Conservatives and Liberals, Tories and Whigs, alternated in office, but the affairs of state and the management of the Empire were entrusted to a self-perpetuating mandarinate of public servants usually drawn from upper class families of independent means. The legal and institutional basis of the capitalist economic order was constructed when the majority of the population had no voice and the vote was severely restricted to owners of property. The control of the ruling classes over British politics was not seriously challenged until the mass unemployment of the inter-war years discredited the old order and sweeping social reforms were introduced by the Labour Party following the Second World War.

Whereas peasant agriculture predominated in Continental Europe, where yields were lower and famines still occurred, agrarian capitalism in England had substantially raised living standards by the end of the eighteenth century. The peasantry had virtually disappeared. Two centuries of enclosures of common lands had transformed the peasantry into wage labour on farms mainly operated by tenant farmers paying rents to an oligarchy of land-owning gentry and squires. A surplus of displaced peasants was redundant to this productivity-enhancing model of capitalist agriculture. They roamed the countryside as vagabonds; they were the new underclass of the "undeserving able-bodied poor." They were shipped to settlement colonies or rounded up in the ports and "spirited" to swell the ranks of sailors. In areas surrounding the port cities of Bristol and Liverpool, industries supplied a variety of simple manufactures for overseas trade on the coast of Africa, the American colonies and the plantations.

The most powerful and influential class of the period was the landed oligarchy of minor nobility; together with the merchant class and West Indian planters they controlled Parliament. In some cases, a seat could be purchased from a mere handful of eligible voters, as in the case of David Ricardo, who bought such a seat in 1819. Unlike their counterparts on the Continent of Europe, English aristocracy was not averse to commerce; they invested in the improvement and cultivation of crops and livestock and advanced working capital to tenant farmers on their estates. Prominent members of the landed oligarchy occupied senior positions in the East India Company. Perhaps the plantations provide the best illustration of an enterprise that benefited both the merchants who advanced the credit and sold a product, and the landed families who profited from the gains of the planters. The accumulation of capital in England took the form of increasing availability of commercial, short-term advances to agriculture, small industry and overseas commerce.

Adam Smith's exposition of the three major classes which constitute the national economy, referring to those who "live by rent, those who live by wages, and those who live by profit," was drawn from his observation of a capitalist market economy which was agrarian and rural, not yet industrial or urban. Smith's seminal work, *An Inquiry into the Nature and Causes of the Wealth of Nations* (1776), made no mention of the revolutionary innovations introduced in the cotton spinning industry. On the cusp of the transition from agrarian to industrial capitalism, Smith turned his invective against the mercantile system and the merchant class. He believed the real source of the wealth of a nation to be the efforts and skills of its people rather than the accumulation of treasure.

It was not until the invention of the rotary steam engine in 1784 that a power revolution replacing wind, water and horses could be introduced to manufacturing industries and transportation. The decisive technological leap to high-productivity manufacturing came in the cotton spinning industry.

Prior to a series of productivity enhancing innovations, it took ten artisanal spinners to supply one weaver. The machinery was simple and the textile mills were initially driven by water power; they were based in rural areas and, in the absence of an effective banking system, the capital required was local in origin. The factory, some four and five stories high, was an innovation in industrial organization assembling hundreds of workers — mostly women and children — under one roof operating machinery which controlled and dictated the pace of work. The increase in productivity was extraordinary, reflected in the ten-fold decline in the cost of one pound of spun yarn. By the 1830s, the cotton industry contributed more to national income than all other industries and accounted for approximately one-half of total British exports. Rapid mechanization and massive employment of cheap labour yielded high profits; the value of net output increased eight times more than the wage bill in the textile industry.

Production greatly exceeded domestic demand but due to the poor quality of the cloth, foreign sales were limited to captive colonial markets of slave traders on the coast of Africa, the American colonies and most importantly India, whose economy was reorganized to supply Britain with cotton, jute, other raw materials and foodstuffs, including wheat, sugar and tea. The economic historian Eric Hobsbawm has suggested that the Industrial Revolution could not have occurred without pre-existing mercantilist relations of colonial trade. Without the Empire there could not have been a cotton industry, and without the cotton industry there might not have been the Industrial Revolution. No wonder the Brazilian economist and historian Celso Furtado called the Industrial Revolution a "genuine mutation" (1983: 35).

As noted by Patel, the Industrial Revolution did not raise real wages in England until the middle of the nineteenth century, and its impact on the rest of the world — with the important exception of India — was not significant until 1850–70. The first fifty years of nineteenth-century England were haunted by the fear of social upheaval, riot or even revolution. The established elites were terrified that subversive ideas of the French Revolution might cross the Channel as the rising price of bread during the long years of the Napoleonic Wars further immiserized the dispossessed, unemployed and impoverished wage earners. Agricultural labourers who organized trade unions were deported to the colonies. Even after the Reform Act of 1832, which extended the vote to the urban bourgeoisie, the franchise was severely restricted to the propertied classes. Social movements, including Luddism, radicalism, trade unionism, Utopian Socialism and Chartism, brought the country to the brink of revolution.

The most striking evidence of the contrast between the optimism of Adam Smith and the gloomy doctrines of the political economists who followed him was Smith's natalist belief in the benefits of a growing population and that working people could and should enjoy rising wages and an improved standard of living. In the early nineteenth century, a new breed of political economists, preoccupied with an explosive increase in population, turned their attention to the reform of the Poor Law, which had provided assistance since Elizabethan times. The New Poor Law of 1834, introduced by the reformed Parliament, prohibited outdoor poor relief and effectively criminalized poverty. The poor were to be forced into employment, however low the wages and long the hours, on penalty of consignment to draconian workhouses designed to be more inhospitable than prisons, a fate which carried serious social stigma. An architect of this legislation, Nassau Senior, was the first professor of political economy to be appointed at Oxford University. The doctrines of the new political economists held that attempts to relieve the corrective pattern of misery could only make things worse for the poor. The idle and improvident working classes must not be encouraged to become dependent on the taxpaying classes, whose profits were required to finance productive investment. Labour markets must be free to depress wages to subsistence. It is difficult to escape comparison with prevailing neoliberal economic philosophy in the United States, where deep cuts of taxation of the rich are justified by their supposed contribution to productive investment, "flexible wages" of the working poor have reduced incomes of some wage earners below poverty levels and state support for the unemployed and the poor is demonized as socialism.

The pressure of the population on the food supply and the real cost of providing even a subsistence wage gave rise to the demand for the abolition of the so-called Corn Laws, which restricted the import of wheat. The movement for the abolition of the Corn Laws enjoyed wide popular support, including that of the rising industrial classes, while the increasing engagement of the landed upper classes in industrial enterprise may explain the absence of significant opposition to their abolition. Ricardo supported the movement on the grounds that it would benefit both labour and capital because the importation of cheap food would reduce the cost of providing subsistence wages and thus sustain profits. The abolition of the Corn Laws in 1846 and the subsequent removal of duties on timber, sugar and other raw materials owed nothing to Ricardo's famous theory of comparative advantage because it was unilateral and demanded no concessions from trading partners. With an undisputed supremacy in manufacturing, England had everything to gain from a regime of free trade.

In the transition from the rural world of Adam Smith and the age of Enlightenment to the raw industrial capitalism of the early nineteenth century, political economy played an active role. Karl Polanyi insisted that the discovery of political economy as a science was more important than the simple mechanical inventions of the early Industrial Revolution because it fashioned an ideology which became an active agent in the social transformation toward a capitalist market system. His famous dictum that "laissez-faire was planned" referred to the role of the state in the restructuring of society by political intervention to conform to the requirements of the calculus of private profit in agricultural and industrial production. The role of economics in furnishing a scientific rationale for acquisitive individualism, the role of the state in constructing the institutional framework of global capitalism and the role of the mass media in celebrating fame and fortune are a powerful defence of contemporary corporate capitalism. Together, they constrain the limits of the possible in the popular imagination and disempower resistance.

Perhaps the most influential political economist of the nineteenth century was Jeremy Bentham, high priest of utilitarian philosophy and father of *homo economicus*. He believed that a person was a utility calculator perpetually weighing the advantages and disadvantages of pleasure and pain; when acting in free competitive markets individual choice would produce the optimal social outcome. By peeling away the institutional context of classical political economy, neoclassical economics — based on the axioms of methodological individualism — became the accepted view of rational economic behaviour and serves as the logical foundation of modern economics. It is here that we locate the ideological taproot of the neoliberalism of our times, which has transformed and debased the ideals of freedom and equality of the Enlightenment to the freedom of capital and private enterprise to unlimited access to reconstruct societies in their image and interests.

When Marx arrived in England in 1849, the new system of industrial capitalism had clearly set the world on a course of extraordinary increase in productive capacity. It is difficult to imagine more extravagant praise to the achievements of the bourgeoisie than can be found in the *Communist Manifesto* (1848): "The forces of production have increased more in a hundred years than they have since the dawn of human history, nature has been subjected to man, science has transformed both agriculture and industry, whole continents have been cleared for cultivation to sustain a vast increase in population."

Marx was the first political economist of industrial capitalism. The principal source of the accumulation of capital was no longer in commerce or agriculture, but in investment in machinery employing ever-increasing numbers of workers at subsistence wages. A workday of twelve to sixteen hours was not uncommon until legislation introduced in 1847 limited the working hours of women and children to ten hours a day. Whereas Ricardo targeted the landlord as the parasitical class, Marx used the Ricardian model to reveal the capitalist as the exploiter of labour, and surplus value as the source of profit under prevailing conditions of competition. The dominance of capital over labour is due to the private ownership of the means of production, which invests the capitalist with full ownership of the product of social labour. The idea of exploitation in capitalist production was not original to Marx; it was current in French socialist thought and succinctly expressed by Pierre-Joseph Proudhon in the famous epithet "property is theft."

Marxism never took root in England, where Marx lived and wrote his most important work. In mid-Victorian times economic benefits began to accrue to the working people of Britain. Working men aspired to social status in their habits of dress as associations and trade unions based along craft lines organized insurance for funeral expenses, saving societies, consumer cooperatives and measures to improve working conditions. A political party representing the interests of labour in Britain was not established until 1906, long after socialist parties on the continent were represented in the Parliaments of Germany and France. Socialist critics of an increasingly commercialized capitalist society included Christian Socialists, William Morris and the Fabian Society, who shared the hope of French socialist philosopher Saint Simon that industrialization could "assure the happiness of all by spreading industrial arts and by submitting the world to the peaceful laws of industry" (Gerschenkron 1962: 24). They believed that the universal franchise, and with it the entry into representation of the working class in Parliament and government, could attain these objectives. Extension of the franchise was resisted by the propertied classes, who maintained that only those with a stake in society could be trusted with control over government. Although qualifications regarding property were gradually relaxed, prior to 1872 there was no secret ballot and 40 percent of British males — including veterans of the First World War — were still disenfranchised in 1918, when the right to vote was granted to all males. Britain was among the last of the Western countries to introduce universal male franchise, long enjoyed by citizens of France and Switzerland (since 1848), and Germany (since 1871). In the United States discriminatory restrictions on the universal franchise were not eliminated until 1965.

TECHNOLOGICAL TRANSFORMATION OF LATE-COMER INDUSTRIALIZERS

The way in which industrialization and modern capitalist economic development spread from northwest Europe to the late-comers varied significantly according to historical and cultural legacy, resource endowment and the period in which these countries entered the world economy. Britain was the model to be emulated. Industrialization spread to the older pioneers of France, Belgium, and adjoining regions of Western Europe. Free trade was greeted as a liberating doctrine to break down feudal barriers of princely states and monopolies of corporate guilds. It was associated with the Enlightenment and radical movements challenging *ancien régimes*. The revolutions of 1848 enjoyed wide ranging popular support, and economic liberalism was seen as freedom from oppressive constraints. The Free Trade Agreement of historical enemies France and Britain, signed in 1860, symbolized a new age of prosperity and freedom in Western Europe, and as noted industrialization was embraced by both bourgeois and socialist thinkers alike.

Conscious of the advantages which accrued to England by virtue of its headstart in international competition, Friedrich List concluded that a less developed country, such as Germany, should protect its productive potential against competition until such time as its industries could successfully compete with stronger nations. List acknowledged that protection had a cost in terms of higher domestic prices, but that duties could "awaken the sleeping energies of a country" and attract productive powers of foreign capital and skills. List, author of *National System of Political Economy* (1841), was an early advocate of national economic planning and has been called the "official economist of Bismarckian development" (Lipietz 1987: 54).

The political moments which marked the consolidation of the nation-states of the major world powers of the twentieth century occurred within an extraordinarily short space of time in the decade of the 1860s. Although the United States was founded in 1776, it was the victory of the more dynamic and industrially advanced Yankee North over the wealthy but backward plantation economy of the South in the American Civil War (1861–65) that consolidated American capitalist development and cleared the way for the realization of its Manifest Destiny. In Germany, the strong nation-state was both an instrument and an objective of modernization. German economic and military power was built by an alliance of the landed classes of Prussia with the industrialists of the Western provinces in the unification of Germany in 1871. The modernization of Czarist Russia, the most backward country of Europe, starting with the emancipation of the serfs in 1861, was motivated more by national aspirations to be recognized as a great power of Europe than by consideration of private profit; the virtual non-existence of an indigenous bourgeoisie accorded the leading developmental role to the state bureaucracy. In Japan, the Meiji restoration of 1868 sought to counter Western power by modelling reforms on Bismarck's Germany; modernization and industrialization were a defensive reaction by the traditional ruling classes to resist Westernization by the strategic adaptation of Western technology and institutions to Japanese national objectives. To the above list of political moments of the 1860s, we could add the unification of Italy (1861); equal status of the Kingdom of Hungary within the Austro-Hungarian Empire (1868); and the creation of the Canadian state by the confederation of the remaining British provinces of North America (1867).

In all the late-comers, economic development went hand in hand with the consolidation and territorial expansion of the nation-state. In all cases the precondition for economic development was the subordination of traditional elites to national strategies of accelerated industrialization, although the United States was exceptional in its adherence to a philosophy of economic liberalism and a belief in an adversarial relationship between government and business. Alexander Gerschenkron and also Celso Furtado emphasized the role of ideology in national economic development; the motives of the late industrializers were not only economic but also political. Not only was national unification a precondition for economic development but economic development was a means — an instrument to further the national project.

Lessons of Nineteenth-Century Industrialization for the Global South

Alexander Gerschenkron's seminal work, *Economic Backwardness in Historical Perspective* (1962), was written to retrieve the lessons of the experience of the nineteenth-century late industrializers for the new nations emerging from colonialism after the Second World War. His reading of the industrialization of the late-comer nations of Germany, Imperial Austria and Russia antici- pated by several decades the recognition of the fundamental importance of institutional innovation, leapfrogging of technology, educational and social policy and the role of ideology in the mobilization of individual and collective national energies for the escape from economic backwardness. Opportunities inherent in industrialization vary directly with the degree of backwardness: the greater the technological gap, the greater the opportunity to "leapfrog" by means of the adoption of the most modern and efficient technology available. For this reason European countries at a relatively early stage of industrialization concentrated on branches of industry in which technology was most modern, "while the more advanced countries, either from inertia or unwillingness to require or impose sacrifices implicit in a large investment program, were more hesitant to carry out continual modernizations of their plant" (Gerschenkron 1962: 9–10).

Above all, what emerges from the success of the first generation of late industrializers is a long-term strategic — rather than a short-term profit maximizing — approach to economic development. The Germans devel- oped the universal bank, which became the dominant form of banking on the Continent of Europe, combining long-term investment banking with traditional English-style short-term commercial credit. These banks were not averse to risk taking. They borrowed short and lent long but accompa- nied the borrowing enterprises with technical advice from establishment to liquidation. German, Austrian and Italian banks exercised ascendancy over the industrial enterprises which they financed — a practice which, in the context of shortage of capital and of entrepreneurship, was highly suited to the industrialization of a backward country. Similar banking institutions were found in mid-nineteenth-century France.[3] The banks were attracted to heavy industry: coal mining, iron and steel making, electrical and general engineer- ing and the chemical industries, and complemented an investment strategy based on the development of a domestic capital goods industry.

Gerschenkron observes that investment in social and physical infrastruc- ture preceded investment in directly productive activity in Continental Europe and that the polarizing effects of early industrialization were moderated by social legislation. Contradicting commonly held beliefs that poor countries cannot afford to expend resources on social investment, it is interesting to note that Germany and also Austria, Sweden, Denmark and Switzerland enacted social welfare legislation in the late nineteenth century, when per capita income was similar to levels prevailing in India, Pakistan, Central Asia and Central America, or Cuba today. These European countries are now more than ten times richer than they were at that time. Britain — then the wealthiest country of Europe — did not introduce national insurance until 1911, and France and the United States not until the 1930s.

Gerschenkron's account of the strategies of German modernization and industrialization continues to illuminate important differences with the dominant Anglo-American model. Compared to the disasters of other European countries sucked in to excess financialization, the differences are not unimportant in explaining the success of Germany in adapting to and benefiting from the expansion of the now-global world economy.

Japan: Asia's First Industrializing Nation

In a time sequence of modernization and industrialization, Japan was both the last of the nineteenth-century late-comers and the first of Asia's twentieth-century industrializers, serving as a model and a driver for the economic development of East Asia. While Britain led the first Industrial Revolution by the application of indigenous invention, and Germany and the United States led the Second Industrial Revolution of science-based technologies by a stream of product, process and organizational innovations, the industrialization of Japan has proceeded by the application, modification and improvement of existing technology.

From the Meiji Restoration, the Samurai elites set the country on a course of replicating the success of the West in industrial and military technology. Building on the traditional value placed on primary education and a 30 percent literacy rate, Japan systematically engaged in the transfer and adaptation of the industrial textile industry of Lancashire. Japan imported the military technology of Bismarck's Germany, which also served as a model of economic development. We base our account of the industrial strategy of Japan on the reflections of Saburo Okita, known as the architect of the 1960 "National Income Doubling Plan." We are indebted to Surendra Patel for recommending Okita as the most authoritative and insightful source by an insider economist.[4] Interestingly, Okita initially trained as an engineer.

Japan was able to exploit competitive advantage in colonial and neighbouring low income export markets for textiles and other light manufactures, while developing state supported heavy industry closely related to its war economy. The forward looking view of the dynamics of competition which motivated large Japanese firms to equip and re-equip their factories with the best and most up-to-date machinery was first manifested in the cotton textile industry. In the first four decades of the twentieth century, Japan drove Lancashire out of the China market, and by 1935 had invaded and captured world markets that in the past were the cherished preserves of the West.

There is no doubt that cheap wages played an important role in reducing Japan's costs of production to levels previously unknown. However, it was by means of the industrial organization and the technology policy of Japanese business groups that the potential asset of cheap labour was converted into an effective instrument of competition. We note that cheap labour did not deter the textile industry from investing in expensive imported equipment. Nor did the availability of Western equipment prevent Japan from developing textile machinery, which was exported to China and other poorer neighbouring countries as they mechanized cotton spinning.[5] In the depression of the 1930s, Japan could improve its competitive position by devaluation because it was not dependent on imports of capital goods.[6] Neither in the textile nor in the machinery industries did Japanese firms follow the short view dictated by static comparative advantage.

> Our government and our business people very carefully studied the industrial field, carefully searching out those industries with future potential. The automobile industry is one such example. The government closed the door to foreign firms who wanted to invest in the industry in Japan.… Until our industry became competitive, no foreign investment should be allowed in that sector.… The policy was: careful selection of industries; prevent ruinous competition at the infancy stage, nurse them up to competitive stature and then we expose them to outside competition. (*Okita 1981: 3–4*)

Okita insisted that economic development based on values that are not compatible with the historical ethos of a society is unlikely to succeed: "Each country has its own background, history, religion and tradition... modernization is not a synonym for Westernization" (Okita 1979: 13). Ultimately, Okita stressed the importance of the organizational capacity of the public sector, "capital, raw material, and other material considerations are not themselves the determining factors of development. Rather it is the capacity of government to organize the available resources for productive purposes that is the most crucial factor" (1993: 274).[7]

These lessons were well understood by the next generation of East Asian late industrializers, South Korea and Taiwan. They had the added advantage of the sweeping land reforms imposed by the United States on defeated Japan and its former colonies, which endowed them with the advantages of the most equitable distribution of income in the region with the sole exception of Mao's China. Korea's rise to become Asia's "Next Giant"[8] was largely modelled on the industrial strategies described by Okita.

Nineteenth-Century Globalization

By the middle of the nineteenth century Britain was the workshop of the world and the undisputed pioneer of industrial capitalism, leading in all aspects of mechanical and civil engineering, including general and specialized machinery and, of course, bridge and railway construction, soon to be followed by the telegraph, permitting instantaneous transmission of information in the railway age. The achievements of nineteenth-century industry were celebrated by the Crystal Palace, the Eiffel Tower and the magnificent railway stations of iron and glass of the major cities of Europe and the United States. These monuments to the marvels of engineering contrast with the skylines of today's cities, dominated by edifices celebrating commerce, finance and, in the United States, also advertising and corporate media.

From the 1870s, the newly industrializing countries entered the world economy with the superior technology of science-based industrial production and the advantage of a revolution in communication of railways and telegraphs, which greatly reduced transaction costs. Germany led in steel and chemicals, including photography and pharmaceuticals, and innovations in explosives are associated with Alfred Nobel of Sweden. The United States led the transformation from coal to petroleum as the principal fuel of road, sea and air transportation and pioneered the horizontally and vertically integrated modern corporation — initially within a growing domestic market and later on a transnational scale. In the large continental countries, still predominantly rural, the majority of the population gained their livelihood from agricultural activity. When steamships flooded European markets with cheap grain and other foodstuffs from the Americas, the peasantry was impoverished and swelled the ranks of the growing urban proletariat. In the interest of social stability, Bismarck's Germany protected both the agricultural producers of Prussia and the industrialists of Western Germany in the so-called marriage of rye and iron.

The entry of late-comer nations into the world economy, with Germany and the United States in the lead, challenged British industrial supremacy. European output doubled from 1870 to 1900, when Europe reached the pinnacle of its dominance. As technological innovation in production and communication increased productivity and lowered costs, and ever more producers entered the world economy, increasing volumes of output and intensified competition depressed prices and profits. A crisis of overproduction was triggered by bank failures in Vienna and New York in the wake of excessive real estate construction in 1873, and prices and profits did not recover until the 1890s. The Long Depression (1873–96) was aggravated by the deflationary effects of the Gold Standard in conditions of a relative shortage of this precious metal and abated with the gold rushes of the 1890s.

Declining rates of profit in the capitalist heartlands was countered by the concentration of capital in mergers, trusts and cartels. All major countries, with the important exception of Britain, abandoned free trade and adopted protectionism. Low rates of return on capital in domestic economies led the major powers to seek new markets and investment opportunities in Africa and Asia. In 1886 the European powers divided Africa into arbitrarily delineated colonies, with Britain, France, Belgium and Portugal receiving the lion's share; colonialism was extended to regions of Asia not previously under European rule. The United States also acquired colonies in the Pacific and Latin American and Caribbean regions.

While temperate and tropical primary commodity exporters suffered deteriorating terms of trade, Britain — dependent on imported food and raw materials — benefited from the declining prices. India became ever more important to Britain, as a market for manufactured exports, a source of cheap food and raw materials and the Indian Army to fight in its many wars. Despite Britain's loss of industrial supremacy, its prosperity and hegemony was sustained by revenues from shipping, insurance and commerce, and the backflow of interest on portfolio investments in its far-flung formal and informal empire. Britain was still the richest country in the world in 1914; the principal beneficiaries of a growing volume of rentier incomes were the propertied classes and the financial services industry of the City of London. The increasing incomes and the social status of persons of independent means sustained the lifestyles and cultural achievements of the Belle Époque in Britain as in France. In the United States, which profited immensely from the Great War, the 1920s were a gilded age, with income inequality not surpassed until the 2000s.

The technological transformation associated with industrial capitalism in Europe, the United States and the British dominions resulted in a combined sixteenfold increase in their output and a threefold increase in their population over the 130 years from 1820 to 1950. By contrast, the larger population of Asia barely doubled from 1820 to 1950, while GDP increased only two and a half times. The dramatic reversal in the relative importance of Europe and its overseas offshoots on the one hand and Asia on the other is illustrated by the fact that in 1950 Asia's contribution to world output was a mere 19 percent whereas 130 years earlier, in 1820, Asia's share of world output was 59 percent. The slow ascent of the Global South from exploitation and humiliation was enabled by imperial rivalry of the great powers, two world wars and revolutions which consigned kings and kaisers, czars and sultans to the dustbin of history.

THE TRANSFORMATIVE CRISIS OF 1914–45

When Europe emerged from the First World War, the nineteenth-century political and economic order had collapsed. The Russian Revolution of 1917 sent shock waves throughout the capitalist world, and the Wilsonian doctrine of self-determination gave legitimacy to aspirations of oppressed peoples and nations. Imperial Germany was defeated and the Western powers imposed unpayable war reparations on the Weimar Republic. The Hapsburg Empire fractured into small national succession states supported by Western credits. England and France hijacked the Arab revolutions and acquired control over the remnants of the Ottoman Empire in North Africa and the Middle East as protectorates or client states.

The Western powers attempted to restore the pre-1914 economic order, including the Gold Standard. Protecting the value of their overseas investments, the rentier interests of the propertied classes of Britain prevailed in the restoration of the pound sterling at its traditional — but now overvalued — level in relation to gold. Its mining, shipping, ship-building and engineering industries became uncompetitive in world markets and unemployment remained high throughout the inter-war years. When employers demanded a cut in wages, workers resisted, most dramatically in the General Strike of 1926, which lasted for ten days. In the language of Keynes, the Gold Standard was a juggernaut depressing wages to the benefit of the upper tier of society. In the interests of the rentier classes, the pound was sustained by short-term American capital attracted by the high rates of interest of the Bank of England. When funds were recalled to the U.S. to benefit from a stock market boom and to cover the losses of 1929, a major bank in Vienna failed and Britain was forced to abandon gold convertibility, and the whole house of cards of politically negotiated European debts collapsed in the world economic crisis of 1931–33.

The literature on the Great Depression has largely been drawn from the experience of the United States, where the Roaring Twenties preceded the crash of 1929. But it was not until the pound sterling collapsed in 1931 that thousands of banks closed their doors and the real economy fell into precipitous decline. Industrial production fell by over 50 percent and millions of workers lost employment. When Roosevelt assumed office in 1933, the traumatic impact of the crisis, including the failure of over ten thousand banks, demanded emergency measures. All banks were closed for one week. When they re-opened, the surviving banks were ordered to extend credit. Extensive New Deal programs were launched to provide a measure of social security, labour legislation favouring trade union organization and direct public employment for millions of workers. All of this, together with comprehensive regulation of industry and a large increase in public deficit spending, constituted a break with the traditionally minimalist role of the government. When under pressure from the opposition Roosevelt moved toward balancing the budget in 1937, the economy relapsed into a slump. In the years preceding and during the war, private-public partnerships in defence procurement created what Eisenhower later called the military-industrial complex.

Conditions were very different in Europe, which had never recovered from the consequences of the First World War; both in the victorious and in the defeated countries massive unemployment existed from 1918 to rearmament prior to the Second World War. In both Britain and France, monetary policies favouring the interests of financial creditors contributed to unemployment. Britain abandoned free trade for imperial preferential trading and a sterling bloc embracing their colonies and regions of economic influence. France, together with Belgium and some other Western European countries, founded a gold bloc, with similar deflationary effects on employment.

Keynes and a small band of colleagues and graduate students at Cambridge fashioned economic theories that challenged prevailing doctrines and advocated deficit spending on public works to alleviate unemployment. These ideas were received more favourably by American economists implementing New Deal policies than by the more conservative British economics profession. When I was a student at the London School of Economics in wartime England, Keynes was not on the curriculum. Like Marxist economics, the theories of Keynes and also Kalecki were taught in unofficial seminars by young lecturers or off-campus PhD students.

In Germany, a population traumatized by post-war hyperinflation, punishing war reparations and mass unemployment responded to Nazi populist rhetoric directed against communists, Jews and capitalists. Financed by Germany's largest businesses, Hitler was elected to office in 1933. In Nazi Germany unemployment was eliminated in two years by large public expenditures on infrastructure and rearmament. In other countries of central, eastern and southern Europe, nationalist fascist governments acceded to power in the wake of the world economic crisis. Currency convertibility was suspended and industries were protected. Mussolini's Italy invaded Abyssinia in 1935, and General Franco launched a civil war against the republican government of Spain in 1936 with the military assistance of Germany and the tacit support of Britain and France. Throughout the 1930s, the contrast between unemployment in Europe and the successful socialist Soviet five year plans initiated in 1929 gained wide support for communist parties in the West.

It was not until Germany occupied France in 1940 and threatened to invade Britain that the ruling classes abandoned hopes of peace with Hitler and replaced the old Conservative leadership with Winston Churchill. With other senior economists, Keynes was called to London to plan Britain's war economy. Like snow in the spring, unemployment vanished as all human resources were mobilized for production of essential goods and services. With all available men enlisted in the armed services and women in the war factories, and with wage and price controls and rationing of food, the contrast with the laissez-faire capitalism of the inter-war years is best illustrated by the fact that the nutrition of the population improved during the war, as measured by weight and height of industrial workers in large surveys.[9] Expectant mothers and infants received orange juice and vitamins. The best of English high culture was available to the populations of all major cities in concerts and theatre productions performed at minimal cost or for free.

Even before the decisive defeat of Hitler's armies at Stalingrad in 1943, planning for the post-war order was the topic of discussion in British — and refugee and colonial — intellectual circles in London. There was the Beveridge Report on full employment and social security from cradle to grave, and plans for the independence of all of Britain's colonies. The Keynes plan for an International Clearing Union, with a special purpose currency called bancor solely for transactions between national central banks and backed not by gold but by stockpiles of commodities, would enable countries with different socioeconomic systems to pursue policies of full employment while engaging in international trade. It was simply inconceivable that the world could ever return to the misery and inequalities of pre-war Britain. The rejection of Churchill's Conservatives and the election of the Labour Party in 1945 was unexpected, but it should not have been a surprise.

While post-war planning in Britain was concerned with maintaining full employment and the construction of an international economic and political order which would avoid a return to the chaos of the inter-war years, and the U.S. was dedicated to dismantling European empires and their preferential commercial and currency blocs, the peoples of the future Global South did not win their independence without protracted struggles. The leaders of the Indian National Congress, established in 1885, were rounded up and imprisoned by the British during the Second World War, and some Indian nationalists allied with the Japanese to drive out the British. In Asia, the war was widely regarded as a conflict between rival imperialist powers, and national liberation movements fought for political independence from all varieties of imperialism. In Africa, the fiercest struggles for liberation were in countries of European settlement, including Algeria, Kenya and southern Africa. The Russian Revolution of 1917 and the waning of British and French imperial power accorded Marxist and communist parties a significant role in struggles for liberation from oppressive colonial regimes. The Indian sub-continent achieved political independence in 1947 and was tragically divided by British manipulation of local political forces into India and Pakistan. Political independence of the countries of Southeast Asia followed years of resistance and armed struggles against Japanese, British, Dutch and French imperialism. When Indonesia gained independence, its communist party was the third largest in the world. The formation of the Non-Aligned Movement of Asian and African countries in 1955 in Bandung consolidated the determination of the presidents of those participating to chart a course of development independent of influence from the United States or the Soviet Union.

FROM THE TAMING TO THE UNLEASHING OF GLOBAL CAPITAL

In a book entitled *Escape from Empire,* Alice Amsden, best known for her path-breaking study of the rise of South Korea, *Asia's Next Giant* (1989), divided post-war American hegemony into three decades of Good (1950–1980) followed by Evil (1980–) Empire. The first encouraged the economic development of the Global South; the second rolled back many gains. We do not have to agree with the language, but the divide which distinguishes the first thirty years of post-war order from the neoliberal era which followed is generally accepted by analysts, whether mainstream or critical. We prefer Patel's characterization of the "Golden Years" as the Taming of Capitalism, and we may call the regime change of the 1980s the Unleashing of Global Capital. Interestingly, Amsden's cosmology envisaged the approach of other Giants to challenge the fading star of the Empire.

When the West emerged from the transformational crisis of two major wars and the descent of the capitalist economic order into depression and chaos, the defeat of Germany and Japan, the heavy losses suffered by the Soviet Union and the economic costs of the war to Britain, only the United States had the resources necessary for the reconstruction of Europe. The design of the post-war international political and economic order was influenced by the New Deal and the wartime alliance with the Soviet Union. The establishment of the United Nations with a veto for the five major victorious powers, and the Bretton Woods financial order, based on a gold exchange standard with provision for orderly changes in exchange rates, created the international political and financial framework which sustained three decades of unprecedented growth of the world economy.

In the industrialized countries, full employment was proclaimed as the principal objective of national economic policy. Comprehensive measures of social welfare financed by progressive income tax greatly increased the role of government in national expenditure from 10–20 percent of GDP to 30–50 percent, and almost one-third of the incomes of the rich was transferred through progressive taxation and social programs to lower income groups (Patel 1993: 24). In Europe, social expenditures constituted the largest single item of government spending; in the United States, Cold War-related military expenditure played a more important role.

In this model of regulated corporate capitalism based on an implicit social contract variously known as social democracy or embedded liberalism, productivity gains were shared by capital and labour. Rising real wages sustained effective demand for increased output of consumer goods, and capitalists had incentives to invest in increased industrial capacity. The model varied according to historic and ideological circumstances, from the most egalitarian in Scandinavia to the least in the United States. Even so, in the latter, highest earners were taxed at 70 percent as recently as 1980.

In the first three decades of the United Nations, the Group of 77, comprised of the republics of Latin America and the newly independent nations of Africa and Asia, achieved overall growth of 5 percent per annum and confronted the Global North with a demand for a fairer new international economic order. This marked the high point of the Global South in the United Nations system. The oil producing countries of the Middle East had successfully formed a cartel that raised prices above prevailing historical lows. Commodity exporters of bauxite threatened to follow the example of OPEC. Revolutions in the Middle East, the collapse of Portuguese rule in Africa, Cuban intervention in Angola to fight South African military forces, and above all the United States defeat in Vietnam and the 1979 overthrow of the Shah in the Iranian Revolution appeared to herald a loss of Northern control over the Global South.

While all of the above considerations played a role, the fundamental reasons for the neoliberal regime change of 1980 were economic. From the mid-1960s, increased government expenditure on social infrastructure in response to the civil rights movement and the cost of the Vietnam War created inflationary pressures and a loss of gold to cover the U.S. external payments deficit. The latter was further aggravated by the strong outflow of U.S. direct investment to benefit from high growth in reconstructed Europe. To avoid painful adjustment to the continuing loss of gold, Nixon invoked the privilege of seigniorage and terminated gold convertibility in 1971. Because the U.S. dollar served as virtually the only international reserve currency, American foreign expenditures could be made in their national currency. The resulting increase in international liquidity was a permissive condition for rising prices, including the OPEC oil shocks, which impacted more severely on European importers of petroleum than on the U.S. To maintain competitiveness, European countries abandoned the gold peg and floated their currencies, ratified by the IMF in 1973. This marked the end of the Bretton Woods financial order and ultimately of national control over the global money supply.

Capital Unleashed: The Neoliberal Counter-Revolution

Three decades of full employment and social security had virtually eliminated the business cycle and unemployment as an effective means to control the power of organized labour. Rising wages and declining productivity reduced corporate profitability while endemic inflation reduced the value of financial assets. Interest rates could barely keep up with inflation, and throughout the 1970s real rates were very low — often negative. The principal objective of monetary policy became the elimination of inflation by the suppression of aggregate demand to create a surplus in the labour market. Economists advised that inflation could not be suppressed unless unemployment was permitted to rise to its "natural" or "non-inflationary" rate (NAIRU), then approximately 7 percent. Social expenditure, which had sustained full employment, and progressive taxation, which had provided the fiscal resources, were deemed to be incompatible with a rate of return on capital sufficient to sustain economic growth. A counter-revolution in economics was in the making. Keynes was dismissed. Funded by major corporations, the neoliberal paradigm was created in the 1970s in think-tanks, universities and institutes, principally in the United States and Britain. The doctrinal clock was turned back to neoclassical price clearing markets reminiscent of ideas prevailing before the Great Depression.

The objective of the neoliberal counter-revolution was to restore the discipline of capital over labour, and the principal means of achieving it were deregulation, liberalization, privatization and explicit attacks on trade unions. These policies were successfully implemented by Thatcher (1979) and Reagan (1980) in the neoliberal regime change of the 1980s. Thatcher understood the importance of the ownership of property in the class-structured society of England. She gained popularity and won three elections by a wide distribution of shares through the privatization of railways, public utilities and other state enterprises and converting council house rents into titles of property. She legitimated the exercise of acquisitive individualism without social responsibility, granting respectability to fortunes however — and by whomever — they were made. By this minor social revolution, she both diminished the status of the upper classes and brought Britain culturally closer to the United States. In the more socially mobile culture of the U.S., it was the right of individuals to the proceeds of earned income — as wages, salaries or profit — that gained popularity for policies of radical income tax reductions. Supply-side economic theories of questionable validity claimed that these policies would not only increase investment and employment but might also increase total taxation revenues.

A new set of policy prescriptions was fostered in universities and the World Bank to promote "outward looking development" and demonize import substituting industrialization in the Global South. The developmental state and development economics were trashed. Structural Adjustment Programs were imposed on weak indebted countries to restructure their economies to become even more export dependent, whether on primary commodities or cheap labour manufactures.

The implosion of the Soviet Union put new wind in the sails of Western capitalism. Thatcher famously pronounced that there is no alternative to capitalism and there is no such thing as society. Socialism of all varieties was in deep retreat, and neoliberal policies gained general acceptance by political parties and governments of all persuasions. The peace dividend was invested in escalating military expenditures, and NATO was accorded a new role in the extension of U.S. geopolitical presence from the Balkans to Central Asia, beginning with the dismantling of Yugoslavia. On the economic front, the OECD unsuccessfully championed the Multilateral Agreement on Investment

(MAI), intended as a charter of rights of multinational corporations.

The World Development Report of 1995, entitled *Workers in an Integrating World*, suggested that globalization promised a return to a "golden age" of 1870–1914, which could bring untold prosperity to developing countries provided they opened their economies to unrestricted imports and Foreign Direct Investment and removed subsidies and other domestic obstacles to free market forces. Globalization was presented as an irreversible trend toward a borderless world free from national interference with free trade and free capital flows. While the liberalization of capital proceeded by unilateral dismantling of regulation and controls, the liberalization of trade required intergovernmental negotiation. In 1994, a trade agreement between Canada, the U.S. and Mexico (NAFTA), with extraordinary provisions for rights of foreign corporations to sue host governments for potential loss of profit on account of domestic regulation, was the template of subsequent Free Trade Agreements. The U.S.-proposed the extension of NAFTA to cover all the Americas, from Canada to Chile, but was blocked by Latin American opposition. The GATT was transformed into the WTO, which committed member countries to open markets to trade and, most importantly, was intended to protect foreign investments from regulation and control by host national governments. The revolution in information technology facilitated the internationalization of production chains by transnational corporations. In the 1990s and 2000s, international trade and Foreign Direct Investment increased very much faster than world production. The importance of developing countries in world trade increased from less than a quarter to one-third, and the composition shifted from primary commodities to manufactured exports (UNCTAD 2008: 46).

Of all the aspects of globalization, the liberation of capital from regulatory constraint or supervision has had the most profound consequences. The drastic reduction of taxation on upper incomes in the U.S. created ever-larger pools of savings seeking higher returns in global markets than those prevailing domestically. Returns on portfolio investments and the opportunities for capital gains exceeded profits from investment in non-financial enterprise: corporations moved assets from production to finance. Iconic companies, once providing thousands of decent — mostly unionized — jobs, engaged in downsizing, subcontracting and outsourcing to cheaper labour locations to boost shareholder value and compete on stock markets with financial service industries. General Electric, once known for its heavy engineering and production of household durables, is now among the top financial corporations and owns one of the handful of major U.S. mass communication networks. From the mid-1980s to 2000, the share of financial corporations in total corporate profits increased from 16 to 40 percent in the U.S. (Johnson 2009).

A seminal article (Jensen and Meckling) in 1976 by two business economists advocated the practice of providing stock options as remuneration, thereby creating pecuniary incentives for management to gain from maximizing short-term shareholder value and speculating in stock markets. This replaced the previous strategic objective of maximizing corporate production and sales. This predatory style of capitalism operating on a short time horizon achieved higher returns by drawing capital out of productive enterprise and profited by manipulating markets and devising financial innovations, whereby the stock market became a casino rather than a guide to the long-term prospects of non-financial corporations.

The Asian Crisis of 1997 might have served as a warning, but United States authorities lifted remaining constraints on financial liberalization in 1998 by permitting the consolidation of commercial and investment banking. Rising stock markets and real estate values were sustained and encouraged by easy credit available from central banks. Financialization assumed unimaginable proportions; the estimated value of total derivatives in 2007 was $600 trillion according to the United Nations — 964 percent of world GDP.

Grotesque fortunes were made in this gilded age of financial prosperity. Asset inflation in real estate and the stock market gave the illusion of ever increasing wealth, encouraging ever more risky financial investment and ever more debt-financed consumption. Although the bubble of asset inflation was obviously unsustainable, it was sustained by expectations of continued gain and fortified by economic theories of the self-correcting trend of free markets toward equilibrium. Dissenting voices were drowned in the noise of corporate media feeding the fantasies of the population with the fortunes and misfortunes of celebrities. In contrast with the Belle Époque in the closing years of British and French imperial power, the Belle Époque of the decline of American power surely marked a low point in the history of cultural achievement of the United States.

The immediate source of the financial crisis of 2008 was Wall Street, and the transmission of the crisis was through London, the principal financial centre for international transactions. Political, economic and financial links between the U.S. and the U.K. are close. It is no accident that Britain has been the closest ally of the United States in the wars in Iraq and Afghanistan.

Since the demise of the Bretton Woods financial order in 1971, capital has been progressively freed from discipline and oversight both in North America and Europe. Control over the creation of credit passed from central banks to financial markets. Productivity increases accrued to upper-income groups, and inequality levels in the U.S. surpassed those prevailing before the Great Depression. The richest 1 percent of Americans own 40 percent of national wealth, more than the bottom 90 percent. Real median wages and salaries did not increase in the thirty years from 1980. In the years preceding the crisis, finance, insurance and real estate accounted for more than 20 percent of GDP in the U.S., rising from 15 percent in 1971, while manufacturing declined from 23 percent to 12 percent, of which some 80 percent was directly or indirectly related to defence expenditure (Johnson 2008).[10] The hollowing out of manufacturing was even more severe in Britain, where it declined from 32 percent to 11 percent in the same period. Consumption expenditures have been sustained by ever-expanding debt while gross fixed capital formation as a percentage of GDP has been in secular decline in industrialized countries. In the U.S. economy, with some 15 percent unemployed or underemployed and barely more than half of the potential labour force at work three years after the financial crisis of 2008,[11] only a massive increase of public expenditure could rekindle economic growth. Instead a government captive to financial and corporate interests is slashing spending. The fragility of overleveraged European banks and resistance of local populations to bear the burden of paying for debts they did not incur threatens the existence of the Eurozone and could result in another — and more serious — financial crisis. Because credit is the lifeblood of a modern economy, the financial system cannot be permitted to implode. Financial markets have acquired an effective veto over government policy. Markets rule. Democracy is in suspense in the heartlands of capitalism.

DIVERGENT DEVELOPMENT IN THE GLOBAL SOUTH

The first three decades following the end of the Second World War were favourable to national economic development in the Global South, which experienced an average growth rate exceeding that of the North. In the 1980s and 1990s, growth stalled in Latin America and the Caribbean, and Africa was impoverished by neoliberal policies imposed by the Washington Consensus. By contrast, India and China, and also Korea and Taiwan, were set on a high growth path.

Earlier in this text we noted the difference between the incorporation of Latin America and Africa into the world economy as peripheral suppliers of raw materials to the centres on the one hand and the role of the older civilizations of South and East Asia, initially as sources of desirable fine manufactures and later as captive markets for Europe's industrial exports, on the other. With experience in manufacturing and the benefit of assets abandoned by departing colonial powers, the latter were better positioned to nurture domestic manufacturing industries with increasing proprietary technology and value-added. They were able to benefit from the liberalization of trade in the 1980s and 90s by the export of manufactures while maintaining control over financial, economic and social policies through autonomous development strategies. It is not by accident that forty-six of the fifty IMF Structural Adjustment Programs in the 1980s were found in the countries of Latin America, the Caribbean and Africa, and only three were in Asia (Ali 2004).

In the independent republics of Latin America, landed oligarchs profited from their insertion in the world economy as suppliers of agricultural and mineral raw materials since the late nineteenth century. The income generated from exports sustained significant industrialization and urbanization in the Southern Cone countries. By 1950, Latin America was by far the richest of the South, with GDP per capita on a level with Mediterranean Europe and one-quarter that of the United States. Latin America accounted for 8 percent of world production in 1950, more than half of the exports of the Global South, and some two-thirds of the value added in the manufacturing industries of the South (Amsden 2003: 247).

Following the Great Depression and the breakdown of world trade and investment before and during the Second World War, laissez-faire liberal capitalism was almost universally discredited. Escape from underdevelopment and export dependence was the objective of all nations of the Global South, and the developmental state and development planning was the means. The early United Nations provided a supportive environment both in New York, where Patel was employed, and in the Economic Commission for Latin America in Santiago, Chile. As commodity prices declined in the 1920s and collapsed in the Great Depression, Latin American countries declared moratoria on debt service, suspended currency convertibility and channelled resources to industrial production for the domestic market. Drawing on the success of these policies, Raul Prebisch and his team of young economists at the U.N. Economic Commission for Latin America outlined a strategy of escape from export dependence by import substituting industrialization, known as the Prebisch Manifesto (1950).[12]

In the context of the Cold War, the attraction of Soviet planning, especially in Asia, persuaded U.S. policy-makers to lend support to development planning, notwithstanding opponents from Chicago-based advocates of free markets. The principal policy tool was the development bank providing concessional credit and access to foreign exchange, which was conditional on performance criteria, including provision for domestic content, upgrading of managerial and technological capacity and — where appropriate — achievement of export targets. Development banks financed public and private enterprise, initially in large projects of infrastructure such as roads, water, sewage and other essential public utilities. Domestic industries were sheltered by negative lists and tariffs.

The economic model of Brazil, under military dictatorship from 1964 to 1985, was based on state support for heavy industry supplying inputs to industrial production of consumer goods for a growing middle-class domestic market. Large state enterprises in petroleum, electricity, steel and mining and more than a hundred smaller ones formed the industrial base while multinational corporations were attracted to Brazil's growing and protected middle-class market. By 1980, the level of industrialization was similar to that of South Korea, acknowledged as the most successful newly industrializing country (Hewitt, Johnson and Wield 1992). Unlike South Korea, however, whose national conglomerates engaged in manufacturing activity for domestic and export markets, Brazil's commercial and landed oligarchies profited from commodity export revenues and lacked incentives to engage in industrial activity capable of competing internationally. The majority of the population was excluded from this model of economic growth and remained poor.

From 1950 to 1980, GDP growth averaging 6 percent per annum in Latin America and the Caribbean raised its share of the world economy from 8 percent to 10 percent. The average rate of annual per capita income growth over these thirty years was 2.7 percent (Cardoso and Fishlow 1992). The strong growth of Latin America in the 1970s and promising export markets for petroleum and other commodities had attracted large volumes of (mostly American) commercial bank finance on floating rates of interest. Mexico's announcement in August 1982 that it was unable to service external debt sent shock waves through Wall Street. The proximate cause of the Latin American debt crisis was the Volker Shock of 1979, which raised interest rates into the teens, resulting in a stronger U.S. dollar and a serious recession that weakened export markets. American banks were rescued from insolvency by the intervention of the Federal Reserve and the IMF, while the entire costs of adjustment were borne by the populations of the debtor countries. In the lost decade of the 1980s, GDP per capita declined by 8 percent for the region as a whole, in some countries by very much more. In this period, and also in the 1990s, hundreds of public and private sector businesses were auctioned to multinational corporations. Nowhere else was there such a bonanza of privatization of state assets, in some cases just to meet the next payroll of the public service. In the 1990s neoliberal economic theories gained popularity among Latin American economists, as high rates of inflation were eliminated by strong monetary policies. Economic crises of increasing frequency and severity, growing income disparities and chronic poverty resulted in the election of a new generation of Left-leaning politicians more responsive to popular discontent than to doctrines of neoclassical economics. In the 2000s poverty was reduced by targeted social expenditures in Brazil and other countries, but inequality remains higher than in any other region of the Global South.

Release of political and economic energy following the decolonization of Africa resulted in average annual growth rates of 5 percent and average growth of per capita income of 2.4 percent from 1950 to 1975 (Morawetz 1977). Strong demand for primary export commodities was the engine of growth, and import substitution in food processing and household products, as well as expenditure on physical and social infrastructure, provided growing urban employment in the private (informal and formal alike) and especially public sectors. Achievements in education were critical in raising the number of qualified professional personnel as teachers, health workers and public administrators at every level of government; we may recall that independence endowed the Belgian Congo with a grand total of thirty university graduates, and conditions in other former colonies were not very much better (Galbraith

1965). The first generation of independence leaders were nationalists espousing variants of African socialism and self-reliance.

Sub-Saharan Africa was indebted almost exclusively to multilateral and bilateral donor agencies. The recession of the 1980s in the United States and Europe precipitated a deep debt crisis, and Africa became a laboratory of failed policies of liberalization and privatization, which further increased the vulnerability of fragile economies to shocks of civil wars and the HIV/AIDS epidemic. The majority of all IMF programs from 1980 to 2000 were imposed on Africa. Economies stagnated, per capita incomes failed to grow (World Bank 2004: Chap. 4), and the number of poor almost doubled (Ravallion and Chen 2008). Of all the regions of the Global South, Africa suffered the greatest reversal of progress made between 1950 and 1980. For all its great resource and mineral wealth, the continent's share of world output in 2006 was a mere 3 percent.

In the 1950s, India was the Mecca of development planning. The founding Nehru development model of post-independence India was based on socialist and secular values of equity, coexistence and tolerance in a mixed economy combining private business with public enterprise and state planning. Early development plans in India were influenced by Soviet industrialization, with emphasis on basic industry and the production of capital as well as consumer goods for the domestic market. Full employment was a stated objective of development plans, as was reduction of income inequality. For these reasons industrial policy favoured small and medium enterprise rather than support for modernization of large business concerns. The economy was highly regulated and controlled; economic growth for the entire subcontinent was modest from 1950 to 1980, with average per capita growth of only 1.6 percent per annum.[13] With a large population, but very low levels of average income per capita, India's share of the world economy was only 4 percent in 1950 and even lower, at 3 percent, in 1980.

India was barely affected by the slowing down of growth in the North Atlantic in the 1970s and 1980s. Liberalization policies in the 1990s increased growth rates from levels averaging 5.7 percent in the 1980s to 6.9 percent in the 2000s and reaching 10 percent in 2010.[14] Prior to 1990 there was virtually no Foreign Direct Investment (FDI). Following the liberalization of the early 1990s, FDI inflows increased slowly to 3 percent of gross fixed capital formation by the turn of the century and a substantial increase in the late 2000s, by which time the accumulated stock of foreign assets as a percentage of GDP reached 12 percent in 2010 (UNCTAD 2011). The export of information technology services is a rapidly growing sector that has gained international attention. It employs skilled professionals and holds out the possibility of important externalities in raising productivity in India's domestic industries, but employment is two million at most. Income disparities, which were moderate until the liberalization of the 1990s, have widened substantially. Strong economic growth has been based on a growing domestic middle-class market of some 300 million people, where incomes have grown at rates of 15 to 25 percent annually. For the remaining 70 percent of the population, growth has been more like 2 percent per annum, and many have suffered declines (Akbar 2008). The majority of people living in poverty are rural, and agricultural output is scarcely increasing. Of all the world's poor, one-third are found in India, more than in Sub-Saharan Africa (Ravallion and Chen 2008).

The Rise of East Asia

The most extraordinary achievement of the Global South since 1950 has been the ascent of East Asia, with historically unprecedented growth rates. As noted above, Japan was both a model and a driver for the entire East Asian region. With GDP per capita only 20 percent of U.S. levels in 1950, somewhat lower than in Latin America, Japan's high growth ascent to major industrial power achieved 72 percent of U.S. incomes by 1980, becoming a serious competitor to U.S. supremacy in automobile and state-of-the-art electronic equipment. Preferential access to U.S. technology and markets certainly played a role, as did U.S. defence procurement, but the success of Japan is attributable to the policies described earlier in this text which had enabled Japan to become a modern imperial power prior to the Second World War.

Following Japan, its former colonies of Korea and Taiwan embarked on industrial policies that combined import substitution with the export of manufactures under state guidance and support. In both these countries, radical land reforms — imposed on defeated Japan and its former colonies by the U.S. — and consequent equitable income distribution contributed to the mobilization of national resources to achieve rapid industrialization. Both countries benefited from the nationalization of Imperial Japanese industrial and commercial assets. Taiwan was the most statist of East Asia countries; Korean development was modelled on Japan, where large conglomerate groups were the dominant form of national enterprise guided by large and effective planning agencies with the full support and direct participation of political authorities. Foreign Direct Investment was restricted. Selected enterprises were encouraged to adopt the most advanced technologies available. All these firms were nurtured in sheltered domestic markets, but were required to meet export targets in more challenging conditions of international competition. Access to domestic markets was controlled by licensing to limit wasteful competition. Research and development was rewarded. Growth rates of output and of manufactures exports was very high. In Korea, as in Japan, a strong labour movement engaged employers in militant industrial action to achieve a share in the rising productivity of the economic model. Perhaps the most extraordinary achievement of Korea and Taiwan was the 8 percent per annum increase of real earnings per worker in manufacturing from 1975 to 1990 (Amsden 2003: 246), attesting both to rapid productivity increases and the equitable distribution of the gains therefrom. This contrasts with considerably lower increases in other newly industrializing countries and near zero increases in wages in the United States.

Korea and Taiwan, together with Singapore and Hong Kong, were in the first tier of a flying-geese formation headed by Japan, with the ASEAN countries in the next tier, thus forming dense networks of vertical and horizontal trade and investment throughout East Asia and mainland China. With variations regarding relations with multinational corporations and banks, they also practised combinations of domestic industrialization with the export of manufactures. In all these cases, nationally owned enterprises were critical to successful economic development (Amsden 2007; Sioh 2010). The forced march to high growth was achieved by high rates of savings and domestic investment, long hours of work and authoritarian governments driven by a national project to overcome the stigma of backwardness and inferiority to former colonial powers, whether Japanese, American or European.

After fifteen years of struggle to free China from Japanese occupation and a civil war, Mao's communists emerged victorious in 1949. In the three decades following the founding of the People's Republic, the Mao-era laid the foundations for the later ascent of China, but economic growth was slow and Chinese per capita income was still very low, rising from 5 to 6 percent of U.S. levels in the thirty years from 1950 to 1980, when its share of the world economy was a mere 5 percent. Building on the infrastructure, literacy and educational attainments of the Mao-era, Deng Xiaoping's change of course launched an industrial revolution greatly surpassing both the scale and the speed of that of Western Europe two hundred years earlier. China launched a program of economic reform and opening in 1978, combining private with state enterprise in a unique model that cannot be described as either capitalist or socialist, but has features of both, designated by Deng Xiaoping as "socialism with Chinese characteristics." High rates of growth in the 1980s were based almost exclusively on domestic savings and investment. In the early 1990s China relaxed regulations to encourage foreign investment. Foreign Direct Investment inflows as a percentage of gross fixed capital formation rose sharply, reaching 17 percent in 1994, declining slowly to 10 percent in 2002 and more rapidly to 4 percent in 2010. The accumulated value of foreign assets reached its peak in 1999, at 17 percent of GDP, declining steadily to less than 10 percent in recent years. Multinational engagement in China principally takes the form of joint ventures (UNCTAD 2011). Internal migration from agricultural regions to the coastal provinces surpasses anything previously recorded in history. Three decades averaging 10 percent per annum growth have brought substantial improvement to the material standard of living of the majority of the population and has reduced poverty from 53 percent to 4 percent (Ravallion and Chen 2008). Income inequality, however, has rapidly been increasing.

By 1995 Asia's share of value-added in the manufacturing activity of the Global South had increased to 48 percent from twenty-six twenty years earlier, while Latin America's had declined to 35 percent (Amsden 2003: 247). In East and South Asia, manufactures account for 80 to 90 percent of all exports, a significant component of which is high value-added (World Bank 2004: 65–66). By contrast, seventeen Latin American and Caribbean countries were dependent on three or fewer commodities for the majority of their export earnings (Common Fund for Commodities 2005), and for the region as a whole manufactures accounted for less than 60 percent of exports with lesser high value-added (World Bank 2004: 63–64). In Africa, the majority of countries remain dependent on primary exports, although some engage in low value-added manufacturing exports.

DECLINE OF THE WEST AND RISE OF THE REST

It was widely expected that the crisis and the consequent recession in the major capitalist countries would be transmitted to the Global South by declining export earnings, FDI, remittances and tourism, and that it would be poor people in poor countries who would be most seriously affected. What actually happened illustrates the degree to which traditional relations of trade and finance between capitalist centres and the Global South are undergoing a historic change. Contrary to predictions — with the exception of the southern periphery of the United States (Mexico, Central America and the Caribbean) — few countries of the Global South dipped into negative growth, and those that did, including exporters of manufactures, swiftly recovered.

In the recession year of 2009, developing economies were the sole drivers of world growth, while advanced economies and adjacent regions had fallen into deep decline: the United States -3.5 percent; Japan -6.3 percent; the Eurozone -4.3 percent; Britain -4.9 percent.[15] In a ranking of 150 cities according to recovery of income and employment from the crisis, fifteen of the top twenty-five were from Asia, seven were from Latin America, and Istanbul ranked number one (*Global Metro Monitor* 2010). Some $100 billion of IMF assistance was required in Europe. Aside from a $72 billion line of credit extended to Mexico, smaller programs in Central America and the Caribbean, and a mere $6 billion dispersed over thirty African countries associated with the effects of the 2008 food crisis, no other countries of the Global South required IMF assistance. The small number of IMF programs in Asia were related to problems of populations displaced by war.

Evidence of the increasing role of the Global South in world production is reflected in the comparison of average growth rates in the decade 2000 to 2010. In India, China and throughout Developing Asia — comprising over half of the world's population — high growth rates barely diminished in the Great Recession and averaged 8 to 9 percent over the decade; increased demand and higher prices for mineral resources raised Sub-Saharan African rates to 5.5 percent; led by the oil exporting states, Middle East and North Africa saw almost 5 percent growth; Latin America and the Caribbean, more closely integrated with Europe and North America than other regions of the South, averaged 3.5 percent. These growth rates contrast with average growth over the decade for the United States (2 percent), European Union (1.5 percent) and Japan (1 percent).[16]

There has been a dramatic shift in patterns of world trade. As recently as 1985, trade between countries of the North constituted two-thirds of world trade, while trade between countries of the South was negligible. In the past twenty-five years, trade within the North declined to one-third of world trade, while trade within the South increased to one-quarter. Over the same period, traditional dependence on the markets of the North declined from 80 to 60 percent of the trade of the South.[17]

Of equal if not greater significance is the increased capacity of developing countries to raise their rates of domestic savings and investment. According to a 2008 UNCTAD report, accumulation of surpluses together with rates of domestic investment higher than at any time in the last thirty years attest to the capacity of countries with relatively low GDP/capita to mobilize national resources and attain a high rate of gross capital formation, which is the basis for sustainable long-term growth. Increasing flows of FDI were attracted to export manufacturing, extractive industries and communication infrastructure, but benefits accruing to host countries varied according to the ability of governments to negotiate positive developmental terms. Experience of costly exchange rate and financial crises in the 1990s encouraged central banks of middle-income and also poorer developing countries to accumulate reserves from strong export earnings (invested at low yields of interest in U.S. securities) as a precaution against speculative attacks on their currencies. These precautionary surpluses are very large and represent a sacrifice of resources that could otherwise have been used for public and private investment and consumption. Together with Japan, the Global South is currently sustaining the external account deficit of the United States. The total value of these reserves exceeds $5 trillion.

The most dramatic illustration of the shift of growth momentum from the West and North to the East and South is China's sixteen-fold increase in GDP in thirty years. This invites comparison with the sixteen-fold increase of Europe and North America over a period of 130 years. Since 2010, China has surpassed Germany as the world's largest exporter of manufactures and Japan as the world's second largest economy in market value. Estimates suggest that China will surpass the U.S. in the market value of its economy by 2020.[18] As in India, in China there is a growing middle-class market. To correct the imbalance of an economy excessively dependent on export manufacturing, China's Twelfth Five Year Plan (2011) proposes a greater emphasis on the domestic market and extension of the services sector, which is both more labour intensive to create more employment and less resource intensive to curtail environmental degradation. To increase the rate of consumption it is proposed to increase wages and reduce the very high rate of personal savings. Because personal savings are motivated by fear of ill health and old age, the plan proposes to widen and deepen the social safety net. But China is still a developing country with a low per capita income faced by a long road to the attainment of what Chinese authorities term "moderate prosperity" for all its peoples. China may rival the Global North in terms of the size of its economy, but as a relatively poor developing country humiliated by nineteenth-century Western imperialism, China defines itself politically as part of the Global South. While the greater part of China's 10 percent share of world trade is with the North, China has become an important trading partner in Asia, the Middle East, Africa, and Latin America and the Caribbean. China accounts for one-tenth of world demand for commodities and supplies one-tenth of the world's middle- and high-technology goods. It is the largest supplier to the U.S. of consumer electronics (Arora and Vamvakidis 2010).

At the turn of the century, the Bush administration harboured ambitions to create a new world order under the military and economic control of American Empire. Ten years later, uncontrolled financialization, unsustainable military expenditures and a state captured by corporate power have resulted in a crisis with no prospect of recovery in the foreseeable future. Vast financial fortunes have been created. Transnational corporations have consolidated their power. But the social and political institutions that sustained the American dream are corrupted and broken. The economy of the U.S. is still the largest in the world, but thirty years of neoliberal policies have severely compromised, if not destroyed, the financial and political institutions which led to its pre-eminence. The future of the Eurozone — if not the economic union itself — is threatened. Prospects for the entire North Atlantic economy are, at best, slow growth for the next ten years; North America and the European Union will still be large and important markets for the Global South, but traditional dependence is unravelling.

CONCLUSION

An earlier version of this paper, presented at the Autonomous University of Zacatecas in 2009, has been elaborated here as a one-sided conversation with our friend and colleague, Surendra Patel. The main body of his work related to the transfer of technology to the Global South, and, as noted, in the early 1990s he foresaw the return of Asia to the world economy — long before shifting power relations became the subject of current journalistic and academic preoccupation. Following Alexander Gerschenkron, Surendra noted that late-comers entering the world economy with the most recent technology and lower transaction costs attain growth rates exceeding those of previously industrializing countries. In our daily lives we observe that information technology has accelerated time and compressed space. History is speeding up. The growing points of the world economy are now in the East and South, but the planet clearly cannot sustain the spread of the wasteful lifestyle and exorbitant dependence on carbon fuels from the West to the Rest.

Europe gave birth to industrial capitalism, but the European world has exhausted its historic role in the application of science and technology to the production of socially useful goods and services. The instrumental rationality of the West which increased the productive capacity manifold is destroying the natural environment that sustains life on Earth. The West has abandoned leadership in international negotiations to combat climate change and is engaging in dangerous technological experiments which threaten the delicate balance of industrial activity and the ecological carrying capacity of the globe. Escalating military intervention to secure control of hydrocarbons and other scarce natural resources — including land and water — threatens the fragile peace of a world in rapid transition from 200 years of Western hegemony.

As rampant financial capital is devouring and corrupting the social and political pillars that sustained the golden post-war years, we recall that Keynes's greatest fear was that finance would destroy capitalism. He believed that the love of money was a mental illness and spoke of the euthanasia of the rentier. When the Soviet Union imploded, the master spy novelist of the Cold War, John le Carré remarked that the fact that communism has failed does not mean that capitalism cannot also fail. Indeed, the scale of the destruction of economic livelihoods by a virtual tsunami of capital unleashed from control suggests a slow motion crumbling of the foundations that sustained Western capitalism. It has reverted to its mercantilist origins of the accumulation of wealth by commerce, finance and conquest.

In this essay we have emphasized the specific circumstances of the birth of capitalism in the mercantile system of trade and war, and the importance of Britain (and later the United States) in fashioning an ideology of economism that subordinates all other human aspirations to material acquisition. Science and technology in the service of accumulation of material wealth and the culture of consumerism is degrading and subordinating human lives to the false God of endless accumulation. Scarcity must forever be created where there was once abundance. Poverty is created where it did not exist. Beyond material necessities of food and shelter, poverty is a social construct inherent in a system that values individual achievement by economic success. Sufficiency is the enemy of unlimited accumulation of wealth.

The financial and economic crisis of 2008 has accelerated the concentration of financial and economic power in ever fewer and larger agglomerations of corporate wealth. The gross inequality of economic power is undeniable, but so is the crumbling of the social and political pillars on which Western capitalism has rested. Governments are hostage to finance; the bonds of the social contract are broken; and democracy is in suspense. Ultimately it is the society that sustains the economy. Major Latin American countries have adopted a variety of policies to secure a fairer share for the majority populations in the still grossly inequitable distribution of national wealth. North Africa and the Greater Middle East, with potential to become the next region of strong economic development, is engaged in a struggle to regain freedom from Western military and political control of client states. In Africa, the struggle to regain sovereignty over land and mineral resources from Western corporations and kleptocratic elites may engender new forms of resistance and liberation. As anticipated by Surendra, East Asia is returning to the place it occupied in the world economy four hundred years ago. Will this usher in a new era of history as he envisioned? Will the ambitions of India's middle classes to be part of the global elite extinguish Gandhi and Nehru's foundational values of an equitable society respectful of all its citizens? Will the political authorities in China be able to restrain the acquisitive capitalism they have encouraged in the project of catch-up growth with the West? These are questions I would have liked to ask Surendra.

The only remaining area of undisputed superiority of the West is military. In all other respects, the globe is moving toward a more balanced and multipolar political and economic order. The countries of the Global South are demonstrating an increased capacity to exercise leadership by example and cooperation to combat the great challenges posed by the limited resources of the natural environment to sustain moderate prosperity for all of its nations and populations. This is not the end of capitalism, but the end of 200 years of Western ascendancy and Western institutions as a model for the rest of the world. As new giants are rising, they are fashioning original social, economic and political institutions in conformity with their diverse histories and cultures and new forms of the participation of populations in the determination of their futures, which is the only universally valid meaning of democracy.

NOTES

This chapter is an elaboration of a lecture delivered to a summer school in Critical Development Studies at the Autonomous University of Zacatecas, 2009, and a Patel Memorial lecture delivered at Saint Mary's University, Halifax, 2010. It was completed in February 2012. It is published here for the first time.

1. In 1950 China's and India's GDP per capita as a percentage of that of the U.S. stood at 5 and 7 percent respectively (Maddison 2006). Note that in this paper Maddison is used for all historical population, GDP, GDP as a share of world production and GDP per capita data. He uses 1990 Geary-Khamis dollars with purchasing power parity. A full explanation of Maddison's background methodology and reasoning can be found at <http://www.ggdc.net/maddison/Historical_Statistics/BackgroundHistoricalStatistics_03-2010.pdf>.

2. 1950 GDP per capita as a percentage of that of the U.S.: South and East Asia*: 7%; Africa (all): 9%; West Asia (Middle East without North Africa): 19%; Latin America and the Caribbean 26%.
    * Using Maddison's categories, this grouping is composed of China, India, Indonesia, Japan, Philippines, South Korea, Thailand, Taiwan, Bangladesh, Burma, Hong Kong, Malaysia, Nepal Pakistan, Singapore and Sri Lanka.

3. The innovative development of industrial banking, pioneered by Credit Mobilizer under Napoleon III of France, should be understood as a creative response to the specific conditions of a relatively backward economy. This financial organization was designed to "build thousands of miles of railroads, drill mines, erect factories, pierce canals, construct ports and modernize cities" and challenged conservative "old wealth" banking confined to floating government bonds and foreign exchange transactions (Gerschenkron 1962: 12).

4. Okita was director general of the Planning Bureau of the Economic Planning Agency, president of the Overseas Economic Co-operation Fund and chair of the governing board of the United Nations University World Institute for Development Economics Research (UNU-WIDER). Patel was personally acquainted with him.

5. By 1929 some 80 percent of Japan's manufactured exports went to China and other regional markets.

6. Imports of machinery to Japan in 1929 comprised only 8 percent of all imports — by 1936 down to 6 percent. This contrasts with Korea in the mid-1960s, when machinery was 16 percent of imports, rising to 29 percent by 1971. In the 1970s, Korea undertook a "great spurt" of investment in heavy and chemical industry to reduce import dependence and deepen the structure of production.

7. On a visit to Japan in the early 1980s, the author asked the obvious question: to what do you subscribe the success of Japan? On more than one occasion the answer came back that it was due to the scarcity of land and virtual absence of mineral and petroleum resources, and thus the necessity to develop human resources and strong industrial and manufacturing capacity for domestic and export markets.

8. See, for example, Amsden (1989).

9. These annual surveys were organized by the Ministry of Food and employed several hundred university students during summer vacations. I was assigned to Nottingham and Coventry. We had to get agreement from the employer to weigh and measure the workers. Where no scales were available at the factory, he had to grant time for participants to go to the nearest pharmacy for their measurements. In some small enterprises, particularly in the chemical industries, conditions were appalling.

10. Finance, insurance and real estate figures calculated based on Bureau of Economic Analysis data. The figure relating to defence expenditure dates from 1990 but is likely to have increased rather than diminished since that time.

11. U.S. U6 rate (total unemployed, plus all marginally attached workers plus total employed part-time for economic reasons) as of January 2012: 15.2 percent; United States Civilian Participation Rate as January 2012: 64.0 percent. Source: U.S. Department of Labour, Bureau of Labour Statistics.

12. *The Economic Development of Latin America and Its Principal Problems* was originally

published in Spanish in 1949, with English-language translation in 1950.

13. Calculation based on World Bank data.

14. IMF data.

15. IMF figures, September 2011.

16. Calculated from IMF figures.

17. ECLAC, on the basis of United Nations Commodity Trade Database (COMTRADE).

18. *The Economist* estimates the date may be as early as 2019, see "Dating Game: When Will China Overtake America?" 16 December 2010. For a thorough review of recent estimates, see Ross (2011). Of course all such estimates are contingent on assumptions, but the similar results obtained by numerous independent projections are striking.

11. THE GREAT FINANCIALIZATION OF 2008

I am honoured and delighted that the Progressive Economics Forum has awarded me the John Kenneth Galbraith prize, and I am especially pleased that it is shared with my friend and colleague Mel Watkins. We go back a long way and we have come through many struggles together. My principal contribution to Canadian political economy, *Silent Surrender: The Multinational Corporation in Canada* (1970), would never have seen the light of day without Mel Watkins. The project began when Charles Taylor asked me to draft a paper on the issue of foreign ownership for a policy committee of the, then recently founded, New Democratic Party. Influential economists close to the NDP argued that foreign capital of any kind was obviously beneficial because it would increase national output, and the gains of economic growth could be redistributed by fiscal measures. They maintained that concerns regarding the loss of cultural identity were misplaced because revenue from economic growth could enhance government support to Canadian cultural industries. The most influential proponent of this conventional wisdom was the Canadian economist Harry Johnson, commuting between Chicago and the LSE.

In the course of several meetings, including a weekend retreat with members of the national executive of the NDP, I explained that the essential difference between incoming portfolio capital and Foreign Direct Investment was one of control. A subsidiary or affiliate of a multinational corporation located in Canada is not simply a firm whose owners are non-resident. It is an integral part of a larger enterprise and subject to its strategic considerations. A Canada dominated by subsidiaries and branch plants of mainly American companies could not undertake coherent long-term strategies of industrial development and thus was destined to remain dependent on primary resource exports. As I amassed more material to strengthen my argument, the initial policy paper became a small monograph published by my colleague Lloyd Best in 1968 in the *New World Quarterly*, under the title "Economic Dependence and National Disintegration: the Case of Canada." This little known Caribbean publication began to circulate among Canadian students and was reprinted by Cy Gonick in Winnipeg. With additional material it was submitted to Macmillan of Canada. The manuscript was sent to a University of Toronto economist, who rejected it with comments that it was ideological, it was not economics, and it had no value. By this time, the publisher rather liked the manuscript and asked me to name another reader. I suggested Mel Watkins and the rest is history. Mel wrote a wonderful introduction and a second one when the book was reissued in 2002.

Mel will surely remember Lloyd Best. We all met at the invitation of Chilean economist Osvaldo Sunkel at Hamburg in a remarkable workshop in 1970. Scholars from diverse places of the world who did not know each other but were working in one form or another with concepts of dependency, were brought together: from Canada, Watkins, myself and the brilliant Stephen Hymer, who died far too young in a tragic accident; Lloyd Best from the West Indies; Arghiri Emmanuel known for his *Unequal Exchange*; Giovanni Arrighi, then recently returned from East Africa and later associated with Wallerstein, Frank and Amin; and Froebel, Heinrichs and Krey, who we called the three musketeers and who jointly published a pioneering study on the migration of manufacturing activity to the Third World. It was the best workshop I have ever attended. There were no papers, just the excitement of the exchange of ideas. Stephen Hymer kept us up until three in the morning in animated discussion.

The chapter in *Silent Surrender* entitled "From the Old Mercantilism to the New," suggested that the foreign operations of multinational corporations resembled in some respects those of the old chartered companies in extending the territorial reach of the metropole into foreign lands, a comparison also made by other authors. Although foreign mining companies with concessions over vast territories employing private militias with de facto judicial power do indeed resemble the old chartered companies, corporate manufacturing has no counterpart in the preindustrial era.

Historically, the United States was a high wage economy compared to Europe. The modern corporation, whether horizontally or vertically integrated, was an innovative organizational response to these special conditions of continental expansion in the large domestic economy of the United States. Because labour was scarce in relation to land, businesses were motivated to undertake constant technological improvement, and unionized labour was able to share the gains of increased productivity. In the post-war era, the typical multinational manufacturing corporation engaged in Schumpeterian strategies of innovation in process and product and the creation of new consumers for these products by advertising and marketing. Corporations had long-term planning horizons; strategies were designed to increase sales and market share; profits were generally reinvested; dividend payments were conservative; and shareholders of blue-chip stock considered it a long-term investment. Increased sales and market-share, and not shareholder value of assets, was the objective pursued by the managerial technostructure. This was well described in Galbraith's then recently published *The New Industrial State.*

What I found particularly interesting in this work was his insight into the mutually supportive relationship between the managerial technostructure of the corporations and their counterparts in the bureaucratic apparatus of the state.

These "mighty engines of capitalism," as they were once referred to by Henry Fowler, with their networks of production facilities in many countries, contributed positively to the U.S. balance of payments by the backflow of profits and interest and the generation of demand for U.S. exports. For the host country, the outflow of interest and profit exceeded the inflow of FDI. Firms established as affiliates could not engage in research and development, they were not permitted to compete with the parent company, and they did not have the decision-making power to engage in national industrial strategies. My analysis of the effects of increasing foreign control over Canada's manufacturing industries was not essentially different from the Watkins Report, commissioned by Walter Gordon on behalf of the Privy Council of Canada. The Watkins Report was shelved. Walter Gordon resigned and established the Committee for an Independent Canada. The national energy policy proposed by Prime Minister Trudeau was resoundingly rejected by the Canadian business elite. With few exceptions, like Walter Gordon and Eric Kierans, the Canadian business elite did not have a long-term view of developing independent national industries or a coherent Canadian national economy. Nor did the labour movement.

By and large the Canadian labour movement did not support policies of economic nationalism. The Canadian subsidiaries of major U.S. manufacturing corporations, like General Motors and General Electric, generated substantial employment at good wages. They were unionized. Workers could expect employment in one company for a lifetime; real wages increased annually. Working conditions in U.S. affiliates were usually better than those in Canadian-owned companies. Leftist critics of Canadian economic nationalism saw no advantage in Canadian ownership or control of industry. A capitalist is a capitalist. What is the difference?

The Auto Pact of 1965 was a unique legally binding international agreement negotiated between the Big Three American automobile companies and the governments of the United States and Canada. In this continental rationalization of production facilities, Canada secured provisions for 60 percent domestic content favouring the Canadian production of parts and components. Skilful negotiation and good luck in the choice of production of popular models in Canada yielded substantial gains for Canadian autoworkers. There was a large increase in Canadian production and exports of cars, trucks and parts accounting for approximately one-quarter of Canadian merchandise exports — exclusively to the United States.

But, the ultimate result of opting for a "special relationship" with the Big Three, rather than encouraging a genuine Canadian industry, was vulnerability to decisions by American companies to scale down their operations in

Canada, with attendant loss of employment. The implicit decision not to opt for an indigenous car industry because it would have been more costly and risky was characteristic of the mercantile nature of the Canadian business classes. Among developed countries, Canada is unique in not having even one national brand. Almost all the developed and many developing countries, much poorer than Canada, established genuinely independent automobile industries, gaining a competitive advantage in the uniqueness of their products.

Canadian autoworkers and communities dependent on the industry are now paying the price of the special relationship. In the course of the past ten years, there have been plant closures and major reductions in employment. In Ontario, where most of the industry is located, 30,000 jobs have been lost since 2001, with 10,000 more scheduled to disappear. The share of transportation equipment in Canada's exports has decreased from 21 percent in 2003 to 16 percent in 2007. Within this total, all the sub-sectors of the industry have declined. There is speculation that in the future there may not be a single assembly plant remaining in Canada. Only the independently owned auto parts industry has a chance of survival. The desperate situation of the Canadian autoworkers was signalled by the recent agreement between the CAW and the largest auto parts producer, who guaranteed security of employment in exchange for the abrogation of the right to strike.

Ontario has suffered a loss of 200,000 manufacturing jobs in the past four years, and the trend continues. Ontario, the industrial heartland of Canada, with the largest population, has historically been the richest province. No longer so. Its GDP per capita is now $1000 below the national average; $30,000 below that of Alberta and $12,000 below Newfoundland. For years, Ontario attracted migrants from poorer provinces. For the first time since records were kept, there has been a net out-migration from Ontario to other provinces. Some people maintain that the loss of manufacturing jobs is no cause for alarm because there has been a compensating growth of employment in the service sectors, which now employ more than five million people in Ontario. But no country can sustain a decent standard of living for its working population without dynamic, nationally owned enterprises engaged in manufacturing.

The recent sale of what is left of iconic Canadian business to foreign mega-corporations or private equity funds is cause for serious concern. The critical importance of policies favouring nationally owned enterprise is the lesson of successful economic development both in Europe and in Asia. In countries that have succeeded in maintaining employment in manufacturing, governments have engaged in strategic industrial policies that offer assistance to innovative technological development in business and educational institutions. This is better understood in Quebec — which has successfully nurtured Quebec-based world-class manufacturing and engineering corporations — than in the rest of Canada. Indeed, it is questionable whether Canada still has a national economy in any meaningful sense of the term. We have to ask how it can be that Canada, the largest supplier of petroleum to the United States at a time when oil prices are at record highs, is experiencing a melting down of its industrial heartland? In any rationally organized national economy, the rents from the resource sector would be invested in the long-term development of human resources and cutting edge technologies of manufacturing activity.

The Canadian national economy constructed in the nineteenth century on an east-west corridor was a political project known by historians as the Canadian National Policy. Its three principal instruments were a transcontinental railway, commercial policy to promote industrialization in Ontario and Quebec, and assisted immigration and land grants to develop the agricultural resources of the Prairies. Over the years, this east-west economy, based on a special relationship with Britain, was transformed by north-south links of trade and investment with the United States along the 3000 miles of shared border. The political fragmentation implied in these changing patterns of trade required deliberate policy measures by the federal government to counteract the disintegrating effects of the pull of economic forces. Canada emerged from the Second World War with a strengthened industrial base in Ontario and Quebec. The introduction of social security measures, including old age pensions and universal health care, financed by progressive taxation; transfer payments from richer to poorer provinces; welcoming immigration policies; federal expenditures on communication and the arts, including the National Film Board and the Canadian Broadcasting Corporation; and participation in all aspects of the United Nations system, gained Canada international respect. Expo '67 marked the high point of Canadian post-war achievement.

This model of "embedded liberalism," which yielded three decades of high growth, was underpinned by an institutional framework that regulated and restricted both the power and the mobility of capital. Finance was subservient to production. Financial institutions channelled savings to investment and were strictly regulated. Central banks served as instruments of the government, with full employment as primary objective; price stability was secondary. Banks were not permitted to charge more than 6 percent interest on loans or to engage in mortgage or investment banking. There were exchange controls and no private trading in foreign currencies. Social expenditures were financed by progressive income taxation. In Canada, the highest tax bracket was 80 percent; in the United States it was even higher, at 94 percent.

From 1945 to the mid-1970s, the distribution of income in North America was more equitable than ever before or since. At that time, in the United States, the average earnings of the super rich 0.01 percent of families was only 200 times greater than the average earnings of 90 percent of American families. In the 1980s, this measure of income disparity increased from 300 to 500, and continued to increase throughout the 1990s. In 2006 the income of the super rich was 976 times greater than that of 90 percent of American families. Income inequality is now even more extreme than it was in 1929, when the ratio was 892 to one. In the United States, median family income has increased by only $8000 since 1980, and this increase is primarily due to more family members contributing to family income. In Canada, trends are similar. Median family income has increased somewhat, but Statistics Canada reported that median earnings of full-time wage and salary earners have stagnated in the twenty-five years since 1980. Median earnings of the top quintile rose by 16 percent, while the highest .01 percent of wage and salary earners doubled their income from $3 million to $6 million in the same period. The bottom quintile suffered a decline of 21 percent. In these twenty-five years, GDP has doubled, but the gains from economic growth have largely accrued to high-income earners, while low income earners have been impoverished. These statistics stand in strong contrast to the prevailing trends from the 1950s to the 1980s, when GDP growth in the U.S. and Canada was accompanied by rising real earnings of full-time wage and salary earners.

So what has happened to the good unionized jobs in iconic corporations like General Motors and General Electric? These companies today are not the same as they were in the 1960s and 1970s. For all the faults we found with them, those times were good compared with the present. Why do productivity increases no longer result in higher labour incomes? How have the gains of labour been rolled back since the 1980s? How has the power of labour so declined that the once mighty UAW/CAW negotiated a no-strike agreement? How has the distribution of income so deteriorated, with similarities to the "dance of the millions" — now billions — which preceded the crash of 1929? How have we arrived at a financial crisis that threatens to project the real economy into a deflationary spiral of rising unemployment and increasing poverty? Why have democratic institutions in Canada and the U.S. failed to protect the economic security of the majority of the population?

For the last two hundred years, and most spectacularly in the three decades following the Second World War, investment in productive capacity achieved remarkable increases in the material standard of living. Although profitability was the criterion for success in the private sector, it was by innovation in the production and marketing of useful goods and services that profit was earned and reinvested. Capital had a stake in the communities, indeed in the countries, in which its production facilities were located.

Since the early 1980s we have witnessed a reversion to accumulation by dispossession, reminiscent of the old days of the mercantilist era, which preceded industrial capitalism. Transnational corporations have increasingly secured monopolistic control over markets on a global scale. In many respects, they are more powerful than governments. The largest of these companies, such as Monsanto, do indeed resemble the old chartered trading companies. Millions of farmers are in bondage to this and similar companies, and thousands have been dispossessed of their land. In the industrialized world, transnational corporations have outsourced production to cheap labour countries, and millions of workers have been dispossessed of good jobs. This is reflected in the declining contribution of manufacturing and the increasing contribution of finance, distribution and business services to GDP, most dramatically in the United States and Britain. Progressive financialization of capital has substituted short-term market based considerations of shareholder value for the long-term strategic planning horizon of corporations producing for mass markets. In this Anglo-American variety of capitalism, finance has become decoupled from production, and the capital market has lost its useful function of judging the long-term productive capabilities of different firms. Once the criterion of shareholder value became the objective of good management of a company, the capital market became a gigantic casino where people attempted to guess the market with confidence that it would maintain a secular rising trend. Of all the aspects of globalization, it is the financialization of capital that has had the most profound consequences in the West.

Galbraith's most important book was *The Great Crash*. I suggest that the transformational process, which has unravelled the institutional framework that sustained the good times of the 1960s and 1970s, might be called The Great Financialization. It had its origins in the dissolution of the Bretton Woods financial order, gathered momentum in the 1980s and exploded in the mid-1990s. Ever since dollar convertibility to gold was abandoned, the United States was able to sustain an ever-increasing external deficit by issuing ever-larger amounts of dollars. International liquidity increased, and deregulation of financial institutions encouraged the progressive expansion of credit. Soon, cross-border capital movements and trading in foreign currencies greatly exceeded the requirements of trade in goods and services. Short term capital movements rather than trade determined exchange rates and contributed to financial and banking crises in Mexico, Argentina, Brazil, Turkey, East Asia and Russia. These crises were more severe than anything previously experienced. Millions were plunged into poverty, and private and state assets passed into foreign hands at fire-sale prices. In all of these cases, including a large intervention to save banks from the impending failure of the Long-Term Capital Management hedge fund, overexposed international financial institutions were rescued by central bank and IMF intervention. The Asian Crisis threatened the stability of the global financial order, but progressive financialization was able to sustain economic growth in the heartlands of capitalism. The real costs of capital account liberalization were borne by the rest of world.

In the 1970s, inflationary pressures reduced the profitability of financial investment, and full employment increased the bargaining power of labour. As anticipated by Michael Kalecki, Keynesian solutions became inoperative as the rate of return on capital declined. These economic trends, combined with rising radicalism in the Third World and the defeat in Vietnam, were countered by a political decision to institute an economic regime change to restore the discipline of capital over labour. Princeton economist and *New York Times* columnist Paul Krugman drew attention to the imbalance of political power within American democratic institutions which enabled a small number of conservative, wealthy activists, backed by anti-union businesses, to redefine the policy direction of the government. Neoliberal policies, introduced by Thatcher and Reagan, were designed by economists in university research institutes and think-tanks financed by business interests. They were crafted with political skill and bated with promises of tax reduction. The doctrine of supply-side economics, which maintained that a reduction of income tax rates would induce an increase in output and thus increase total tax receipts, was a seductive ideological construct with populist appeal but no scientific validity.

Public expenditures were increasingly financed by the sale of securities to domestic and foreign creditors, and public sector savings were negative. Household savings were also negative and consumer expenditures were sustained by an increasing volume of mortgage and household finance, including credit cards at usurious rates of interest. The volume of debt further ballooned by financial innovation of derivative debt instruments. If financial liberalization was the primary mechanism undermining the Keynesian historic compromise of capital and labour, the erosion of progressive income taxation both contributed to financialization and exacerbated inequality.

The burden of taxation was shifted from corporations and the wealthy to middle and lower income groups by means of regressive sales taxes. High-income earners with greater discretional income generated pools of capital seeking returns in emerging markets and other financial investments. Investment in infrastructure and productive capacity of the real economy stagnated as returns in global financial markets exceeded those in the domestic economy. Iconic American corporations, which once engaged in mass production for mass consumption, increasingly derived income from distributional, financial and other business services associated with the import of manufactures from countries where labour costs are substantially lower. Wal-Mart, which directly produces none of the vast array of products it retails, and does not tolerate unions, is at the extreme end of this model. The prosperity of the United States has been increasingly sustained by military and consumption expenditures, financed by mountains of domestic and foreign credit. American consumers became the driving force of the world economy, but American producers have slipped from the predominant role they played in the early post-war years.

The financialization of capital is most extreme in Britain and the United States, where incomes deriving from financial markets have contributed disproportionately to GDP growth, while the real economy has been hollowed out. This is reflected in changes in the relative contributions to GDP of manufacturing on the one hand and finance, insurance and real estate on the other. In Britain, value added by manufacturing declined from 32 percent in

1971 to 14 percent in 2006, while in the United States it declined from 23 to 13 percent in the same period. Income derived from finance, insurance and real estate in the United States increased from 15 percent in 1970 to 21 percent in 2007. Finance and insurance alone doubled from 4 percent of value added to GDP in 1971 to 8 percent in 2007; as a proportion of value added in manufacturing, this represents an increase from 18 to 65 percent in the same period.

Once capital markets were deregulated, the initiative of macro-economic policy passed from national governments to financial markets. Central banks were reconfigured to be "independent" of ministers of finance; they henceforth became instruments for the protection of creditor interests of financial institutions, and governments became more sensitive to their credit rating than to opinion polls or election results. Contending political parties dance to the same tune. Democracy is now in suspense, effectively hostage to financial markets.

For the past twenty-five years, financialization of capital has been encouraged by disinflationary policies of central banks, which systemically favour creditors over debtors. Neoliberal objectives of zero inflation and pressure on governments for fiscal surpluses contrast with previous commitments of central banks to macro-economic policies designed to ensure full employment. Central banks have contributed to the sustained profitability of mushrooming global financial transactions, resulting in the increasing vulnerability of the real economy — private and public — to debt finance. As an increasing volume of capital has shifted into financial circuits by the lure of inordinate profits, manufacturing and other productive sectors have come under pressure to sustain profitability by mergers and acquisitions, downsizing, outsourcing and the search for new markets. International competitiveness has become the criterion of success for the private sector and the measure of responsible public policy by governments.

The liberalization of capital has been accompanied by measures to break down barriers to trade and investment on an international scale. It is important to note however that the dynamics of financial liberalization are significantly different from trade liberalization. Whereas the liberalization of capital proceeds by stealth as a progressive process of unilateral reduction of national regulatory constraint, the liberalization of trade requires negotiated agreement between governments. Where negotiations take the form of free-trade agreements, they are legally binding international treaties of indefinite duration.

Governmental and business elites fearing that Canada would be left out in a world of competing economic blocs, called on the "special relationship" with the U.S. to obtain exemption from American protectionism. Canada initiated negotiations for a free trade agreement to secure American markets for Canadian products, which eventually resulted in the Canada-U.S. Free

Trade Agreement of 1988. It is not accidental that Canada, the first industrialized country to host a massive inflow of U.S. direct investment, was also the first to negotiate an a new kind of free trade agreement, which went far beyond conventional commercial agreements to protect the interests of foreign investors from the exercise of sovereignty by the host governments. Canadian export dependence on the U.S. market increased from 65 percent in the mid-70s to some 85 percent by the end of the century, and American ownership of Canadian industry also increased significantly. My colleague Dorval Brunelle has suggested that the Canada-U.S. Free Trade Agreement was the template for globalization.

Victory of the West in the Cold War gave a tremendous political lift to the doctrines of market fundamentalism. There appeared to be no alternatives to compliance with the demands for capital and trade liberalization. A new institutional regime of multilateral and bilateral treaties was launched in 1994 with the signing of NAFTA, the initiation of a Free Trade Area of the Americas and the transformation of the GATT into the WTO. The WTO provides the framework for a consensus-based regime regulating world trade, with mechanisms to enforce compliance by member countries.

Trade liberalization has forced developing countries to open their markets to cheap — often subsidized — imports which had a destructive effect on their agricultural and industrial capacities and cut short the promises of development. Liberalization conditionalities attached to successive IMF programs have almost completely destroyed the once flourishing domestic manufacturing industries in Jamaica. Factory shells are now warehouses where containers of imported products are repackaged for sale on the domestic market. Many developing countries have experienced similar loss of industrial capacity.

Trade liberalization is not the only, or perhaps not even the most important, element in efforts to open economies to trade and capital flows. Concessions obtained in two decades of Structural Adjustment Programs imposed on debtor countries, and in bilateral free trade agreements, guaranteeing the rights of investors, have gone far beyond WTO rules. Large and powerful developing countries, including Brazil, India and South Africa, have refused to sign onto a WTO agenda which would include granting national treatment to foreign investors, intellectual property rights, limitations on government procurement and so-called unfair competition by state enterprises. The new style of free trade agreement, of which the Canada-U.S. FTA was the template, secures all of the above for foreign investors.

With increasing turbulence and uncertainty in financials markets, funds moved into commodities, including petroleum, copper and other minerals and more recently into food and land. Whereas biofuels have contributed to a secular rising trend in prices of corn and soy, only speculative forward purchases can account for the spike in rice, wheat and many other food products since 2007. The financial crisis is impacting in the first instance on the value of personal and institutional savings and threatens recession in the North; the Global South appeared to be relatively insulated. However, speculative activity in commodity markets was directly responsible for the food crisis of 2008, which according to the World Bank plunged one hundred million people into dire poverty. Food prices doubled and tripled, and poor people in developing countries, where food expenditures account for some 70 percent of income, have been the victims of a crisis originating in the financialization of the major capitalist economies. Food riots erupted in thirty-three countries, and the World Bank expressed concern regarding the social stability of the developing world. The FAO considered thirty-seven countries in need of food aid, but the U.N. had difficulty in meeting its target of $500 million. Contrast this with Cargill's posted profit of $1.2 billion in the first quarter of 2008. Indeed the dominance of multinational agribusiness in world markets is a manifestation of the subordinate position of producers to corporations, which control access to inputs of high yielding seeds, pesticides and fertilizers, and access to markets including processing facilities. Their profits greatly exceed the incomes of agricultural producers. This is the case also in Canada, where a large increase in exports of agricultural products has failed to raise the net income of farmers, which has been stationary for the last twenty years.

But the disparity between agricultural incomes of farmers and the mega-profits of corporations is very much more extreme in developing countries. The food crisis of 2008 has extinguished the gains of poverty reduction programs and has put the entire free trade agenda into question. According to Fred Bergsten, trade liberalization has come to a "screeching halt." Developing countries blocked the FTAA and suspended the WTO Doha round, and the objectives of food self-reliance will require some reversal of economic liberalization. India and many other developing countries have suspended the export of food in order to meet domestic demand, and food sovereignty has become an important objective of many developing countries. Programs to increase domestic production will require land reform and protection from the destructive effects of the imports of subsidized food and food products.

There are questions to be asked about the responsibility of economists and the relevance of economics. The fundamental tenet of economics is that the free market is the most efficient mechanism for the allocation of scarce resources. Over the past twenty-five years in which capital and commodity markets have been liberated from regulatory constraint, income inequality has greatly increased. In the 1970s, CEO compensation was forty times greater than average worker salaries in the U.S. Since that time, free markets have revalued the services of CEOs to amount to three hundred times those of worker salaries today.

Specifically, we must ask what has been the real contribution of the recipients of the explosive growth of financial incomes? The huge increase in incomes derived from financial services contributed significantly to GDP growth. Our accounting conventions record incomes generated in finance, insurance and real estate as an addition to national production as measured by GDP. By these conventions the services of the top hedge fund managers are forty times more valuable than those of the top corporate CEOs, and roughly 13,000 times more valuable than the highest paid members of U.S. Congress, who earn just under $200,000. Thus, individuals and corporations engaged in financial services, who receive one fifth of all incomes generated in the U.S., appear to have contributed one fifth of the value of all goods and services of the national economy. But what useful goods or services have been produced by the financial sector to merit this reward?

The actual contribution of financialization has been the ability to sustain economic growth by the ever-increasing volume of debt, facilitated by easy money from the Federal Reserve. The near doubling of GDP barely raised median family incomes and reduced industrial employment and earnings, while the physical and social infrastructure of the country deteriorated. The permissive condition has been the willingness of the rest of the world to finance the external payments deficits of 6–7 percent of GDP by purchasing U.S. securities and holding increasing amounts of dollar reserves. This situation is plainly unsustainable and is unravelling. According to George Soros, the "current crisis is the culmination of a super-boom that has lasted for more than 60 years" and was aided by authorities who intervened to rescue the global financial system whenever it was at risk.

We need to rethink economics. More fundamentally, we have to rethink the real value of goods and services. Feminists have drawn our attention to the fact that the market assigns no value to the useful services performed in the household, principally by women. While personal services of caring are grossly undervalued, financial services have become grossly overvalued. We need to return to some basic questions of use-value and exchange value. Economics should abandon its a priori deductive methodology. It should study real economies in the context of the societies in which they exist and the power relations between private and public authority. This was the approach of John Kenneth Galbraith.

NOTE

This chapter is based on a different, earlier paper published in *Unconventional Wisdom: Lectures from the John Kenneth Galbraith Prize in Economics* (2009). Also originally titled "The Great Financialization," it was published in Ottawa by the Canadian Centre for Policy Alternatives.

12. DEVELOPMENT ECONOMICS IN PERSPECTIVE

I wish to express my sincerest thanks to the Consortium Graduate School of Social Science and most particularly to Professor Norman Girvan for the opportunity to engage in an ongoing process of reflection on a subject which has been central to my work for the past twenty-five years: economic development. Within the discipline of economics, this translates to "development economics." More broadly, we are concerned with the contribution of economics to the understanding of the process of economic development, and specifically with developmental policies for the large and varied set of Third World countries.[1]

Although I have taught courses on economic development for many years at McGill University, and also here in the Department of Economics in the late 1970s, I have never enjoyed teaching as much as I did when I was able to work with the Consortium students. I can think of three reasons for this: first, because we share a Caribbean experience and a common interest in exploring solutions to the problems of the region; second, because the Consortium approach to development studies is consciously and deliberately multidisciplinary, thus inviting the transgression of disciplinary boundaries, which are progressively more restrictive as mainstream economics has become more abstract, mathematical and non-institutional; and third, because I have found the Consortium students to be bright, hardworking and genuinely interested in expanding their understanding of the world around them.

Development economics emerged as a sub-discipline of economics in the 1940s and 1950s as the Third World was forming from the shambles of the disintegrating European colonial empires. The communist victory in China, the decolonization of the Middle East, the Indian sub-continent and the former Dutch East Indies (Indonesia), followed by Africa in the 1950s and 1960s, created a number of new nation-states. Economic development was top priority on their agendas. The United States, as the new hegemonic power, was faced with the challenge of managing the emergence of these states without colonial political authority over their affairs. As Gerald Meier put it, "the pedigree of development economics reads 'from colonial economics out of political expediency'."

Development economics has an intimate relationship with the politics of policy prescription. What then is the role of economics and of economists in the formulation of theories and policies pertaining to development? There is no simple answer because economists are diversely motivated by values, ideologies and collective generational experience. Does this mean, then, that there is no such thing as a "science" of economics? Yes and no, but more yes than no. As far as I am concerned, there is no such thing as a "science" of economics, or a "science" of society, if by "science" we mean a set of "laws" that can be proved or disproved in the manner of the laws believed to govern natural phenomena. If however we interpret "science" in its older meaning of a body of knowledge and a set of propositions which can be developed from this body of knowledge, then economics can serve a useful purpose if applied with propriety and relevance. This leads me to the position that the body of knowledge we know as political economy, or economics, has to be stripped of its ideological baggage and also of its extravagant claims to universality. Economics is important, but we must understand its basic ideas and concepts to be able to use its theoretical constructs appropriately and intelligently.

We are here particularly concerned with the intellectual roots and historical context of the body of propositions that formed the sub-discipline of "development economics." Derived from the classics of economics and the historical experience of industrialized countries, development economics emphasized the role of the state as the catalytic agent of economic development. In the current climate of deregulation and emphasis on the private sector as principal agent of development, this body of propositions has gone out of style, along with the Keynesian management of the mixed economy with which it was closely associated. This resulted in a shift in emphasis from national development (structural transformation) to active policies of adjustment to international market forces (structural adjustment). Not surprisingly, considerations of finance and the management of external payments, including debt service, has replaced development as the major concern of international development agencies and the governments of scores of heavily indebted developing countries. Market-oriented policies are dressed up in the language of the "science of economics," and technocrats in developing countries are accorded the role of "sherpas" to guide governments along the precipitous paths of implementing such policies.

ECONOMICS, IDEOLOGY AND DEVELOPMENT

I follow Schumpeter in his proposition that, in the social sciences, theories are based on an initial "vision" or intuitive insight inferred from the realities of a specific moment in human history, bounded in space and time. Unlike natural science, social science does not proceed by discarding one vision (theory/paradigm) in favour of a subsequently developed one. This is because these theories illuminate different aspects of the diversity and complexity of social reality. Nowhere is this more evident than in development studies, where competing paradigms and competing ideologies continue to nourish this field of study. Contrary to popular belief however, there is no simple relationship between social science paradigms and their role in lending "scientific" legitimation to ideological positions. Indeed, the conflation of methodology and ideology has served to sow confusion and disorientation.

It is essential that we understand the origins of economic theories and locate them within the problematique that gave rise to them. The starting point of each body of theory is related to contemporary political-economic-social realities and prevailing philosophies. This introduces the element of "ideology" in a twofold manner: (1) the discourse of the dominant paradigm reflects the agenda of the intellectual strata which formulated it; and (2) theories or paradigms are called upon to serve the interests of contending forces in the political struggle to maintain, reform or overthrow existing relations of power. Thus, social science paradigms may act as a powerful conservative force to lock the mind into acceptance of the status quo as "scientifically determined" or "rational" — or they may act as a powerful radical force to mobilize solidarity and legitimize popular movements of resistance to oppression.

However there is no permanent association between social science theories and paradigms on the one hand, and the ideological roles that they are called upon to play on the other. Take, for example, neoclassical economics. This elegant apparatus of economic theory carries the hidden message that "the market knows best," and governments should not interfere with market forces. But this body of theory, when stripped of ideology, can serve other purposes. Interestingly, Leon Walras, one of the founders of neoclassical economics, was a socialist; and Wassily Leontief developed a Walrasian general equilibrium model into input-output analysis that has been widely used in economic planning. Conversely Marxism, devised as a theory to empower the working class, regressed into a mumbo jumbo of textual citation when it became the official ideology of the Soviet Union.

Economics is the most influential of the social sciences, and its approach now extends into the disciplines of political science (public choice theory) and sociology (human capital theory). The calculating "rational" individual is an intellectual construct that supports a view of economic activity as disembodied transactions of "factors of production" guided by the price signals of the market. Hence, economics is no longer about real people living in real communities or societies bound by ties of cultural commonalities and participating in a multitude of formal and informal associations. The disembodied "rational" individual of modern economics is the intellectual reflection of the "disembedded" economy. The only truly disembodied factor of production is money capital. Money can move across the world, forever seeking the largest, quickest or safest return on investment. Money capital is not interested in where productive activity is located, what is produced, who is employed or who is rendered unemployed as a result of this or that investment. Money capital has no concern for environmental degradation or the geographic distribution of the results of its international mobility.

My argument here is not directed at the role of ideology in the struggle for liberation and human development. It is precisely because ideas are so powerful that we must be able to separate the scientific elements in the corpus of economic theory from the ideological baggage that has attached itself to it. The ideology, which can move a people or a nation to construct its own history, to "take charge" of its affairs, or if you prefer, to "develop," must be centred and rooted within its own culture if a people is to be the subject, not the object, of its history. Only thus can its technocrats and planners and businesses constructively draw on the corpus of economic theory for the good management of the affairs of state. Economic theory is important for the understanding of the mechanisms of economic interdependence, the functioning of markets and the management of the modern mixed economy. It is a tool and must never become a master. As a tool, it must serve the collective purpose of the society. It goes without saying that these purposes and objectives cannot be defined by some external agency, as is increasingly the case for countries under IMF/World Bank management.

My critique is directed at the arrogance of the practitioners of a disembodied "economic science" advocating universal prescriptions divorced from institutional context. It is directed also at a scholastic Marxism that is blind to realities because it is blinkered by the categories of its discourse. I believe that we must lay claim to all the important insights of the work of all the "classics" of economics. Each has cast the light of understanding upon a particular facet or aspect of economic life; each has contributed something of importance, whether in methodology or substance, or both.

Fortunately, there are a finite number of important ideas that are associated with the insights of economists. I suggest that all the truly great economists have some place in our understanding of the complexity of contemporary reality: they enable us to illuminate a particular aspect of our reality. However their insights and theories have to be understood in the context of the times that gave rise to them and the particular problems they sought to address. This is why I adopt a historical approach in my survey of the contribution of economics to an understanding of development. Because there has always been a close relationship between the paradigms or "visions" of economists and the interests of the ruling classes, their theories have been vulgarized and transformed into ideologies to serve vested interests — or those who oppose them. The transformation of neoclassical economics into an ideology of economic liberalism in the service of transnational financial capital is a case in point.

EARLY DEVELOPMENT ECONOMICS

In the 1940s and 1950s, before development economics became institution-alized in the service of national and multilateral development agencies, a number of independent scholars addressed the problems of development and underdevelopment. They came to the problem with their individual agendas, social philosophies and generational experiences. Received economic theory was marshalled to provide a framework on which to hang their insights and policy prescriptions.

Thus Rostow, the most influential of the American modernizers, was a cold warrior interested primarily in developing an American foreign policy response to the attraction of the Soviet model of industrialization to the countries of Asia. His theory of stages was cobbled together from simple growth theory and the Schumpeterian notion of leading sectors. In the late 1950s, he was instrumental in persuading the U.S. administration to engage in development assistance and technical advice in development planning to counter communist influence.

Many of the group of early development economists, best described as European Structuralist, were products of the diasporas of Continental European emigration to England and the United States in the years preced-ing the Second World War.

The role of the state in the development of the European "late industrial-izers," including the successes of the planned Soviet economy; Continental traditions of economic thought, including the theories of Joseph Schumpeter; chronic underemployment of labour and the evident incapacity of the market to lift "backward" economies out of economic underdevelopment; long-term trends of the declining role of raw materials in international trade; and the influence of the doctrines of J.M. Keynes served as points of departure of their contributions to early development economics. Hirschman's "Rise and Decline of Development Economics" (1981) is the best single article distin-guishing early development economics from one-size-fits-all "monoeconom-ics." It argued the case for active government intervention and economic planning in a mixed economy aided by development assistance to augment the inadequate capital resources of developing countries. These economists were internationalist in outlook and social democratic in philosophy, in the broad and non-partisan sense of that term (or politically "liberal" in American parlance).

The Classical Model in a Tropical Setting

In 1949, using the neoclassical theory of comparative advantage, W. Arthur Lewis argued that densely populated countries poorly endowed with land should export manufactures and import their food requirements. In the con-text of Jamaica, structured by centuries of sugar plantation economy and a society burnt with the stigma of slavery, this was a liberating project, which moreover held out the promise of providing work and incomes for labour made redundant by declining employment in the sugar industry. We must bear in mind that in those days it was widely believed that underdeveloped countries were not capable of undertaking manufacturing activity, which was believed to require superior skills and work discipline and had spin-off benefits of "learning by doing." The transformation of Puerto Rico's derelict sugar economy into an export manufacturing economy by Operation Bootstrap was to be the model.

In practical terms, industrialization had to start by addressing the domestic market, whether in Jamaica or in Africa, where Lewis, as the first economic advisor to the newly established state of Ghana, stressed the need for import substitution combined with agricultural development. It was wrong to have blamed Lewis for the excesses of "industrialization by invitation," a term coined by Lloyd Best. Nor was his advocacy of export manufacturing predicated on a permanent supply of cheap labour. Indeed, he was emphatic in his view that "international trade cannot substitute for technological change, so those who depend on it for their major hope are doomed to frustration... the most important item on the agenda of development is to transform the food sector, create agricultural surpluses to feed the urban population, and thereby create the domestic basis for industry and modern services" (Lewis 1978).

Equipped with a thorough grounding in classical and neoclassical economics and the study of English economic history, Lewis addressed a question which, he tells us, had troubled him for a long time: why labour engaged in the production of exports of colonial countries (coffee) is paid so much less than labour producing the exports of developed countries (steel), when workers work equally hard? And why the relative prices of coffee and steel are so unfavourable to the producers of coffee? It was from Arthur Lewis, then a young lecturer at the LSE, that I first learnt that primary commodity prices of Latin American export commodities started to decline in the mid-1920s — well before the onset of the Great Depression.

Lewis tells us that in August 1952, walking down a street in Bangkok, the explanation of the dual problem of economic development and adverse terms of trade revealed itself to him: "so in three minutes I had solved two of my problems with one change of assumption" — the rejection of the neoclassical assumption of a fixed supply of labour in favour of the classical model of capital accumulation, drawing on an infinitely elastic supply of labour in the tradition of Ricardo and Marx. The famous Lewis model is essentially Ricardian, with the addition of technical progress and productivity increases in the capitalist sector.

However the "originality of the copy," to borrow Cardoso's felicitous phrase in describing CEPAL developmentalism, is revealed in the open or "tropical" version of the model, which concludes that in the trade relationship between a labour-surplus (underdeveloped) and labour-scarce (developed) country, the gains in productivity increase in the export sector will accrue to the developed trading partner in the form of cheap imports, because prices and wages are not determined by productivity but by the opportunity cost of (surplus) labour. Thus, factoral terms of trade offer the tropical countries the opportunity to stay poor — at any rate until the labour reserves of China and India are exhausted. Lewis concludes that "tropical countries cannot escape unfavourable terms of trade by increasing productivity in the commodities they export, since this will simply reduce the prices of such commodities. The terms of trade can be improved only by raising productivity in domestic foodstuffs" (1978a). In other words, trade is not a highway to development for poor countries. It is not a substitute for raising the productivity of domestic agriculture, nor can the import of foodstuffs be of help if it is obtained by unfavourable terms of exchange in trade. With the passage of time, tropical countries steadily lost ground in export markets, "because the tropics can only compete where the difference in wages exceeds the difference in productivity. This left a rather narrow range of agricultural exports, and contributed to the over-specialization of tropical countries in one or sometimes two export crops" (Lewis 1978a). Here is the fundamental explanation of the crisis that today faces the peripheral commodity exporting countries of Africa. Starting with experiential observation of the basic injustice of the unequal rewards of labour in "tropical" and "temperate" countries, proceeding by reasoning from basic economic theory, corroborated by careful research in economic history, in *Growth and Fluctuations 1870–1913*, Lewis laid bare the elements of the basic problem of "trade and development" in clear, lucid language. He spelled out the policy implications and "the fundamental sense in which the leaders of the less developed world denounce the current economic order as unjust, namely that the factoral terms of trade are based on market forces of opportunity cost, and not on the just principle of equal pay for equal work" (Lewis 1978b).

He was not among those who believed that inequality in international economic relations between developed and developing countries could be ameliorated by international negotiation. He believed in self-reliance. He tells us that his mother brought him up to believe that "anything they can do, we can do too." He concluded his Schumpeter lectures with the well known passage that the development of the LDCs does not depend on the developed countries, and their potential for growth would be unaffected if they were to sink under the sea. Only autocentric development, starting with the modernization of the food-producing sector, can bring about a rise in the supply price of labour, and "automatically, we shall have a new international economic order" (Lewis 1978a). In his 1979 Nobel lecture, *The Slowing Down of the Engine of Growth*, Lewis returned to the theme of trade and development and challenged prevailing ideas concerning the feasibility of trade as an engine of growth in the context of the world economy of our time. This does not mean that foreign exchange is not essential as an input to the economy of "tropical" countries; it means that external markets cannot supply the growth dynamic — as was the case in the era of classical imperialism from 1870 to 1914.

The Structuralist Developmentalism of Raúl Prebisch and CEPAL

Raúl Prebisch, who had served during the Great Depression as director general of Argentina's central bank, tells us that he lost faith in the doctrines of neoclassical economics when the "great industrial centres," as he called them, plunged the old economic order into crisis and chaos. He concluded that the "peripheries," as he termed them, should no longer rely on the traditional export economy and should actively seek to industrialize by replacing imports from the metropoles. He challenged the traditional international division of labour between peripheral exporters of raw materials and industrialized exporters of manufactures with theories of deteriorating terms of trade. In 1950, as executive secretary of the recently established United Nations Economic Commission for Latin America (CEPAL), Prebisch used Keynesian constructs of the transmission of cycles to the periphery and structuralist assumptions concerning labour and commodity markets to argue that "the fruits of technical progress" accrue to the centres, resulting in a cumulative bias against economic development in the peripheries. In later versions, he elaborated his theories, placing increasing emphasis on the wasteful consumption of the upper classes and the detrimental effects of the unequal distribution of income in Latin America.

The pioneering work of Prebisch and the group of Latin American economists associated — whether formally or more loosely — with the early CEPAL, constitutes the "open economy" counterpart to the European structuralists. Whereas the latter were concerned with strategies of development of large semi-continental regions, the starting point of Prebisch and his associates was the economic development of the Latin American periphery. *Latin America and Its Principal Problems*, published in Spanish in 1950 and termed the "CEPAL Manifesto" by Hirschman, and the companion *Survey of Economic Development of Latin America in the 1930s and 1940s*, cover the major themes and propositions of Latin American Structuralism, which subsequently gave rise to dependency theory. In 1964, Prebisch became the first Secretary General of the United Nations Conference on Trade and Development.

In the mid-1970s, as the world entered an economic crisis which he described as "more profound, complex, and difficult than the Great Depression," Prebisch returned to Santiago. In retrospect it was his opinion that little had been achieved in the ten years he spent in the service of international institutions and numerous North-South dialogues, "nothing important was achieved then or later." From 1976 until his death in 1986 he contributed an important set of articles to the *CEPAL Review* restating and elaborating his original analyses of the problems of peripheral capitalism. He challenged monetarism and the revival of neoclassical economics with the explicit intent of stemming the galloping tide of the appeal of economic liberalism to younger generations of Latin American economists, the so-called Chicago Boys. The following passage from the closing pages of an article published in 1982 is testimony to the importance that Prebisch accorded independent thought and intellectual emancipation from economic theories which do not serve the best interests of Latin American development:

> Thirty years ago, the periphery had begun a tenacious and difficult attempt to emancipate itself intellectually. It was learning to question those theories developed in the centres that did not fit with the basic interests of peripheral development. The return to conventional theories in recent years has represented an attempt to counteract this effort aimed at independent thinking about development. The seductiveness of these theories is very powerful, and it clouds their proponents' view of reality so they are not able to perceive clearly the interplay of internal and external interests behind these new manifestations of conventional thinking. Now is the time to pursue this effort at intellectual emancipation. We must now advance on broader fields and include in our thinking and examination the structure of society, without which both the theory and practice of development will continue to drift from their proper paths. (Prebisch 1982: 151)

During his term as director of CEPAL (1948–63), Prebisch and his team of economists made four distinct contributions to economic theory and policy, of which the first is ultimately the key to the rest:

1. The Centre–Periphery System

This system is the historical outcome of the way in which technical progress is propagated in the world economy. In the peripheries it penetrates only where the industrial centres need imports of foodstuffs and agricultural and mineral raw materials at low cost, thus creating outward directed, externally propelled development. In Latin America this happened in the second half, particularly the last quarter of the nineteenth century. We note that on this definition, important regions of the Third World, principally in Asia, are not and never were, peripheries. The centre-periphery paradigm thus applies to Latin America, the Caribbean, most of Africa and some Southeast Asian countries. The same is true for dependency theory, which derived from the CEPALIST centre-periphery paradigm.

Implicit in the early CEPAL studies are the following characteristics of peripheral economic structures: production structures are disarticulated and specialized, with few internal linkages; technologies are heterogeneous, resulting in a wide range of productivities; the spread between the highest and lowest wage labour incomes is greater than in the centres; and the centres generate and the peripheries receive technology, consumption styles and external shocks which they cannot absorb without instability and disequilibrium due to their fragile, vulnerable and over-specialized economic structures.

2. Deteriorating Terms of Trade for the Periphery

The thesis of deteriorating terms of trade associated with Prebisch and also Hans Singer is too well known to require repetition. During the "golden years" of post-war economic growth, the business cycle was dormant, and trade acted once more as an engine of growth. Since the mid-1970s, when the Keynesian consensus model in the industrialized countries broke down, together with the accompanying Bretton Woods international order, disequilibrium forces in the terms of exchange between industrialized and developing countries re-asserted themselves with ferocity. Commodity terms of trade have fallen disastrously, plunging surplus labour countries depending on primary exports into deep crisis. They are forced to suffer the lion's share of adjustment to a thoroughly disordered international system, puffed up by vast pools of debt-creating private finance, bailed out and sustained — from time to time — by the central banks of the industrialized countries, acting individually or in concert as the Group of Seven or — when dealing with indebted developing countries — as the executive board of the International Monetary Fund.

3. Peripheral Industrialization

The CEPAL analysis recognized that peripheral industrialization has a structural tendency to external disequilibrium due to maladjustments between a high rate of growth of demand for industrial imports and the low rate of growth of external demand for primary commodity exports. Moreover, it was recognized that imported capital intensive technology was likely to be labour-displacing, thus pushing down wage levels and limiting the purchasing power of the masses. Sectoral bottlenecks inherited from outward-directed development in terms of land tenure patterns, transportation systems of rail and port designed to service the requirements of primary commodity exports, and associated inelastic supply of domestic foodstuffs, were recognized as problems to be addressed. It follows that devaluations are generally ineffective as policies designed to switch resources to export production or to substitute domestic for imported goods. Where import volumes are constrained to decline due to lack of foreign exchange to pay for them, production levels also decline, as does aggregate consumption. Potential output and potential savings are wasted. This is the burden of the "two gap" model, developed by Chenery and associates, which formalized the structuralist arguments of the CEPAListas in the context of the Alliance For Progress.

4. Obstacles to Economic Development and the Inflation Debate

Toward the end of the 1950s industrialization in Latin America, particularly in the Southern Cone countries, was moving toward stagnation, diagnosed as "the end of easy import substitution." Slow growth was accompanied by inflation, balance of payments crises, rising unemployment, social tensions and political unrest. In response to the crisis, CEPAL developmentalists advocated more intensive industrialization, regional economic integration, redistributive income policies, land reform, social welfare measures, economic planning and programming and increased external assistance. Reformist and radical critics noted that CEPAL developmentalist policies were creating a new kind of dependence as multinationals installed themselves in protected domestic markets.

The first encounter between orthodox monetarism and Latin American Structuralism occurred in the context of a slowing down of growth, accompanied by internal (inflation) and external (payments) disequilibria. While the debate started in Chile in the mid-1950s, the increasing role of the IMF in the lending policies of international agencies, including USAID, brought the Chile debate to the fore in other Latin American countries from 1957 onward as governments had to conform to monetarist IMF guidelines to be eligible for loans.

At the heart of the monetarist-structuralist debate was the issue of stabilization and growth: the structuralists did not dispute the fact that high interest rates and tight credit can suppress inflation. However, they maintained that such measures could secure no more than a temporary abatement of inflationary pressures and that price stability could ultimately be achieved only by positive developmental policies of increased production and economic growth. Moreover, deflationary monetary policies are a disincentive to producers and result in the wasteful underutilization of resources (unemployment) and the compression of output.

The monetarist response (which subsequently found favour with the military regimes of Chile, Argentina and Uruguay) consisted of neoclassical ("get prices right") arguments. Briefly, the "structural rigidities" or "bottlenecks," considered by the structuralists to be inherent in the condition of underdevelopment, are the result of price distortions arising from excessive controls. Thus, food subsidies are a disincentive to farmers; low utility rates are a disincentive to investors in utilities; and overvalued exchange rates are a disincentive to exporters; low (negative real) interest rates discourage savings, encourage wasteful consumption, lead to deficit financing and result in investment in real estate or foreign currency. The monetarist approach was supported by local private business groups, influential newspapers, visiting US dignitaries, and rightist political parties. Monetarists maintain that there is a latent dynamism in the private sector, and untapped possibilities for attracting large volumes of foreign investment. To realize this potential however, the economy must undergo a painful but necessary anti-inflationary therapy to purge itself of distortions and obstacles induced by inflation.

According to structuralist analysis, the underlying causes of internal and external disequilibria were the following: inelastic supplies of domestic foodstuffs; foreign exchange shortages due to excess of marginal coefficient of imports over exports; unequal distribution of income requiring redistributional policies with budgetary implications; and inelastic fiscal system of inelastic expenditures (salaries, debt service) accompanied by variable (export sector) revenues, regressive indirect taxes and tax evasion. In this view, monetary expansion and the propagation of inflation is not a primary but a derivative cause of inflation resulting from the efforts of various sectional interests to defend their real incomes in the context of slow growth or contraction: credit creation to accommodate the business sector; indexation to protect labour incomes; and deficit financing to maintain expenditures of state and parastatal sectors.

The issue is ultimately a political one. As Prebisch was at pains to point out, the monetary mechanism is not neutral but operates in favour of the privileged classes — at the national and also the international level. Monetary measures cause a contraction in the economy until unemployment forces labour to accept lower wages, but there are no mechanisms to contain the privileged consumption of the favoured classes. Similarly, exchange rate policy, which favours exporters while reducing the real wages of the working people, is not distribution neutral. The debate between monetarists and neoclassical orthodoxy on the one hand, and Structuralism and the search for heterodox macro-economic policies on the other, continues to dominate Latin American economics.

It is important to note that the vigorous debates concerning the nature of Latin American dependence and underdevelopment were conducted by Latin American social scientists — some "structuralist," some Marxist — who shared a common intellectual formation, as well as common experiences. Much of these debates were lost in translation to English, where the popularization of dependency theory emphasized exploitation by unequal trade to the neglect of the originality of its insights of internal class structures specific to peripheral capitalist economies. Prebisch and his CEPAL associates had laid the foundations of a common discourse, which enabled the Latin American structuralist view to survive the inhospitable climate of the hardline monetarist revival of the 1970s and the Structural Adjustment Programs of the 1980s.

THE ATTACK ON DEVELOPMENT ECONOMICS

In our review of the classics of development economics we have emphasized those contributions that have stood the test of time and the sea change in the "rules of the game" of the international economy, which first manifested itself in the late 1960s. We assign particular significance to the work of those pioneers of modern development economics who stayed the course for forty years and more, whose point of departure and abiding concerns were the welfare of the masses of the people of the countries which they termed "peripheral" (Prebisch), and "tropical" (Lewis). Because Caribbean countries are both peripheral and tropical, in the sense defined by Prebisch and Lewis, Caribbean social scientists would make a great mistake in dismissing the body of development economics associated with the pioneers as dépassé — as is now fashionable. This does not mean that we do not need to go beyond the excessively limiting concepts of economics, which form the building blocks of much of their work. Indeed, in their parting words to us both Prebisch and Lewis pointed to the need to advance on broader fields and include in our studies the structure of society.

From the mid-1960s to the mid-1970s, development economics became fashionable and institutionalized, giving rise to a proliferation of journals, academic teaching programs and textbooks. Work became increasingly quantitative and, most importantly, became the handmaiden of national and international development agencies. Of all of these, the World Bank assumed the status of *primus inter pares*, which it enjoys to this day. On another occasion we shall examine and evaluate progress made toward the understanding of development and underdevelopment during this period. Here we simply list some of the themes which occupied the attention of development economists: growth and structural transformation; growth and income distribution; growth and employment/unemployment; policies of redistribution with growth and basic human needs; and the meaning of GNP and alternate measures of development.

In the context of the dissolution of the Bretton Woods system and consequent instability of prices and exchange rates, it appeared that developing countries might be able to exercise commodity power, which created reformist illusions of a new international economic order and radical illusions of delinking from the grip of dominant external economic and financial control. Most importantly, the macro-economic and monetary policies of the United States and other industrial countries created a vast pool of private banking capital in search of profitable investment, which enabled semi-industrialized developing countries and oil exporters to access private bank finance on easy terms and without strings. This is the origin of the debt problem, which hit with hurricane force in the summer of 1982 when Mexico announced its incapacity to meet debt payments. From that time onward, the international agencies, whose task it is to administer the economic affairs of the developing world on behalf of the industrialized creditor countries, have moved "adjustment" to the top of the agenda and put "development" on the back burner.

In retrospect it is not difficult to identify the event whose cumulative effects blew up the storm that triggered the debt crisis. It was the Volker Shock, of 1979 — the reversal of U.S. monetary policy, which caused interest rates to leap into double digit figures and precipitated the recession of 1981–82.

This hit oil importers and oil exporters alike. The developing countries which escaped this sea change in the international economic environment were those either relatively sheltered from international entanglement in trade and payments, such as China and India, or countries which had built strong manufacturing export capacity in the course of the 1970s, such as the East Asian Tigers. In another essay I have drawn attention to the fact that only one of a World Bank list of some forty "seriously indebted countries" is in Asia — the Philippines. I have also argued that the era of trade as engine of growth for primary exporting peripheries is finished and that the era of significant development aid is likewise finished. This was so even before the end of the Cold War and the evident attraction of the vast natural and human resources of the Soviet Union and East Europe to private and governmental investors.

As stated at the beginning of this essay, trends in economic theory are closely related with the policy positions of governments. Nowhere is this more evident than in the neoclassical attack on development economics of the early 1980s. The groundwork was laid earlier, beginning with Little, Scott and Scitovski (1970), who started the attack on import substituting industrialization and the revival of neoclassical trade theory in the service of policies of "outward-orientation." Ballassa and Krueger are names of economists closely associated with these positions. The axe directed against the body of classical development economics however was first wielded by Deepak Lal, a relatively obscure economist then enjoying a senior position in the World Bank: "The demise of development economics is likely to be conducive to the health of both the economics and the economies of developing countries" (Lal 1983: 109). Further respectability was lent to the attack by Little (1982) and by the Swedish economist Assar Lindbeck, chair of the Nobel Prize Committee for Economics, who was engaged as a consultant to prepare a new research agenda for the World Bank in 1984 (World Bank 1984). The pioneers of development economics are listed and paraded before the court of "mainstream economics" and charged with "Structuralism." Little identifies Rosenstein-Rodan, Ragnar Nurkse, Arthur Lewis, Raul Prebisch, Hans Singer and Gunnar Myrdal as formulators of the initial set of structuralist hypotheses, which sees the world as inhibited by bottlenecks and constraints, requiring transformation of production structures by administrative means.

The structuralist view, according to Little, shares with socialism a distrust of the market. Lindbeck lists the same set of offenders, adding also Alexander Gershenkron's "great spurts," Hirschman's "backward and forward linkages" and Chenery's "two gap" theory of savings and balance-of payments constraints. The structuralists are faulted because they suffer from a strong distrust of the price mechanism; experience has shown, Lindbeck argues, that relative price signals are highly effective in allocating resources in developing countries, and "standard economic theory as developed in the West over some two centuries is highly relevant to developing countries, as well" (World Bank

1984). Lindbeck placed "policy-induced distortions and incentives" high on the list of the research agenda of the World Bank. According to Little (1982), "neoclassical economics may be defined as a vision of the world that is the opposite of the structuralist vision." As a "vision of the world" neoclassical economics has become more than a paradigm; it has become an ideology premised on the superiority of the market economy.

Underlying the attack on development economics is the attack on Keynesian theory, with its social democratic redistributional implications. The 1970s spawned an anti-Keynesian counter-revolution in economic theory that now forms a crucial component of economic theory courses in Western universities. The theory of rational expectations has defined Keynesian un-employment out of existence: leading to the simple but strong policy conclusion that attempts to reduce unemployment below its "natural rate" would only aggravate the situation, thus leaving the self-regulating market system to take its "natural" course regardless of social and human costs. The classical development economics of the pioneers has close affinity with the Keynesian rejection of economic orthodoxy. Both were born from the experience of the crises of the inter-war years. Thus, Hirschman (1981: 7): "The claim of development economics to stand as a separate body of economic analysis and policy-derived intellectual legitimacy and nurture from the prior success and parallel features of the Keynesian revolution." Thus Singer (1985: 277): "In some sense Keynes was the real creator of development economics, insofar as he broke with monoeconomics." The defence of development economics has become a rearguard action to preserve the insights of its pioneers from elimination from the curricula of economics departments that are aping, in sheepish fashion, the anti-institutionalist trends of academic mainstream economics. We must enhance the education of our students by introducing them to the history of economic thought in the context of the history of the world, as it has affected our present and will shape our futures.

THE FUTURE OF DEVELOPMENT STUDIES

The study of economic development will however have to break out to reach beyond the limits of its economistic approach. Today, Adam Smith is lionized as the prophet of the miracles of unconstrained market capitalism, while Karl Marx has been demonized and held morally responsible for the atrocities of Stalinism and the failure of the Russian Revolution of 1917 to realize the socialist dream of an economic order based on cooperation, solidarity and equality. It is my view that economic liberalism and Marxism share Karl Polanyi's "economistic fallacy," the belief that the development of society is ultimately governed by economic forces. Smith believed there was a natural order of things, an invisible hand, which could harmonize the natural propensity of human beings to seek their individual economic self-interest, resulting in economic growth and progress. Marx, whose theories were more complex and less mechanistic, presented the capitalist economy as governed by laws whose inherent contradictions would eventually result in its breakdown, giving rise to a higher social order.

Liberalism and Marxism both suffer from excessive abstraction of institutional, historical and cultural realities. Both of these doctrines lay claim to a universalism that reflects the dominance and self-confidence of nineteenth-century Western industrial civilization. It is a conceit of modernity that there exists a universal science of society on the basis of which economic development and social change can be programmed. It is a positive deceit that macro-economic gimmickry, such as underlies the Structural Adjustment Programs, can substitute for societal mobilization of collective energy, which is the essence of development.

In the case of the liberal tradition, which forms the basis of modern neoclassical economics, the point of departure is the proposition that the pursuit of individual self-interest in the form of economic gain is a natural human inclination and that "an invisible hand" harmoniously coordinates the self-interested behaviour of individuals, so long as there is competition in markets for goods, labour, land and money. The liberal view abstracts from the fact that the elevation of material self-interest over other human motives is the result of the institutionalization of "rules of the game" designed to force people into instrumental "economic" behaviour. The producer is severed from the means of subsistence; needs are defined to be unlimited; scarcity is instituted where it did not previously exist; tradition and custom are deemed to be obstacles to a rationally organized economy; the economy is "disembedded" from society. Work is divorced from creativity and is redefined as a "disutility," a disagreeable necessity motivated exclusively by material incentives. Consumerism is elevated to the status of the supreme objective governing rational human behaviour. Motivations ranging from love to religion, from civic pride to neighbourliness, are redefined as "altruistic" — subordinate to, if not directly in conflict with, rational "economic" behaviour.

As an ideology, economic liberalism enjoyed a remarkable renaissance in the 1980s, particularly in Third World countries forced by external indebtedness to institute neoliberal policies in order to maintain access to external finance, and in Central and Eastern Europe, where the rejection of "really existing socialism" raised expectations that market-oriented policies would rescue their economies from stagnation and corruption. Closer examination however reveals that belief in economic liberalism is by no means universal. Only in the United States do its principal tenets form an integral component of a national ideology that holds that capitalism is synonymous with democracy, the market with efficiency, and free trade with development. Only the Americans believe that their national ideology can and should serve the world as a model. Only the Americans believe that their particular value system, born of their particular historical experience as a vast and virtually empty continent populated by Europeans seeking to escape poverty and oppression, is universal and free of cultural specificity. The United States is the only industrialized country where philosophic individualism is so deeply entrenched that socialist movements have never taken root. It is ironic that the legitimating power of this belief system has supported a remarkable level of uniformity of opinion and lifestyle, reflected in a mass media that strikes the foreign observer as being highly controlled. The United States however, remains a very powerful force in the world, particularly with respect to small and weak Third World states, which are critically dependent on the good will of Washington. This remains a fact in spite of the dismal failures of neoliberal policy measures, particularly in Africa.

The collapse of the centrally planned models of economic organization in Eastern Europe and the Soviet Union have resulted in the end of the Cold War, which provided the overarching framework of the international system for half a century, leaving the world with only one military superpower. There is a widely shared fear that the awesome arsenal of high technology armaments will be deployed to reimpose Western imperialist control over strategic regions of the Third World. "Police actions" in the service of a "new world order" suggest that the United States will continue to pump up its deficit-ridden economy with military expenditures. The fate of the Soviet Union remains suspended in uncertainty. National and ethnic forces are challenging the authority of the central government, which has been unable to reorganize the over-planned economy to produce and distribute basic consumer goods to the population. The possibility of civil war in the Soviet Union is a frightening prospect given the large arsenal of nuclear weapons in the control of the army. The relative stability provided by the military superpower standoff since 1945 has terminated.

While Marx explained capitalism in terms of social and class relationships supported by law and ideology, and criticized the "commodity fetishism" of classical political economy for its mechanistic presentation of disembodied commodities and "factors of production" moving in and out of markets in response to supply and demand, the predominant Marxist tradition itself suffers from an excessively mechanistic and ahistorical approach. In seeking to identify the essential "laws of motion" of the capitalist economy, institutional arrangements are consigned to the "superstructure" and are treated as derivative of basic economic forces and relationships. Capitalism thus appears as unchanging in its essential aspects. This is also the flaw in so-called world systems theory. Carried to its logical extreme, there would be little difference between the capitalism of nineteenth-century England and that of contemporary America, Sweden, Austria, Japan, Brazil or Jamaica. The treatment of the superstructure as derivative of the economic base in mainstream Marxism is a serious flaw. It underestimates the power of the people to force the state to respond to societal stress by the introduction of social democratic reforms within a capitalist mixed economy, and grossly underrates the importance of political democracy as a basic need and human right. It has served to legitimate the bureaucratic socialist state and to reject the possibility that it can become a direct instrument of exploitation and oppression. The teleological element in Marxism, derived from the assumption of progress in human affairs, sustained the belief that the breakdown of capitalism would inevitably usher in a better and higher social order. As an ideology, Marxism has served as a powerful critique of the evils of capitalism. As a guide to an alternative and higher form of social organization, Marxism has failed. The socialist dream remains unrealized. Marxism as "scientific socialism" has overwritten the moral critique of capitalism that underlies the work of Karl Marx with an economic determinism that resembles capitalist modernization theory. Socialism as a vision of a human social order based on fraternity, solidarity and the social values of community, has an inescapable moral element derived from its European Hebraic-Christian tradition that is not inconsistent with all religious thought and tradition. Socialism as an alternative to oppression and injustice based on profit and greed never conceived of the replacement of capitalist exploitation by the rule of an all-powerful state. The association of socialism with the authoritarian state has been a contributing factor to the popular appeal of economic liberalism.

CONCLUSION

As the twentieth century draws to a close there is a widespread sense of foreboding concerning our capacity to control the modernizing forces that have been unleashed since industrial capitalism was born in England some two hundred years ago. The world has witnessed historically unprecedented economic growth — accompanied by inequality on a scale never before experienced by humankind. Industrial production has increased seventy-fivefold, most of it since the end of the Second World War. Fear for the degradation and destruction of the natural environment is universally recognized as a justified concern. "Sustainable development" has become a fashionable buzzword. Any meaningful notion of sustainable development, however, must begin with the recognition that the diversity of cultures which nourish human creativity is as precious an inheritance as the diversity of plant and animal life. It is the repository of collective wisdom from which springs the capacity of individuals and societies to survive adversity and renew commitment to future generations.

The "market magic" paradigm is seductive because the logical coherence of neoclassical economics lends intellectual respectability to the pursuit of self-interest by the economically powerful. It is appealing because it appears to offer a personal and individual solution to economic pressure. This is a tragic illusion. In reality it serves as an instrument whereby the rich and powerful seek to impose on whole societies a set of values and "rules of the game" which reinforce inequality and injustice and dismantle the capacity for social solidarity. Governments are disempowered and become the unwilling debt collectors for international capital, while millions are condemned to misery without end. We believe that the "market magic" paradigm will, in time, yield pride of place to a vision of the world which takes account of our fundamental need to be rooted in society, to be sustained and supported by relations of solidarity, and to live in dignity and harmony with the physical environment. This does not mean that markets are not important and necessary. It does, however, mean that our lives cannot be ruled primarily by the pressures of market forces. The extension of the division of labour to the international level whereby whole societies are under pressure to produce what they do not consume, and consume what they do not produce, has replaced traditional motivations of economic activity by consumerism. As already stated, any meaningful notion of sustainable development must begin with the understanding that it is our cultural environment which nourishes our creativity and energy.

Development cannot be imposed from without. It is a creative process and its central nervous system, the matrix that nourishes it, is located in the cultural sphere. Development is ultimately not a matter of physical capital, or foreign exchange, but of the capacity of a society to tap the root of popular creativity, to free up and empower people to exercise their intelligence and collective wisdom. It is the responsibility of those who aspire to exercise leadership, whether in government or working in the private sector, or in educational, cultural, trade union, religious or other nongovernmental institutions or associations, to protect the cultural, social and political institutions of society from the disintegrating forces of external market criteria. Societies and nation states that do not have the social cohesion to chart a coherent strategy of survival in the difficult years to come will not survive. They will disintegrate. This is true for rich and poor countries alike.

NOTES

This chapter is based on an unpublished paper originally prepared in 1991 for a presentation to the Consortium Graduate School of the University of the West Indies, Jamaica.

1. On terminology, there has been a succession of appellations for the countries of Asia, Africa and Latin America which emerged from overt or quasi-colonialism after the Second World War, starting with the "new countries," the "backward," "underdeveloped" and more recently the "developing" countries. None of this terminology is satisfactory. I prefer "Third World" because it derived as a political category within the United Nations system during the Cold War. For convenience, I use these terms interchangeably, as is current practice.

13. RECLAIMING POLICY SPACE FOR EQUITABLE ECONOMIC DEVELOPMENT

Economics is perhaps the most important and certainly the most influential of the social sciences. The early political economists and their predecessors addressed the great issues of economic growth and development: capital accumulation and the distribution of the product between major economic classes; population growth and food supply; free trade and national development; and even the long-term viability of capitalism itself. Their theories informed the bourgeois state as well as social movements opposed to exploitation and oppression. The marginalist revolution in economics of the 1870s was born in the more prosperous and stable environment of the mid-nineteenth century. It gave birth to neoclassical economics, which addressed the efficient allocation of a given set of resources and the marginal adjustment of prices and output to restore market equilibrium. The ideological implication was that distribution was fair because each factor of production was rewarded according to its contribution to the product. Issues of growth and stagnation, aggregate employment and unemployment, and business cycles disappeared from the mainstream economic discourse. This body of doctrine dominated until the advent of the Great Depression, the Second World War and the wave of decolonization of Asia and Africa that followed.

Keynes and his associates and students in Cambridge challenged prevailing doctrines, most famously by the publication of *The General Theory of Employment, Interest and Money* (1936), which proved that an economy could reach equilibrium with underutilized capacity of labour and capital. During the war Keynes was instrumental in directing the British war economy. His small volume *How to Pay for the War* (1940) illustrated the analytical power of the macro-economic categories of modern national income accounting: production and consumption, savings and investment. It informed fiscal, monetary and administrative policies to successfully repress inflation in conditions of supply shortages. Although Keynes did not concern himself with post-war planning for underdeveloped regions, his influence was pervasive. Many of the best and brightest Indian economists studied at Cambridge, and the intellectual links between Cambridge and Indian economic planners and policy-makers remained important. At this time also, students and future political leaders from Asia, Africa and the West Indies turned their thoughts to the economic transformation that would have to follow political decolonization.

One of Keynes's closest intellectual collaborators was Joan Robinson, who was quick to recognise that it was not unemployment of labour de-clared redundant but rather the vast pool of wasted human resources in the form of underemployment in low productivity activities which charac-terized the emerging new nations. A similar observation was made by the Norwegian trade economist working for the League of Nations, Ragnar Nurkse, who suggested that surplus labour be mobilized for large, labour-intensive public works, as was done in China after the revolution. Another of Keynes's students was Hans Singer, whose initial interest in unemploy-ment in chronically depressed areas of Britain turned to underemployment and underdevelopment. He is perhaps best known for the Prebisch-Singer thesis on terms of trade.

A number of emigré economists in Britain, influenced by their personal experience of late industrialization in Central and Eastern Europe, conceived plans for the post-war transformation of underdeveloped regions. The con-tributions of Michael Kalecki, Kurt Mandelbaum, E.F. Schumacher and Joseph Steindl of Oxford University and Paul Rosenstein-Rodan of the Royal Institute of International Affairs laid the basis of development economics as a formal sub-discipline. These Central European economists were as familiar with Marx as with Keynes, and the success of Soviet five year plans played a significant role in approaches to development planning. It is well known that Kalecki's model of an economy with underutilized resources of labour and capital was similar to Keynes's, but presented in Marxist rather than the more familiar Anglo-Saxon analytical categories. His contribution to planning for economic development deserves to be more widely acknowledged.

An imaginative plan for a radically new international financial order was designed by Keynes and, notwithstanding opposition including from the City, his proposal for an International Clearing Union was published as an official government document in 1942, and officials from Canada and other dominions were invited to London for discussion. The intention was to permit policy space for nations to secure full employment without engaging in competitive devaluations or subjecting their economies to the punishing deflationary measures required by the Gold Standard and imposed on weak succession states by the League of Nations.

A special purpose money (Bancor) exclusively for clearing international payments between central banks, and backed by commodity stocks, would have precluded private trade in national currencies. Such an international financial architecture would have enabled countries with widely different economic and financial institutions to engage in international exchange. The resources proposed in the Keynes plan were six times larger than those allocated to the International Monetary Fund, established in 1944 — a modified version of the White plan, proposed by the United States. Keynes considered he had failed and offered his resignation, which was not accepted.

In 1945, Karl Polanyi, best known for *The Great Transformation* (1944), wrote that only the United States believed in universal capitalism — now known as globalization. In "Universal Capitalism versus Regional Planning," he envisaged a world of regional blocs, including communist Russia, social democratic Western Europe and the United States, to be followed by other emerging regions of the world.

The United Nations, founded in San Francisco in 1945, brought together economists concerned with the eradication of underdevelopment and poverty in Africa, Asia and Latin America. It was charged with responsibility for financial and technical assistance to the underdeveloped regions. Responsibility for financial development assistance, however, was soon transferred to the World Bank, where the principal donor countries controlled policy — and the United States had an effective veto.

Outstanding among the regional commissions of the U.N. was the Santiago-based Economic Commission for Latin America, under the direction of Raul Prebisch. *The Economic Development of Latin America and Its Principal Problems*, accompanied by background studies of the experience of Latin American export economies in the 1930s and 1940s, was drafted by Prebisch with the assistance of a team of brilliant young Latin American economists and published by the United Nations in 1949. It made the case for reducing export dependence by domestic industrialization and came to be known as the Prebisch Manifesto.

In the 1940s and 1950s, great minds applied themselves to the great problems of economic development, and students chose to study economics to make the world a better place. Econometrics as a scientific tool of economic planning was pioneered by Jan Tinbergen and Ragnar Frisch, who advised the government of Egypt in the construction of an innovative multisectoral development plan. Development economists such as Celso Furtado, Arthur Lewis, Albert Hirschman and Gunnar Myrdal approached the problem of underdevelopment from a historical, structuralist and institutional perspective, while Alexander Gerschenkron examined the lessons of the late industrializers of the nineteenth century as a guide to industrialization policies for the developing countries. My generation of students of economics was interested in understanding the functioning of economies with a view to achieving full employment and social security from cradle to grave, not personal gain or how to invest or play the stock market. Favoured career options were university or public service; only the weakest students opted for the private sector.

By the mid-1950s development economics had gained recognition as a distinct sub-discipline of economics. Books were published and academic journals and institutes were established in American and British universities. A representative collection of papers by development economists from many countries, *The Economics of Underdevelopment*, edited by Agarwhala and Singh, was published in 1958. Three major themes dominated the discourse: *market and state*, *trade and development* and *growth and equity*. Underlying these themes is the deeper issue of the relationship of the economy to society, which requires an approach beyond the scope of economic analysis. Karl Polanyi's warning of the consequences of disembedding the economy from its social matrix, inherent in a capitalist market economy, points to the critical role of social policy in the design of equitable economic development.

The 1950s and 1960s witnessed the decolonization of Asia, Africa and the West Indies and the determination of post-colonial countries to engage in national projects of economic transformation. In the context of the superpower rivalry of the Cold War, the Non-Aligned Movement of Asian and African countries was convened in Bandung by Indonesia's President Sukarno in 1954. The establishment of the United Nations Conference on Trade and Development (UNCTAD) under the directorship of Prebisch in 1964 served as a forum for Third World countries to fashion a common program for a new international economic order (NIEO). The early post-war decades were, on the whole, favourable to national economic development, and high average growth rates of the developing world, including Africa, surpassed those of the industrial countries.

It was generally accepted that the state must play a central role in economic transformation because the private sector was either dominated by landed and commercial oligarchies with vested interests in the status quo or was simply too weak and disorganized. The degree of state involvement in the economy varied across countries, but it was common practice that the provision of basic public infrastructure and its financing was universally undertaken by the state, accompanied by some form of long-term economic planning. In the first three post-war decades, countries were able to privilege domestic agriculture and industry by discretionary access to credit and foreign exchange, subsidies and a variety of protective commercial policies. The principal of sovereignty regarding natural resources and, more generally, the sovereign right of nations to formulate fiscal, monetary, commercial and all other aspects of government policy was not questioned — although in practice it was often violated.

Issues of trade and development were contentious from the start. Policies of import substituting industrialization (ISI) — successful to varying degrees — met the unwavering opposition of international trade theorists with reference to the theory of comparative advantage, and Prebisch was considered a dangerous radical. Indeed, the asymmetry of gains from international trade formed the bond which united countries of different ideologies in the formulation of the UNCTAD agendas. However, a decade of international conferences aimed at reform of the international economic order failed to produce tangible results. Arthur Lewis declined to participate in these negotiations. In his view, the South collectively had all the resources required for economic development and when this potential was realized a more equitable international order would ensue.

In the 1970s, Taiwan and South Korea followed the example of Japan in strategies of late industrialization. The city-states of Hong Kong and Singapore were also highly successful, and Southeast Asian countries embarked on programs of industrialization for domestic and export markets according to their different geographical and historical endowments. China made the turn to its unique model of communist market capitalism in 1978. In each of these cases of "late industrialization," governments instituted incentives specific to the circumstances and development objectives of their respective countries.

With the notable exception of Nehru's India, development economists and development planners were not directly concerned with issues of equity or poverty. It was thought that capital accumulation would create employment opportunities on a scale sufficient to absorb underemployed surplus labour. Perhaps the most profound disappointment was that economic growth failed to do so, giving rise to the phenomenon of "growth without development," reformist and radical critiques of developmentalism and the search for revolutionary solutions. The use of per capita gross national product as an implicit measure of the welfare of nations was challenged by alternative measures of the "quality of life." As it became evident that capital-intensive technology could produce growth without employment, the significance of the informal sector — whether as problem or solution — came into focus. It was found that import substitution industrialization (ISI) had effectively increased external dependence by requirements of imported inputs and capital goods to sustain industrialization. The foreign exchange constraint became the principal bottleneck to growth. The phenomena of marginalization and social exclusion inherent in developmentalist approaches to economic growth pointed to the economistic bias of prevailing doctrines of development economics. The eminent Swedish economist Gunnar Myrdal was among the first to identify social expenditures on health and education as investments in the expansion of the human capacity of the working population. Under pressure from critics of growth without development, the World Bank identified basic human needs as priority areas of expenditure, although the bulk of development assistance continued to finance large-scale industrial infrastructure.

In the fractured decade of the 1970s, the demise of the Bretton Woods financial order released constraints on international liquidity as capital was freed from national control. The flood of liquidity was a permissive condition of commodity booms, benefiting petroleum, bauxite, sugar and other commodity exporting countries, and sovereign lending by commercial banks to middle-income developing countries. In the industrial heartlands of capitalism, inflationary pressures eroded the value of financial assets and the profitability of capital in the real economy. Slow growth and economic instability in the industrial world and political revolutions, from Afghanistan to Nicaragua, from Angola and Mozambique to Grenada and ultimately in Iran, were the catalyst for a profound regime change signalled by the accession of Thatcher and Reagan to office. The Volker Shock, which raised interest rates into the teens, precipitated the Latin American debt crisis of the 1980s.

An ideological counter-revolution in economics replaced Keynes with policies of monetarism, deregulation, liberalization and privatization. Capital was enabled to reverse the gains made by labour in the industrial world and national developmental gains in Latin America and Africa. The policy leverage exerted by international financial institutions over Latin American countries indebted to commercial banks and African countries indebted to the multilateral agencies progressively constrained national policy space. As Ha-Joon Chang pointed out, the policies which served late industrializers of the nineteenth century and more recently the East Asian countries are now precluded by commitments made in bilateral or multilateral agreements.

Keynes was banished and development economics was demonized as structuralist heresy bordering on socialism. The World Bank declared that that there was one and only one economics, and that economic science could explain the functioning of the economy anytime, anyplace, anywhere, regardless of institutions. Developing countries as diverse as anything you can find from Asia, Africa and Latin America were no different from the leading industrial countries, only poorer. There was a changing of the guard at the World Bank; reformist economists, including Hollis Chennery, Paul Streeten and Mahbub Ul Haq, were replaced by Anne Krueger, Deepak Lal and a team of consultant trade theorists, including Jagdish Baghwati, Bala Belassa and Swedish economist Lindbeck, who wrote a research memorandum placing the entire blame for the debt crisis on erroneous domestic policies pursued by Latin American governments.

From 1980, priorities regarding the three major themes of development economics have been reversed. The market has been elevated to the principal economic mechanism and the state has been downsized, stripped of fiscal resources and bound by a multitude of commitments made in bilateral or multilateral negotiations with creditors, including national treatment for foreign investors. The provision of basic infrastructure, both physical and social, has been privatized and/or subjected to criteria of cost recovery. Trade has been enthroned as the engine of growth, and economies restructured to privilege exports over production for the domestic market. Competitiveness rather than national welfare has become the objective of economic policy. In many countries, liberalization of imports has destroyed agricultural and industrial capacity. In Jamaica, for example, 30 percent of jobs in agriculture, fishing and forestry and 48 percent of jobs in manufacturing disappeared in the decade of the 1990s (Levitt 2005: xxi).

The neoliberal experience has brought financial crises of increasing severity and frequency. The human costs have been enormous. Where growth has occurred, it has been accompanied by polarization of income and the social exclusion of poor people from economic circuits of production and consumption. The prevailing doctrine is that trade liberalization and Foreign Direct Investment engender economic growth, inequality is perhaps inevitable, and poverty should be addressed directly by targeted programs to ensure social stability — a necessary condition for a favourable investment climate.

It is now widely recognized that these policies have failed. I am sometimes asked how development experts in the multilateral agencies could possibly believe that one set of policies — the so-called Washington Consensus — could fit the great diversity of countries. The answer is simple: the policies serve the interests of creditors and provide a favourable environment for foreign investors. These requirements are indeed rather uniform. The problem is that the assumption that such an environment engenders growth and development does not accord with experience.

A paper by Harvard economist Dani Rodrik states that most economists would now agree that: the reforms of the 1980s and 1990s have produced disappointing results; the most successful countries in terms of growth have followed heterodox policies; most successful countries have adhered to some generally recognized principles; policies appropriate to a particular situation cannot be inferred from these principles; and policy diversity is desirable (2004: 1).

In an exhaustive study of the relationship between episodes of growth and significant economic reforms, Rodrik found that the majority of growth take-offs are not produced by significant economic reforms — and the vast majority of significant economic reforms do not produce growth take-offs (3). Rodrik proposes a diagnostic approach to identify bottlenecks to economic growth specific to a country and to develop policies directed at these, rather than an attempt to implement a comprehensive set of reforms which may, moreover, fail to yield results. This is reminiscent of the structuralist approach of earlier Latin American economists.

If indeed countries that have been successful have followed heterodox policies, and those that have followed the prescriptions of the World Bank and the IMF have generally failed, we may conclude that policy formulation and implementation should be returned to national authorities, who are politically accountable to their populations for success or failure — regardless of the nature of political institutions. The multilateral agencies and the economists they employ are not accountable to the populations that have suffered the consequences of their failed policies. The World Bank is directly accountable only to the creditors who provide it with operational finance.

The experience of the past twenty years has produced an unprecedented degree of inequality and social exclusion, both between nations and most significantly within nations, whether accompanied by high growth, low growth or no growth. While economic globalization gives the impression of a world more uniform and homogeneous than it was fifty years ago, the realities of daily life of the majority of people are characterized by diversity and difference. Contrary to the general belief both of mainstream economists and Marxists that the economy forms the base of society, I suggest that, ultimately, it is the cultural, social and institutional relations of a society that sustain a strong economy. An equitable economic order must rest on an equitable political and social order. This requires a longer view and an analysis of the political and social structures that underlie the national and international economies. Until the cleavages arising from the displacement of indigenous peoples of the Americas and plantation slavery are addressed, a modern market economy will be neither stable nor equitable; the chronic instability of Latin American economies is ultimately a product of the social and political exclusion of majority populations. In Africa, the promising beginnings of the 1950s and 1960s have been rolled back by neocolonial Structural Adjustment Programs, crude appropriation of natural resources and the human tragedy of the devastating HIV/AIDS epidemic, particularly scandalous in view of the unavailability of affordable treatment.

The historical legacies of the incorporation of peripheral regions into the world economy are profound. Notwithstanding the reality and desirability of diversity of political, social and economic structures, a revaluation of the three themes of development economics points to a reversal of priorities prevailing in the past twenty-five years. The emphasis on economic growth must be replaced with an emphasis on the quality of life of the people.

Market and State

The state must take responsibility for the provision of basic infrastructure, starting with universal access to clean water and other essential services that most directly affect the lives of people. The state must reclaim its sovereign right over natural resources and ensure that all citizens benefit from the national heritage. All modern economies are mixed economies, and the institutional forms of private, public and community involvement in the economy offer fruitful areas of institutional experimentation.

In the neoliberal era, governments have been forced to abrogate monetary, fiscal and administrative policy instruments, constraining their capacity to respond to the demands of their constituents for elementary social justice. Politically, the devolution of power and resources to the private sector and non-governmental organizations reduces the public space within which democracy can operate.

Trade and Development

Trade is beneficial, but the extreme export orientation of many countries has destroyed domestic capacity and measures should be taken to restore priority to agriculture and industry serving the domestic market. Where entrepreneurs and businesses produce only for export markets, labour is simply a cost to be reduced, but where production is for the domestic market, their employees are also customers, so there is a collective interest in maintaining the purchasing power of the population.

Domestic production of food for domestic consumption must be protected from destructive competition by imports, not only for important reasons of individual and national food security but because agriculture, forestry and fishing are industries which by their nature bring people into contact with the natural environment.

Foreign investment is desirable but should be required to comply with national regulations concerning employment of nationals, purchase of local materials and adherence to environmental standards. On no account should foreign investors and non-nationals receive treatment more favourable than nationals.

Control over entry and exit of capital flows is a basic instrument of macro-economic management, and countries should reclaim the sovereign right to exercise it.

Growth and Equity

The biggest challenge we face is to address the enormous inequities that have characterized the experience of the neoliberal model. It is an every-day observance in many countries, including those that have experienced substantial economic growth, that the quality of life has deteriorated, that the bonds that link us in society have loosened and that insecurity — both physical and economic — has increased. This suggests prioritizing measures that directly impact the quality of life, not only of the poor but of the whole society. Investment in the provision of universal primary health care and primary education, and the provision of other essential public services of water, sanitation and transportation address not only the needs of the poorer sections of the population but, when universally used, can help to restore social cohesion.

In many countries, including the developed economies of the North, intensified competition has led to perpetual downsizing of employment, and productivity gains have increasingly accrued to capital and persons employed in professional, commercial and business services. Where people cannot se-cure gainful employment, they join the ever increasing ranks of the informal sector. While some can earn a reasonable living, many are consigned to work which cannot secure a basic livelihood. The vast range of productivities and remuneration typical of a developing country calls for institutions to secure a more equitable distribution of national output. Proposals for basic income merit consideration as means of instituting entitlements.

As Myrdal pointed out a long time ago, a population that is lacking good health and basic education is limited in its ability to contribute to the economy. Years of deteriorating social infrastructure call for priority expenditures in these areas that directly impact both on the well-being and the productivity of the population. Ultimately, people are the most valuable economic resource of any country.

In the context of the pressures of globalization, shared common historical experience of distinct, large regions suggests that equitable economic development should be conceived on a regional scale. We are reminded of the project of "extended nationalism" of regional blocs — based on geographic, historical and cultural commonalities — proposed by Dudley Seers in the early 1980s as a response to the evident failure of international negotiations for a more equitable economic order:

> If and when nationalism is extended in this way, and a world of regional blocs replaces the neo-colonial system, the governments of the superpowers will feel less compulsion to meddle (whether by financial aid, diplomatic pressure or military force) in the affairs of other countries, and also be less able to do so: world peace will be more secure. (1983: 165)

Dudley Seers was an eminent development practitioner and consultant to U.N. Economic Commissions in Latin America and Africa and also British development agencies in Africa, Asia and the West Indies. He was the founder and first director of the Institute of Development Studies at the University of Sussex (1963). A lifetime of experience led him to reject external assistance by international development experts, and he spent later years of work in the expansion of the European Community to include the peripheral nations of Mediterranean Europe.

Seers was not the only development economist to become disillusioned with international development assistance. In the early 1980s, Gunnar Myrdal expressed the view that development assistance should not be directed toward building up the modern industrial sector, which could only employ "a minimal part of the total growing workforce" while the rest became "economic refugees" from the agricultural sector (1984: 160). Because money is fungible, external assistance may serve to support corrupt and unpopular political regimes. Myrdal believed that assistance should be more effectively controlled by donors and directed exclusively at social sectors:

> The only "development aid" I would find room for under present circumstances would be directed to the simplest and least costly mea-

> sures to increase food production, to provide sanitation facilities and to increase their utilisation, generally to supply pure water, and also as far as possible to improve health care, particularly for poor families, and to give their children somewhat more of better schooling. This together with securing the availability of contraceptives could well claim the whole part of any so-called development aid. (161)

The approach we have taken departs from current practice, where policies of economic and social development for many countries are designed by the international development industry. Responsibility for the welfare of the people must return to national political authorities, in the context of regional cooperation. This however, does not dispose of the responsibility of the rich countries of the North to share in the financial burden of human development. They should take prime responsibility for the provision of global public goods, by fiscal contributions and effective taxation of the operations of transnational corporations. What is suggested here is that the international community take collective responsibility for those truly global problems, which clearly require global action and far exceed the financial capacities of individual countries. The appropriate agencies are those of the United Nations — the only international institution where all countries have a voice.

These requirements far exceed current levels of development assistance. Specifically, I suggest the following areas: permanent provision for relief of victims of natural disasters, which are likely to occur with increasing frequency due to environmental degradation; action on issues of public health, which respect no borders: eradication and prevention of communicable diseases including HIV/AIDS and reducing toxicity from industrial and agricultural pollution; and restoration and preservation of the biosphere and long term management of natural resources.

The coordination of functional cooperation in these areas would be facilitated by the establishment of regional authorities. This approach to international development assistance addresses the critiques of Seers and Myrdal. It restores a measure of policy space to national and regional political authorities — relinquished in unequal negotiations over the past twenty-five years — and places the responsibility for financing urgent human needs that can only be addressed on a global scale on the countries that have the resources to do so.

NOTE

This chapter incorporates information and ideas presented at the North-South Institute (January 19, 2006) and the VIII International Meeting of Economists in Havana (February 6–10, 2006).

14. INTELLECTUAL INDEPENDENCE AND TRANSFORMATIVE CHANGE IN THE SOUTH

In 1986 the United Nations adopted a declaration on the "right to development" as an inalienable human right, embracing all civil, economic, social, cultural and other human rights enumerated in the Universal Declaration of Human Rights. Since this Declaration was adopted globalization has devalued sovereign equality and stripped states of monetary, fiscal and administrative policy instruments essential to the formulation and implementation of proactive strategies of economic and social development.

The authority of the United Nations has declined. Private global capital flows have displaced official development assistance as a major source of external finance. Market criteria of profitability (cost-recovery) have prevailed over egalitarian social criteria in the provision of public goods directly affecting the well-being of people. International inequalities have escalated. Domestic disparities have widened. Finance has been privileged over productive activity, and countries open to capital flows have borne the full economic, social and human costs of adjustment to ever more frequent and damaging financial and economic crises.

Since the end of the Cold War, the only remaining superpower has acted as self-appointed global police force. Military interventions targeted at physical and social infrastructure have punished civilian populations for the alleged misdeeds of their leaders. The George W. Bush administration flaunted an extreme posture of unilateralism, with disregard of the views of even the closest allies. The influence of financial and corporate power at the highest levels of government calls for new initiatives to protect populations and societies of the developing world from exploitation and societal collapse.

There is a crying need for creative thinking and new initiatives to protect the gains of development from devastation by financial hurricanes fed by institutional investors who freely move funds in and out of countries at the tap of a keyboard with no responsibility for the impact of their operations on "host" countries. The IMF, BIS, G7 and so on are captive to the overriding interest of protecting the value of global financial investments regardless of collateral damage to shattered lives and the hopes of millions.

RECLAIMING POLICY AUTONOMY

For the past twenty years, the developing world has been adjusting to the agendas of the IMF and the World Bank. It is time to reclaim the right of nations to policy autonomy, the right to make the best use of their own resources (Lewis) and the right to engage in the international economy on their own terms (Rodrik). The right to development is a citizen right, and its realization is a priority obligation of national governments. States — not the IMF or the World Bank — have the right and the duty to formulate appropriate national development policies.

The aspirations to equity and social justice which motivated the call for a new international economic order twenty-five years ago remain a fundamental motivation of all human rights claims, including the right to development. This requires an international rule-based regime that permits space for developing countries to follow different and divergent paths to development according to their own philosophies, institutions, cultures and societal priorities.

Subordinating Finance to Production

Finance must be subordinate to the productive economy, globally and nationally. The productive economy must provide the basic needs of the entire population in an integrated society where there is not one economy for the privileged and another for the poor. Poverty alleviation is no substitute for development as a social project of all citizens. Economic growth must be subordinate to long-term sustainable development. Private profitability criteria are inappropriate for the provision of universally available educational, health care and other essential public services. All modern economies are mixed economies combining the private sector, state enterprise, self-employment and diverse forms of cooperative and associational community economic organization. Democracy and pluralism implies diversity of social and economic organization of societies.

The first requirement for restoring the right to development is the establishment, within a reconstructed United Nations system, of a multilateral world financial authority to track, oversee and regulate global financial markets on principles which restore "market risk" to creditors and limit the "socialization" of private (unguaranteed) debt. Global capital markets cannot be permitted to capsize economies or override the social priorities of national societies. The rights of financial investors must be subordinated to the rights of citizens — nationally and internationally. Until such time, developing countries must reclaim policy autonomy yielded in unequal negotiations with official creditors.

Accountability of the IMF and the World Bank

The International Monetary Fund should return to its original mandate to provide medium-term finance for countries with temporary balance-of-payments problems to enable them to undertake adjustment without deepening a crisis by restrictive monetary and fiscal measures which have long-term effects in eroding social infrastructure — as intended by the architects of the Bretton Woods Institutions. The right to impose capital controls should be re-affirmed and initiatives to bind countries to capital account liberalization suspended.

All official debt to poor countries should be cancelled, and financial restitution made to Sub-Sahara Africa for slavery, colonialism and the imposition of inappropriate programs and policies by the IMF and World Bank in the past two decades. Development assistance should not be conditional on trade and investment liberalization or privatization of state assets; it should be greatly increased and granted to poor countries on highly concessional terms for physical and social infrastructure, as was the practice prior to the 1980s. The World Bank should be brought under the direction of the Social and Economic Council of the United Nations. Development assistance should be governed by principles of parity between donors and recipients. International funding for "global public goods" and disaster relief should be increased. The United Nations must be strengthened and reformed to accord with the demographic realities of the twenty-first century with no permanent seats on an elected Security Council. Nothing less can assure peace, which is the ultimate prerequisite of development.

A Development-Oriented WTO

Developing countries must have an effective voice in the making and the implementation of the rules of the WTO, which should be restricted to cross-border trade in its conventional sense with no extension into "trade-related" matters, which raises questions of the permissible limits of interference in domestic social and cultural norms and institutions. Policy options are reduced. Indeed, this is the explicit purpose. The intention is to lock states into irreversible commitments through the sanctity of contract. Investor rights prevail over fundamental human rights. Trade enforceable regulations concerning intellectual property rights to pharmaceuticals must be amended to permit — and encourage — the production of generic drugs by and for developing countries. The right to health is a sacred right to life. The WTO should support, not frustrate, development initiatives of member countries.

Regional Co-operation of Developing Countries

Because it is obvious that small countries can only implement developmental policies in the context of larger regional entities, all barriers to regional economic integration of developing countries should be eliminated from the rules of the WTO. Developing countries should become less reliant on exports that impoverish the rural economy and the environment, or on destabilizing external financial flows as a substitute for a high rate of domestic savings and progressive and equitable taxation. Regional monetary arrangements for mutual assistance should be encouraged. Indeed, strong regional institutions not only provide a degree of mutual support to countries with limited power in the international arena, but a network of regional institutions may serve to offset the gross imbalance of power in the international system.

Globalization and Democracy

The above is a minimal agenda of international reform to enable societies to determine their own economic, political and social goals in accordance with their specific needs and social priorities. It is also an agenda for democratic accountability and popular voice. Globalization of finance and trade has reduced the capacity of states to govern markets at the national level, but enhanced the capacity of the major capitalist powers to set the rules which govern markets at the global level. At the national level, governments are under pressure from productive enterprise, labour and civil society to respond to the real needs of the population, however reluctantly or incompletely. At the global level, capital is insulated from popular pressure and the constraints of democratic accountability.

The argument that popular voice (democracy) is incompatible with un-limited openness to global trade and finance has been presented by Rodrik (2000) in an elegant transposition of the familiar trilemma. A similar view regarding respect for diversity, space for policy autonomy, and democracy was expressed by the executive director of the United Nations Economic Commission for Latin America:

> Weaker actors should continue to demand national autonomy in crucial areas, particularly in the choice of the social and economic development strategy. Moreover, national autonomy is the only system that is consistent with the promotion of democracy at the world level. There is indeed no sense in promoting democracy if the representative and participatory processes at the national level are given no role in determining economic and social development strategies. This is also consistent with the view that institution building, social cohesion, and the accumulation of human capital and technological capabilities (knowledge capital) are essentially endogenous processes. To borrow a term from Latin American structuralism, development can only come "from within." Support for these endogenous processes, respect for diversity, and the design of rules that allow it to flourish are essential rules of a democratic, development-oriented world order. (Ocampo 2000: 9)

For peoples and nations, as for individuals, the right to development is ultimately the right to be autonomous, the right to be free, the right to the fruits of individual and collective work, and the right to live in harmony in a society of peace and mutual support and respect. The revolution in communication and information has diminished distance and speeded time. We know more about what is happening to other people in other countries. In that sense, "globalization" is not menacing. What is menacing is the tide of global finance that is sloshing in and out of currency and securities markets in search of short-term gains with no responsibility for the fate of the majority of people who gain no benefits but pay the costs of this casino capitalism. There is no limit to the damage that international finance can inflict on small — and not so small — economies. Even the most successful countries have been brought to their knees by changes in market sentiment.

Global markets in bonds and equities are undermining "stakeholder" capitalism — even in major capitalist countries of Western Europe and Asia. Shareholder profitability trumps social security, social justice, redistributive equity and fundamental human rights. Exit trumps Voice. Global capital mobility is subverting democracy even where formal institutions of representative government are deeply rooted in the political culture. The provenance of this virulent style of predatory accumulation is Anglo-American, and the permissive condition was the destruction of an orderly international monetary system in the early 1970s when Washington, New York and London cooperated in freeing capital from the constraints of the Bretton Woods system.

RECLAIMING DEVELOPMENT ECONOMICS

Development economics emerged in the late 1940s and 1950s as a Third World was forming from the new nations of former European colonial empires. Its pioneers were independent scholars who addressed the problem of "underdevelopment" from their respective experiences, regions, and intellectual formations. They came from India, Latin America, Asia, the Caribbean and Continental Europe and its diasporas in Britain and the United States. Keynes was an important influence, but so was Marx and other Continental European schools of economics. The nineteenth-century late industrializers, Soviet economic planning and the management of the British war economy were among the historical experiences which informed their work. They addressed the central problem of the role of the state in economic development.

"Market and state," "trade and development," and "growth and equity" have been the three grand themes of development economics. For the peripheral export economies emerging from colonialism and for the Latin American republics, "trade and development" have been primary issues. In these commodity exporting countries, which constituted the majority of post-colonial states, industrialization did not progress from craft to modern production, but by the encouragement of import substitution and by nationalizations and other measures to increase "national value added" from export activities. These developmental strategies were never accepted by mainstream trade theorists. Raul Prebisch was considered a dangerous heretic.

In the early 1960s development economics became institutionalized, giving rise to specialized journals, academic teaching programs and textbooks. Research became increasingly empirical and quantitative in the service of national development agencies and the international donor community. In the 1970s, the World Bank assumed increasing importance in policy analysis and prescription. Themes that occupied the attention of Bank researchers included "developmentalist" issues of structural transformation, income distribution, employment and unemployment, redistribution with growth and basic human needs. Although conditions were favourable to high growth, income disparities widened and employment failed to increase as expected — a condition known as "growth without development." In the 1970s, the G77 bloc of developing countries within the U.N. and the non-aligned movement of Asian and African states raised the demand for a more equitable new International Economic Order. In retrospect, much energy was wasted in interminable negotiations with the North. The reaction of the United States to the upsurge of radicalism on a world scale was political intervention by counter-insurgency, as in support of the military coup in Chile in 1973. The masterminds of the neoliberal policies introduced by the Pinochet dictatorship were Milton Friedman and Friedrich Hayek.

It would be difficult to find a more striking illustration of the close relationship between economic theory and the policy prescriptions of the major powers than the concerted attack on development economics in the early 1980s, as described in the previous chapter. The 1970s spawned a counter-revolution in economic theory which continues to dominate university curricula. Economic history and the history of economic thought are no longer required subjects in most honours or graduate programs. Development economics survived as a special field of study, although impoverished by excessive econometric empiricism.

In the 1990s, issues pushed off the agenda in the 1980s resurfaced like archaeological finds in the intellectual desert. Work on measurement of the "quality of life" and "basic human needs" was resumed by the authors of the *Human Development Reports* (UNDP 1990). At the initiative of Mabub Ul Haq, with help from Amartya Sen and others, a human development indicator (HDI) based on social statistics was constructed as a measure of human welfare to challenge the productionist bias of GDP per capita. Critiques of "growth without development" and "growth without employment," raised by Myrdal, Seers and others in the mid-1960s, returned to the discourse in the Copenhagen Social Summit (1995). Under the influence of Joseph Stiglitz, the World Bank initiated annual conferences on development economics, and the *World Development Report 1997* adopted a more socially and environmentally sensitive definition of development and returned the state to the development discourse.

But the moment of truth came with the Asian Crisis of 1997, which capsized some of the most successful economies of East Asia and raised a storm of controversy about the competence and the motives of the IMF and the U.S. Treasury. The chief economist of the World Bank broke protocol by a stinging public critique of ideological "market fundamentalism," including "shock therapy" and "asset stripping" in Russia. Debates concerning "miracle growth" and crisis in East Asia and the consequences of financial and capital account liberalization raged in the corridors of power and the pages of journals and newspapers. For a while it appeared that the Asian Crisis could precipitate the first general world recession since the 1930s. Instead, it fed the stock market boom in the United States. But a creeping world recession is casting a long shadow over developing countries excessively dependent on export markets and external finance.

Although the lights went out at the Bank with the departure of Stiglitz, critiques of the IMF/Bank doctrine that "growth is good for the poor and liberalization is good for growth" are gaining intellectual ground as financial crises jump like wildfire from country to country — today Argentina and Turkey, tomorrow East Asia, and then back to Latin America. Each crisis savages millions of lives as jobs are lost, businesses bankrupted, wages reduced and savings destroyed. Three years of talk about a "new financial architecture" has produced no significant progress. The G7, IMF, BIS and so on are intellectually bankrupt. Interestingly, these crises have not hurt the U.S. because trouble in any part of the world generates capital flight to safe havens in dollar deposits, while the flood of cheap tropical food and cheap manufactures from crisis stricken economies contribute to sustaining the long, low inflation boom in the United States. When Britain was the top metropole, its imports were financed, in part, by backflow of interest and profits from overseas investment, while savings remained high and capital continued to be exported. In contrast, U.S. savings are low and the huge American payments deficit is financed by large capital inflows from the four corners of the world. Artificially high yields, which raise the supply price of funds for productive enterprise, encourage speculative investment in acquisitions, mergers and takeovers. Moreover, this perverse international financial system is chronically deflationary. Japan has been in chronic stagnation for over a decade and overall world growth slowed in the 1990s.

The Arthur Lewis Legacy

The imperial style of governance whereby some 15,000 assorted professionals employed by the IMF and the World Bank design economic and financial programs and approve the budgets of scores of independent countries is an experiment destined to fail. For many countries it has been a disaster. Asian countries — including China — which succeeded in sustained decades of growth and escaped the debt crisis of the 1980s, managed their economies in their own way. They owed nothing to advice from the IMF or the World

Bank. The crisis came when they opened their capital markets. Interestingly, when Malaysia re-imposed exchange control, the dire predictions of the world business press fizzled. It was reluctantly admitted that this measure had contributed to regional stability.

We believe that civil society and governments of the developing world will have to take the initiative in reclaiming the right to development in regional cooperation, on a scale eventually perhaps as large as all of Africa, all of Southern Cone America, or the Caribbean together with Central America and the Andean countries. Until the trend toward an extreme imbalance of power in the world is reversed, little can be expected from international nego-tiation. This was also the view expressed by Arthur Lewis and Raul Prebisch twenty-five years ago. Nothing that has happened since that time suggests that the North is more inclined to make concessions. On the contrary, the international imbalance of power has greatly increased.

Arthur Lewis believed that the South has all the resources required for its own development. In his seminal article "Economic Development with Unlimited Supplies of Labour" (1954), he grounded development econom-ics in a model that established the subject as a distinct branch of economics. Lewis was conservative and pragmatic in temperament, practical in delivering policy advice, but radically anti-imperialist in his conviction that the peoples and societies of the South have the capacity to chart their own paths to de-velopment. In an autobiographical note written late in life, he stated: "What matters most to growth is to make the best use of one's own resources, and exterior events are secondary" (Breit and Hirsh 1995: 11). Trade is useful, but export performance should not be the principal criterion of good developmen-tal economic management. In the context of globalization and unrelenting pressures for export competitiveness, the teachings of Lewis present a radical challenge to the developing world to reclaim the right to development — the right to make the best use of one's own resources.

The Prebisch Legacy

While a young Arthur Lewis witnessed the riots sweeping through the West Indies in the 1930s and asked why workers cutting cane in the hot sun were paid so much less than industrial workers in England for equal — perhaps even harder — work, Raul Prebisch encountered declining commodity prices and collapsing export markets as director-general of Argentina's central bank. In a series of important articles he wrote for the *CEPAL Review*, he revisited his rejection of the economic doctrines of the great industrial centres:

> In those far off days when I was a young man, I felt positive reverence for the economic theories of the centres. I began to lose this dur-ing the depression, however, and I have continued to lose it, so that very little of it remains. On the contrary, I think I have acquired an

acute critical sense regarding what they do and what they think, for the impressive advance registered in other scientific disciplines has not yet reached that of theories of economic development, caught as they are in the musty toils of over a century ago. (*Cepal Review*, December 1982).

In the last years of his life, he admonished the younger generations of Latin American economists for their enthusiastic adoption of "lines of thought promoted from other latitudes" and warned of the consequences of "the flagrant manifestation of the hegemony of the centres: the intellectual dependence of the periphery." The centres, he noted, "are simply not interested in our achieving a socially satisfactory form of development." Prebisch castigated the intellectual high priests of neoliberalism in the following words:

> Let Milton Friedman understand! Let Friedrich Hayek also understand! A genuine process of democratization was moving forward in our Latin America, with great difficulty, and frequent delays. But its incompatibility with a system of accumulation and distribution of income is leading toward crisis. And crisis brings about an interruption in the process and the suppression of political freedom; just the right conditions for the promotion of the unrestricted play of the laws of the market. What a paradox! You praise political freedom and individual rights. But you don't realize that in these lands of the periphery, your preaching can only bear fruit through the suppression of freedom and the violation of those rights? Because not only do the ideologies you preach perpetuate and aggravate social inequalities, they also conspire flagrantly against the efforts that must be made to reach new forms of understanding and articulation between North and South. The damage you are doing with your dogmas is immeasurable. Over thirty years ago we demonstrated the falseness of that long past scheme of the international division of labour to which neoclassical theoreticians would have us return. And in the name of economic freedom they would justify sacrificing political freedom.

These words were written in December 1981, a year before the start of the great Latin American debt crisis. The massive restructuring of economies by international creditors savaged the living standards of the majority of the population, and the intellectual initiative passed to the "neoclassical theoreticians" employed by powerful international institutions to legitimate policies which have sacrificed political freedom to the economic freedom of global international capital.

Prebisch and CEPAL laid the foundations of a common discourse of Latin American (economic) Structuralism, which gave rise to a rich critical literature of dependency more familiar to students of political science and sociology than to economists. The disappointing results of monetarism, budgetary contractions, deep liberalization, massive privatizations and ever more frequent financial crises have turned the tide against the hegemony of neoliberalism. Intellectual independence is returning with a call to rethink the development agenda (Ocampo 2000).

REGAINING THE INTELLECTUAL INITIATIVE IN DEVELOPMENT THEORY

Following the victory of the West in the Cold War, it was pronounced that "globalization" has made it impossible for countries to replicate any of the development strategies which in the historical — or even in the recent — past enabled late industrializers to transform and modernize their economies to give hope of a better life to the majority of the population.

A seductive new lexicon was invented and brilliantly marketed to displace an older discourse of the sovereignty of states, national economic development and governments that make and enforce laws. In less than a decade, "globalization," "civil society" and "governance" have become common language of official reports and popular journalism. "Globalization," as noted above, first appeared in the two-volume Shorter Oxford English Dictionary in 1995! Associated with the Internet and the revolution in communication, it has become a household word in less than a decade. Financial markets have indeed become global, but the proposition that two hundred years of history have come to an end is manifestly absurd. The liberalization of finance was instituted by governments. It is unstable, socially irresponsible and ultimately politically unsustainable. Globalization is both a description of the increased interdependence of economies and a prescriptive agenda in the service of capital.

The attack on development as a proactive political and economic project has come from several quarters, including a post-modern post-development critique that dismisses development together with industrialization and nation-states as yesterday's story. As argued in this paper, if we accept "the end of history" of endogenously directed economic and social development, we effectively deliver fragile societies to domination by a non-territorial imperialism, enforced by financial and economic sanctions, sweetened by a seductive discourse of micro-economic grassroots community development, but ultimately backed by rapid-strike military capacity to extinguish dissent, protest and rebellion anywhere in the world.

Because the systemic imbalance of power in the international system, reinforced by free trade, finance and invasive policy reforms, does not and will not for a long time present the possibility of democratic global governance, the right to development must be defended, reclaimed and advanced by co-operation of civil society and developing country states on a regional scale.

Commitments made under duress to international creditors or in unequal trade negotiations will have to be abrogated or renegotiated. In that struggle, international public opinion and advocacy NGOs can play an important role, as illustrated by the retreat forced on pharmaceutical companies in the matter of patent rights to HIV/AIDS medicines.

There is a new generation of young people out there, bright and serious, and anxious to understand the causes of poverty and injustice in the world, wishing to know how they can contribute to the struggle for justice. We of an older generation have a responsibility to counter the pervasive influence of a de-humanized economics based on false premises of methodological individualism and divorced from the realities of life as it is lived by real people in real societies.

There is no better way to liberate students of economics from the sterile orthodoxies of monoeconomics than the study of economic development in all its dimensions. This must include the history of economic thought; the history of capitalism since its beginnings in the mercantilist era of conquest, European settlement and political colonialism; and the experiences of developing countries and regions since the end of the Second World War. Dissent from economic orthodoxy has a proud tradition. Lewis and Prebisch were the targets of conservative — but also radical — critiques in their day. Many of the latter opted for the privilege of high office and high remuneration of international clerkdom. But how many of these politicians and technocrats are now uncomfortable because as insiders they know that the central bankers and ministries of finance of the major powers who dominate the Bretton Woods Institutions care little for the welfare of the populations of the developing world?

In recent years, the excesses of globalization have rekindled a spirit of resistance reminiscent of the struggles of the 1970s. In the intellectual arena, outstanding economists have challenged prevailing orthodoxies. Fundamental issues of economy and democracy; economy and society; market and the economy of care; and more generally the relation of economic and social policy are returning to development economics in its broadest sense. We need to open channels of dialogue and discussion, free from financial and intellectual dependence on the great industrial centres. Could we hope to see the establishment of an institute of development economics dedicated to research, publication and teaching programs to serve the interests of the South?

NOTE

This chapter was originally presented at the UNRISD conference "The Need to Rethink Development Economics," Cape Town, South Africa, September 7–8, 2001.

PART 3

Conclusion

15. GLOBALIZATION AND DEVELOPMENT
Decline of the West and Rise of the Rest

The world has witnessed three global eruptions since Columbus sailed west to find a new route to China. The epicentre of the voyages of discovery, conquest and trade in the mercantile era (1500–1800) were the emerging nation-states of the Atlantic seaboard of Europe. Indigenous peoples of the Americas and their civilizations were destroyed. The continent was folded into European overseas economies of conquest, settlement and exploitation of African slave labour. The chartered companies, an early form of public-private partnerships and forerunners of the modern transnational corporation, established ports, forts and trading posts to access spices and fine cottons and silks of Asia. Technological improvement did not occur in production but rather in shipping and maritime warfare. Prior to the nineteenth century, living standards were hardly above subsistence in Asia, the Middle East, the Americas and Europe, although they were somewhat higher in England and lower in Sub-Saharan Africa, where neither the plough nor irrigated agriculture were in use.

At the opening of the nineteenth century, China was still the largest and most developed civilization, and in 1820 its production equalled that of all of Europe, including Russia.[1] But the outlines of the future Third World were taking shape in the three centuries of this first globalization of European conquest and commerce. Latin America and Africa were destined to become food and raw-material exporting peripheries, while Asian civilizations, although exploited, were not uprooted or destroyed. Although ravaged in the Age of Imperialism, with notable exceptions, they were not transformed into raw material supplying peripheries to the industrial centres of Europe.

England was the pioneer of the social transformation, which dispossessed the peasantry and created a working class of wage-employed labour, initially in agriculture. Ownership of land was stripped of traditional obligations to the rural population. According to Polanyi, the commodification of land and labour was more important than the simple mechanical inventions of the early Industrial Revolution in enhancing productivity. Industrialization spread to the Continent of Europe, creating demand for food to feed the growing urban proletariat. From the mid-nineteenth century, the entry of late industrializing nations with the superior technology of the science-based Second Industrial Revolution challenged Britain's initial lead in industrial production. But it was the commercial revolution in communication of railways, telegraphs and steamships that created a world economy of European industrial centres and primary commodity exporting peripheries.

Nineteenth-century globalization had no over-arching governing institutions. Britain was the principal source of overseas investment, with France in second place. The United States and other exporters of primary commodities in the Americas were importers of capital. The integrating mechanism was the pound sterling and the Gold Standard, albeit with the assistance of British and French naval power, as required. Exports of capital, principally in long-term portfolio investment in physical infrastructure, were large in relation to world production, as also was international migration in relation to world population. In the Age of Imperialism, Europe was at the pinnacle of its power, with a third of the world's population and almost half of the world's output.

As increasing world output reduced prices and profits in the late-nineteenth century, European powers extended imperial control to embrace Africa and large swaths of Asia in the search for new investment opportunities. Nineteenth century globalization was quintessentially European, and its collapse in the imperialist war of 1914–1918 transformed the political, economic, and social landscape in Europe. Kings, kaisers, czars and sultans bit the dust. The Russian Revolution traumatized the ruling classes.

Prior to the Second World War, American participation in world trade and investment was marginal. American capitalism evolved within a large domestic economy, although economic influence and territorial control extended into neighbouring regions of Mexico, Central America, and the Caribbean. Accumulation of economic power by the family concerns of robber baron capitalism, gigantic profits made in the First World War, and the gilded age of the Roaring Twenties, eventuated in the Great Crash of 1929. Under the leadership of Franklin Delano Roosevelt, American capitalism had the resilience to reflate the economy with New Deal measures which introduced social security, raised minimum wages, enacted pro-labour legislation, undertook public works, and directly employed labour in a large variety of projects until the Second World War lifted the U.S. economy into prosperity. With the exception of ultra-conservative Republicans in the United States, the laissez faire, self-regulating capitalism that had created the world economic crisis of 1929–33 was universally discredited. Socialism appeared to offer an alternative in Europe and the new nations emerging from colonialism. Cold War competition of the two superpowers for influence and the practice of long-term social and economic planning by European governments favoured state-led initiatives of economic development in the Third World.

After 130 years of industrial capitalism the world saw a fiftyfold increase in production and a sevenfold increase in world population, but over three-quarters of the gains were accrued to Europe and its offshoots in the Americas. Asia's share of 59 percent of world output in 1820 was reduced to a mere 19 percent by 1950. China was now the poorest country in the world, with GDP per capita lower than that of Sub-Saharan Africa.

NATIONAL ECONOMIC DEVELOPMENT IN THE THIRD WORLD

In the early post-war years, economic development to lift countries emerging from colonialism out of stagnation attracted the best and the brightest economists, as illustrated by our friend Surendra Patel. The United Nations, where the General Assembly was soon dominated by the new nations of the Third World, provided a supportive environment. India was the Mecca of development planning. In Latin America, the United Nations Economic Commission (CEPAL) under the leadership of Raul Prebisch, assembled a team of brilliant young structuralist economists, including Celso Furtado, Osvaldo Sunkel, Anibal Pinto and Maria Conceição Tavares, who challenged monetarist doctrine and advocated industrialization. Together with other independent-minded economists, many from Scandinavia and Central Europe, and others including Arthur Lewis, they produced the heterodox body of development economics. In the superpower contestation of the era, most of these economists chose to be non-aligned and all of them would have supported coexistence in a world of peace. *Co-Existence* was the name of the journal initiated by Karl Polanyi in the early 1960s, and seven of the eleven editorial advisors were eminent development economists in the comprehensive sense of the term. I cannot think of a better way to mark the deterioration of economics from those days than to list these remarkable economists: Ragnar Frisch, Oskar Lange, P.C Mahalanobis, Gunnar Myrdal, Joan Robinson, Jan Tinbergen and Shigeto Tsuru. My father died as the proofs of the first issue arrived in Canada. Shortly before his death he wrote: "My work is for the new nations of Asia and Africa." From his appointment at Columbia University in 1947 until his death, Polanyi's research on economic institutions in primitive and archaic societies, where no individual family was destitute unless the whole community fell on hard times, was motivated to show that our economistic market society is unique in historical experience in raising love of gain and fear of hunger to the organizing principle of economic life.

In the 1940s and 1950s the intellectual centres of discussion of issues of development were New Delhi and Cairo, Rio de Janeiro and Santiago in Chile. State centred industrialization was financed from domestic savings while India and Egypt also had accumulated resources of British war debts in sterling balances. When the Non-aligned Conference of Asian and African nations was convened by President Sukharno of Indonesia in 1955 in Bandung the

Communist Party of Indonesia was the third largest in the world. Presidents Nehru, Nasser and Nkrumah embraced socialist economic planning of one kind or another and the invitation extended to Tito of Yugoslavia attests to the non-aligned credentials of the movement. The obliteration of this relatively recent history from the development discourse and its replacement by President Truman's 1949 so-called Point Four Declaration of American assistance to underdeveloped countries has become the received wisdom of development practitioners of all persuasions. In fact the Eisenhower administration and also the World Bank in the 1950s were firmly opposed to foreign economic aid. The Kennedy administration's Alliance for Progress in Latin America was a response to the Cuban Revolution, and W.W. Rostow of MIT was influential in persuading Kennedy to support concessional development assistance to India, Pakistan and Indonesia following the military coup which overthrew the Sukarno regime and the massacre of a million Indonesian citizens.

In the Cold War, which framed American foreign economic policy in the post-war years, Germany and Japan were integrated into the American security system in Europe and Asia. Japan was permitted to reconstruct its heavy industries and served as a logistical supply base for American military engagements in wars in Korea and Indochina. Large U.S. expenditures and favoured access to markets and technology assisted in the ascent of Japan as a major industrial power and the dynamic centre of growth in East and Southeast Asia. The radical land reform imposed by the U.S. occupation of Japan and its colonies contributed to an inclusive model of development where labour shared in gains of productivity, albeit not without militant industrial struggles. Political authorities in the former Japanese colonies of Korea and Taiwan engaged in strategies of industrialization, combining import substitution with export promotion. In both cases, acquisition of the most advanced technology was a priority. Korea constructed the most modern steel complex in the world, while in Taiwan the state provided science parks catering to medium- and small-scale enterprises. World Bank advice regarding comparative advantage in labour-intensive technology was definitively dismissed. Korea and Taiwan were among the first of the newly industrializing countries of the Third World to compete effectively in the strong revival of world trade in the 1960s and 1970s. The Japan-Korea-Taiwan complex, together with the *entrepôt* economy of Hong Kong, provided a platform for the subsequent opening of China to trade and investment.

In Latin America, industrialization was initially more advanced and GDP per capita very much higher than in East Asia (excepting Japan). In the 1930s and 1940s, when export markets collapsed or were interrupted by war, the Latin American countries of the Southern Cone engaged in strategies of industrialization for domestic markets. This experience, together with the Prebisch-Singer thesis of declining terms of trade for exporters of primary commodities, challenged prevailing doctrines of comparative advantage. As world trade revived, Latin American growth reverted to the export of primary commodities with growth averaging 6 percent in the first three post-war decades. Industrialization was directed to an urban middle class market with purchasing power. The majority rural population lived at the margin of subsistence. The business classes, dominated by landed and commercial oligarchies had little incentive to risk their capital in manufacturing activity. For these reasons state enterprises and foreign companies played an important role in strategies of industrial development, most notably in Brazil, which according to Unido had attained a degree of industrialization equal to that of Korea by 1980. In both these countries "miracle" high growth was orchestrated by authoritarian governments, with tacit support of the United States.

In 1964 Prebisch was appointed head of the newly established United Nations Conference on Trade and Development (UNCTAD) to address the problems of deteriorating terms of trade of developing countries dependent on the export of primary commodities. As former colonies in Sub-Saharan Africa and the Caribbean joined the United Nations, the Group of 77 united the newly independent states of Asia, Africa and the Caribbean with the Latin American republics to form a bloc of Third World countries within the United Nations system. The establishment of OPEC, followed by producer cartels in bauxite, raised the confidence of Third World commodity producers in the call for a fairer new international economic order, adopted by the General Assembly of the United Nations in the 1970s. At this time also, the 1972 Stockholm Conference on the Human Environment raised issues of ecological sustainability, following the earlier Club of Rome (1968). But the many international conferences of the 1970s were frustrated by the determination of the leading countries of the North to institute an economic regime change to re-introduce the discipline of capital over labour. In his Nobel lecture "The Slowing Down of the Engine of Growth" (1979) and the Shumpeter lecture "The Evolution of the International Economic Order" (1978), Arthur Lewis concluded that in the long run, the countries of the developing world had within them all the resources for economic growth. They should not have to depend on exports to the developed countries, but rather reorganize their agriculture to feed their populations, providing the basis for their manufacturing and service industries: "International trade cannot substitute for technological change, so those who depend on it for their major hope, are doomed to frustration."

The state-led national economic development of the first three post-war decades laid the foundations of the contemporary rising powers of the Global South, led by China, whose historic industrial revolution increased GDP sixteenfold from 1980 to the 2000s. China was relatively isolated from the world economy before opening to foreign trade and investment in the 1990s. Interestingly, China has been more successful in benefiting from the globalization of trade and investment than countries that embraced the market paradigm. As Arthur Lewis predicted, countries that embraced free trade and free markets as the highway to growth and development suffered serious setbacks. He understood that only the effective combination of the resources of the South for technological advance in domestic agriculture and industry could create a more equitable international economic order. Arthur Lewis and the early development economists stand tall compared with the poverty, sterility and market myopia of contemporary mainstream economics.

HISTORIC COMPROMISE OF CAPITAL AND LABOUR

From the end of the Second World War to the mid-70s full employment was achieved in Britain by the subordination of capital to national policy objectives: full employment with price stability and the reduction of income inequality. The central bank was mandated to serve these policies and also acted as the banker of the government. Capital controls were maintained. In the literature of economic policy planning, the policy objectives were known as the "social welfare function." For Hayek, this departure from the minimalist "law and order" government of nineteenth-century laissez-faire capitalism was the *Road to Serfdom*. For Polanyi, the self-regulating market was the road to the ruin of the Western democracies.

Full employment and the welfare state were mutually supportive, and progressive income taxation acted as an automatic stabilizer that virtually eliminated the business cycle in the 1950s and 1960s. Shortly after I joined McGill in 1961, I was assigned a course on business cycles and informed myself of the large and interesting literature. The business cycle, however, had apparently vanished and the course morphed into Theories of Economic Growth.

In the United States, three decades of full employment, close to 50 percent unionization and progressive income taxation had significantly increased labour's share in the national product. By the 1970s income inequality had reached historic lows. From the mid-1960s, rising prices due to expenditure on social programs in response to the civil rights movement and the war in Indochina reduced the value of financial assets, while saturated markets and stagflation reduced profits in the real economy. To the economic elites the situation appeared to be a "crisis of democracy" with President Carter too weak to reassert control (Crozier, Huntington and Watanuk 1975). With the election of Reagan in 1980, it was in his words, "morning in America." In Britain, where inflation reached 25 percent, the combination of strong labour unions and the second oil shock created an economic and political crisis for the incumbent Labour government, and IMF intervention paved the way for the election of Margaret Thatcher in 1979. As predicted by Kalecki in 1942 several decades of full employment had diminished both the power and the profitability of capital (Kalecki 1942).

Inflationary pressures and declining returns to capital in the domestic economy were not the only problems in the late 1960s. Competition from Europe, and later also from Japan, combined with rising foreign expenditures on the war in Vietnam and large outflows of direct investment to Canada and Europe resulted in an ever-larger external payments gap and the drain of gold from America's reserves. To avoid painful adjustment to the country's external payments deficit, President Nixon terminated gold convertibility of the U.S. dollar in 1971. From this time to the present, the United States could use its domestic currency to make foreign payments. When followed in 1973 by the floating of all major exchange rates, national control over the money supply passed to a global market in short-term capital including speculation in foreign exchange. The third globalization had its origins in the dissolution of the Anglo-American capital controls in the 1970s, and was characterized by the progressive financialization of corporate capitalism and the role of the U.S. dollar now liberated from the discipline of gold convertibility.

All of the above was accompanied by an upsurge of radicalism in the Third World: revolutions from Afghanistan to Nicaragua, and even tiny Grenada; the establishment of Leftist governments in the former Portuguese African colonies in 1975; defeat of South African intervention in Angola with Cuban assistance; above all, defeat of the United States in Vietnam; and finally the Iranian Revolution, which ousted the Shah and humiliated the United States in the hostage crisis of 1979. At this time the Third World reached the zenith of its influence within the United Nations system. The Trilateral Commission, but most importantly the first convocation of the G5 in 1975, signalled the common concern of the governments of the West with their apparent loss of control both domestically and in the Third World.

NEOLIBERALISM, GLOBALIZATION AND THE UNRESOLVED CRISIS OF CAPITALISM

The neoliberal counter-revolution of the 1980s was prepared in think-tanks and universities. It was signalled by the 1976 award of a Nobel Prize to Hayek. Policies included deregulation, liberalization and privatization; the elimination of progressive income taxation; regressive sales taxes; and monetary policy to create excess supply in the labour market (high interest rates). The World Bank launched an intellectual attack on development economics as interventionist interference with the free market and advocated the removal of all subsidies on essential foods or concessionary credit extended to small farmers. This ideological attack on policies that had achieved successful economic development in Latin America, the Caribbean and Africa was enforced by Structural Adjustment Programs that privileged exports over domestic production by devaluation of currencies.

A drastic monetary compression by the U.S. Federal Reserve in the early 1980s raised interest rates to two digits. The principal objective was to check inflation and inflationary expectations by compressing aggregate demand. The consequent recession served to re-introduce unemployment as a discipline in the labour market. Economists declared that non-inflationary growth required an unemployment rate of 7 percent. Progressive taxation was dismantled. War was declared on labour organizations. The social contract was broken. Median wages, which had risen with increased productivity for the past thirty years, ceased to rise. From 1980 to the financial crisis of 2008/9, real median wages and salaries in the United States and also Canada have not increased. On the eve of the 2008/9 crisis income inequality in the United States reached the 1929 peak, and almost one-quarter of GDP went to the top 1 percent. The entire increase in productivity and economic growth since the early 1980s accrued to high income earners whether as interest, profit, rents, fees, royalties, stock options, bonuses or high salaries of managerial elites including lawyers, accountants and others employed in business and financial services. In the United States over 90 percent of the population did not benefit from economic growth for the previous thirty years. Where household incomes increased it was through the contribution of two or more income earners, and in recent years also through debt finance, asset inflation in real estate and the stock market.

The contribution of manufacturing to GDP had declined to 12 percent or less while finance, insurance and real estate increased to 20 percent or more. The industrial base is now so hollowed out that it is largely dependent on government defence contracts. Returns to financial capital exceeded returns to productive investment in the real economy, until profits of financial corporations accounted for 40 percent of total corporate profits, compared with less than 10 percent in the 1960s. As median wages and salaries stagnated or even declined, consumption was maintained by ever increasing household debt and the illusion of wealth by asset inflation. Economists embraced a doctrine of the efficient market hypothesis and pronounced that the post-industrial new economy of services industries represented a higher stage of development. The illusion that this predatory model of financial wealth creation could sustain economic growth without limit was most fully held in Britain, where household debt in relation to income surpassed levels in the United States; one in nine households in London were reported to be dependent on the financial services industry for their incomes, and de-industrialization had progressed even further than in the United States. The belief that financial services could sustain Britain's economy was shared by Labour and Conservative governments alike. Nor was Europe exempt from the illusion of sustainable economic growth by asset inflation in real estate and the stock market.

The neoliberal reforms of deregulation, privatization and liberalization initiated in the United States and Britain by Reagan and Thatcher in the 1980s together with a growing global market in financial assets and the end of the Bretton Woods financial order opened the era of the third economic globalization. But it was not until the demise of the Soviet Union in 1991 that the full force of the globalization of trade and capital was unleashed. Deregulation, mergers and acquisitions, and the elimination of progressive income taxation created ever growing agglomerations of financial capital seeking high returns in global markets and transnational corporations engaged in outsourcing of production to cheaper labour locations and other strategies to reduce labour costs. This resulted in the impoverishment of the industrial working class and ultimately the destruction of a viable manufacturing industry.

The growth of a global market in foreign exchange and other financial assets was facilitated by the unilateral liberalization of capital controls by national monetary authorities. The liberalization of trade and direct invest-ment requires negotiation with governments, starting with the Structural Adjustment Programs imposed by the IMF and the World Bank on indebted developing countries of Latin America, the Caribbean and Africa in the 1980s, and continuing in the 1990s. The creation of the World Trade Organization together with IMF and World Bank programs and the negotiation of a network of Free Trade Agreements required an elaborate administrative structure staffed with tens of thousands of highly trained professionals at the multilateral and national levels. This elaborate and expensive bureaucracy of technocrats reminds us of Polanyi's observation that nineteenth-century laissez-faire was planned by a strong state, but resistance to the dictates of the market was spontaneous. When transposed from the national to the international scene, resistance of societies to domination by supranational institutions which fa-vour transnational corporate power can only be effectively mobilized within the political arena of the nation state. This is currently the issue in Europe, where democracy is in suspense. It is the reason why developing countries have accumulated reserves and paid down IMF debts to maintain policy in-dependence. The construction of supranational rules to secure the freedom of financial capital from control and regulation by national governments distinguishes globalization as an agenda of corporate capitalism from the technological revolution in communication.

When the word "globalization" first appeared in the early 1990s, the process was already well advanced. It was facilitated by the revolution in information technology and driven by corporate capital in search of new investment frontiers, domestic and overseas. The introduction of "global-ization" to describe the internationalization of production under control of transnational corporations is a brilliant example of the importance of language in the marketing of the neoliberal project. It is a seductive term that suggests a world without borders and communication across the globe. When "globalization" is used to replace "accelerating international trade and investment," the nation and its borders disappear from view. In language if not in reality, economics has obliterated the political jurisdiction of the nation-state. The elimination of national sovereignty over the allocation of national resources, including the control and regulation of capital, defines globalization as a project whose objective is the subordination of peoples and nations to capital accumulation on a global scale.

A borderless world is a reality for global finance, restlessly trading financial assets and foreign exchange across time and space. It also describes the network of connectivity of the major transnational corporations created by an incessant process of mergers and acquisitions. The cross-border mergers of major corporations are reminiscent of feudal alliances of princely families. Forty-nine of the fifty most connected agglomerations of capital are financial entities, almost all headquartered in Europe or the United States (Vitali, Glattfelder and Battiston 2011). This structure of a concentration of corporate power in the Global North, with affiliated production facilities across the globe resembles the extension of metropolitan control over overseas dependencies from the era of mercantile capitalism and imperialism to the present. The differences between our globalization and that of the nineteenth century, however, are more important than the similarities. Competing national capitalisms of the nineteenth century have given way to the agglomeration of corporate capital of the advanced economies of the West. It is inconceivable today that the nations of the West would engage in war with each other.

The CEOs at the pinnacle of power have no allegiance to any particular nation or people. They may reside in the country of their citizenship and their companies may receive assistance from their home governments, as in the case of General Motors and others in the recent financial crisis, but they acknowledge no responsibility to provide employment. Apple is an American business headquartered in the United States, but the company clearly states that it does not have "an obligation to solve America's problems. Our only obligation is making the best product possible." Low wages are not the only issue. Due to the lack of highly skilled American workers, over a third of the final cost of an iPhone goes to Japan, 17 percent to Germany and 13 percent to South Korea, countries where wages are higher, or at least almost equal to the United States. A mere 6 percent of the retail price of an Apple iPhone accrues to American product designers, lawyers, accountants and other specialized professionals. In China wages are substantially lower but the contracting companies are able to supply several hundred thousand assembly workers as required (Reich 2012). The example of this outstandingly successful company is perhaps extreme in its independence from support by its home government. American companies in the pharmaceutical industry have vital interest in free trade negotiations that protect their intellectual property, and defence-related aerospace industries clearly have a direct relationship to government purchases. Nevertheless, the relative delinking of transnational corporations from employment of the domestic labour force is a distinguishing feature of contemporary globalization.

In the case of the great financial conglomerates, there is only a tenuous connection with the real economy. The names of the American Robber Baron capitalists of the nineteenth century are associated with railways, petroleum or chemical industries. The only physical manifestation of the fortunes of the financial barons of our times are the tall edifices of cement and glass of our cityscapes celebrating the dominion of commerce and finance over the real economy, which as Adam Smith told us is the real source of the wealth of nations.

The West is in decline in relation to the rest of the world, facing at best a decade of stalled economic growth, at worst a catastrophic social implosion. The Great Financialization radiating from its Anglo American epicentre in Wall Street and London, has created a global market trading 24/7 in foreign exchange, bonds, various exotic derivatives, commodity futures and equities, of which some 70 percent are now automated, short-term trades. The markets and the rating agencies exert discipline over governments by attacks on bonds or currencies and demand deflationary contraction of government expenditure. The culture of greed and the power of the creditors to impose adjustment on debtor states, and more generally the extraction of economic rents from productive enterprises, recall Keynes's greatest fear that finance would destroy industry. He believed that love of money was a mental illness. The British-based Tax Justice Network reports that some $20–$30 trillion is currently deposited in tax havens, of which some $10 trillion belongs to only 92,000 individuals (Stewart 2012). This mega-trillion accumulation of wealth represents a surplus extracted from the productive activity of millions of people in scores of countries, a financialized capitalist economic order that cannot secure a satisfactory return without creating inequality on this scale. From its beginnings in commerce and conquest to its achievements in the creation of industrial civilization, the West has reverted to its mercantile origins of trade and war, commerce and conquest. Since the demise of the Soviet Union the principal objective of the West has been the maintenance of control over the petroleum resources of the greater Middle East by wars in Afghanistan and Iraq, and political and military intervention in civil conflict in Libya and Syria. The only remaining superiority of the West is the military might of the United States. The attempt to extend military power to sustain the wasteful lifestyle of the West by control over the natural resources of the globe threatens the fragile peace of the world and the civilizational contributions of its many peoples and nations.

THE CAPTURE OF GOVERNMENT: DEMOCRACY IN SUSPENSE

The coexistence of capitalist economic institutions with universal franchise and representative government by election of political parties has been referred to as democratic capitalism. In the nineteenth-century capitalist order, none of the European powers were democracies. In the first three decades following the Second World War, lessons learnt from the Great Depression placed restrictions on capital, which, as noted, strengthened the power of labour, and full employment was the principal objective of economic policies of Western governments. In the course of the last three decades, and especially since the demise of the Soviet Union, neoliberal ideologies gained control over the policies of major contending political parties, which have increasingly reflected the priorities of the corporate world: economic growth over environmental sustainability, competitiveness in external markets, creation of a favourable investment climate, cost-effectiveness criteria or privatization for social infrastructure, the negotiation of Free Trade Agreements, and the elimination of deficits of governments and public sector enterprises. There is little change to these priorities when incumbent parties are replaced by opposition parties in Western democracies. Politics and politicians are devalued. Celebrity success is lionized.

How, we may ask, has capital succeeded in capturing governments while maintaining institutions of representative democracy? How has capital gained the initiative in determining the policy priorities of governments in the West? Rising income inequality created large pools of finance concentrated and managed by investment banks employing thousands of highly paid financial analysts assessing risks on high returns on other people's money. A broad stratum of the middle class invest their savings in pension or mutual funds for the education of their children or for retirement. They identify the security of their savings with the state of global capital markets as detailed in daily business newscasts. The financialization of wealth created in the real economy is now a defining feature of corporate capitalism.

Financial markets have become engines of mass destruction of social coherence, which is the glue that binds the democratic market society. Polanyi's contention that the self-regulating market is ultimately incompatible with democracy requires no further proof today. In a 1932 article entitled *"Economy and Democracy,"* Polanyi maintained that the conflict between the captains of industry and working-class political and trade union organizations in Continental Europe could be resolved either by socialism or fascism. In the crisis of capitalism of the 1930s, a number of fascist regimes were established in Central, Eastern and Mediterranean Europe. Polanyi attributed the virulence and inhumanity of German fascism to the socially disintegrating consequences of the self-regulating market: "Market society was born in England — yet it was on the Continent that its weaknesses engendered the most tragic complications. In order to comprehend German fascism, we must revert to Ricardian England." Fascism may be described as the intervention of the state to protect corporate capital by the suppression of labour and popular organization and the suspension of civil liberties, accompanied by populist nationalistic rhetoric with appeal to the lower classes of society. In the United States today, the concentration of corporate power, including the mass media; the militarization of the economy; unlimited contributions to political parties and campaigns; and the limitations on civil liberties in the undefined and open-ended war on terror have been described as a silent (Johnson 2008) or a slow-motion (Saul 1995) coup d'état of corporate capitalism. It also has features of a national security state. As a European with a long memory I see it as creeping fascism.

It has not been sufficiently noticed that in the past sixty years, until the crash of Lehman Brothers in 2008, major financial institutions have not been permitted to fail. Unlike the frequent financial crises of nineteenth-century capitalism, most dramatically in 1873 and again in 1929, when more than 10,000 American banks went under, monetary authorities have intervened to rescue or reorganize large financial institutions. In 1982 and again in 1997, the Federal Reserve intervened to save insolvent American banks in the Latin American and East Asian debt crises. The great majority of banks are profit-making enterprises owned by shareholders engaged in creating money and credit advanced to businesses, households and governments. If losses exceed their capital reserves they are insolvent, and have failed. In the past, central banks imposed conservative reserve ratios on banks. The globalization of finance and the mergers of commercial and investment banks have enabled them to engulf businesses and households in a mega-trillion dollar web of debt. Because credit is the lifeblood of a modern market economy, the failure of a large investment bank can trigger a general financial meltdown, as almost happened in 2008. The intimate relations of CEOs of banks with the Federal Reserve and more generally with top officials of the government explains the trillions of public funds advanced to the banks, while the government did not come to the assistance of millions of families who lost their homes by writing down mortgages.

In the four years which have passed since 2008, neoliberal financialization has created an economic, political and social crisis more profound than that of the 1930s because governments are now captive to financial markets and incapable of restoring the purchasing power of consumers, which is the driver of economic growth in the market economies of the West. In the United States impoverished households can no longer supplement their stagnant or declining incomes by borrowing; businesses are reluctant to undertake investment in uncertain prospects of recovery from recession; and the government is constrained by a Congress committed to deficit reduction, while banks are more powerful than ever and continue to pay mega-bonuses.

In Europe, which was forced into premature adoption of the Euro as a defence against speculative attacks on national currencies without the prior construction of a European fiscal system, the situation is even more intractable and now threatens the future of the Eurozone. The full burden of adjustment to imbalances of external surpluses of Germany and other strong member countries and payments deficits of weaker peripheral countries has been imposed on the populations of the latter. The situation is reminiscent of the

Latin American debt crisis of the 1970s but more intractable because any solution, short of the exit of Greece, Spain and other peripheral countries from the Eurozone, requires lengthy and complex political negotiations by governments whose rich and powerful citizens have secured their wealth in tax havens beyond the control of their national governments.

DECLINE OF THE WEST AND RISE OF THE REST

Perhaps the most revealing aspect of the Great Recession which followed the financial crisis of 2008/9 was the contrast between its deep impact on the heartlands of capitalism and regions closely integrated by trade and finance on the one hand, and the rapid recovery in the rest of the world, on the other. For the first time since its establishment, IMF assistance was required in a large number of countries in Europe. With the exception of the southern peripheries of the United States — Mexico, Central America and the Caribbean — no countries of Latin America requested IMF programs and a mere $6 billion was disbursed over thirty countries in Africa, in connection with the steep rise in food prices in 2008. High growth in China and India was only marginally affected and all of Developing Asia, constituting over half the population of the world, averaged annual growth of 8–9 percent in the first decade of the twenty-first century.

Although the advanced countries appeared to have recovered from the Great Recession by 2010, and world growth rebounded to 5.3 percent, the recovery was weak and short-lived because the fundamental causes of the Great Recession have not been addressed. Four years after the financial crisis of 2008/9, growth in all advanced countries was a mere 1.9 percent, with growth hovering around zero in the Eurozone and Britain in 2012. World growth of 3.5 percent continues to be sustained by the Global South (China at 8 percent, India 6.7 percent, the ASEAN Five at 5 percent, Latin America 3.9 percent, Sub-Saharan Africa 5.4 percent). These very high growth rates will certainly decline, but with the shift of world production to the South and relative stagnation in the North, it is expected that the South will continue to contribute 75 percent to annual world growth for the foreseeable future, compared with 50 percent before the crisis. This shift in the growing points of the world economy reflects both the dynamics growth of the South and the relative stagnation of the North. It is unmistakeable that world growth is no longer driven by the rich markets of Europe and North America, although they continue to be important to the export economies of the South.

When North America and Europe achieved unprecedented growth with full employment in the 1950s and 1960s, and Latin America engaged in industrialization for the domestic market primarily with Foreign Direct Investment, international trade had barely recovered from the Great Depression and the Second World War. As profitability in the heartlands of capitalism declined and Keynesian consensus unravelled, capital sought higher returns in Latin America, the OPEC petroleum economies and the rising export manufacturing countries of East Asia. The revolution in communication offered opportunities for the location of production facilities in a number of newly industrializing countries (NICs). Capital flows to Mexico in 1982 were running higher than ever before in the history of the country, and the announcement in August 1982 that Mexico was unable to disperse billions of debt service was an unexpected shock to Wall Street, the IMF and the World Bank. Over-exposed American banks were rescued by the Federal Reserve and the IMF. Latin American countries lost a decade of growth and the monetarist austerity policies of the Washington Consensus gained reluctant acceptance by economists and technocrats in Latin America, the Caribbean and Africa. Asia was not significantly affected. India's economy was overwhelmingly national and domestic, while the export manufacturing "miracle" economies of East Asia did not experience their debt crisis until 1997.

World trade revived from the 1970s, and from 1980 to the present, trade grew roughly twice as fast as world production, and cross-border capital flows are now many times greater than what is required to clear international balances of trade, increasing the vulnerability of all open economies, large and small. In all countries the global liberalization of trade and capital flows has increased inequality, because the dollar value of internationally traded goods including real estate tends to be the same in all participating countries of the global economy. This is known as the "law of one price" in a fully competitive international market freed from all trade barriers. In small countries dependent on tourism, prices in supermarkets and real estate values are higher than in the capitalist centres.

But it was not until the implosion of the Soviet Union in 1991 that the South was folded into a global economy by the replacement of the General Agreement on Tariffs and Trade (GATT) in 1994 by the WTO, with enforceable rules for all member countries. In the same year Mexico was added to the previously existing Canada-U.S. Free Trade Agreement of 1988 by the establishment of the North American Free Trade Agreement. President Bush initiated its extension to embrace all of the Americas as the Free Trade Area of the Americas, which was effectively blocked by Brazil. NAFTA became the template of a new generation of enhanced Free Trade Agreements with invasive conditionalities intended to secure foreign investors from regulation by national governments. The word "globalization" appeared for the first time in the World Development Report of 1995, entitled *Workers in an Integrated World*.

The unexpected disappearance of the Soviet Union from the economic and political landscape sent shock waves throughout the Third World. The perception that there is no alternative to universal capitalism led many developing countries to abandon capital controls and embrace the Washington Consensus as the only game in the global village. In Jamaica, Prime Minister

Manley freed the exchange rate, and the currency promptly went into free fall, followed by a stock market bubble and ponzi banks and the inevitable rescue packages extended to failed banks and other businesses. Many other small, and not so small, countries responded to free market triumphalism in similar fashion in the early 1990s. The neoliberal counter-revolution of belief in markets free from government controls gained compliance, if not whole-hearted support from economists and technocrats in developing countries. India undertook important measures of liberalization, and it is perhaps no coincidence that Deng Xiaoping announced the opening of China to foreign investment at that time.

The GATT had provided a framework for the voluntary negotiation of concessions to the mutual advantage of equal partners, principally indus-trialized countries. It was familiarly referred to as "the rich man's club." By contrast, where Free Trade Agreements are negotiated between the United States or the European Union and developing economies, they favour the stronger over the weaker partner. In Central America, the Caribbean and Africa, which opened their markets to free trade, domestic agriculture was displaced by imported food. Economies of scale and corporate links to large retail chains enable agribusiness to deliver at prices that cannot be matched by independent farmers. Local industries producing for the domestic market are converted into warehouses, breaking down, packaging and selling imported manufactures; while manufacturers aspiring to export exotic tropical products to the rich markets of the North cannot compete with scale economies of large companies, which can put similar products on supermarket shelves at prices below their cost of production.

Although Mexico is not a small country, the asymmetric effect of a free trade area encompassing weaker economies is illustrated by NAFTA — and more recently by the European Union. Canadian manufacturing companies relocated to the Southern United States. American industrial workers lost employment to the assembly plants on the Mexican border. But the two million jobs in the maquiladora zones cannot compensate for the damage inflicted on Mexico by this Free Trade Agreement. Three million peasant families were displaced by imported American corn and swelled the ranks of immigrant labourers in the United States. Rural poverty increased and food security diminished. Mexican industries serving the domestic market were adversely affected by American imports, and financial integration as-sisted the laundering of profits from drugs exported to the American market. The social coherence of the country was further undermined by American insistence on the War on Drugs, which has claimed the lives of some 20,000 Mexicans. What appears to be a trade agreement of mutual benefit is better understood as a class issue; it redistributed power and income from the work-ing population of all three countries, including small and medium businesses, to transnational corporate capital.

Following Mexico's entry to NAFTA, financial liberalization precipitated the Tequila crisis in 1995, and once again intervention by the Federal Reserve and the IMF rescued overexposed American banks. The increasing volume of short-term capital seeking high returns in liberalized emerging markets created a series of financial crises in Latin America and ultimately also in East Asia, where none of the countries affected had fiscal deficits. Conformity with the Washington Consensus was most extreme in Argentina, where following a series of political crises, the economy was dollarized. The East Asian crisis rebounded to Russia, and back to Latin America, where the dollarized Argentine economy collapsed, and the government declared a unilateral moratorium on debt service in 2002. The painful lesson of IMF-inspired adjustment to these crises in the troubled 1990s resulted in decisions by Latin American governments to accumulate reserves and pay down debt to the IMF to regain policy space. This was facilitated by rising prices of Latin America's primary commodity exports and measures of regional cooperation, including assistance from Venezuela.

The crisis of 2008/9 revealed, as noted above, a rift between the Southern peripheries of the United States on the one hand, and the rest of Latin America on the other. A study by the Inter-American Development Bank, entitled *One Region, Two Speeds,* ascribes the difference between the slow-growing Mexican and the faster-growing Brazilian clusters of countries to differences in the nature and destination of their exports. The former depended on exports of manufactures and other goods and services to the United States while the latter had a net export of commodities to diverse markets, including other developing countries. The study confirms our observation that the Southern peripheries of the United States were more severely affected by the crisis than the rest of Latin America or indeed any other region of the Global South. These peripheries, with close ties of trade and finance and also remittances with the United States, fell into deep recession, with declining growth of 6 percent in Mexico, while the rest of Latin America was less profoundly affected and recovered quickly. The slow growth cluster of Mexico, Central America and the Caribbean is also the principal source of emigration of surplus labour to the United States. With the elections of Left-leaning governments in the Andean region and in the Southern Cone of the Americas, neoliberal policies of the Washington Consensus were rejected. The establishment of the Union of South American Nations in 2008, consisting of twelve countries uniting MERCOSUR with the Andean Community of Nations, signalled the assertion of Latin American identity, cooperation and solidarity. A Bank of the South is headquartered in Venezuela, while the capital of the union will be in Ecuador and the Parliament in Bolivia. This is a significant break with the previous inclusion of the United States and Canada in inter-American political and economic institutions.

Only countries that maintained control over their domestic economy and most importantly over the external capital account have been successful in gaining benefits from the liberalization of global trade and investment. China may have gained the greatest advantage because it has a strong political directorate that nurtured an industrial base with a high rate of domestic investment before opening the economy to trade and partnerships with foreign companies. As in Japan, Korea and Taiwan, where a relatively equal distribution of income was favourable to the achievement of high rates of inclusive economic growth, the Maoist legacy of radical land reform and universal literacy laid the foundation for China's industrial revolution and ascent to world power. China's economic model of development is unique in combining state control and state enterprises with the release of the productive energy of the private sector, with strategic control over banks and the external current and capital accounts. A successful economy must rest on a socially cohesive society where governments command respect and legitimacy by popular support in charting the difficult course toward what the Chinese called the achievement of moderate prosperity for all.

China has surpassed Germany as the world's largest exporter and now accounts for 10 percent of world trade. But China's economy is fragile. Extraordinary rates of domestic investment of over 50 percent, low rates of consumption, internal migration and urbanization on a scale unsurpassed in modern history and the rapid rise of inequality all threaten social stability. China is still a relatively poor developing country experiencing its unique great transformation in a world in precarious transition from Western hegemony to an uncertain future.

Economists have attributed the success of India to the liberalization of extensive government controls over access to foreign exchange, credit and licences to industries in the early 1990s. The political and economic system of India is very different from that of China but the success of Shining India similarly rests on the construction of domestic industries for the domestic market in the period of Nehruvian socialism. A network of tertiary educational institutions has endowed the country with a broad base of scientific and technical personnel fluent in the English language contributing to India's achievements in the pharmaceutical and information technology software industries. Transnational corporations have not played a significant role in Indian economic development. The magnet that in recent years has attracted them is the rapid growth of a middle-class market for the brand name products of Western corporate capitalism. But high growth based on a middle-class market of some 300 million has not lifted 500 million Indians out of poverty, and income inequality is now greater than when growth was slower and government policies more inclusive and equitable.

Of the BRICS (Brazil, Russia, India, China and South Africa), Brazil stands out as a democracy that recovered swiftly from the recession and has sustained economic growth while somewhat reducing income inequality and significantly reducing poverty by innovative social transfers. Chapter 10 of this volume included a brief account of industrial policies in Brazil in the years preceding the return of democracy in 1985. And we have noted the lessons learned from the costly neoliberal policies of the 1990s. With the election of President Lula da Silva in 2002, Brazil embarked on policies of a "new developmentalism" based on the Latin American structuralist approach of the 1950s and 1960s but adapted to Brazil as a rising industrial power in the global economy. Policies of structural development macro-economics aim to reduce dependence on foreign capital and achieve technological improvement in all industries and an increase in income and purchasing power of the entire population. A policy of zero hunger by significant cash transfers to families has lifted thirty million Brazilians out of poverty. Strong export earnings from rising prices of commodities and large inflows of portfolio capital enabled the government to undertake counter-cyclical expenditures from accumulated reserves during the crisis of 2008/9 without undesirable appreciation of the exchange rate. From the blocking of the Bush initiative to extend NAFTA to embrace all of the Americas, to Brazilian support of Latin American solidarity and cooperation with China, India, Russia and South Africa, Brazil offers hope of a new international economic order which will no longer be dominated by Washington and its discredited consensus.

In *The Rise of the Rest*, Alice Amsden has defined development as the shift from resource-based to knowledge-based assets and compared the industrial policies of seven countries that, together with China and India, constitute the rising economies of the Global South. (In addition to India and China, these are South Korea, Taiwan, Turkey, Mexico, Brazil, Chile and Argentina.) Technological know-how can be bought by licences, imported by inviting foreign companies or developed through investing in research and development, enhancing domestic capacity to adapt technical information to the country's specific requirements. Only the last of these options enables a developing country to advance to the technological frontier and bargain advantageously with transnational corporations.

In that regard countries richly endowed with resources of land and minerals may achieve strong economic growth, but where powerful economic interests, whether domestic or foreign, dominate primary export activities, there is little incentive for the development of manufacturing industries based on human skills and knowledge. Because of this and also because of excessive reliance on transnational corporations, which contribute little to national research and development, equitable economic development in Latin America remains frustrated by powerful land-owning and commercial oligarchies and high levels of inequality associated with the exclusion of indigenous populations by the legacy of European conquest and settlement. Interestingly, South Africa was not included in Amsden's list of the Rest, perhaps because the legacy of settlement colonialism and Apartheid, which has not yet been overcome to create a socially coherent national society with capacity to develop manufacturing industries based on the enterprise of the majority population. In the rest of Sub-Saharan Africa, extractive activity by foreign companies has set back diversified manufacturing.

KNOWLEDGE, TECHNOLOGY AND DEVELOPMENT

The Indian economist Surendra Patel noted that externalities of knowledge and infrastructure generated by earlier industrializing countries assisted later ones to reach a given level of economic development in a shorter time with higher rates of growth. He was among the few economists on the political Left to celebrate the social and economic achievements of the Third World in the forty years since decolonization. Where others could see only failure and the increasing economic gap with the North, he documented the significant decline in the social gap as measured by life expectancy and other social indicators. His optimism has been amply confirmed by the high growth economies of the late twentieth and early twenty-first centuries. He predicted in the early 1990s that the rate of technological advance could close the social gap between the West and the rest of the world in the space of seventy years, one human lifetime. If he had lived longer he might have thought that it would take even less time.

The revolution in information technology of computers, software and the Internet has been compared with the nineteenth-century revolution in communication, but it is more profound. It has not only shortened distances and compressed time, but it has affected every aspect of the production of goods and services and speeded up the very rate of technological change. Because information technology can treat ever larger and more complex data sets at accelerating speeds, ever-new areas of knowledge are opened. Automation and ever more clever robots are displacing labour in the production of goods and services. Japan, with an aging population, is in the forefront in the automation of industrial production, and robots are also common in households.

The displacement of labour by automation is not confined to the advanced economies. In China, industrial output has doubled since 2004 but employment has stagnated at 230 million workers; in the high growth economy of India over half the non-agricultural labour force remains in the informal sector and the number of poor has not declined (Ghosh 2011). While competition in global markets continues to favour regions with lower wages, they cannot maintain their competitive advantage without investing in efficiency-enhancing technology. As wages have stagnated in the United States but continued to rise in China, some manufacturing industries are returning to the United States, where unit costs of production have been reduced by labour-saving technology. But the jobs created will be far fewer than was the case when they were outsourced.

It is ultimately the labour-saving technology in all industries which presents a challenge to an economic system based on continuous cost reductions to maintain profitability. Globalization has placed no limits on the commodification of labour, land and money, and now also knowledge, with patenting extending to forms of life. As labour becomes increasingly redundant to the production of internationally traded goods, the exploitation of the natural resources of the globe has become the new investment frontier of corporate capital. The exploitation of natural resources is not new, but the financial crisis and high degree of uncertainty about the future have accelerated the rush for ownership of natural resources, with increasingly damaging social and environmental consequences. The ongoing financial crisis, fears of inflation, China's growing demand for natural resources and fears of food insecurity due to climate change all combine to raise the value of land and minerals, including gold as a hedge against inflation. In the ten years between 2002 and 2012, petroleum prices increased more than tenfold, minerals more than fourfold, and food prices more than doubled. The index of all primary commodities increased more than three times. Million hectare tracts of land have been bought by corporate funds. Landscapes are devastated, people displaced from their land, and water and soil polluted by large-scale operations of international mining companies. Canada and Russia are poised to take advantage of climate change to exploit the fragile Arctic environment with exploration for petroleum and minerals.

Globalization of trade and investment was initiated in the United States to sustain corporate profitability by capturing new markets and extending investment to regions of the Global South. Enormous fortunes were made. A concentration of financial and non-financial corporations gained power over the global market. But three decades of neoliberal policies have created a grossly inequitable distribution of income in the United States. Consumer expenditures have stagnated due to the impoverishment of the working and middle classes, and ceased to be the driver of economic growth, as was the case in the past. It is widely acknowledged that income inequality is the fundamental cause of the persistence of economic stagnation. There is no solution to this deep-rooted structural imbalance short of a reconstruction of America's financial, economic and political order from the bottom up. This may take a generation or more.

The United States has been able to maintain private and public expenditure in excess of national production by the import of capital from China and other surplus countries to cover external and also fiscal deficits. In that regard, and also because infrastructure was not maintained and production capacity was destroyed, the United States was able to maintain private and public consumption, including military expenditure, by consuming capital — financial, physical, social and political. With a national debt of over 90 percent of GDP, a mere 50 percent of the eligible labour force employed and ambitions to project military power across the globe, is this financialized corporate capitalism now hollow at its core? It is only the continuing role of the dollar as the world's principal reserve currency that has enabled the Federal Reserve to create dollars in payment for imports and military expenditures overseas, recycled by the purchase of Treasury bills by exporting surplus economies.

CAN THE BRICS MOVE US TOWARD A MORE EQUITABLE AND SUSTAINABLE WORLD?

In a passage quoted in Chapter 10, Surendra Patel pointed to the importance of inter-country trade in the rise of East Asia and predicted that other developing countries might also benefit by building trade links with the growth pole of East Asian economies. Trade between the BRICS is increasing at 28 percent per year and is projected to reach $500 billion by 2015. China's development assistance equalled that of the World Bank in 2009 and is likely to surpass it in light of the demands of the financial crisis. The recent decision by the BRICS to establish a common development bank with participation of their national development banks is a significant step toward the expansion of trade among them and with other developing countries by providing finance in the currencies of the BRICS.

There is a crying need in Africa for infrastructure to strengthen links of trade among countries, to provide clean water both for households and for agriculture, and for primary health care and public transportation by road and rail. To date infrastructure has served primarily the extractive industries. The BRICS bank could make a transformative contribution to a continent whose development is blocked by thirty years of the imposition of the Washington Consensus. The financial crisis which has weakened the dollar and the euro opens a window of opportunity for the BRICS development bank to change priorities from freedom of markets to freedom of people and nations to determine their own futures. Colonial and neocolonial rule has fragmented the continent. The most important priority is the internal opening of Africa to inter-country trade and locally controlled manufacturing for the domestic market and for export.

The five countries of the BRICS, with 45 percent of world population and combined a GDP equalling that of the United States, are very different from each other. China and the neighbouring countries of Taiwan, Korea, Hong Kong and also Japan form a complex and dense network of trade in East Asia. Although divided by external political affiliations, they share, to one degree or another, a common civilizational history. China has charted its own course to world power, and China's entry to world trade has made a significant contribution to the diversification of economic relations in countries of the South, including small countries of the Caribbean and Africa. China has the capacity to develop new and sustainable technologies to address the environmental consequences of rapid urbanization. Most importantly, throughout history China's rulers have placed the highest priority on political stability and territorial integrity. China has no interest in becoming a hegemonic world power.

India is the dominant country of South Asia, and it shared a common history with Pakistan prior to the partition of 1947. It was more profoundly influenced by its colonial relationship with Britain than any other county of the South, and the political elites are more Westernized than in any other country of Asia. The founders of independent India were socialist and secularist but India's secularism was one of tolerance and coexistence of diverse religious communities. Situated between the old metropoles of Europe and the rising power of East Asia, India fears isolation. Its ties with the United States and Israel in the areas of defence and nuclear energy are countered by participation in the BRICS group. India, like Russia and China, is fearful that American ambition to control the greater Middle East, including neighbouring Iran, is a threat to peace and stability. In that regard, the rising economic power of the BRICS may lead toward a world of mutual coexistence.

Russia's participation in the BRICS, including the Central Asian former Soviet republics, derives from common security interests with China, cemented in the Shanghai Agreement of 2001. Russia is unique as a former great power with a permanent seat in the U.N. Security Council, but is a transition country recovering from the shocks of the disintegration of its former over-centralized economy and the rapid introduction of capitalism, which created instant multibillionaires and instant widespread impoverishment, reflected in a dramatic decline in life expectancy. Russia's large resources of energy could be important in mutual cooperation with other BRICS parties.

In many respects it is the participation of Brazil with the rising economic power of Asia that has created a multipolar alternative to a globalization which has attempted to impose Western institutions, lifestyles and values on the rest of the world, proclaiming them to be universal human rights. With the addition of South Africa, the BRICS have acquired a tri-continental presence. However, unlike Brazil, whose large and strong economy represents Latin America's move toward policy independence, South Africa is too closely integrated with commercial and economic interests of the West to be truly independent and cannot adequately represent the interests of all of Africa. South Africa joined the BRICS at the invitation of China in 2011. China has engaged bi-laterally with South Africa to assist in diversifying African economies through manufacturing for domestic markets including China. With all these reservations, the BRICS represent a new and important platform for the collective rise of the South, and most especially for the liberation of Africa from imperial tutelage and underdevelopment. It is inconceivable that the values of Anglo American capitalism, whose greed and pursuit of short-term gain has precipitated a crisis more profound than that of the 1930s, can continue to dominate the rest of the world.

CONCLUSION

This book, and especially the chapter dedicated to the memory of Surendra Patel, has tracked the decline of the West and the achievements of the rest from the dissolution of colonialism in the 1940s and 1950s to the rise of China and India and the achievements of the South, where more than half of world output is now produced. It is regrettable that the governments of advanced countries are in denial regarding climate change, but this places greater responsibility on those of the rest of the world to reclaim control over land and resources to create a more equitable and sustainable world. This also requires fashioning an international financial order based on a special currency, as proposed by Keynes many years ago.

Technology is labour-saving and labour-replacing. It can give us leisure or create unemployment. It can restore or destroy the environment. It can restrict our freedom by invasive surveillance or expand it by social networks. Like the economy, it must be subject to social control. Our natural environment is now too fragile and precious to be subjected to market criteria of profitability. The physical environment is real. Nature can be violent and destructive, as in hurricanes and tornados, droughts and floods. The economy, as Polanyi told us, is a social construct of laws and institutions. Its destructive forces of economic crises, dispossession and displacement of peoples, creation of poverty where it did not previously exist, elimination of diversity in plant and animal life and other violations of nature, including climate change, are of our own making. Globalization has created a frightening uniformity of consumerist lifestyles, which has eliminated diversity of cultures and languages. If the economy does not serve the people, it can and will be restructured. Social movements and democratic politics are most effective at the local, and most importantly the national level. Western governments have fashioned supranational institutions whose rules are incompatible with pluralism, democracy and development. Democracy and pluralism require diversity of social, economic and political objectives of societies. Globalization has gone too far. It can and should be rolled back: as is indeed likely to happen as developing countries protect their economies from destabilization from the effects of the continuing economic crisis. International trade has made countries excessively dependent on exports. A reorientation of agriculture and industrial production toward domestic markets and food security may reduce GDP growth, but it will produce a more equitable, socially inclusive and sustainable economy. It would also result in a reduction of pollution in the atmosphere by excessive global transportation of luxury food products to the rich nations of the world.

Any meaningful notion of sustainable development must begin with the understanding that it is our cultural environment that nourishes our creativity and energy. Development cannot be imposed from without. It is a creative process and its central nervous system, the matrix that nourishes it, is located in the cultural sphere. Development is ultimately the capacity of a society to tap the root of popular creativity, to free up and empower people to exercise their intelligence and collective wisdom. Societies and nation-states that do not have the social cohesion to chart a coherent strategy of survival in the difficult years to come will not survive. They will disintegrate. This is true for rich and poor countries alike.

NOTE

1. All figures and data for this postscript are from Maddison (2006).

AFTERWORD

GLOBALIZATION, FINANCIALIZATION AND THE EMERGENCE OF THE GLOBAL SOUTH

BY SAMIR AMIN

Translated from the French by Stuart Anthony Stilitz

Polanyi, Braudel and Marx had this in common: they imparted a historical depth to their analysis of human systems, essential to understanding the trajectory of capitalism. For them, capitalism, like any other previous or perhaps future system, is not the expression of a rationality invented by the human mind, but the product of history: there is no capitalism other than historical capitalism. Building on an intimate knowledge of her father's work, Kari Polanyi Levitt has extended this analysis into the twenty-first century. In this volume of essays, she addresses both the "great financialization" of capitalism and the "great transformation" of the world economy by the emergence of the Global South. The author's approach reveals the striking contrast between the power of the historical method and the futility of Hayek's obsession with some form of transhistorical rationality.

The theses I put forward on the emergence of generalized, globalized and financialized monopolies, whose guiding principles are discussed here, derive from a shared ambition to understand the historically profound transformation of capitalism. I maintain that the implosion of contemporary capitalism (evoking the title of my most recent book) may be attributed to two phenomena. Capitalism has been unable to manage the conflicting objectives of accumulation of financial wealth and of economic growth, as illustrated by the crisis of the euro zone; and the emerging economies of the Global South are engaged in a growing conflict with the traditional centres of capitalism and imperialism. Conventional economic theory is totally sterile in this respect, incapable even of conceptualizing this type of analysis.

My analysis of the challenge facing the peoples of our planet today is based on the central role played by generalized monopoly capitalism. This concept helps to explain every significant development marking capitalism in every region of the world. It gives coherence to a landscape that would otherwise seem to be shaped solely by chance and chaos. The adjective "generalized" describes the nature of this transformation: monopolies are now in a position to reduce all economic activity to subcontracting. This concept allows us to determine the scope of major transformations that have shaped the configuration of class structures and the management of political life. However, the creation of an authentic "Springtime of the Peoples" in the "Autumn of Capitalism" heralded by the collapse of the system calls for audacity in both thought and action.

GENERALIZED MONOPOLY CAPITALISM

The formation of monopoly capitalism dates to the late nineteenth century but first gained primacy in the United States in the 1920s. It spread to Western Europe and Japan in the thirty-year boom following the Second World War. The concept of surplus, discussed by Baran and Sweezy in the 1950s, captures the essence of a capitalism dominated by monopolies. I was won over by their work, which enriched the Marxist critique of capitalism, and in the 1970s I began reformulating it to accord to the emergence of generalized monopoly capitalism.

My first reformulation of generalized monopoly capitalism dates back to 1978, when I gave an interpretation of the response of capital to the new crisis, which started in 1971 to 1975. My interpretation identified three emerging trends: (1) the centralized control of the economy by the monopolies; (2) the growing globalization, including relocation of manufacturing industries to the periphery; and (3) financialization. A book, *Let's Not Wait for 1984!*, co-authored with Andre Gunder Frank in 1978, went unnoticed, probably because our theories were ahead of their time. Today, the three dimensions of the crisis are glaringly obvious to everyone.

We had to give a name to this new phase. We considered the expression "late monopoly capital." However, the modifier "late," like the prefix "post," did not explicitly indicate the content and scope of what was new. The adjective "generalized" on the other hand indicated that the monopolies were now in a position to reduce all or almost all economic activity to subcontracting. Family farming, discussed in my recent writings, is the best example.

The domination of the economy by generalized monopoly capitalism required, and facilitated, changes in the way political life was managed. In the central countries, there arose a new political culture of consensus, which in effect depoliticized politics. It replaced the previous culture of parties on Right and Left, which gave scope and meaning to bourgeois democracy and accommodated class struggle within its framework. The terms "market" and "democracy" are contradictory. The market is in fact a "non-market," because it is managed by generalized monopolies. In the peripheries, the management of the economy by the local dominant super-class similarly negates democracy. There may be a great diversity and variety of political movements, but these rarely challenge in a fundamental way the power of the local ruling class. In that sense, politics are depoliticized here as well.

THE TRIUMPH OF ABSTRACT CAPITAL

Capitalism, in the form it took since the Industrial Revolution of the nine-teenth century, reflected a historical reality crucial to understanding the logic of its *modus operandi*. The new master class, consisting of individuals and families tied to historically determined and defined economic entities, gradually established itself as the dominant class in the political system. They owned the capital, or at least most of it, of their factories and financial and commercial firms. They were a real "concrete" bourgeoisie, which, by its ownership of private property, assumed direct management of the economy through engagement in competitive markets. It was this concrete competi-tion that Marx analyzed to probe the transformation of value systems into price systems. Additionally, the monetary macro-economic management of nineteenth-century capitalism was grounded in the Gold Standard, where gold served as a concrete commodity money. This management of the col-lective interests of capitalism, transcending those of individual capitalists, operated within the political framework of the nation state, thereby ensuring that capital accumulation was consistent with the political management of the nation, ideally through bourgeois democracy.

Today, at every decisive level the reality is quite different. Concreteness is disappearing, while an abstract reproduction of capital is gaining ground. The abstract nature of capitalism today, or more exactly of capital, is tan-tamount to permanent insurmountable chaos. Capitalist accumulation has always been synonymous with disorder, at least in the sense Marx gave to the term, namely, a system that moves from one disequilibrium to another, drift-ing along wherever class struggle and power rivalries carry it. Nevertheless, the disorder was kept within reasonable limits by three factors: effective competition among the diffuse sources of capital; state management of the production system within a national framework; and the discipline imposed by the Gold Standard. Abstract capitalism has erased these limits; the violence of dislocations associated with lurching from crisis to crisis has increased. Analysis of today's abstract capitalism reveals that this system is not viable and that its collapse, already underway, is inevitable. In this sense, contem-porary capitalism deserves to be described as senile. Hence my designation: the Autumn of Capitalism.

THE FINANCIALIZATION AND GLOBALIZATION OF CAPITALISM

Abstract capitalism dominates the global economy today. Globalization is the name that the monopolies have given to the requirements through which they control production systems in the peripheries. By the peripheries, we mean the whole world except the Triad partners — the United States, Europe and Japan. Globalization is a new stage of imperialism. It is another way of abol-ishing the right of peoples to freely choose their economic system. Abstract capitalism is a system that provides monopolies with rent. This rent is levied on the mass of surplus value that capital extracts from the exploitation of labour. To the extent that the monopolies operate on the periphery of the global system, monopoly rent is imperialist rent. The process of capital accumulation characterizing capitalism in all its historical forms is determined by monopolistic and imperialistic rent-maximization. This shift in the centre of gravity of capital accumulation is at the root of the incessant pursuit of revenue concentration for the purpose of securing monopoly rents. These rents are captured primarily by oligarchies, to the detriment of workers' wages and even the earnings of non-monopolistic capital.

This increasing imbalance is driving the financialization of the economic system. A growing proportion of the surplus can no longer be invested in broadening and deepening production systems. Consequently, *financial* investment of the surplus is the only viable outlet available to monopoly-driven accumulation. Institutional changes facilitating financialization include, among others: (1) changing management doctrine from long-term profitability in the real economy to the short-term objective of maximum shareholder value; (2) replacing pay-as-you-go arrangements by funded pensions systems; (3) adoption of flexible exchange rates; and (4) shifting interest rate determination from central banks to supply and demand in the market.

Thirty giant banks located in the Triad have effective control over the creation and reproduction of financial assets. What are euphemistically called "markets" are actually the spheres in which the strategies of these dominant economic agents are deployed. Financialization, which increases inequalities in the distribution of income, also generates the growing surplus on which it then feeds. Financial investments, including speculative investments, continue to grow at dizzying rates far exceeding investment in productive capacity and GDP growth, which in part have become illusory. The colossal growth in financial investment requires — and in turn fuels — debt in all its forms, including sovereign debt. When governments claim they are pursuing the goal of debt reduction, they are deliberately lying. The strategy of the financialized monopolies depends on growth of debt, which they seek rather than oppose, since it is a financially attractive way to absorb surplus monopoly rent. Forced austerity policies allegedly designed to reduce debt actually increase it.

FINANCIAL OLIGARCHY AND GENERALIZED PROLETARIANIZATION

Generalized monopoly capitalism has transformed class structures both in the Triad and in the peripheries. In the centres, social polarization now pits a financial oligarchy, supported by new middle classes, against diverse dominated classes forming a "generalized proletariat." In the peripheries, polarization takes different forms, depending on whether or not the country is a major emerging economy.

Increasing concentration and centralization of capital defines the logic of accumulation on a global scale. It is important to distinguish between ownership and control of capital. For example, individuals may own shares in pension funds, but finance capital controls the management of these assets. Ideology extols the virtues of competition, but the benefits accrue to an increasingly limited number of oligopolies. This competition is neither perfect nor transparent, qualities it never had and which are foreign to capitalism as it continues to expand.

Capitalist domination is now so centralized that the way the bourgeoisie lives and organizes itself is not what it used to be. The bourgeoisie was once made up of stable, middle-class families; it shaped its personality and developed its projects over the long term. The resulting stability promoted confidence in bourgeois values and the influence of these values in society. To a large extent, that ruling class was accepted as such. It seemed to deserve privilege and wealth in return for the services it provided. It was usually a national bourgeoisie, sensitive to the interests of the nation, notwithstanding the ambiguities and limitations of this manipulated concept. The new ruling class has abandoned that vocation.

PLUTOCRACY: THE NEW RULING CLASS OF SENILE CAPITALISM

The new plutocracy is counted in tens of thousands, not in millions, as was the old bourgeoisie. Furthermore, this class includes many newcomers whose reputation is related more to their successful financial transactions than to their entrepreneurial role in technological breakthroughs. Their rapid rise contrasts starkly with that of their predecessors, whose ascent took many decades. The proliferation of new start-ups is noteworthy for their extreme instability, resulting in frequent failures, despite the laudatory and excessive rhetoric developed in their regard.

Centralization and concentration have reinforced the interpenetration of political and economic power. This is nothing new. The class nature of power, even in a democratic setting, dictates that the political class is always at the service of capital, while some powerful politicians have always been attracted by the prospect of a share in the capitalist bounty. This interpenetration is now approaching homogenization. This is a new phenomenon and is reflected in changes in ideological discourse.

The ideology of capitalism in the past focused on the virtues of ownership of property, especially smallholdings, which, because of their stability, were seen as conveyers of technological and social progress. By contrast, the new ideology praises "winners" and dismisses "losers" without further consideration. The image of success promoted by the dominant rhetoric is asymmetrical: success is claimed for the system, but failure is blamed on personal circumstance. This ideology, which supports a sort of "social Darwinism," is similar to that of criminal organizations. In both cases the winners are always right, even when their methods, while not necessarily criminal, border on the illegal and ignore common moral values.

CRONY CAPITALISM GOES GLOBAL

There is collusion between the world of business, auditors and rating agencies, while governments are tacitly complicit. The rating agencies, paid by the monopolies, consider themselves above the fray and vested with exclusive authority to lay down the rules of the game, setting limits for government action. We must dismiss these agencies lest we capitulate in advance, which is unworthy of any Left policy. We must reformulate the issue in a manner befitting a democracy: define the conflicting social interests, formulate proposals for a social compromise drawing on broad popular support, and determine the requirements with which monopoly capital must comply.

The economic and political spheres have merged in the power structure of contemporary capitalism. As Marx, Polanyi and Braudel understood, capitalism cannot be reduced to the market, as dominant discourse repeats *ad nauseam*. In contemporary capitalism, the principal players are oligopolies and the state. Collusion in the new capitalism resembles what it was in its early days, although it waned considerably in the nineteenth and twentieth centuries. Consider the Republic of Venice, which was run as a company of very rich merchants, or the Colbertist and Elizabethan periods, ruled by absolute monarchs. In drawing this parallel, we are suggesting that capitalism is now obsolete and has entered a senile phase.

The logic of contemporary capitalism resembles what some economists, sincere believers in the virtues of liberalism, called crony capitalism. The reference was to countries of East Asia and Latin America, viewed as corrupt in relation to the debt crises of the 1990s. Cronyism now also applies to capitalism in present-day United States and Europe. Again, current ruling class behaviour comes close to what we know about Mafia behaviour.

The system is unable to react to this trend because it is quite simply incapable of challenging the centralization of capital. The measures it takes are reminiscent of late nineteenth century anti-trust laws (the Sherman Act), which had limited effectiveness. A new law (the Sarbanes-Oxley Act) legitimizes greater involvement by judges in business life. It is likely that the judiciary will get involved in the collusion game it claims to be eradicating.

The political system in contemporary capitalism is comfortable with representative democracy, which we may call "low-intensity democracy." You are free to vote for whomever you want but it makes no difference because the market rather than Parliament decides. It also tolerates the autocratic power and farcical elections that exist in other contexts.

THE NEW BUSINESS CLASS IN THE PERIPHERIES

The centre-periphery distinction has been a feature of global capitalist expansion from its inception, five centuries ago. The local ruling classes in the countries of peripheral capitalism, whether colonies or independent nations, have always been subordinate allies who have benefited from their integration into the global capitalist system. There is considerable diversity among these classes, which dominated their societies before their submission to capitalism and imperialism. The transformations they underwent after integration were no less considerable. In some cases, former political masters became major landowners, and old state aristocracies were modernized. Political independence replaced them by new bureaucracies and state bourgeoisies. These new ruling classes, at least initially, had legitimacy in the eyes of the population because of their association with national liberation movements.

Yet here, too, in the pre-1950 colonial period and in the neo-colonial era (1950–1980), the local ruling classes benefited from a relative stability. For a long time, successive generations of the aristocracy and the new bourgeoisie adhered to ethical and national value systems. The new political generation that led national liberations did likewise. The men and, to a lesser extent, the women who served as their representatives enjoyed varying degrees of legitimacy.

The upheavals caused by global oligopolistic capitalism have replaced the old ruling classes in the periphery by a new class of *affairistes*. This term is common in Francophone countries of the South. The *affairistes* are ostensibly engaged in business, but they are not creative entrepreneurs. They derive their wealth from their political contacts, domestic and foreign, government and corporate. They operate as well-remunerated intermediaries, enjoying a politically derived income that constitutes the major part of their wealth. These *affairistes* do not have any system of moral and national values. As caricatures of their alter egos in the dominant centres, their purview is limited to their personal success, money and greed, which they conceal behind their professed praise of free enterprise. Mafia behaviour is not far away. This new class is an integral part of the lumpen-development that characterizes most of the countries of the South. By contrast, in emerging countries, the dominant social bloc is different. The state is committed to a strategy for social transformation, whatever its limitations. This gives the regime a certain legitimacy, which is absent in countries dominated by a comprador state and a comprador bourgeoisie.

However, this is bound up with three illusions. The first pretends that emergence within global capitalism and through capitalist means will allow these countries to catch up; the second ignores the limitations of what would in fact be possible within this framework; and the third involves the possibility of social and political conflict. Together, these illusions open the door to a variety of possible changes, ranging from the best, that is, moving towards socialism, to the worst, entailing failure and re-compradorization.

A GENERALIZED BUT SEGMENTED PROLETARIAT

The segmentation of the proletariat is not new. The concept of the proletariat was more evident when it applied to factory workers in the nineteenth century or to Fordist industrial workers in the twentieth. Their concentration in workplaces facilitated solidarity in struggles and maturation of political consciousness, cultivating certain *ouvriéristes* forms of Marxism. The more recent fragmentation of production, facilitated by technological change, has weakened worker solidarity and created perceptions of divergent interests.

The proletariat appeared to shrink at the very moment it was becoming generalized. Numerous forms of small, independent production, and millions of small traders, farmers and craft workers disappeared, replaced by subcontractors and superstores. Ninety percent of workers, in both goods and services, are now employees, whose wages and salaries show disparities far exceeding the training costs for the qualifications required.

But feelings of solidarity are being revived. "We represent the 99%," claims the Occupy Movement. While 80 percent would be more accurate, this movement represents the overwhelming majority of the working world. There are two important aspects to this phenomenon: it points to the fact that capital exploits everyone, and exploitation and the violence associated with it come in a variety of forms and pose a challenge to the Left. The Left therefore cannot ignore contradictions within the people without abandoning the project of making objectives converge. This in turn suggests a need for diversity in organizational forms and actions deployed by the new, generalized proletariat. The ideology of social movements often ignores these challenges. Going on the offensive inevitably requires the creation of intellectual centres capable of conceptualizing the unity of strategic objectives.

The transformations in the economic basis and class structures of the system have modified the conditions in which power is exercised. Political domination is now expressed through a new kind of ruling class, including a media priesthood, wholly at the service of generalized monopoly capital. The ideology promoting the individual as paramount and the illusions of a movement that seeks to change the world without addressing the question of how workers and peoples are going to capture power, reinforce the hegemony of capital.

A SHIFT IN THE CENTRE OF GRAVITY OF GLOBAL CAPITALISM?

Do the victories of anti-imperialist struggles waged by states and peoples of the peripheries set the stage for socialism or the emergence of new capitalist centres? Current conditions seem to pit the decline of the old centres of the Triad against the rapid development of emerging countries like China. Could the current crisis therefore lead to renewed capitalist growth centred on Asia and South America? In other words, do the successes of the anti-imperialist struggles in emerging countries set the stage not for socialism, but for a new, albeit less polarized, capitalist expansion?

The main argument in my critique of the possibility of catch-up growth in the peripheries is grounded in the specific historical path of industrial capitalism, which many now propose as the sole model. This model was from the outset based on mass expulsion of the peasantry. The model was sustainable only because of a safety valve: mass emigration to the Americas. This experience cannot be replicated today by the peripheries, which account for nearly 80 percent of the world's population. Five or six Americas would be needed to catch up by imitation! Catching up is still an illusion and initiatives that appear to be making headway will inevitably fail. That is why we contend that anti-imperialist struggles are also potentially anti-capitalist. If catching up is impossible, then trying a different approach becomes necessary.

Taking a long-term view of emerging country development, catch-up growth is by no means assured. In the short term, to assess emerging country success in terms of accelerated growth within global capitalism and through capitalist methods reinforces the illusion that catching up is indeed possible. The same illusion accompanied twentieth-century experiments known as the first wave in the "Awakening of the South," presented as "catching up through the socialist path." We analyzed the contradictions of the "Bandung Project" (1955–1980), which strived to unite the working classes and the national bourgeoisies as allies in the liberation struggles with incompatible objectives.

A CONFLICT WITH GREAT POTENTIAL FOR PROGRESS

Today, the collective imperialism of the Triad is deploying all the economic, financial and military means at its disposal to perpetuate its domination over the world. Emerging countries that attempt to counteract the Triad's advantages, including technological superiority, exclusive access to the world's natural resources and military control over the planet, inevitably clash with it. There is a positive side to this clash: it helps to dispel emerging country illusions about their ability to advance within the system. It also provides popular and democratic forces with an opportunity to influence the course of events so as to make headway on the long road to socialism.

Emergence is not measured in terms of long-term high growth rates of GDP or exports, i.e., that last more than a decade. Rather, it involves sustained growth in industrial production and an increasing ability of emerging country industries to be competitive on a global basis. The economic competitiveness of productive activities refers to the production system as a whole, not the competitiveness of certain production facilities considered in isolation. Through relocation or subcontracting, multinationals operating in the South can set up local production facilities, whether they are subsidiaries of these transnational corporations or independent firms, capable of exporting to global markets. It then becomes possible to refer to these local entities as "competitive" — to use the language of conventional economics.

This truncated concept of competitiveness derives from a highly empiricist method. The competitiveness is that of the production system. This assumes that the economy in question is composed of productive firms and industries sufficiently interdependent to constitute a system. The competitiveness depends on a variety of economic and social factors, including the overall levels of worker education and training in every category, and the effectiveness of all institutions managing national economic policy, which encompasses taxation, business law, labour rights, credit, government support and so forth.

EMERGING ECONOMIES AND AFFIRMATION OF SOVEREIGNTY

The concept of emergence involves a holistic and political approach. A country is emerging only to the extent that its government is guided by the goal of building an autocentric economy, albeit one that is open to the world, thereby affirming its national economic sovereignty. Its complex, multifaceted and mutually complementary set of objectives means that the affirmation of sovereignty will involve every aspect of its economic life. This contrasts sharply with the objectives of comprador power, which contents itself with adjusting the country's prevailing growth model to the requirements of the dominant world system.

My proposed definition of emergence has so far said nothing about the overall objective of the political strategy, whether capitalist or socialist, adopted by the state and society concerned. Yet, this issue is an integral part of the debate, for the vision of its ruling class has a major impact on the success of a country's emergence. The relationship between policies shaping emergence and their attendant social changes does not depend only on the internal coherence of these policies, but also on their degree of complementarity or conflict with social changes. Social struggles cannot be expected to accommodate the project of the ruling class; they are in fact one of the determinants of the project.

Current experiments reveal diversity and fluctuation in these relationships. Emergence is often accompanied by even greater inequality. Inequalities, whether benefiting a tiny minority or a larger swath of the middle classes, may contrast with the impoverishment of the majority of workers. On the other hand, inequality may be accompanied by improved living conditions of workers where the rate of growth in wages is lower than that of the incomes of individuals benefiting from the system. In other words, the policies implemented may or may not affect the link between emergence and impoverishment. Emergence is not a fixed and final status describing the country concerned; rather, it is made up of successive stages which may or may not lead to an impasse.

Similarly, the relationship between an emerging economy and the world economy is itself constantly changing. It has the potential to strengthen or weaken sovereignty and social solidarity in the country. For example, growth in exports can weaken or strengthen the relative autonomy of an emerging economy *vis-à-vis* the global system.

Emergence is a political project. Aside from its success in terms of economic indicators, an emerging economy's resilience is tested by its ability to reduce domination by capitalist centres. We have defined dominance in terms of control over technological development, natural resources, the global financial and monetary system, media and weapons of mass destruction. And we have concluded that the objectives of the emerging countries are in conflict with the strategic objectives of the Triad and that the level of violence depends on the degree to which their challenges to the centres are radical and far-reaching. The economic success of emerging countries is therefore inseparable from their foreign policy. Are they aligned with the politico-military coalition of the Triad? Do they accept NATO strategies? Or are they attempting to oppose them?

POLITICAL PROJECTS, SOCIAL BASES AND LEGITIMACY

Emergence is impossible without a state policy. This policy must be founded on a wide social base giving it legitimacy. It must implement a coherent project for an autocentric national production system, assuring the vast majority of the working classes reap the benefits of growth. The opposite of an authentic emergence project of this type is lumpen-development, a unilateral submission to the requirements of global capitalism as organized by the generalized monopolies. We are making free use of this term, which was employed by the late Andre Gunder Frank to analyze a similar trend, though he did so with reference to conditions in a different time and place. Today, lumpen-development is what results from the accelerated social disintegration generated by a model imposed by the imperialist centres. It manifests itself as a dramatic growth in survival activities (the so-called informal sector) or, stated differently, by the impoverishment inherent in the unilateral logic of capital accumulation.

It will be observed that we have not categorized emergence as either capitalist or socialist. Emergence is a process that combines, in a complementary or a conflicting way, the logic of capitalist management of the economy with that of non-capitalist (and potentially socialist) management of society and politics. Certain emerging economies can be categorized as either capitalist or socialist because they have no connection to lumpen-development processes. They have not impoverished the working classes; indeed, they have given rise to a modest or even marked improvement in living conditions. Two of these experiments, carried out in Korea and Taiwan, are plainly capitalist. This is not the place to discuss the specific historical circumstances that led to a successful emergence project in these two countries. Two other countries — China and Vietnam — inherited the legacy of revolutionary aspirations carried out in the name of socialism. Cuba might be included in this group if it could overcome the contradictions it is currently experiencing.

By contrast, there are examples of emergence that have made extensive use of lumpen-development processes. India is the best example. Many aspects of what an emerging economy requires and creates are in evidence here: state policy supporting a large industrial system of production; an expanding middle class associated with this system; growing technological and educational capabilities; and international policies capable of preserving the country's independence on the world stage. However, the vast majority of the population face accelerated impoverishment. What we have here is a hybrid system combining emergence and lumpen-development; one might even contend they have a complementary relationship. Without making too sweeping a generalization, we believe that all other countries considered to be emerging — including Brazil, South Africa and others — belong to this hybrid category. There are also cases, in many other countries of the South, where the elements of emergence are barely noticeable, with the result that lumpen-development processes dominate.

THE IMPLOSION OF CONTEMPORARY CAPITALISM

Generalized, globalized and financialized monopoly capitalism now has nothing to offer the world, other than the sad prospect of humanity's self-destruction, and further deployment of capital accumulation is inexorably heading in this direction. Capitalism has outlived its usefulness, producing conditions that suggest a necessary transition toward a higher stage of civilization. The implosion of the system, caused by the ongoing loss of control over its internal contradictions, signals the "autumn of capitalism." This "Autumn of Capitalism" has not coincided with a "Springtime of the Peoples." This would imply that workers and peoples in struggle have accurately gauged not what is required to "overcome the crisis of capitalism" but rather to "exit from a "capitalism in crisis" (the title of one of my recent works). This has not happened, at least not yet.

The distance between the "Autumn of Capitalism" and a "Springtime of the Peoples" is creating a perilous situation. The battle between defenders of the capitalist order and those who are able to enlist the forces of humanity on the long road to socialism, envisaged as a higher stage of civilization, has barely begun. Every conceivable option is open, from the most civilized to the most barbaric.

The very existence of the gap requires explanation. Capitalism is not only a system based on the exploitation of labour by capital, but also a global system whose deployment gives rise to polarization. Imperialism and capitalism are two sides of the same coin, two inextricably linked aspects of the same phenomenon, namely, historical capitalism. For most of the twentieth century, workers and oppressed peoples challenged this system, achieving much success through a long wave of struggles ending in the 1980s. The successes included revolutions conducted under the banners of Marxism and communism; reforms won with a view to gradual socialist development; and triumphs of national liberation movements of oppressed and colonized peoples. Separately and collectively, they forged power relations that worked to the benefit of workers and peoples. However, the wave faltered without creating conditions that would have facilitated further breakthroughs. In running out of steam, it allowed monopoly capital to resume its offensive and restore its absolute and unilateral power while the contours of a new wave of revolt were barely emerging. In the gray landscape of a night that has not ended, of a morning that has not yet broken, monsters and phantoms emerge. For while the project of generalized monopoly capitalism is indeed abhorrent, the responses of the forces of refusal continue to reside in the shadows.

The contemporary capitalist system is based on the false premise that markets are self-regulating, whereas in reality they are volatile. Nevertheless, the imbalance in the opposing social forces is so great that this ridiculous idea has gained widespread acceptance. In periods when the opposing forces are more evenly balanced, as was the case during the aforementioned wave of the last century, social actors were obliged to develop their intelligence to consolidate their gains. By contrast, periods of extreme imbalance place a high premium on stupidity, allowing capital to imagine it can do whatever it wants for eternity, since history has supposedly reached the apogee of its development following the final defeat of socialism. The astounding mediocrity of the political actors of our era is but a pale reflection of this premium on stupidity.

NOTE

The ideas raised in this afterword were developed by the author in his book, *L'implosion du capitalisme contemporain* (Éditions Delga, Paris 2012).

BIBLIOGRAPHY

Akbar, M.J. 2008. "The Arc of Turbulence." *The India Lectures*. 28 August. Ottawa: IDRC.

Ali, Abdel Gadir. 2004. *Structural Adjustment Programs and Poverty in Sub-Saharan Africa: 1985–1995*. <http://www.idrc.ca/en/ev-56338-201-1-DO_TOPIC.html>.

Amsden, Alice H. 1989. *Asia's Next Giant*. Oxford University Press.

____. 2003. *The Rise of "The Rest": Challenges to the West from Late-Industrializing Economies*. Oxford University Press.

____. 2007. *Escape from Empire: The Developing World's Journey through Heaven and Hell*. Cambridge, MA: MIT Press.

Arora, Vivek, and Athanasios Vamvakidis. 2010. "Gauging China's Influence." *Finance and Development* 47, 4 (December).

Arrighi, Giovanni. 1994. *The Long Twentieth Century: Money, Power and the Origins of Our Times*. London and New York: Verso Publishers.

Ball, Robert 1993. "Hyperactive Asia." 28 June. *Time*.

Barnet, Richard J., and Ronald E. Muller. 1974. *Global Reach*. New York: Simon and Schuster.

Bauer, Otto. 1919. "Der Weg Zum Socialismus." Pamphlet. Vienna.

Beckford, George L. (ed.). 1975. *Caribbean Economy, Dependence and Backwardness*. Kingston, Jamaica: Institute of Social and Economic Research, University of the West Indies.

Beeching, Jack. 1975. *The Chinese Opium Wars*. London: Hutchinson.

Best, Lloyd, and Kari Levitt. 1968. *Export Propelled Growth? Industrialisation in the Carribbean*, Vol. II. *Pure Plantation Economy*. Montreal: McGill University.

____. 2009. *Essays on the Theory of Plantation Economy: A Historical and Institutional Approach to Caribbean Economic Development*. Kingston: University of West Indies Press.

BIS (Bank for International Settlements). 2004. "Triennial Central Bank Survey of Foreign Exchange and Derivatives Market Activity." April. <http://www.bis.org/publ/rpfx05.htm>.

Blanchard, Jean-Marc F. 2007. "China, Multinational Corporations, and Globalization: Beijing and Microsoft Battle Over the Opening of China's Gates." *Asian Perspective* 31, 3: 67–102.

Block, Fred. 2001. "Karl Polanyi and the Writing of the Great Transformation." Presented at the Eight International Karl Polanyi Conference, *Economy and Democracy*, in Mexico City, Mexico.

Borkanau, Frantz. 1938. *Austria and After*. London: Faber & Faber.

Breit, William, and Barry T. Hirsh, eds. 1995. "W. Arthur Lewis." In *Lives of the Laureates: Thirteen Nobel Economists*. Cambridge, MA: MIT Press.

Browne, Martha Steffy. 1981. "Erinnerungen an des Mises-Privatserninar," *Wirtschaftspoluische Blatter* 28, 4: 110–20.

Cannan, Edwin. 1997. *Collected Works of Edwin Cannan*. Vol. VII. Alan Ebenstein (ed.). London: Routledge/Thoemmes Press.

Cardoso, Eliana, and Albert Fishlow. 1992. "Latin American Economic Development: 1950–1980." *Journal of Latin American Studies* 24. Quincentenary Supplement: The Colonial and Post Colonial Experience. Five Centuries of Spanish and

Portuguese America. Cambridge University Press. <http://www.jstor.org/pss/156952>.

Chang, Ha-Joon. 2002. *Kicking Away the Ladder: Development Strategy in Historical Perspective*. London: Anthem Press.

Chapman, Anne. 2010. *European Encounters with the Yamana People of Cape Horn, Before and After Darwin*. New York: Cambridge University Press.

Cohen, R.B., et al., eds. 1979. *The Multinational Corporation: A Radical Approach. Papers by Stephen Herbert Hymer*. Cambridge, MA: Cambridge University Press.

Common Fund for Commodities. 2005. *Basic Facts*, May.

Condliffe, J.B. 1933. *Economic Yearbook of the League of Nations 1932–33*. Geneva: League of Nations.

Craver, Earlene. 1986. "The Emigration of Austrian Economists." *History of Political Economy* 18, 1: 1–32.

Cristi, F.R. 1986. "Hayek on the Impossibility of Socialism." Paper presented at the annual meeting of the Canadian Political Science Association, Winnipeg, June.

Crozier, Michel, Samuel Huntington and Joji Watanuk. 1975. *The Crisis of Democracy. Report on the Governability of Democracies to the Trilateral Commission*. New York: New York University Press.

Davis, Mike. 2000. *Late Victorian Holocausts: El Niño Famines and the Making of the Third World*. London: Verso.

Dillard, D. 1948. "The Keynesian Revolution and Economic Development." *Journal of Economic History* VIII, 2.

Dostaler, Gilles, and Diane Ethier (eds.). 1988. *Friedrich Hayek: Philosophie, Economie et Politique*. Montreal: Association Canadienne-Francaise pour l'Avancement des Sciences.

Drucker, Peter. 1978. "The Polanyis." In *Adventures of a Bystander*. New York: Harper & Row.

Duczynska, Ilona. 1978. *Workers in Arms: The Austrian Schutzbund and the Civil War of 1934*. New York: Monthly Review Press.

Duczyska, Ilona, and Karl Polanyi. 1963. *The Plough and the Pen: Writings from Hungary, 1930–1956*. London: Peter Owen.

Economist. 2010. "Dating Game: When Will China Overtake America?" 16 December.

Eichengreen, Barry. 1996. *Globalizing Capital: A History of the International Monetary System*. Princeton University Press.

Einstein, Albert. 1931. Speech at the California Institute of Technology, Pasadena, California, February 16. *New York Times*, February 17.

Feinstein, C.H. (ed.). 1967. *Socialism, Capitalism and Economic Growth: Essays Presented to Maurice Dobb*. Cambridge University Press.

Fischer, Ernst. 1959 [1974]. *An Opposing Man*. New York: Liveright.

Fischer, George, and Peter Rosner. 1987. *Politische Okonomie und Wirtschaftspoliuk im Austro Marxismus*. Vienna: Osterreichischer Bundesverlag.

Fischer, Stanley. 1999. "The Financial Crisis in Emerging Markets: Some Lessons." Conference of the Economic Strategy Institute, Washington DC, 28 April. <http://www.imf.org/external/np/speeches/1999/042899.htm>.

Furtado, Celso. 1983. *Accumulation and Development: The Logic of Industrial Civilization*. Translated by Suzette Macedo. Oxford: Martin Robertson and Co.

Galbraith, John Kenneth. 1965. *The Underdeveloped Country: The Massey Lectures*.

Canadian Broadcasting Corporation.

Gallagher, John, and Ronald Robinson. 1953. "The Imperialism of Free Trade." *The Economic History Review* 2nd series, VI (1).

Garrison, R.W., and I.M. Kirzner. 1987. "Friedrich August von Hayek (1899 -)." In *The New Palgrave Dictionary of Economics* Vol. 2. London: Macmillan Press.

Gerschenkron, Alexander. 1962. *Economic Backwardness in Historical Perspective: A Book of Essays*. Belknap Press of Harvard University Press.

Ghosh, Jayati. 2011. "The Challenge of Ensuring Full Employment in the Twenty-First Century." *The Indian Journal of Labour Economics* 54, 1.

Global Metro Monitor. 2010. "The Path to Economic Recovery: A Preliminary Overview of 150 Global Metropolitan Economies in the Wake of the Great Recession." December. Brookings Institute and LSE Cities.

Government of Canada. 1968. *Report of the Task Force on the Structure of Canadian Industry* [The Watkins Report]. January. Ottawa: Privy Council Office.

___. 1972. *Foreign Direct Investment in Canada* [the Gray Report]. Ottawa.

Greenspan, Alan. 1998. "Address to the Federal Reserve Bank of Chicago." May 7.

Grenville, Stephen. 1998. "The Asia Crisis, Capital Flows and the International Financial Architecture." May 21. Talk to Monash University Law School, Melbourne.

Haberler, Gottfried von. 1981. "Mises Private Seminar." *Wirtschafispolitische Blatter* 28, 4: 121–26.

Hamilton, Alexander. 1791 [2007]. *Report on the Subject of Manufactures*. New York: Cosimo Inc.

Hartwell, Ronald M. 1995. *A History of the Mont Pelerin Society.* Indianapolis: Liberty Fund.

Hautmann. 1971. *Die Verlorene Raterrepublik,* Vienna: Europaverlag.

Hayek, Friedrich A. 1929. *Das Mieterschutzproblem.* Wien : Steyrermühl-Verl.

___. 1931. *Prices and Production.* New York: Augustus M. Kelly Publishers.

___. 1944. *The Road to Serfdom.* London: Routledge Press.

___. 1949. "The Intellectuals and Socialism." *University of Chicago Law Review* Spring.

___. 1979. *A Conversation with Friedrich von Hayek.* American Enterprise Institute.

Heilbroner, Robert. 1992. "21st Century Capitalism." Massey Lectures. Concord, ON: Anansi.

Hewitt, Tom, Hazel Johnson and Dave Wield (eds.). 1992. *Industrialisation and Development.* Oxford University Press in association with the Open University.

Hicks, John R. 1981. "LSE and the Robbins Circle." In *Collected Essays on Economic Theory.* Vol. I: *Wealth and Welfare.* Oxford: Martin Robertson.

Hirschman, Albert O. 1981. *Essays in Trespassing: Economics to Politics and Beyond.* New York: Cambridge University Press.

Hutcheson, T.W. 1981. *The Politics and Philosophy of Economics:* Marxians, Keynesians, and Austrians. New York: Basil Blackwell.

Hutton, Will. 1994. "Markets Threaten Democracy's Fabric." *The Guardian Weekly* 16 January: 21.

Hymer, Stephen. 1973. "Notes on the United Nations Reports on Multinational Corporations in World Development." 6 Nov. Geneva: United Nations. (Mimeo).

Ingham, Barbara, and Paul Mosley. 2010. "Marvellous Intellectual Feasts: Arthur Lewis at the London School of Economics 1933–1948." Brooks World Poverty

Institute Working Paper 124.

Innis, Harold. 1930. *The Fur Trade in Canada: An Introduction to Canadian Economic History*. New Haven: Yale University Press.

Jensen, Michael, and William Meckling. 1976. "Theory of the Firm: Managerial Behavior, Agency Costs and Ownership Structure." *Journal of Financial Economics* 3, 4 (October).

Johnson, Chalmers. 2008. "Why the US Has Really Gone Broke: The Economic Disaster that Is Military Keynesianism." *Le Monde Diplomatique* Feburary.

Johnson, Elizabeth, and Donald Moggridge (eds.). 1972. *Essays in Biography: The Collected Writings of John Maynard Keynes*. Vol. X. Edited by Elizabeth Johnson and Donald Moggridge. U.K.: Royal Economic Society and Macmillan Press Ltd.

Johnson, Simon. 2009. "The Quiet Coup." *The Atlantic* May.

Kalecki, M. 1943. "The Political Aspects of Full Employment." *Political Quarterly*.

Keynes, John Maynard. 1971a. *The Collected Writings of John Maynard Keynes*. Vol. IX, *Essays in Persuasion*. Edited by A. Robinson, E. Johnson and D. Moggridge. London: Macmillan/New York: St Martin's Press.

____. 1971b. *The Collected Writings of John Maynard Keynes*. Vol. XXV, *Activities: 1940–1944, Shaping the Post-War World: the Clearing Union*. Edited by Austin Robinson, Elizabeth Johnson and Donald Moggridge. London: Macmillan/New York: St Martin's Press.

____. 1944. "Proposal for an International Monetary Fund, Annex A of the Washington Conversations Article VII, Memorandum by the Minister of State." 7 February: 13; <http://discovery.nationalarchives.gov.uk/SearchUI/Details?uri=C9056018>.

Kierans, Eric, and Walter Stewart. 2001. *Remembering*. Toronto: Stoddart.

Kirzner, Israel. 1986. "Ludwig von Mises and Friedrich von Hayek." In N. Leser (ed.), "Der Zeitgeschichtliche Hintergrund des Wien und Osterreich im Fin-de-Siecle."

Kitchen, Martin. 1980. *The Coming of Austrian Fascism*. London: Croom Helm; and Montreal: McGill-Queen's Uiversity Press.

Lal, Deepak. 1983. *The Poverty of Development Economics*. London: Institute of Economic Affairs, Hobart Paperback 16.

Leser, Nobert. 1986. "Der Zeitgeschichtliche Hintergrund des Wien und Osterreich im Fin-de-Siecle." Papers of a conference held in Vienna May 1–3, 1985.

Levitt, Kari. 1964. "Karl Polanyi and *Co-Existence*." *Co-Existence* 2, November.

____. 1970. *Silent Surrender: The Multinational Corporation in Canada*. Toronto: Macmillan.

____. 1982. "Stephen Hymer: A Memoir." *The Review* VI, 2 (Fall): 253–79.

____. 1982. "Culture and Economic Systems." Presented at the 1982 International Conference on Economics and Management, Tokyo, 14–15 July.

____. 1989. "Polanyi's Intellectual Adversary: Hayek from Vienna to Chicago." *Monthly Review* 41, June.

____ (ed.). 1990. *The Life and Work of Karl Polanyi: A Celebration*. Montreal: Black Rose Books.

____. 1992. "Karl Polanyi As Socialist." Paper delivered at the Fourth International Karl Polanyi Conference, Montreal, Canada.

____. 1998. "Back to the Future: Insights from Karl Polanyi's Analysis of the World Economic Crisis of the 1930s." Paper presented at the International Sociological Association XIV Congress of Sociology, Montreal.

___. 2004. "The Transformation of the World System: Some Insights from the Work of Karl Polanyi." Keynote address to a one-day conference on "Karl Polanyi and the Transformation of the Contemporary World System" in Budapest, Hungary, November 5–6.

___. 2005. *Reclaiming Development: Independent Thought and Caribbean Community*. Kingston and Miami: Ian Randle Publishers.

___. 2005. "Les principaux concepts dans le travail de Karl Polanyi et leur pertinence actuelle." In Ph. Clancier, F. Joannès, P. Rouillard and A. Tenu (eds.), *Autour de Polanyi, Vocabulaires, théories et modalités des échanges*. Paris: Colloques de la Maison René-Ginouvès.

___. 2010. "Social Dividend as a Citizen Right." Presentation to the 13th Basic Income Earth Network Congress at a roundtable entitled "Basic Income as a Public Policy to Enhance Democracy and Global Justice." Sao Paulo, Brazil, 30 June–2 July.

Levillm Kari, and Lloyd Best. 1975. "Foundations of Plantation Economy." In G. Beckford (ed.), *Caribbean Economy*. I.S.E.R.: Jamaica.

Levitt, Kari, and Kenneth McRobbie (eds.). 2006 [2000]. *Karl Polanyi in Vienna: The Contemporary Significance of The Great Transformation*. Montreal: Black Rose Books.

Levitt, Kari, and Marguerite Mendell. 1987. "Karl Polanyi his Life and Times," *Studies in Political Economy* 22, Spring.

Lewis, Arthur W. 1978a. "The Evolution of the International Economic Order." *Schumpeter Lectures*. Princeton: Princeton University Press.

___. 1978b. *Growth and fluctuations 1870–1913*. London: George Allen and Unwin.

Lindsey, Brink. 2001. "The Decline and Fall of the First Global Economy." *Reason* December.

Lipietz, Alain. 1987. *Mirages and Miracles: The Crisis in Global Fordism*. London: Verso.

Little, Ian M.D. 1982. *Economic Development: Theory, Policy, and International Relations*. New York: Basic Books.

Little, Ian M.D., Maurice Scott and Tibor Scitovski. 1970. *Industry Trade in Some Developing Countries*. Oxford University Press.

Machlup, Fritz. 1981. "Ludwig von Mises: The Academic Scholar Who Would Not Compromise," *Wirtschaftspolitische Blatter* 28, 4: 6–13.

Maddison, Angus. 2006. *The World Economy*. Paris: OECD.

Marshall, Alfred. 1907. *Principles of Economics: An Introductory Volume*. London: Macmillan.

Marx, Karl. 1959 [1932]. *The Economic and Philosophic Manuscripts of 1844*. Translated by Martin Milligan. Moscow: Progress Publishers.

___. 1973. *Grundrisse*. Penguin Books (Pelican ed.).

Marz, Eduard. 1984. *Autrian Banking and Financial Policy*. London: Weidenfeld Nicholson.

___. 1986. "Joseph A Schumpeter und die Osterreichische Schule der Narional Okonomie." In N. Leser (ed.).

McRobbie, Kenneth, and Kari Polanyi Levitt (eds.). 2006 [2000]. *Karl Polanyi in Vienna. The Contemporary Significance of the Great Transformation*. Montreal: Black Rose Books.

Mendell, Marguerite. 1990. "Karl Polanyi and Feasible Socialism." In Kari Levitt (ed.), *The Life and Work of Karl Polanyi*. Montreal: Black Rose Books.

Mirowski, Philip, and Dieter Plehwe (eds.). 2009. *The Road from Mont Pelerin: The*

Making of the Neoliberal Thought Collective. Cambridge: Harvard University Press.

Mises, Ludwig von. 1920. "Die Wirtschaftsrechnurg in Sozialistischen Gemeinwesen." ("Economic calculation in the Socialist Commonwealth"). *Archiv fur Sorialunssenschaft und Sozialpolitik* 47

___. 1922. *Die Gemeinwirtschaft: Untersuchungen über den Sozialismus*. Jena: Gustav Fischer.

___. 1978. *Notes and Recollections*. South Holland, IL: Libertarian Press.

___. 1924. "Neue Beitrage Zum Problem der Sozialistischen Wirtschaftsrechnung." *Archiv fur Sozialwissenshaft und Sozialpolitik* 51, 2.

Mises, Margit. 1976. *My Years with Ludwig von Mises*. New Rochelle, NY: Arlington House.

Morawetz, David. 1977. *Twenty-Five Years of Economic Development 1950 to 1975*. Baltimore: World Bank and Johns Hopkins University Press.

Mühleisen, Martin and Christopher Towe (eds.). 2004. "US Fiscal Policies and Priorities for Long-Run Sustainability." International Monetary Fund Occasonal Papewr 227. 7 January.

Myrdal, Gunnar. 1984. "International Inequality and Foreign Aid in Retrospect." In Gerald M. Meier and Dudley Seers (eds.) *Pioneers in Development*. Washington, DC and Oxford, UK: World Bank and Oxford University Press.

Needham, Joseph. 1954. *Science and Civilisation in China*. Cambridge: Cambridge University Press.

Nishiyama, Chiaki, and Kurt R. Luebe. 1984. *The Essence of Hayek*. Stanford, CA: Hoover Institute Press.

Nitzan, Jonathan, and Shimshon Bichler. 2004. *New Imperialism of New Capitalism*. Mimeograph. Montreal and Jerusalem. <www.bnarchives.net>.

Nye, Joseph. 1974. "Multinationals: The Game and the Rules: Multinational Corporations in World Politics" *Foreign Affairs* October.

Ocampo, J.A. 2000, "Rethinking the Development Agenda." eclac. <www.eclac. org/publicaciones/xml/1/7281/lcl1503i.pdf]//>.

Okita, Saburo. 1979. *Developing Economies and the Japanese Experience*. New Delhi: Indian Council of Cultural Relations.

___. 1981. "Development Strategy: A Japanese Perspective." In Haruo Nagamine Harua (ed.), *Nation-Building and Regional Development: The Japanese Experience*. Nagoya, Japan: Sukuri Asia for the United Nations Centre for Regional Development.

___. 1993. "Many Paths To Development." In Y Seyyid Abdulai, Samir Amin, Ahmne Ben Salah, Michel Camdessus et al. *Facing the Challenge: Responses to the Report of the South Commission*. Zed Books and the South Centre.

Patel, Surendra. 1993. "The Taming of Capitalism: The Historic Compromise." IDS Working Paper. Halifax, NS: Saint Mary's University.

___. 1995. *Technological Transformation, Volume V: The Historic Process*. Aldershot: Ashgate Publishing.

___. 2007. *Technological Transformation and Development in the South*. Edited by K. Ahooja-Patel and H. Veltmeyer. New Delhi: A.P.H. Publishing.

Patel, Surendra, Krishna Ahooja-Patel and Mahesh S. Patel. 1995. *Development Distance Between Nations*. New Delhi: Ashish Publishing House.

Pettifor, Anne (ed.). 2003. *Real World Economic Outlook: New Economics Foundation*. London: Palgrave.

Pigou, A. C. 1968. *The Theory of Unemployment.* New York: A.M. Kelley.

Polanyi, Karl. 1918 [1954]. "The Calling of this Generation." *Szabad gondolat* (June).

____. 1922. "Der geistesgeschichtliche Hintergrund des Moskauer Prozesses." [The Intellectual-Historical Background of the Moscow Trials.] English translation by Kari Polanyi Levitt. *Die Wage* 25, 29: 393–97.

____. 1925. "Neue Erwagungen zu unserer Theorie von Praxis." *Der Kampf.* [Some Reflections Concerning our Theory and Practice, translation by Kari Polanyi Levitt.] Reprinted as "On the Periphery of Austro-Marxist Theory" in Gerald Mozetic (ed.), *Austro-Marxistische Positionen* [1983]. Wien: Bohlan-Verlag.

____. 1932. "Economy and Democracy." *Oesterreichische Volkswirt* [Vienna].

____. 1933. "Der Mechanismus der Weltwirtschaftskrise." [The Mechanisms of the World Economic Crisis.] Translated by Kari Polanyi Levitt. *Oesterreichische Volkswirt.* [Vienna].

____. 1944 [2001]. *The Great Transformation: The Political and Economic Origins of Our Time.* Boston: Beacon Press.

____. 1945. "Universal Capitalism or Regional Planning?" *London Quarterly of World Affairs* 10, 3: 86–91.

____. 1947 [1968]. "Our Obsolete Market Mentality." In George Dalton (ed.), *Primitive, Archaic, and Modern Economics: Essays of Karl Polanyi.* New York: Anchor Books.

____. 1957. "The economy as instituted process." Polanyi, Arensberg and Pearson, eds.

Polanyi, Karl, with C.M. Arensberg and H.W. Pearson. 1957. *Trade and Market in the Early Empires.* Glencoe, IL: Free Press.

Prebisch, Raul. 1949/50. *The Economic Development of Latin America and Its Principal Problems.* New York: United Nations, Economic Commission for Latin America.

____. 1982. "Monetarism, Open Market Policies, and the Ideological Crisis." *Cepal Review* 17, August

Putzel, James. 2002. "Politics, the State, and the Impulse for Social Protection: The Implication of Karl Polanyi's Ideas for Understanding Development and Crisis." Crisis Working Paper 18, Oct. <http://eprints.lse.ac.uk/840/WP18JP.pdf>.

Rabinbach, Anson. 1983. *The Crisis of Austrian Socialism.* Chicago: University of Chicago Press.

____. (ed.). 1985. *The Austrian Socialist Experiment: Social Democracy and Austro Marxism, 1918–34.* Boulder CO: Western Press.

Ravallion, Martin, and Shaohua Chen. 2008. *The Developing World Is Poorer than We Thought but No Less Successful in the Fight Against Poverty.* World Bank.

Reich, Robert. 2012. "The Problem Isn't Outsourcing: It's that the Prosperity of Big Business Has Become Disconnected from the Well-Being of Most Americans." <http://robertreich.org/post/27527895909>.

Reuber, Grant, et al. 1973. *Private Foreign Investment in Development.* Oxford: Clarendon (for the OECD).

Reventlow, R. 1969 [1985]. *Zwischen Allierten und Bolscheunken: Arbeiterrate in Isterreich 1918 bis 1923.* Vienna: Europaverlag.

Robinson, Joan. 1972. "The Second Crisis in Economics: Richard T. Ely Lecture." *American Economic Review* LXII (2 May): 1–10.

Rodrik, Dani. 2000. "How Far Will International Economic Integration Go?" *Journal of Economic Perspectives* 14, 1. <http://pubs.aeaweb.org/doi/pdfplus/10.1257/jep.14.177>.

___. 2004. "Rethinking Growth Policies in the Developing World." Luca d'Agliano Lecture in Development Economics. Torino, Italy. October.

Rosner, Peter. 1988. "A Note on the Theories of the Business Cycle by Hilferding and Hayek." *History of Political Economy* 20, 2: 309–19.

___. 1990. "Karl Polanyi on Socialist Accounting." In Kari Levitt (ed.), *The Life and Work of Karl Polanyi*. Montreal: Black Rose Books

Rosner, Peter, and Georg Winkler. n.d. "Aspects of Austrian Economics." Working Paper 8407. Department of Economics, University of Vienna.

Ross, John. 2011. "The Central Date for China's GDP to Overtake the US at Market Exchange Rates Is 2019: A Study of Growth Assumptions and Analyses." *Key Trends in Globalisation* 15 February.

Routh, Guy. 1975. *The Origin of Economic Ideas*. London: Macmillan.

Saul, John Ralston. 1995. "1995 Massey Lectures: The Unconscious Civilization." <http://www.cbc.ca/ideas/massey-archives/1995/11/06/massey-lectures-1995-the-unconscious-civilization>.

Schlesinger, Rudolf (ed.). 1964. *Co-Existence*. November. London: Pergamon Press

Schorske, Carl E. 1981. *Fin-de-Sicle Vienna: Politics and Culture*. New York: Random House.

Seers, Dudley. 1983. *The Political Economy of Nationalism*. Oxford, UK: Oxford University Press.

Simon Johnson, Simon. 2008. "The Quiet Coup." *The Altantic Magazine* May. <http://www.theatlantic.com/magazine/archive/2009/05/the-quiet-coup/7364>.

Singer, Hans. 1985. "The Terms of Trade Controversy and the Evolution of Soft Financing: Early Years in the UN." In Meier and Seers (eds.), *Pioneers in Development*. London: Oxford University Press.

Sioh, Maureen. 2010. "The Hollow Within: Anxiety and Performing Postcolonial Financial Policies." *Third World Quarterly* 31, 4 (June): 581–97.

Skidelsky, Robert. 1992. *John Maynard Keynes: The Economist as Saviour*. London: Macmillan.

Soros, George. 1998a. Reuters newswire, June 11.

___. 1998b. Reuters newswire, July 8.

Stewart, Heather. 2012. "Wealth Doesn't Trickle Down — It Just Floods Offshore, Research Reveals." <http://www.guardian.co.uk/business/2012/jul/21/offshore-wealth-global-economy-tax-haven>.

Streissler, E.S. 1986. "Arma virumque cano: Friedrich von Wieser the Bard as economist." In N. Leser (ed.).

Tang, Sumei, E.A. Selvanathan and S. Selvanathan. 2008. "Foreign Direct Investment, Domestic Investment, and Economic Growth in China: A Time Series Analysis." World Institute for Development Economics Research *Research Paper* 2008/19; February. <http://www.wider.unu.edu/stc/repec/pdfs/rp2008/rp2008-19.pdf>.

Time Magazine. 1977. 17 March.

Turner, Louis. 1973. *Multinational Companies & the Third World*. London: Allen Lane.

UNCTAD. 2008. *Development and Globalization: Facts and Figures*. New York and Geneva: United Nations.

___. 2009. *World Investment Report 2009*. New York and Geneva: United Nations.

___. 2011. *World Investment Report*. New York and Geneva: United Nations.

UNDP. 1990. *Human Development Report.* New York: Oxford University Press.
___. 1999. *Human Development Report.* New York: Oxford University Press

United Nations General Assembly. 1974. *Declaration on the Establishment of a New International Economic Order*, 1 May, Resolution 3201 (S-VI).

Vitali, S., J.B. Glattfelder and S. Battiston. 2011. "The Network of Global Corporate Control." PLoS ONE 6, 10: e25995. doi:10.1371/journal.pone.0025995 <www.plosone.org/article/info%3Adoi%2F10.137%Fjournal.pone.0025995>.

Walpen, Bernhard. 2004. *Die offenen Feinde und ihre Gesellschaft: Eine hegemonietheoretische Studie zur Mont Pelerin Society.* Hamburg: VSA-Verlag.

World Bank. 1984. *Report on the World Bank Research Program Part II.* Office of the Vice President, Economics and Research Staff, Report No. 5325.
___. 1992. *World Development Report.* Oxford University Press.
___. 1995a. *World Development Report.* Oxford University Press.
___. 1995b. *Global Economic Prospects.*
___. 2004. *Beyond Economic Growth: An Introduction to Sustainable Development.* Second ed. Washington, DC: World Bank.

Zeisel, Hans. 1985. "The Austro-Marxist in 'Red' Vienna: Reflections and Recollections." In A. Rabinbach (ed.), *The Austrian Socialist Experiment: Social Democracy and Austro Marxism, 1918–34.* Boulder CO: Western Press.

INDEX